Ezra B Chase

Teachings of Patriots And Statesmen

Ezra B Chase

Teachings of Patriots And Statesmen

ISBN/EAN: 9783744732741

Printed in Europe, USA, Canada, Australia, Japan

Cover: Foto ©ninafisch / pixelio.de

More available books at **www.hansebooks.com**

TEACHINGS

OF

PATRIOTS AND STATESMEN;

OR, THE

"FOUNDERS OF THE REPUBLIC"

ON

SLAVERY.

By EZRA B. CHASE, Esq.

"FIAT JUSTITIA"

PHILADELPHIA:
J. W BRADLEY, 48 N. FOURTH STREET.

Entered according to Act of Congress, in the year 1860, by

EZRA B. CHASE,

In the Clerk's Office of the District Court of the United States, in and for the Eastern District of Pennsylvania.

PHILADELPHIA:
STEREOTYPED BY S. A. GEORGE,
607 SANSOM STREET.

PRINTED BY KING & BAIRD.

INTRODUCTORY.

In compiling the following pages, I have not been influenced by partisan purposes; neither have I compiled them for the notoriety of having my name appended to a book. The country is sufficiently flooded already with partisan literature—books written for political advantage, or pecuniary gain, or both. To such authorship I do not aspire. If I have cherished an ambition in reference to this work, it has been an ambition to place before the people information upon the subject that is now agitating the country, upon which they can rely,—the views and opinions of those distinguished patriots and statesmen who formed the government, and whose intentions and principles should be heeded and carried out, if we would preserve it from disruption and decay. This information, or most of it, has hitherto been locked up in scores of huge Congressional volumes, entirely inaccessible to the general mass of readers; or if, by chance or otherwise, accessible, requiring so much time and research as to render it comparatively valueless.

I believe the most that the people—the voters—of this country desire, in reference to the question of slavery, is, to know, from an authentic source, what the framers of the Constitution meant to do with it; what relation they meant the government should hold to the institution, if any; and that, knowing this, regardless of the selfishness and fanaticism of politicians, north or south, east or west, they will steadily pursue the path marked out by their fathers, and perpetuate the principles of Constitutional liberty with every energy and effort in their power.

That there need be no mistake in this matter, I have commenced this compilation with the debates in the congress of the confederation, the first form of a national government adopted by the colonies after the declaration of independence. These "Notes" were kept by Thomas Jefferson. They are meagre, it is true, as are all the debates of those times, for stenography was then unknown; but they furnish all, as well as the best, lights we can get, of the opinions of the statesmen at that time. It will be seen that the "Notes" relate almost exclusively to the slavery question, and hence we may conclude that then, as now, that subject was one of difficulty as well as delicacy. I have given the "Notes" in full, *pro* and *con*—I could do no more; and the reader must form his own opinions,—mine would be superfluous.

Passing from the Articles of the Confederation, I have next taken up the Convention to form the present Constitution. The only debates preserved in that body were taken by Mr. Madison and Mr. Yates; the latter, however, left the Convention before its adjournment, and hence did not take them fully. I have carefully compiled, from both these sources, everything that was said and done relating to slavery, together with such other matter as seemed likely to be of interest at the present time. It will be seen that here, too, difficulties were presented, that for a while seemed likely to preclude the possibility of a union of the States on their present basis; but they were happily arranged, in a spirit of mutual concession and compromise, upon the principle of granting such powers as seemed necessary for the good of the whole, specifically, and "reserving to the people or the States, respectively," all powers not granted. These debates, too, are meagre, but they are sufficient to give the intelligent reader a clear notion of the intentions of the Convention, and what powers are really granted to Congress by that instrument of government which has shed so much happiness upon our beloved country.

Pursuing the same purpose, I have next taken up the conventions of the several States to ratify the Constitution, and given everything relating to the subject of slavery that was said and done in them.

In some of these States the debates are quite full; in others but mere fragments have been preserved; and in a few, none at all. I have given everything I could find, and my facilities have not been very limited, upon this subject. The construction given to the Constitution by the wise and good men who deliberated upon its ratification, many of whom had taken part in its formation, has been carefully and fully noted. I have omitted nothing on this subject within the scope of an ample library, and long, patient, and thorough investigation.

Leaving the Constitution at the period of its ratification by the requisite number of States, I have next taken up the Ordinance of 1787, important in the history of the country as containing the first restriction upon the spread of slavery ever adopted by these States, although it was adopted under the Articles of Confederation, before the present Constitution was framed; still, it is deemed of importance at the present day, as furnishing a precedent for the prohibition of slavery in the Territories by the general government. This chapter was compiled by Hon. Peter Force, of Washington, from original documents, who has spent a lifetime in compiling the archives of the government, under the authority of Congress. It is unquestionably the only authentic history of that famous ordinance ever given to the country; and I desire here to express to the great American compiler, my sincere thanks for his courtesy and kindness in this behalf.

Passing from this, the first action of Congress

upon the subject of slavery is taken up. This occurred in 1790, the first Congress that assembled under the present Constitution, and was had upon the memorial of the Pennsylvania Abolition Society. The report of the committee, and the final action of Congress upon that subject, will be found in this chapter.

The Virginia and Kentucky resolutions, drawn by Messrs. Madison and Jefferson, defining the rights and powers of the general government and the States, are next given.

From this period till the application of Missouri for admission into the Union, in 1820, the question of slavery was not agitated in Congress to any considerable extent. This was the first discussion ever had in that body on the power of Congress to restrict slavery in the territories of the United States. A succinct and careful history of the difficulty is given, together with extracts from the speeches of the most prominent statesmen of that time who participated in it, embracing nearly the entire speech of General Pinckney, who was the only member of Congress, at that time, who was a member of the Convention that framed the Constitution. In this connection, also, the reader will find the opinions of Mr. Madison, Mr, Jefferson, Mr. Monroe, General Harrison, and others, upon the power of Congress to restrict slavery in the national territories.

From this period, down to 1854, the various phases of slavery agitation is traced, and the views of Clay, Calhoun, Benton, Cass, Dickinson, Seward, Marcy, John Quincy Adams, Silas Wright, Daniel Webster, and other of the eminent statesmen of the times, of both political parties, are given. A history of the Kansas-Nebraska bill; extracts from the opinion of the court in the Dred Scott case, and other opinions of the courts in reference to slavery; the inaugural addresses of Washington, Adams, Jefferson, and Madison; and the farewell addresses of Washington and Jackson; may also be found.

Since 1854, the Whig party, as a national organization, has ceased to exist, and the Republican party, organized particularly with reference to the slavery question, has taken its place. I have compiled nothing save the resolutions of the Presidential conventions, subsequent to that period, for the reason that congressional discussions since that time are so familiar to the people, that a synopsis, within the scope of this book, must be too meagre for general interest. I have endeavored to give a fair and faithful compilation of the views and opinions of the eminent statesmen of the country, of both parties, from the organization of the government to 1854, while both of the great political parties were organized upon a basis that embraced the South as well as the North. The base of the structure is laid in the organization of the government itself, and the views of the men who framed it. Let the reader first examine well the base, and then, step by step, ascend to the summit, examining, as he ascends, the best lights he can obtain, and then, like a rational, thinking, independent man, form his own conclusions with reference to this question, and act accordingly. Keeping in view the peace and welfare of the country, he will hardly act amiss, for there can be no safer guides for the present, than the lights and precedents of the past.

I can hardly expect that this volume will escape partisan censure and criticism. Extremists, both North and South, I have no doubt, will condemn it. This I cannot help; I only ask the reader to remember, that it is a compilation of the opinions of those who laid, broad and deep, the foundations of civil and religious liberty, and of those eminent statesmen who succeeded them, and who have shed a halo of fadeless glory around the character of the American nation. If I be the subject of reproach for the compilation, what would be meted out to those patriots and sages, were they now upon earth, and should they again proclaim the doctrines of their day and generation? It is not I who speak, but rather the voice of the immortal dead, a voice from the tombs of those great spirits, who, through the perils of war and revolution, established a government, the freest and the happiest on earth, and bequeathed it to us. Let us heed their admonitions, emulate their virtues, and profit by their examples.

E. B. C.

Wilkesbarre, Penn., June 18, 1860.

CONTENTS.

CHAPTER I.

Occurrences incident to the Act of Confederation—Jefferson's notes of the debates on the Confederation—Mr. Chase's motion in reference to white inhabitants—"White inhabitants"—Slaves—Negroes not considered members of the State—Mr. Adams on the same subject—Free and slave labor contrasted—Mr. Harrison's compromise, that two slaves should be counted as one freeman, and remarks thereon—Mr. Wilson against slavery—Mr. Payne's remarks—Dr Witherspoon against tax on slaves—Mr. Chase on the subject of each colony having one vote in Congress—Dr. Franklin, Dr. Witherspoon, Mr. Adams, Dr. Rush, Mr. Hopkins, Mr. Wilson, on the same subject—Ratification, and the Articles of Confederation..*Page* 21–43.

CHAPTER II.

The causes which led to the formation of the Constitution and wherein the Articles of Confederation were deficient for the purpose of a government, by Mr. Madison—Appointment of delegates to form a Constitution—Organization of the convention—Resolutions of Mr. Randolph, which became the basis of the Constitution—Mr. Madison, on the equality of suffrage—Speech of Alexander Hamilton, advocating monarchical government; also plan of government submitted by him—Discussion continued—Angry discussion between Mr. Madison, Mr. Martin, and others—Dr. Franklin proposes prayer at the opening of the session—His remarks thereon—Mr. Randolph proposes a sermon on the 4th of July—Proposition to adjourn *sine die*—Discussion continued—Report of committee on the construction of Congress—Three-fifths slaves included in representation—Concession of the small States that the House should originate all money bills, in consideration that they should have an equal representation in the Senate—Debate thereon—Mr. Madison's compromise—Further debate on slave representation, and vote—Debate on equality of votes in the Senate—Report of the Committee of the whole House on Mr. Randolph's resolutions—The resolutions as reported—Mr. Rutledge's report from the committee of detail—Discussion thereon by Mr. Madison, Dr. Franklin, and others—Mr. Madison's proposition to give Congress power to institute temporary governments for the territories—Lengthy debate on slavery and the slave trade—Mr. Madison's proposition to give Congress power to institute territorial governments struck out—Mr. Livingston's report on the importation of slaves—Discussion and vote thereon—Fugitive slaves—"Needful rules and regulations respecting the territory," etc.—Report of the Constitution by the committee of revision—The Constitution as reported and adopted—Official letter to Congress—Articles of amendment—When adopted.............................*Page* 44-114.

CHAPTER III.

Debates in the convention of Massachusetts—Rev. Mr. Backus, on the religious test, and the importation of slaves—Mr. Dawes' remarks on slaves, and importation of—Gen. Heath, ditto ; his remarks on the adoption of the Federal Constitution—Mr. King's remarks on representation and taxation—Debate in the convention of the State of New York—Mr. Hamilton's remarks on navigation, commerce, and slave representation—Debate in the convention of the State of Connecticut—Mr. Ellsworth's remarks on the necessity of a Union, and the consequences of disunion—Debate in the convention of Virginia—Objections to the Constitution answered by Mr. Nicholas—Powers of the government—Mr. Mason in opposition to the slave trade—Mr. Madison on the same ; and in reference to fugitive slaves—He prefers union with slavery to disunion without it—Mr. Tyler against the slave trade—

Patrick Henry on the powers of Congress—Fugitive slaves—
Mr. Nicholas on slavery—Mr. Henry replies—Three-fifths of
the negroes represented—Mr. Mason on negro taxes—Mr.
Madison's reply—Mr. Henry against emancipation—Gov.
Randolph on the same subject—Debate in the convention
of North Carolina—Mr. Goudy against negro taxation—
Negroes property—Mr. Davie—Mr. Spaight explains the
views of the Federal Convention—Mr. Iredell on slavery and
the slave trade—Mr. Galloway, Mr. Iredell and others, continue the discussion—Debate in the convention of South
Carolina—Mr. Lowndes on slavery and the slave trade—
Judge Pendleton, Mr. Rutledge, and Mr. Pinckney, on the
same subject............................*Page* 115-154.

CHAPTER IV.

History of the Ordinance of 1787, by Peter Force, Esq., compiler of the American Archives, by authority of Congress............................*Page* 155-178

CHAPTER V.

Memorial of the Pennsylvania Abolition Society to Congress on
the slave trade, and proceedings thereon, 1790..*Page* 179-183

CHAPTER VI.

Virginia and Kentucky Resolutions of 1798, drawn by Messrs.
Madison and Jefferson....................*Page* 184-194.

CHAPTER VII.

The Missouri question in Congress, 1820—Slavery restriction
offered by Mr. Storrs, of New York—Mr. Meiggs opposed—
Mr. Holmes' speech on—Mr. Smyth, Mr. Reid, Mr. Scott,
Mr. Tucker, and Mr. Stevens on—Col. Richard M. Johnson
in the Senate on—Mr. Pinckney, a member of the Federal
Convention that framed the Constitution. on the power of
Congress to restrict slavery—Mr. Whiteman, Mr. Shaw, Mr.
Holmes, and Mr. Barber, on the same subject — Ex-
tracts............................*Page* 195-282.

CONTENTS.

CHAPTER VIII.

Extracts from a letter from Mr. Madison to President Monroe, on the Missouri restriction—Same in reply to Mr. Monroe—Mr. Madison on the Ordinance of 1787—Draft of a veto by Mr. Monroe on the bill establishing the Missouri Compromise line—Extracts from several letters of Mr. Jefferson on the Missouri restriction—Extract from a letter of Gen. Harrison (afterward President) to Mr. Monroe on the same subject..............................*Page* 283-292.

CHAPTER IX

Fugitive slaves—Ordinance of 1787—The Constitution—Act of 1793—Letters of Messrs. Marcy and Seward in favor of allowing owners to hold slaves nine months in the State of New York...............................*Page* 293-306.

CHAPTER X.

Slavery in the District of Columbia in 1831, 1835, and 1836—Remarks of John Quincy Adams, Silas Wright, and James Buchanan on—Mr. Benton's views...........*Page* 307-320.

CHAPTER XI.

Agitation of slavery in the House of Representatives, in 1839, and retiring of Southern members from the hall—"The Gag-Rule," and vote thereon—Extract from Mr. Clay's speech in the Senate...............................*Page* 321-348.

CHAPTER XII.

Resolution of Mr. Calhoun in 1847, and remarks on, Extract—Extract from Mr. Calhoun's speech in 1848—Resolution of Daniel S. Dickinson, and remarks thereon, Extract, 1848—Extracts from the speeches of Henry Clay, Daniel Webster, John C. Calhoun, Gen. Cass, and Gen. Houston, of the Senate, on the Compromise Resolutions of Mr. Clay, in 1850—Also Extracts from the speeches of Mr. Tombs, of Georgia, Mr. Butler and Mr. Ross, of Pennsylvania, of the House of Representatives, on the same subject—Also Extract from "Southern Address."......................*Page* 349-387.

CHAPTER XIII.

The Dred Scott decision—Extracts from the opinions of the Court—Extract from the opinion of the Pennsylvania Supreme Court in 1837, that a negro cannot be a citizen—Prigg vs. the Commonwealth of Pennsylvania, by Judge Story, Extract...................................*Page* 388–408.

CHAPTER XIV.

Inaugural Addresses of Washington, Adams, Jefferson, and Madison, and the Farewell Addresses of Washington and Jackson.....................................*Page* 409–480.

CHAPTER XV.

Repeal of the Missouri Compromise and organization of the Territories of Kansas and Nebraska in 1854...*Page* 481–487.

CHAPTER XVI.

National Conventions—Platforms of the various parties on the subject of slavery, from 1848 to 1860..........*Page* 488–495.

CHAPTER I.

THE ARTICLES OF CONFEDERATION.

PREVIOUS to the adoption of the Declaration of Independence, steps for the formation of a confederated government, by and between the colonies, were taken. A common danger seems to have impressed them with the necessity of a union for the common defense. On the 11th of June, 1776, some three weeks prior to the adoption of the Declaration, a committee of one from each colony was raised for the purpose of preparing a plan of government. The committee soon after made a report, but it was not finally adopted by Congress till the 15th of November, 1777.

It was at the same time resolved by Congress that the Articles of Confederation, as they were called, should be presented to the legislature of each colony; and, if ratified, then their Delegates in Congress should, in that body, approve the same. The colonies seem to have been singularly tardy in ratifying the articles. They were not ratified by Maryland till the 30th of January, 1781; New Jersey and Delaware also withheld their consent till some time during the year 1779; and it was not till after a circular-letter by Congress had been sent to the legislatures of the several colonies, appealing in the most patriotic terms to their love of country and to their sense of common danger, that the Articles of Confederation were adopted by the whole of the thirteen colonies. From that time they took the name of States, a name more sovereign and independent in signification. They were no longer colonies—*dependencies* of Great Britain.

JEFFERSON'S NOTES OF DEBATE ON CONFEDERATION.

On Friday, July 12, 1777, the committee appointed to draw the Articles of Confederation reported them, and on the 22d, the house resolved themselves into a committee to take them into consideration. On the 30th and 31st of that month, and 1st of the ensuing, those articles were debated which determined the proportion or quota of money which each State should furnish to the common treasury, and the manner of voting in Congress. The first of these articles was expressed, in the original draft, in these words:

"ART. XI. All charges of war, and all other expenses that shall be incurred for the common defense or general welfare, and allowed by the United States assembled, shall be defrayed out of a common treasury, which shall be supplied by the several colonies in proportion to the number of inhabitants of every age, sex, and quality, except Indians not paying taxes, in each colony—a true account of which, distinguishing the white inhabitants, shall be triennially taken, and transmitted to the Assembly of the United States."

Mr. Chase moved that the quotas should be fixed, not by the number of inhabitants of every condition, but by that of the "white inhabitants." He admitted that taxation should be always in proportion to property; that this was, in theory, the true rule; but that, from a variety of difficulties, it was a rule which could never be adopted in practice. The value of the property in every State could never be estimated justly and equally. Some other measures for the wealth of the State must therefore be devised, some standard referred to, which would be more simple. He considered the number of inhabitants as a tolerably good criterion of property, and that this might always be obtained. He therefore thought it the best mode which we could adopt, with one exception only; he observed that negroes are property, and as such, cannot be distinguished from the lands or personalties held in those States where there are few slaves; that the surplus of profit which a Northern farmer is able to lay by, he invests in cattle, horses, &c., whereas a Southern farmer lays out the same surplus in slaves. There is no more reason, therefore, for taxing the Southern States on the farmer's head, and on his slave's head, than the Northern ones on their farmer's heads and the heads of their cattle; that the method proposed would therefore tax the Southern States according to their numbers and their wealth conjunctly, while the Northern would be taxed on numbers only; that negroes, in fact, should not be considered as members of the State more than cattle, and that they have no more interest in it.

Mr. John Adams observed, that the numbers of people are taken, by this Article, as an index of the wealth of the State, and not as subjects of taxation; that, as to this matter, it was of no consequence by what name you called your people, whether by that of *freemen* or *slaves;* that in some countries, the laboring poor are called *freemen*, in others they are called *slaves*, but that the difference as to the State was imaginary only. What matters it whether a landlord, employing ten laborers on his farm, give them annually as much money as will buy them the necessaries of life, or give them those necessaries at short hand? The ten laborers add as much wealth to the State, increase its exports as much, in the one case as the other. Certainly five hundred freemen produce no more profits, no greater surplus for the payment of taxes, than five hundred slaves. Therefore, the State in which are the laborers called *freemen* should be taxed no more than that in which are those called *slaves*. Suppose, by an extraordinary operation of nature or of law, one-half the laborers of a State could, in the course of one night, be transformed into slaves, would the State be made the poorer, or the less able to pay taxes? That the condition of the laboring poor in most countries—that of the fishermen, particularly of the Northern States—is as abject as that of slaves. It is the number of laborers which produce the surplus for taxation; and numbers, therefore, indiscriminately, are the fair index to wealth; that it is the use of the word "property" here, and its application to some of the people of the State, which produce the fallacy. How does the Southern farmer procure slaves? Either by importation, or by purchase from his neighbor. If he imports a slave, he adds one to the number of laborers in his country, and, proportionably, to its profits and ability to pay taxes. If he buys from his neighbor, it is only a transfer of a laborer from one farm to another, which does not change the annual produce of the State, and therefore should not change its tax; that if a Northern farmer works ten laborers on his farm, he can, it is true, invest the surplus of ten men's labor in cattle; but so may the Southern farmer, working ten slaves; that a State of one hundred thousand freemen can maintain no more cattle than one of one hundred thousand slaves. Therefore, they have no more of that kind of property. That a slave may, indeed, from the custom of speech, be more properly called the wealth of his master, than the free laborer might be called the wealth of his employers; but as to the State, both were equally its wealth, and should therefore equally add to the quota of its tax.

Mr. Harrison proposed, as a compromise, that two slaves should be counted as one freeman. He affirmed that slaves did not do as much work as freemen, and doubted if two effected more than one; that this was proved by the price of labor—the hire of a laborer in the Southern colonies being from £8 to £12, while in the Northern it was generally £24.

Mr. Wilson said that, if this amendment should take place, the Southern colonies would have all the benefit of slaves, whilst the Northern ones would bear the burden; that slaves increase the profits of a State, which the

Southern States mean to take to themselves; that they also increase the burden of defense, which would of course fall so much the heavier on the Northern; that slaves occupy the places of freemen, and eat their food. Dismiss your slaves, and freemen will take their places. It is our duty to lay every discouragement on the importation of slaves; but this amendment would give the *just rium liberorum* to him who would import slaves; that other kinds of property were pretty equally distributed through all the colonies;— there were as many cattle, horses, and sheep, in the North as the South, and South as North; but not so as to slaves; —that experience has shown that those colonies have been always able to pay most which have the most inhabitants, whether they be black or white; and the practice of the Southern colonies has always been to make every farmer pay poll taxes upon all his laborers, whether they be black or white. He acknowledges, indeed, that freemen work the most, but they consume the most also. They do not produce a greater surplus for taxation. The slave is neither fed nor clothed so expensively as a freeman. Again, white women are exempted from labor generally, but negro women are not. In this, then, the Southern States have an advantage, as the Article now stands. It has sometimes been said that slavery is necessary, because the commodities they raise would be too dear for market, if cultivated by freemen; but now it is said that the labor of the slave is the dearest.

Mr. Payne urged the original resolution of Congress, to proportion the quotas of the States to the number of souls.

Dr. Witherspoon was of opinion that the value of lands and houses was the best estimate of the wealth of a nation, and that it was practicable to obtain such a valuation. This is the true barometer of wealth. The one now proposed is imperfect in itself, and unequal between the States. It has been objected that negroes eat the food of freemen, and therefore should be taxed; horses also eat the food of freemen, therefore they also should be taxed. It has been said, too, that in carrying slaves into the estimate of the taxes the State is to pay, we do no more than those States themselves do, who always take slaves into the estimate of the taxes the individual is to pay. But the cases are not parallel. In the Southern colonies slaves pervade the whole colony, but they do not pervade the whole continent. That as to the original resolution of Congress, to proportion the quotas according to the souls, it was temporary only, and related to the moneys heretofore remitted; whereas we are now entering into a new compact, and therefore stand on original ground.

August 1. The question being put, the amendment proposed was rejected by the votes of New Hampshire, Massachusetts, Rhode Island, Connecticut, New York, New Jersey, and Pennsylvania, against those of Delaware, Maryland, Virginia, North and South Carolina. Georgia was divided.

The other article was in these words:—" Art. XVII. In determining questions, each colony shall have one vote."

July 30, 31, *August* 1. Present forty-one members. Mr. Chase observed, that this Article was the most likely to divide us of any one proposed in the draft then under consideration. That the larger colonies had threatened they would not confederate at all, if their weight in Congress should not be equal to the numbers of people they added to the confederacy, while the smaller ones declared against a union, if they did not retain an equal vote for the protection of their rights. That it was of the utmost consequence to bring the parties together, as, should we sever from each other, either no foreign power will ally with us at all, or the different States will form different alliances, and thus increase the horrors of those scenes of civil war and bloodshed which, in such a state of separation and independence, would render us a miserable people. That our importance, our interests, our peace, required that we should confederate, and that mutual sacrifices should be made to effect a compromise of this difficult question. He was of opinion the smaller colonies would lose their rights, if they were not in some instances allowed an equal vote; and therefore that a discrimination should take place among the questions which would come before Congress. That the smaller States should be secured in all questions concerning life or liberty, and the greater ones in all respecting property. He therefore proposed that, in votes relating to money, the voice of each colony should be proportioned to the number of its inhabitants.

Dr. Franklin thought that the votes should be so proportioned in all cases. He took notice that the Delaware counties had bound up their delegates to disagree to this article. He thought it very extraordinary language to be held by any State, that they would not confederate with us unless we would let them dispose of our money. Certainly, if we vote equally we ought to pay equally; but the smaller States will hardly purchase the privilege at this price. That, had he lived in a State where the representation, originally equal, had become unequal by time and accident, he might have submitted rather than disturb government; but that we should be very wrong to set out in this practice, when it is in our power to establish what is right. That, at the time of the union between England and Scotland, the latter had made the objection which the smaller States now do; but experience had proved that no unfairness had ever been shown them; that their advocates had prognosticated that it would again happen, as in times of old, that the whale would swallow Jonah, but he thought the prediction reversed in event, and that Jonah had swallowed the whale; for the Scotch had, in fact, got possession of the government, and gave laws to the English. He reprobated the original agreement of Congress to vote by colonies, and therefore was for their voting, in all cases, according to the number of taxables.

Dr. Witherspoon opposed every alteration of the article. All men admit that a confederacy is necessary. Should the idea get abroad that there is likely to be no union among us, it will damp the minds of the people, diminish the glory of our struggle, and lessen its importance; because it will open to our view future prospects of war and dissension among ourselves. If an equal vote be refused, the smaller States will become vassals to the larger; and all experience has shown that the vassals and subjects of Free States are the most enslaved. He instanced the helots of Sparta and the provinces of Rome. He observed that foreign powers, discovering this blemish, would make it a handle for disengaging the smaller States from so unequal a confederacy. That the colonies should, in fact, be considered as individuals; and that, as such, in all disputes they should have an equal vote; that they are now collected as individuals making a bargain with each other, and, of course, had a right to vote as individuals. That in the East India Company they voted by persons, and not by their proportion of stock. That the Belgic confederacy voted by provinces. That in questions of war the smaller States were as much interested as the larger, and therefore should vote equally; and indeed, that the larger States were more likely to bring war on the confederacy, in proportion as their frontier was more extensive. He admitted that equality of representation was an excellent principle, but then it must be of things which are co-ordinate; that is, of things similar, and of the same nature; that nothing relating to individuals could ever come before Congress; nothing but what would respect Colonies. He distinguished between an incorporating and a federal union. The union of England was an incorporating one;

yet Scotland had suffered by that union ; for that its inhabitants were drawn from it by the hopes of places and employments; nor was it an instance of equality of representation ; because while Scotland was allowed nearly a thirteenth of representation, they were to pay only one-fortieth of the land-tax. He expressed his hopes that, in the present enlightened state of men's minds, we might expect a lasting confederacy, if it was founded on fair principles.

John Adams advocated the voting in proportion to numbers. He said, that we stand here as the representatives of the people ; that in some States the people are many, in others they are few ; that therefore their vote here should be proportioned to the numbers from whom it comes. Reason, justice, and equity, never had weight enough, on the face of the earth, to govern the councils of men. It is interest alone which does it, and it is interest alone which can be trusted ; that therefore the interests within doors should be the mathematical representatives of the interests without doors; that the individuality of the colonies is a mere sound. Does the individuality of a colony increase its wealth or numbers ? If it does, pay equally. If it does not add weight in the scale of the confederacy, it cannot add to their rights, nor weigh in argument. A has £50, B £500, C £1000, in partnership. Is it just they should equally dispose of the moneys of the partnership ? It has been said we are independent individuals, making a bargain together. The question is not what we are now, but what we ought to be when our bargain shall be made. The confederacy is to make us one individual only ; it is to form us, like separate parcels of metal, into one common mass. We shall no longer retain our separate individuality, but become a single individual, as to all questions submitted to the confederacy. Therefore all those reasons which prove the justice and expediency of equal representation in other assemblies hold good here. It has been objected that a proportional vote will endanger the smaller States. We answer, that an equal vote will endanger the larger. Virginia, Pennsylvania, and Massachusetts, are the three greater colonies. Consider their distance, their difference of produce, of interests, and of manners, and it is apparent they can never have an interest or inclination to combine for the oppression of the smaller; that the smaller will naturally divide on all questions with the larger. Rhode Island, from its relation, similarity, and intercourse, will generally pursue the same objects with Massachusetts; Jersey, Delaware, and Maryland, with Pennsylvania.

Dr. Rush took notice, that the decay of the liberties of the *Dutch* republic proceeded from three causes—1. The perfect unanimity requisite on all occasions; 2. Their obligation to consult their constituents; 3. Their voting by provinces. This last destroyed the equality of representation; and the liberties of Great Britain, also, are sinking from the same defect. That a part of our rights is deposited, in the hands of our legislatures. There, it was admitted, there should be an equality of representation. Another part of our rights is deposited in the hands of Congress. Why is it not equally necessary there should be an equal representation there? Were it possible to collect the whole body of the people together, they would determine the question submitted to them by their authority. Why should not the same majority decide, when voting here by their representatives? The larger colonies are so providentially divided in situation, as to render every fear of their combining visionary. Their interests are different, and their circumstances dissimilar. It is more probable they will become rivals, and leave it in the power of the smaller States to give preponderance to any scale they please. The voting by the number of free inhabitants will have one excellent effect—that of inducing the colonies to discourage slavery and to encourage the increase of their free inhabitants.

Mr. Hopkins observed, there were four larger, four smaller, and four middle-sized colonies. That the four largest would contain more than half the inhabitants of the confederating States, and therefore would govern the others as they should please. That history affords no instance of such a thing as equal representation. The Germanic body votes by States; the Helvetic body does the same; and so does the Belgic confederacy. That too little is known of the ancient confederations to say what was their practice.

Mr. Wilson thought that taxation should be in proportion to wealth, but that representation should accord with the number of freemen.

That government is a collection or result of the wills of all; that if any government could speak the will of all, it would be perfect; and that, so far as it departs from this, it becomes imperfect. It has been said that Congress is a representation of States, not of individuals.

I say, that the objects of its care are all the individuals of the States. It is strange that annexing the name of "State" to ten thousand men, should give them an equal right with forty thousand. This must be the effect of magic, not of reason. As to those matters which are referred to Congress, we are not so many States; we are one large State. We lay aside our individuality whenever we come here.

The Germanic body is a burlesque on government, and their practice on any point is a sufficient authority and proof that it is wrong. The greatest imperfection in the constitution of the Belgic confederacy is their voting by provinces. The interest of the whole is constantly sacrificed to that of the small States.

The history of the war in the reign of Queen Anne sufficiently proves this. It is asked, Shall nine colonies put it into the power of four to govern them as they please?

I invert the question, and ask, Shall two millions of people put it into the power of one million to govern them as they please? It is pretended, too, that the smaller colonies will be in danger from the greater. Speak in honest language, and say, the minority will be in danger from the majority. And is there an assembly on earth where this danger may not be equally pretended? The truth is, that our proceedings will then be consentaneous with the interests of the majority, and so they ought to be. The probability is much greater that the larger States will disagree, than that they will combine.

I defy the wit of man to invent a possible case, or to suggest any one thing on earth, which shall be for the interests of Virginia, Pennsylvania and Massachusetts, and which will not also be for the interests of the other States.

These Articles, reported July 12, '76, were debated from day to day, and time to time, for two years; were ratified July 9, '78, by ten States; by New Jersey, on the 26th of November of the same year; and by Delaware, on the 23d of February following. Maryland, alone, held off two years more, acceding to them, March 1, '81, and thus closing the obligation. Following are the Articles:—

ARTICLES OF CONFEDERATION AND PERPETUAL UNION BETWEEN THE STATES.

To all to whom these Presents shall come, We, the undersigned Delegates of the States affixed to our names, send greeting.—Whereas, the Delegates of the United States of America, in Congress assembled, did, on the 15th day of November, in the Year of our Lord 1777, and in the Second Year of the Independence of America, agree to certain Articles of Confederation and perpetual Union between the States of New Hampshire, Massachusetts-bay, Rhode Island and Providence Plantations, Connecticut, New York, New Jersey, Pennsylvania, Delaware, Maryland, Virginia, North Carolina, South Carolina, and Georgia, in the words following, viz.:

"*Articles of Confederation and Perpetual Union between the States of New Hampshire, Massachusetts Bay, Rhode Island and Providence Plantations, Connecticut, New York, New Jersey, Pennsylvania, Delaware, Maryland, Virginia, North Carolina, South Carolina and Georgia.*

ARTICLE 1. The style of this Confederacy shall be " The United States of America."

ARTICLE 2. Each State retains its sovereignty, freedom and independence, and every power, jurisdiction and right, which is not by this confederation expressly delegated to the United States in Congress assembled.

ARTICLE 3. The said States hereby severally enter into a firm league of friendship with each other, for their common defense, the security of their liberties, and their mutual and general welfare, binding themselves to assist each other against all force offered to, or attacks made upon them, or any of them, on account of religion, sovereignty, trade, or any other pretense whatever.

ARTICLE 4. The better to secure and perpetuate mutual friendship and intercourse among the people of the different States in this Union, the free inhabitants of each of these States—paupers, vagabonds, and fugitives from justice excepted—shall be entitled to all privileges and immunities of free citizens in the several States; and the people of each State shall have free ingress and regress to and from any other State, and shall enjoy therein all the privileges of trade and commerce, subject to the same duties, impositions and restrictions, as the inhabitants thereof respectively, provided that such restriction shall not extend so far as to prevent the removal of property, imported into any State, to any other State of which the owner is an inhabitant;

provided, also, that no imposition, duties or restriction shall be laid by any State on the property of the United States, or either of them.

If any person guilty of, or charged with treason, felony, or other high misdemeanor in any State, shall flee from justice, and be found in any of the United States, he shall upon demand of the Governor, or executive power of the State from which he fled, be delivered up and removed to the State having jurisdiction of his offense.

Full faith and credit shall be given in each of these States, to the records, acts and judicial proceedings of the courts and magistrates of every other State.

ARTICLE 5. For the more convenient management of the general interest of the United States, Delegates shall be annually appointed, in such manner as the legislature of each State shall direct, to meet in Congress on the first Monday in November, in every year, with a power reserved to each State, to recall its Delegates, or any of them, at any time within the year, and to send others in their stead, for the remainder of the year.

No State shall be represented in Congress by less than two, nor by more than seven members ; and no person shall be capable of being a Delegate for more than three years in any term of six years ; nor shall any person, being a Delegate, be capable of holding any office under the United States, for which he, or another for his benefit, receives any salary, fees or emolument of any kind.

Each State shall maintain its own Delegates in any meeting of the States, and while they act as members of the Committee of the States.

In determining questions in the United States, in Congress assembled, each State shall have one vote.

Freedom of speech and debate in Congress shall not be impeached or questioned in any court or place, out of Congress, and the members of Congress shall be protected in their persons from arrests and imprisonments, during the time of their going to and from, and attendance on Congress, except for treason, felony, or breach of the peace.

ARTICLE 6. No State without the consent of the United States in Congress assembled, shall send any embassy to, or receive any embassy from, or enter into any conference, agreement, alliance or treaty with any King, Prince or State; nor shall any person holding any office of profit or trust under the United States, or any of them, accept of any present, emolument, office or title of any kind whatever from any King, Prince or Foreign State; nor shall the United States in Congress assembled, or any of them, grant any title of nobility.

No two or more States shall enter into any treaty, confederation or alliance whatever between them, without the consent of the United States in Congress assembled, specifying accurately the purposes for which the same is to be entered into, and how long it shall continue.

No State shall lay any imposts or duties which may interfere with any stipulations in treaties, entered into by the United States in Congress assembled, with any King, Prince or State, in pursuance of any treaties already proposed by Congress, to the Courts of France and Spain.

No vessels of war shall be kept up in time of peace by any State, except such number only, as shall be deemed necessary by the United States in Congress assembled, for the defense of such State, or its trade; nor shall any body of forces be kept up by any State, in time of peace, except such number only, as in the judgment of the United States, in Congress assembled, shall be deemed requisite to garrison the forts necessary for the defense of such State; but every State shall always keep up a well regulated and disciplined militia, sufficiently armed and accoutred, and shall provide and have constantly ready for use, in public stores. a due number of field pieces and tents, and a proper quantity of arms, ammunition and camp equipage.

No State shall engage in any war without the consent of the United States in Congress assembled, unless such State e actually invaded by enemies, or shall have received ertain advice of a resolution being formed by some nation)f Indians to invade such State, and the danger is so imminent as not to admit of a delay, till the United States in Congress assembled can be consulted : nor shall any State grant commissions to any ships or vessels of war, nor letters of marque or reprisal, except it be after a declaration of war by the United States in Congress assembled, and then only against the kingdom or State, and the subjects thereof, against which war has been so declared, and under such regulations as shall be established by the United States in Congress assembled, unless such State be infested by pirates, in which case vessels of war may be fitted out for that occasion, and kept so long as the danger shall continue, or until the United States in Congress assembled shall determine otherwise.

ARTICLE 7. When land-forces are raised by any State for the common defense, all officers of or under the rank of colonel, shall be appointed by the legislature of each State respectively by whom such forces shall be raised, or in such manner as such State shall direct, and all vacancies shall be filled up by the State which first made the appointment.

ARTICLE 8. All charges of war, and all other expenses that shall be incurred for the common defense or general welfare, and allowed by the United States in Congress assembled, shall be defrayed out of a common treasury, which shall be supplied by the several States, in proportion to the value of all land within each State, granted to or surveyed for any person, as such land and the buildings and improvements thereon shall be estimated according to such mode as the United States in Congress assembled, shall from time to time, direct and appoint. The taxes for paying that proportion shall be laid and levied by the authority and direction of the Legislatures of the several States within the time agreed upon by the United States in Congress assembled.

ARTICLE 9. The United States in Congress assembled shall have the sole and exclusive right and power of determining on peace and war, except in the cases mentioned in the 6th article—of sending and receiving ambassadors—entering into treaties and alliances, provided that no treaty of commerce shall be made whereby the legislative power of the respective States shall be restrained from imposing such imposts and duties on foreigners, as their own people are subjected to, or from prohibiting the exportation or importation of any species of goods or commodities whatsoever—of establishing rules for deciding in all cases what captures on land or water shall be legal, and in what manner prizes taken by land or naval forces in the service of the United States shall be divided or appropriated—of granting letters of marque and reprisal in times of peace—appointing courts for the trial of piracies and felonies committed on the high seas and establishing courts for receiving and determining finally appeals in all cases of captures, provided that no member of Congress shall be appointed a judge of any of the said courts.

The United States in Congress assembled shall also be the last resort on appeal in all disputes and differences now subsisting or that hereafter may arise between two or more States concerning boundary, jurisdiction, or any other cause whatever; which authority shall always be exercised in the manner following:—Whenever the legislative or executive authority or lawful agent of any State in controversy with another shall present a petition to Congress, stating the matter in question and praying for a hearing, notice thereof shall be given by order of Congress, to the legislative or executive authority of the other State in controversy, and a day assigned for the appearance of the parties by their lawful agents, who shall then be directed to appoint by joint consent, commissioners or judges to constitute a court for hearing and determining the matter in question: but if they cannot agree, Congress shall name three persons out of each of the United States, and from the list of such persons each party shall alternately strike out one, the petitioners beginning, until the number shall be reduced to thirteen; and from that number not less than seven, nor more than nine names as Congress shall direct, shall in the presence of Congress be drawn out by lot, and the persons whose names shall be so drawn or any five of them, shall be commissioners or judges, to hear and finally determine the controversy, so always as a major part of the judges who shall hear the cause shall agree in the determination: and if either party shall neglect to attend at the day appointed, without showing reasons which Congress shall judge sufficient, or being present shall refuse to strike, the Congress shall proceed to nominate three persons out of each State, and the Secretary of Congress shall strike in behalf of such party absent or refusing; and the judgment and sentence of the court to be appointed, in the manner before prescribed, shall be final and conclusive; and if any of the parties shall refuse to submit to the authority of such court, or to appear or defend their claim or cause, the court shall nevertheless proceed to pronounce sentence, or judgment, which shall in like manner be final and decisive, the judgment or sentence and other proceedings being in either case transmitted to Congress, and lodged among the acts of Congress for the security of the parties concerned: provided that every commissioner, before he sits in judgment, shall take an oath to be administered by one of the judges of the Supreme or Superior Court of the State where the cause shall be tried, "well and truly to hear and determine the matter in question, according to the best of his judgment, without favor, affection, or hope of reward :" provided also that no State shall be deprived of territory for the benefit of the United States.

All controversies concerning the private right of soil claimed under different grants of two or more States, whose jurisdictions as they may respect such lands, and the States which passed such grants, are adjusted; the said grants or either of them being at the same time claimed to have originated antecedent to such settlement of jurisdiction, shall, on the petition of either party to the Congress of the United States, be finally determined as near as may be in the same manner as is before prescribed for deciding disputes respecting territorial jurisdiction between different States.

The United States in Congress assembled shall also have the sole and exclusive right and power of regulating the alloy and value of coin struck by their own authority, or by that of the respective States—fixing the standard of weights and measures throughout the United States—regulating the trade and managing all affairs with the Indians, not members of any of the States; provided that the legislative right of any State within its own limits be not infringed or violated—establishing or regulating post-offices from one State to another, throughout all the United States, and exacting such postage on the papers passing through the same as may be requisite to defray the expenses of the said office—appointing all officers of the land forces, in the service of the United States, excepting regimental officers—appointing all the officers of the naval forces, and commissioning all officers whatever in the service of the United States—making rules for the government and regulation of the said land and naval forces, and directing their operations.

The United States in Congress assembled shall have authority to appoint a committee, to sit in the recess of Congress, to be denominated "A Committee of the States," and to consist of one delegate from each State; and to appoint such other committees and civil officers as may be necessary for managing the general affairs of the United States under their direction—to appoint one of their number to preside; provided that no person be allowed to serve in the office of president more than one year in any term of three years—to ascertain the necessary sums of money to be raised for the service of the United States, and to appropriate and apply the same for defraying the public expenses—to borrow money, or emit bills on the credit of the United States, transmitting every half year to the respective States an account of the sums of money so borrowed or emitted—to build and equip a navy—to agree upon the number of land forces, and to make requisitions from each State for its quota, in proportion to the number of white inhabitants in such State; which requisition shall be binding, and thereupon the legislature of each State shall appoint the regimental officers, raise the men and clothe, arm and equip them in a soldier-like manner, at the expense of the United States; and the officers and men so clothed, armed and equipped, shall march to the place appointed, and within the time agreed on by the United States in Congress assembled: But if the United States in Congress assembled shall, on consideration of circumstances, judge proper that any State should not raise men, or should raise a smaller number than its quota, and that any other State should raise a greater number of men than the quota thereof, such extra number shall be raised, officered, clothed, armed and equipped in the same manner as the quota of such State, unless the legislature of such State shall judge that such extra number cannot be safely spared out of the same, in which case they shall raise, officer, clothe, arm and equip as many of such extra number as they judge can be safely spared. And the officers and men so clothed, armed and equipped, shall march to the place appointed, and within the time agreed on by the United States in Congress assembled.

The United States in Congress assembled shall never engage in a war, nor grant letters of marque and reprisal in time of peace, nor enter into any treaties or alliances, nor coin money, nor regulate the value thereof, nor ascertain the sums and expenses necessary for the defense and welfare of the United States, or any of them, nor emit bills, nor borrow money on the credit of the United States, nor appropriate money, nor agree upon the number of vessels of war to be built or purchased, or the number of land or sea forces to be raised, nor appoint a commander-in-chief of the army or navy, unless nine States assent to the same: nor shall a question on any other point, except for adjourning from day to day, be determined, unless by the votes of a majority of the United States in Congress assembled.

The Congress of the United States shall have power to adjourn to any time within the year, and to any place within the United States, so that no period of adjournment be for a longer duration than the space of six months, and shall publish the journal of their proceedings monthly, except such parts thereof relating to treaties, alliances, or military operations, as in their judgment require secrecy; and the yeas and nays of the delegates of each State on any question shall be entered on the journal, when it is desired by any delegate; and the delegates of a State, or any of them, at his or their request, shall be furnished with a transcript of the said journal, except such parts as are above excepted, to lay before the legislatures of the several States.

ARTICLE 10. The committee of the States, or any nine of them, shall be authorized to execute, in the recess of Congress, such of the powers of Congress as the United States in Congress assembled, by the consent of nine States, shall, from time to time think expedient to vest them with; provided that no power be delegated to the said committee, for the exercise of which, by the Articles of Confederation, the voice of nine States in the Congress of the United States assembled is requisite.

ARTICLE 11. Canada, acceding to this confederation and joining in the measures of the United States, shall be admitted into, and entitled to all the advantages of this union; but no other colony shall be admitted into the same, unless such admission be agreed to by nine States.

ARTICLE 12. All bills of credit emitted, moneys borrowed and debts contracted by, or under the authority of Congress, before the assembling of the United States, in pursuance of the present confederation, shall be deemed and considered as a charge against the United States, for payment and satisfaction whereof the said United States and the public faith are hereby solemnly pledged.

ARTICLE 13. Every State shall abide by the determinations of the United States in Congress assembled, on all questions which by this confederation is submitted to them. And the articles of this confederation shall be inviolably observed by every State, and the union shall be perpetual; nor shall any alteration at any time hereafter be made in any of them; unless such alteration be agreed to in a Congress of the United States, and be afterward confirmed by the legislatures of every State.

And Whereas it hath pleased the Great Governor of the World to incline the hearts of the legislatures we respectively represent in Congress, to approve of, and to authorize us to ratify the said Articles of Confederation and perpetual union. Know Ye that we, the undersigned delegates, by virtue of the power and authority to us given for that purpose, do by these presents, in the name and in behalf of our respective constituents, fully and entirely ratify and confirm each and every of the said Articles of Confederation and perpetual union, and all and singular the matters and things therein contained: And we do further solemnly plight and engage the faith of our respective constituents, that they shall abide by the determinations of the United States in Congress assembled, on all questions, which by the said confederation are submitted to them. And that the articles thereof shall be inviolably observed by the States we respectively represent, and that the union shall be perpetual. In witness whereof we have hereunto set our hands in Congress. Done at Philadelphia, in the State of Pennsylvania, the 9th day of July, in the Year of our Lord, 1778, and in the 3d year of the Independence of America.

CHAPTER II.

THE FEDERAL CONVENTION.

The following, from the papers of Mr. Madison, is the concluding portion of an article by him, detailing the causes which led to the formation of the Constitution :

A resort to a general convention to re-model the confederacy, was not a new idea. It had entered at an early date into the conversations and speculations of the most reflecting and foreseeing observers of the inadequacy of the powers allowed to Congress. In a pamphlet published in May, 1781, at the seat of Congress, Peletiah Webster, an able though not conspicuous citizen, after discussing the fiscal system of the United States, and suggesting, among other remedial provisions, one including a national bank, remarks, that "the authority of Congress at present is very inadequate to the performance of their duties; and this indicates the necessity of their calling a *Continental Convention* for the express purpose of ascertaining, defining, enlarging, and limiting the duties and powers of their Constitution."

On the 1st of April, 1783, Col. Hamilton, in a debate in in Congress, observed, "That he wished, instead of them, (partial conventions), to see a general convention take place ; and that he should soon, in pursuance of his instructions from his constituents, propose to Congress a plan for that purpose, the object of which would be to strengthen the Federal Constitution." He alluded, probably, to the resolutions introduced by General Schuyler, in the Senate, and passed unanimously by the Legislature of New York, in the summer of 1782, declaring "that the confederation was defective, in not giving Congress power to provide a revenue for itself, or in not investing them with funds from established and productive sources; and that it would be advisable for Congress to recommend to the States to call a general convention, to revise and amend the confederation." It does not appear, however, that his expectation had been fulfilled.

In a letter to James Madison from R. H. Lee, then president of Congress, dated the 26th of November, 1784, he says: "it is by many here suggested, as a very necessary step for Congress to take, the calling on the States to form a convention, for the sole purpose of revising the confederation, so far as to enable Congress to execute, with more energy, effect, and vigor, the powers assigned to it, than it appears by experience that they can do under the present state of things." The answer of Mr. Madison remarks: "I hold it for a maxim, that the Union of the States is essential to their safety against foreign danger and internal contention; and that the perpetuity and efficacy of the present system cannot be confided in. The question, therefore, is in what mode and at what moment, the experiment for supplying the defects ought to be made."

In the winter of 1784–5, Noah Webster, whose political and other valuable writings had made him known to the public, proposed, in one of his publications, "A new system of government, which should act, not on the States, but directly on individuals, and vest in Congress full power to carry its laws into effect."

The proposed and expected Convention at Annapolis, the first of a general character that appears to have been realized, and the state of the public mind awakened by it, had attracted the particular attention of Congress, and favored the idea there of a Convention with fuller powers for amending the confederacy.

It does not appear that in any of these cases the reformed system was to be otherwise sanctioned than by the legislative authority of the States; nor whether, nor how far, a change was to be made in the structure of the depository of federal powers.

The Act of Virginia, providing for the Convention at Philadelphia, was succeeded by appointments from the other States, as their legislatures were assembled, the appointments being selections from the most experienced and high-standing citizens. Rhode Island was the only exception to a compliance with the recommendation from Annapolis, well known to have been swayed by an obdurate adherence to an advantage, which her position gave her, of taxing her neighbors through their consumption of imported supplies—an advantage which it was foreseen would be taken from her by a revisal of the Articles of Confederation.

As the public mind had been ripened for a salutary reform of the political system, in the interval between the proposal and the meeting of the Commissioners at Annapolis, the interval between this last event and the meeting of Deputies at Philadelphia, had continued to develop more and more the necessity and the extent of a systematic provision for the preservation and government of the Union. Among the ripening incidents, was the insurrection of Shays, in Massachusetts, against her government, which was with difficulty suppressed, notwithstanding the influence on the insurgents of an apprehended interposition of the federal troops.

At the date of the Convention, the aspect and retrospect of the political condition of the United States could not but fill the public mind with a gloom, which was relieved only by a hope that so select a body would devise an adequate remedy for the existing and prospective evils so impressively demanding it.

It was seen that the public debt, rendered so sacred by the cause in which it had been incurred, remained without any provision for its payment. The reiterated and elaborate efforts of Congress, to procure from the States a more adequate power to raise the means of payment, had failed. The effect of the ordinary requisitions of Congress had only displayed the inefficiency of the authority making them; none of the States having duly complied with them, some having failed altogether, or nearly so, while in one instance, that of New Jersey, a compliance was *expressly* refused; nor was more yielded to the expostulations of members of Congress, deputed to her legislature, than a mere repeal of the law, without a compliance. The want of authority in Congress to regulate commerce had produced in foreign nations, particularly Great Britain, a monopolizing policy, injurious to the trade of the United States, and destructive to their navigation; the imbecility, and anticipated dissolution of the Confederacy, extinguishing all apprehensions of a countervailing policy on the part of the United States. The same want of a general power over commerce, led to an exercise of the power, separately, by the States, which not only proved abortive, but engendered rival, conflicting, and angry regulations. Beside the vain attempts to supply their respective treasuries by imposts, which turned their commerce into the neighboring ports, and to coerce a relaxation of the British monopoly of the West India navigation, which was attempted by Virginia, the States having ports for foreign commerce, taxed and irritated the adjoining States trading through them—as New York, Pennsylvania, Virginia, and South Carolina. Some of the States, as Connecticut, taxed imports from others, as from Massachusetts, which complained in a letter to the Executive of Virginia, and doubtless to those of other States. In sundry instances, as of New York, New Jersey, Pennsylvania, and Maryland, the navigation laws treated the citizens of other States as aliens. In certain cases, the authority of the confederacy was disregarded—as in violation, not only of the treaty of peace, but of treaties with France and Holland ; which were complained of to Congress. In other cases, the Federal authority was violated by treaties and wars with Indians, as by Georgia ; by troops raised and kept up without the consent of Congress, as by Massachusetts ; by compacts without the consent of Congress, as between Pennsylvania and New Jersey, and between Virginia and Maryland. From the legislative journals of Virginia, it appears, that a vote, refusing to apply for a sanction of Congress, was followed by a vote against the communication of the compact to Congress. In the internal administration of the States, a violation of contracts had become familiar, in the form of depreciated paper, made a legal tender, of property substituted for money, of instalment laws, and of the occlusions of the courts of justice, although evident that all such interferences affected the rights of other States, relatively creditors, as well as citizen creditors within the State. Among the defects which had been severely felt, was want of a uniformity in cases requiring it, as laws of naturalization and bankruptcy ; a coercive authority operating on individuals ; and a guarantee of the internal tranquillity of the States.

As a natural consequence of this distracted and disheartening condition of the Union, the federal authority had ceased to be respected abroad, and dispositions were shown, particularly in Great Britain, to take advantage of imbecility, and to speculate on its approaching downfall. At home, it had lost all confidence and credit ; the unstable and unjust career of the States had also forfeited the respect and confidence essential to order and good government, involving a general decay of confidence and credit between man and man. It was found, moreover, that those least partial to popular government, or most distrustful of its efficacy, were yielding to anticipations, that, from an increase of the confusion, a government might result more congenial with their taste or their opinions; whilst those most devoted to the principles and forms of republics were alarmed for the cause of liberty itself, at stake in the American experiment, and anxious for a system that would avoid the inefficacy of a mere loose confederacy, without passing into the opposite extreme of a consolidated government. It was known that there were individuals who had betrayed a bias toward monarchy, and there had always been some not unfavorable to a partition of the Union into several confederacies, either from a better chance of *figuring on a sectional theatre*, or that the sections would require stronger governments, or, by their hostile conflicts, lead to a monarchical consolidation. The idea of dismemberment had recently made its appearance in the newspapers.

Such were the defects, the deformities, the diseases, and the ominous prospects, for which the Convention was to provide a remedy, and which ought never to be overlooked in expounding and appreciating the constitutional charter, the remedy that was provided.

As a sketch on paper, the earliest, perhaps, of a constitutional government for the Union, (organized into regular departments, with physical means operating on individuals,) to be sanctioned by *the people of the States*, acting in their original and sovereign character, was contained in the letters of James Madison to Thomas Jefferson, of the 19th of March; to Governor Randolph, of the 8th of April; and to General Washington, of the 16th of April, 1787.

The feature in these letters which vested in the general authority a negative on the laws of the States, was suggested by the negative in the head of the British Empire, which prevented collisions between the parts and the whole, and between the parts themselves. It was supposed that the substitution of an elective and responsible authority for an hereditary and irresponsible one would avoid the appearance even of a departure from republicanism. But, although the subject was so viewed in the Convention, and the votes on it were more than once equally divided, it was finally and justly abandoned, as, apart from other objections, it was not practicable among so many States, increasing in number, and enacting, each of them, so many laws. Instead of the proposed negative, the objects of it were left as finally provided for in the Constitution.

On the arrival of the Virginia deputies at Philadelphia, it occurred to them, that from the early and prominent part taken by that State in bringing about the Convention, some initiative step might be expected from them. The resolutions introduced by Governor Randolph were the result of a consultation on the subject, with an understanding that they left all the deputies entirely open to the lights of discussion, and free to concur in any alterations or modifications which their reflections and judgments might approve. The resolutions, as the journals show, became the basis on which the proceedings of the Convention commenced, and to the developments, variations, and modifications of which, the plan of government proposed by the Convention may be traced.

* * * * * * * * * *

APPOINTMENT OF DELEGATES BY STATES.

NEW HAMPSHIRE.—By Act of June 27, 1787, John Langdon, John Pickering, Nicholas Gilman, and Benjamin West, or any two of them, were " appointed and authorized to act as deputies from this State to meet at Philadelphia, delegates from the other States of this Confederacy, to devise ways to avert the dangers which threaten our existence as a free people."

MASSACHUSETTS.—Francis Dana, Elbridge Gerry, Nathaniel Gorham, Rufus King, and Caleb Strong were chosen by the General Court, April 9, 1787, and any three of them authorized to act.

CONNECTICUT.—William S. Johnson, Roger Sherman, and Oliver Ellsworth, appointed by Act of the General Assembly of the second Thursday of May, 1787.

NEW YORK.—Robert Yates, John Lansing, Jr., and Alexander Hamilton, appointed by Act of Assembly, March 6, 1787.

NEW JERSEY.—David Brearly, Wm. C. Houston, William Patterson, and John Neilson, appointed by the Council and Assembly, November 23, 1786. On the 18th May, 1787, William Livingston and Abraham Clark,—and on the 5th June following, Jonathan Dayton, were added to those first appointed, and any three of them empowered to act.

PENNSYLVANIA.—December 30, 1786, Thomas Mifflin, Robert Morris, George Clymer, Jared Ingersoll, Thomas Fitzsimmons, James Wilson, and Gouverneur Morris were appointed by an Act of the General Assembly; and by Act of 28th March, 1787, Benjamin Franklin was added to the list.

DELAWARE.—George Read, Gunning Bedford, John Dickinson, Richard Basset, and Jacob Broom, or any three of them, were appointed by Act of Assembly of February 8, 1787.

MARYLAND.—James McHenry, Daniel of St. Thomas Jenifer, Daniel Carroll, John Francis Mercer, and Luther Martin were appointed by the House of Delegates and Senate, May 26, 1787.

VIRGINIA.—On the 4th December, 1786, by the House of Delegates, with the concurrence of the Senate, George Washington, Patrick Henry, Edmund Randolph, John Blair, James Madison, George Mason, and George Wythe, were appointed. Mr. Henry declined, and James McClurg was appointed by Governor Randolph, in his place on the 2d May, 1787.

NORTH CAROLINA.—By Act of the Senate and House of Commons, in January, 1787, Richard Caswell, Alexander Martin, William Richardson Davie, Richard Dobbs Spaight, and Willie Jones were appointed. Mr. Caswell resigned, and on the twenty-third of April William Blount was appointed in his stead; Willie Jones declining the appointment, Hugh Williamson was appointed by the Governor in his place.

SOUTH CAROLINA.—By Act of March 8, 1787, Charles Pinckney, John Rutledge, Charles C. Pinckney, and Pierce Butler were commissioned.

GEORGIA.—By an ordinance of 10th February, 1787, William Few, Abraham Baldwin, William Pierce, George Walton, William Houston, and Nathaniel Pendleton appointed deputies from this State.

ABSTRACT OF THE JOURNAL AND DEBATES IN THE FEDERAL CONVENTION.

On Monday the 14th of May, A. D., 1787, and in the eleventh year of the Independence of the United States of America, at the State House in the city of Philadelphia, in virtue of appointments from their respective States, sundry deputies to the Federal Convention appeared; but a majority of States not being represented, the members present adjourned from day to day until Friday the 25th of the said month, when, in virtue of the said appointments, appeared from the State of

MASSACHUSETTS.—The Hon. Rufus King, Esq.

NEW YORK.—The Hon. Robert Yates, and Alexander Hamilton, Esqs.

NEW JERSEY.—The Hon. David Brearly, William Churchhill Houston, and William Patterson, Esqs.

PENNSYLVANIA.—The Hon. Robert Morris, Thomas Fitzsimmons, James Wilson, and Gouverneur Morris, Esqs.

DELAWARE.—The Hon. George Read, Richard Bassett, and Jacob Broom, Esqs.

VIRGINIA.—His Excellency George Washington, Esq., His Excellency E. Randolph, Esq., The Hon. John Blair, James Madison, George Mason, George Wythe, and James McClurg, Esqs.

NORTH CAROLINA.—The Hon. Alexander Martin, William Richardson Davie, Richard Dobbs Spaight, and Hugh Williamson, Esqs.

SOUTH CAROLINA.—The Hon. John Rutledge, Charles Cotesworth Pinckney, Pierce Butler, and Charles Pinckney, Esqs.

GEORGIA.—The Hon. William Few, Esq.

Hon. Robert Morris of Pennsylvania moved that a President be elected by ballot, and nominated GEORGE WASHINGTON. A ballot was taken and he was declared unanimously elected, and was conducted to the Chair by Mr. Morris and Mr. Rutledge. William Jackson was elected Secretary, Nicholas Weaver, Messenger, and Joseph Frye, Door-Keeper.

Mr. Wythe, Mr. Hamilton, and Mr. C. Pinckney were appointed a Committee on Rules, and the Convention adjourned till Monday at 10 o'clock.

Monday, May 28, 1787.—The Convention met; Nathaniel Gorham and Caleb Strong, deputies from Massachusetts, Oliver Ellsworth from the State of Connecticut, Gunning Bedford from Delaware, James McHenry from Maryland; Benjamin Franklin, George Clymer, Thomas Mifflin, and Jared Ingersoll, of Pennsylvania, took their seats. Rules for the government of the Convention were reported and adopted.

Mr. Randolph then opened the business of the Convention by offering the following resolutions:

Resolutions offered by Edward Randolph to the Convention, May 29, 1787.

"1. *Resolved*, That the Articles of the Confederation ought to be so corrected and enlarged as to accomplish the objects proposed by their institution; namely, common defense, security of liberty, and general welfare.

"2. *Resolved*, Therefore, that the right of suffrage, in the national legislature ought to be proportioned to the quotas of contribution, or to the number of free inhabitants, as the one or the other may seem best, in different cases.

"3. *Resolved*, That the national legislature ought to consist of two branches.

"4. *Resolved*, That the members of the first branch of the national legislature ought to be elected by the people of the several States every   for the term of   to be of the age of   years, at least; to receive liberal stipends, by which they may be compensated for the devotion of their time to the public service; to be ineligible to any office established by a particular State; or under the authority of the United States, (except those peculiarly belonging to the functions of the first branch,) during the term of service and for the space of   after its expiration; to be incapable of re-election for the space of   after the expiration of their term of service; and to be subject to recall.

"5. *Resolved*, that the members of the second branch of the national legislature ought to be elected by those of the first, out of a proper number of persons nominated by the individual legislatures; to be of the age of   years, at least; to hold their offices for a term sufficient to insure their independency; to receive liberal stipends, by which they may be compensated for the devotion of their time to the public service; and to be ineligible to any office established by a particular State, or under the authority of the United States, (except those particularly belonging to the functions of the second branch,) during the term of service; and for the space of   after the expiration thereof.

"6. *Resolved*, That each branch ought to possess the right of originating acts; that the national legislature ought to be empowered to enjoy the legislative right vested in Congress by the Confederation; and moreover, to legislate in all cases to which the separate States are incompetent, or in which the harmony of the United States may be interrupted by the exercise of individual legislation; to negative all laws passed by the several States, contravening, in the opinion of the national legislature, the articles of union, or any treaty subsisting under the authority of the Union; and to call forth the force of the Union against any member of the Union failing to fulfill its duty under the articles thereof.

"7. *Resolved*, That a national executive be instituted, to be chosen by the national legislature for the term of   years, to receive punctually, at stated times, a fixed compensation for the services rendered, in which no increase or diminution shall be made, so as to affect the magistracy existing at the time of the increase or diminution; to be ineligible a second time; and that, beside a general authority to execute the national laws, it ought to enjoy the executive rights vested in Congress by the Confederation.

"8. *Resolved*, That the executive and a convenient number of the national judiciary ought to compose a council of revision, with authority to examine every act of the national legislature before it shall operate, and every act of a particular legislature, before a negative thereon shall be final; and that the dissent of the said council shall amount to a rejection, unless the act of the national legislature be again passed, or that of a particular legislature be again negatived by   of the members of each branch.

"9. *Resolved*, That a national judiciary be established, to hold their offices during good behavior, and to receive punctually, at stated times, a fixed compensation for their services, in which no increase or diminution shall be made, so as to affect the persons actually in office at the time of such increase or diminution. That the jurisdiction of the inferior tribunals, shall be to hear and determine in the first instance, and of the supreme tribunal to hear and determine in the *dernier ressort*, all piracies and felonies on the seas; captures from an enemy; cases in which foreigners, or citizens of other States, applying to such jurisdictions, may be interested or which respect the collection of the national revenue; impeachments of any national officer; and questions which involve the national peace or harmony.

"10. *Resolved*, That provision ought to be made for the admission of States lawfully arising within the limits of the United States, whether from a voluntary junction of government or territory, or otherwise, with the consent of a number of voices in the national legislature less than the whole.

"11. *Resolved*, That a republican government, and the territory of each State, (except in the instance of a voluntary junction of government, and territory,) ought to be guaranteed by the United States to each State.

"12. *Resolved*, That provision ought to be made for the continuance of Congress, and their authorities and privileges, until a given day, after the reform of the articles of union shall be adopted, and for the completion of all their engagements.

"13. *Resolved*, That provision ought to be made for the amendment of the articles of union, whensoever it shall seem necessary; and that the assent of the national legislature ought not to be required thereto.

"14. *Resolved*, That the legislative, executive, and judiciary powers within the several States ought to be bound by oath to support the articles of union.

"15. *Resolved*, That the amendments which shall be offered to the Confederation by the Convention, ought, at a proper time or times, after the approbation of Congress, to be submitted to an assembly or assemblies of representatives, recommended by the several legislatures, to be expressly chosen by the people to consider and decide thereon.

"16. *Resolved*, That the House will to-morrow resolve itself into a committee of the whole House, to consider of the state of the American Union."

Wednesday, May 30. The Hon. Roger Sherman, a deputy from the State of Connecticut, appeared and took his seat.

The House went into Committee of the Whole, Mr. Gorham in the Chair, on the resolutions of Mr. Randolph.

Mr. Madison moved "that the equality of suffrage established by the Articles of Confederation, ought not to prevail in the national legislature; and that an equitable ratio of representation ought to be substituted." This was opposed, on the ground that the deputies from Delaware were instructed not to assent to such a change, and they would therefore retire should it be adopted. After some discussion the Committee rose and the House adjourned.

Thursday, May 1. The Hon. William Pierce, of Georgia, took his seat.

Mr. Randolph's third resolution, "that the national legislature ought to consist of two branches," was agreed to without dissent, except from Dr. Franklin of Pennsylvania.

The first clause of the fourth resolution, "that the members of the first branch of the national legislature ought to be elected by the people of the several States," was taken up.

Mr. Sherman opposed election by the people, and said it ought to be by the State legislatures; that the people were constantly liable to be misled.

Mr. Gerry also opposed election by the people, saying that we had been having an excess of democracy heretofore. Pretended patriots would dupe and deceive the people— that they had done it heretofore in Massachusetts.

Mr. Madison considered the election of one branch by the people as essential to every plan of a free government. He thought that the great fabric to be raised would be more stable and durable, if it should rest on the solid foundation of the people themselves, than if it should stand merely on the pillars of the legislatures.

On the question for election by the people, Ayes 6, Noes 2, Connecticut and Delaware divided.

[The reader will here observe that the votes of the Convention in all cases were taken by States.]

It was then moved to elect the members of the second branch by the members of the first. This, after considerable discussion, was voted down.

Friday, June 1. The Hon. William Houstoun, from Georgia, took his seat.

The Committee of the Whole proceeded to the seventh resolution, "that a national executive be instituted, to be chosen by the national legislature for the term of   years, to be ineligible thereafter, &c."

Mr. Pinckney was for a vigorous executive, but was afraid it might run into a monarchy.

Mr. Wilson was for a single executive.

Dr. Franklin wanted the question discussed, as it was very important.

Mr. Sherman thought the executive should be elected by Congress.

Mr. Madison opposed fixing the executive till his powers were first agreed upon. Pending the discussion the House adjourned.

Saturday, June 2. William S. Johnson, from Connecticut, Daniel of St. Thomas Jenifer, from Maryland, and John Lansing, Jr., from New York, took their seats.

The motion to elect the executive by the national legislature for the term of seven years was agreed to.

Monday, June 4. It was agreed that the executive should consist of but one person, New York, Delaware and Maryland voting No. It was also agreed that the executive should have the right of veto. It was also agreed that a national judiciary, to consist of one supreme tribunal, and one or more inferior, should be constituted.

Tuesday, June 5. On the question of choosing the judiciary by the national legislature,

Dr. Franklin suggested the Scotch mode of letting the lawyers choose the judges, as they would always choose the ablest of the profession in order to get his practice themselves.

Mr. Madison was opposed to electing judges by the legislature, or by any numerous body, and was inclined to give it to the Senate.

William Livingston, from New Jersey, took his seat.

Wednesday, June 6. Mr. Pinckney moved "that the first branch of the national legislature be elected by the State legislatures, and not by the people."

Mr. Mason spoke against this motion. He said that under the confederacy Congress represented the States, not the people; under the present plan of government Congress should represent the *people*, therefore should be chosen by the people.

Mr. Dickinson proposed that the two systems should be blended. Let one branch come directly from the people, and the other be chosen by the State legislatures. One would thus represent the people, and the other the interests of the States, and being independent they would operate as checks upon each other.

Mr. Read thought too much attachment was betrayed for the State governments. The national government must of necessity swallow them up. If we do not establish a good and strong government we should soon have to do the work over again.

Mr. Pinckney and Mr. Wilson were for preserving the State governments. The motion of Mr. Pinckney to elect the first branch by the State legislatures was then negatived.*

From June 7th till the 14th, the Convention was engaged in the discussion of the remainder of Mr. Randolph's resolutions, when they were reported to the House with amendments.

June 15. Mr. Patterson submitted a series of resolutions, which were afterward designated as "the Jersey plan." They were postponed, however, and on the 19th voted down, receiving but three votes.

June 18. Mr. Hamilton addressed the Convention, and at the close of his remarks, offered his plan of government. We give both the speech and the plan, from Mr. Yates' notes, who observes that Mr. Hamilton saw and corrected

---

* The reader cannot fail to observe, from this discussion, the design of the framers of the Constitution in giving each State an equal representation in the Senate, and of electing that branch (the second branch) by the State legislatures, viz.: that the Senate should be the conservator of State sovereignty, as suggested by Mr. Dickinson, while the House (the first branch) should represent the people. A happy blending of the two systems proposed, and a full answer to the objection so frequently raised in large States, that they have no more power in the Senate than the smallest. It is here that the strongest barrier against the despotism of a central government is erected. May it never be pulled down!

the speech at the time. It is worthy of note that, from this speech and plan of government sprang the political animosity between Mr. Jefferson and Mr. Hamilton, that finally resulted in the organization of two great political parties, Federal and Republican, under the lead of those truly great men. Mr. Hamilton, it will be seen, was cautious as to trusting power in the hands of the people, and advocated a kind of elective monarchy. Mr. Jefferson took the opposite view, and, in some form or other, those distinctive ideas, modified, it is true, have pervaded the politics of the country ever since.

Mr. Hamilton said: To deliver my sentiments on so important a subject, when the first characters of the Union have gone before me, inspires me with the greatest diffidence, especially when my own ideas are so materially dissimilar to the plans now before the committee. My situation is disagreeable; but it would be criminal not to come forward on a question of so much magnitude. I have well considered the subject, and am convinced that no amendment of the Confederation can answer the purpose of a good government, so long as the State sovereignties do, in any shape exist; and I have great doubts whether a national government on the Virginia plan, can be made effectual. What is federal? An association of several independent States into one. How or in what manner this association is formed, is not so clearly distinguishable. We find that the diet of Germany has, in some instances, the power of legislation on individuals. We find the United States of America have it in an extensive degree in the case of piracies.

Let us now review the powers with which we are invested. We are appointed with the sole and express purpose of revising the Confederation, and to alter or amend it, so as to render it effectual for the purpose of a good government. Those who suppose it to be federal, lay great stress on the terms *sole* and *express*, as if these words intended a confinement to a federal government, when the manifest import is no more than that the institution of a good government must be the *sole* and *express* object of your deliberations. Nor can we suppose an annihilation of our powers by forming a national government, as many of the States have made in their constitutions no proper provisions for any alterations, and thus much I can say for the State I have the honor to represent, that when our credentials were under consideration in the Senate, some members were for inserting a restriction in the powers, to prevent an encroachment on the constitution: it was answered by others, and thereupon the resolve carried on the credentials, that it might abridge the constitutional powers of the State, and that possibly in the formation of a new Union, it would be found necessary. This seems reasonable, and leaves us at liberty to form such a national government as we think best adapted to the whole. I have therefore no difficulty as to the extent of our powers, nor do I feel myself restrained in the exercise of my judgment under them. We can only propose and recommend;—the power of ratifying or rejecting is still in the States. But on this great question I am still embarrassed. I have before observed my apprehension of the inefficacy of either plan, and I have doubts whether a more energetic government can pervade this wide and extensive country. I shall now show that both plans are materially defective.

1. A good government ought to be constant, and ought to contain an active principle. 2. Utility and necessity. 3. An habitual sense of obligation. 4. Force. 5. Influence. I hold it that different societies have all different views and interests to pursue, and always prefer local to general concerns. For example, the New York Legislature made an external compliance lately to a requisition of Congress; but do they not, at the same time, counteract

their compliance by gratifying the local objects of the State, so as to defeat their concession ? And this will ever be the case. Men always love power, and States will prefer their particular concerns to the general welfare; and as the States become large and important, will they not be less attentive to the general government? What, in process of time, will Virginia be ? She contains now half a million inhabitants; in twenty-five years she will double that number. Feeling her own weight and importance, must she not become indifferent to the concerns of the Union ? And where in such a situation will be found national attachment to the general government ?

By *force* I mean the *coercion* of law and the coercion of arms. Will this remark apply to the power invested to be instituted by their plan ? A delinquent must be compelled to obedience by force of arms. How is this to be done ? If you are unsuccessful, a dissolution of your government must be the consequence; and in that case the individual legislatures will resume their powers; nay, will not the interests of the States be thrown into the State governments ?

By *influence* I mean the regular weight and support it will receive from those who find it their interest to support a government intended to preserve the peace and happiness of the community on the whole. The State governments, by either plan, will exert the means to counteract it. They have their State judges and militia, all combined to support their State interests; and these will be influenced to oppose a national government. Either plan therefore is precarious. The national government cannot long exist, opposed by so weighty a rival. The experience of ancient and modern confederacies evinces this point, and throws considerable light on the subject. The Amphictyonic council of Greece had a right to require of its members troops, money, and the force of the country. Were they obeyed in the exercise of those powers? Could they preserve the peace of the greater States and republics? Or, where were they obeyed? History shows that their decrees were disregarded, and that the stronger States, regardless of their power, gave law to the lesser.

Let us examine the Federal Institutions of Germany. It was instituted upon the laudable principle of securing the independency of the several States of which it was composed, and to protect them against foreign invasion. Has it answered these good intentions? Do we not see that their councils are weak and distracted, and that it cannot prevent the wars and confusions which the respective electors carry on against each other? The Swiss Cantons, or the Helvetic Union, are equally insufficient.

Such are the lessons which the experience of others affords us, and from whence results the evident conclusion that all Federal Governments are weak and distracted. To avoid the evils deducible from these observations, we must establish a general and national government, completely sovereign, and annihilate the State distinctions and State operations; and unless we do this, no good purpose can be answered. What does the Jersey plan propose? It surely has not this for its object. By this we grant the regulations of trade and a more effectual collection of the revenue, and some partial duties. These, at five or ten per cent., would only perhaps amount to a fund to discharge the debt of the corporation.

Let us take a review of the variety of important objects which must necessarily engage the attention of a national government. You have to protect your rights against Canada on the North, Spain on the South, and your western frontier against the savages, you have to adopt necessary plans for the settlement of your frontiers, and to institute the mode in which settlements and good governments are to be made.

How is the expense of supporting and regulating these important matters to be defrayed? By requisition on the States according to the Jersey plan? Will this do it. We have already found it ineffectual. Let one state prove delinquent, and it will encourage others to follow the example; and thus the whole will fail. And what is the standard by which to quota among the States their respective proportions? Can lands be the standard? How would that apply between Russia and Holland? Compare Pennsylvania with North Carolina, or Connecticut with New York. Does not commerce or industry in the one or the other make a great disparity, between these different countries, and may not the comparative value of the States, from these circumstances, make an unequal disproportion when the data are numbers? I therefore conclude that either system would ultimately destroy the Confederation, or any other government which is established on such fallacious principles. Perhaps imposts—taxes on specific articles—would produce a more equal system of drawing a revenue.

Another objection against the Jersey plan is, the unequal representation. Can the great States consent to this? If they did, it would eventually work its own destruction. How are forces to be raised by the Jersey plan? By quotas? Will the States comply with the requisition? As much as they will with the taxes.

Examine the present Confederation, and it is evident they can raise no troops, and equip no vessels, before war is actually declared. They cannot, therefore, take any preparatory measure before an enemy is at your door. How unwise and inadequate their powers! And this must ever be the case when you attempt to define powers; something will always be wanting. Congress, by being annually elected, and subject to recall, will ever come with the prejudices of their States, rather than the good of the Union. Add therefore, additional powers to a body organized, and you establish a *sovereignty* of the worst kind consisting of a single body. Where are the checks? None. They must either prevail over the State governments, or the prevalence of the State governments must end in their dissolution. This is a conclusive objection to the Jersey plan.

Such are the insuperable objections to both plans, and what is to be done on this occasion? I confess I am at a loss. I foresee the difficulty, on a consolidated plan, of drawing a representation from so extensive a continent to one place. What can be the inducements for gentlemen to come six hundred miles to a legislature? The expense would at least amount to a hundred thousand pounds. This, however, can be no conclusive objection, if it eventuates in an extinction of State governments: reduced to corporations, and with very limited powers, they might be necessary, and the expense of the national government less burdensome.

Yet, I confess, I see great difficulty of drawing forth a good representation. What, for example, will be the inducements for gentlemen of fortune and abilities to leave their houses and business to attend annually and long? It cannot be the wages; for these, I presume, must be small. Will not the power, therefore, be thrown into the hands of the demagogue or middling politician—who, for the sake of a small stipend and the hopes of advancement, will offer himself as a candidate, and the real men of weight and influence, by remaining at home, add strength to the State governments? I am at a loss to know what must be done. I despair that a republican form of government can remove the difficulties. Whatever may be my opinion, I would hold it, however, unwise to change that form of government. I believe the British Government forms the best model the world ever produced; and such has been its progress in the minds of many, that the truth gradually gains ground. This government has for its object *public strength* and *individual security*. It is said with us to be unattainable. If it was once formed, it would maintain itself. All communities divide themselves into the few and the many. The first are the rich and well born, the others the mass of the people. The voice of the people is said to be the voice of God; and, however generally this maxim has been quoted and believed, it is not true in fact. The people are turbulent and changing; they seldom judge or determine rightly. Give, therefore, the first class a distinct and permanent share in the government. They will check the unsteadiness of the second, and as they cannot receive any advantage by change, they therefore will ever maintain good government. Can a democratic assembly, who annually revolve in the mass of people, be supposed steadily to pursue the public good? Nothing but a permanent body can check the imprudence of democracy; their turbulent and incontrollable disposition requires checks. The Senate of New York, although chosen for four years, we have found to be inefficient. Will, on the Virginia plan, a continuance of seven years do it? It is admitted that you cannot have a good executive upon a democratic plan. See the excellency of the British executive. He is above temptation—he can have no distinct interest from the public welfare. Nothing short of such an executive can be efficient. The weak side of a republican government is the danger of foreign influence. This is unavoidable, unless it is so constructed as to bring forward its first characters in its support. I am, therefore, for a general government, yet would wish to go the full length of the republican principle.

Let one body of the legislature be constituted during good behavior, or life.

Let one executive be appointed, who dares execute his powers. It may be asked, Is this a republican system? It is strictly so, as long as they remain elective.

And let me observe, that an executive is less dangerous

to the liberties of the people, when in office during life, than for seven years.

It may be said this constitutes an elective monarchy. Pray what is a monarch? May not the governors of the respective States be considered in that light? But by making the executive subject to impeachment, the term *monarch* cannot apply. These elective monarchs have produced tumults in Rome, and are equally dangerous to peace in Poland; but this cannot apply to the mode in which I propose the election. Let electors be appointed in each of the States, to elect the legislature, to consist of two branches; and I would give them the power of passing *all laws*, without exception. The assembly to be elected for three years, by the people, in districts; the senate to be elected by electors, to be chosen for that purpose by the people, and to remain in office during life. The executive to have the power of negativing all laws; to make war or peace, with the advice of the senate; to make treaties, with their advice; but to have the sole directions in all military operations, and to send ambassadors, and appoint all military officers, and to pardon all offenders, treason excepted, unless by the advice of the senate. On his death, or removal, the president of the senate to officiate, with the same powers, until another is elected. Supreme judicial officers to be appointed by the executive and the senate. The legislature to appoint courts in each state, so as to make the State government unnecessary to it.

All State laws to be absolutely void, which contravene the general laws. An officer appointed in each State to have a negative on all laws. All the militia, and the appointment of officers, to be under the national government.

I confess that this plan, and that from Virginia, are very remote from the idea of the people; perhaps the Jersey plan is nearest their expectation. But the people are gradually ripening in their opinions of government—they begin to be tired of an excess of democracy—and what even is the Virginia plan, but *pork still, with a little change of the sauce?*

The following is Mr. Hamilton's plan:

" 1. The supreme legislative power of the United States of America to be vested in two different bodies of men; the one to be called the assembly, the other the senate; who, together, shall form the legislature of the United States, with power to pass all laws whatsoever, subject to the negative hereafter mentioned.

"2. The assembly to consist of persons elected by the people, to serve for three years.

" 3. The senate to consist of persons elected to serve during good behavior; their election to be made by electors chosen for that purpose by the people. In order to this, the states to be divided into election districts. On the death, removal, or resignation of any senator, his place to be filled out of the district from which he came.

" 4. The supreme executive authority of the United States to be vested in a governor, to be elected to serve during good behavior; the election to be made by electors chosen by the people in the election districts aforesaid. The authorities and functions of the executive to be as follows: To have a negative on all laws about to be passed, and the execution of all laws passed; to have the direction of war when authorized or begun; to have, with the advice and approbation of the senate, the power of making all treaties; to have the sole appointment of the heads or chief officers of the departments of finance, war, and foreign affairs; to have the nomination of all other officers, (ambassadors to foreign nations included,) subject to the approbation or rejection of the senate; to have the power of pardoning all offenses except treason, which he shall not pardon without the approbation of the senate.

"5. On the death, resignation, or removal of the governor, his authorities to be exercised by the president of the senate till a successor be appointed.

"6. The senate to have the sole power of declaring war; the power of advising and approving all treaties; the power of approving or rejecting all appointments of officers, except the heads or chiefs of the departments of finance, war, and foreign affairs.

"7. The supreme judicial authority to be vested in judges, to hold their offices during good behavior, with adequate and permanent salaries. This court to have original jurisdiction in all causes of capture, and an appellative jurisdiction in all causes in which the revenues of the general government, or the citizens of foreign nations, are concerned.

"8. The legislature of the United States to have power to institute courts in each state for the determination of all matters of general concern.

"9. The governor, senators, and all officers of the United States, to be liable to impeachment for mal and corrupt conduct; and, upon conviction, to be removed from office, and disqualified for holding any place of trust or profit; all impeachments to be tried by a court to consist of the chief ———, or judge of the superior court of law of each State, provided such judge shall hold his place during good behavior, and have a permanent salary.

"10. All laws of the particular States contrary to the Constitution or laws of the United States, to be utterly void; and, the better to prevent such laws being passed, the governor or president of each State shall be appointed by the general government, and shall have a negative upon the laws about to be passed in the State of which he is the governor or president.

"11. No State to have any forces, land or naval; and the militia of all the States to be under the sole and exclusive direction of the United States, the officers of which to be appointed and commissioned by them."

June 20. Hon. William Blount, from North Carolina, took his seat.

Mr. Lansing moved "that the power of legislation be vested in the United States in Congress." This proposition was discussed all day. It was adopted.

June 21. Hon. Jonathan Dayton, of New Jersey, took his seat.

The second resolution—"that the legislature shall consist of two branches," was taken up and discussed by Dr. Johnson, Mr. Wilson and Mr. Madison, and was adopted.

Gen. Pinckney moved that the first branch should be elected in such manner as the State legislatures should direct. This was opposed by Mr. Mason, Mr. Sherman and others, who advocated election by the people. The motion was lost.

On the original question of election of the first branch by the people, it was carried,—New Jersey alone voting No, and Maryland divided.

On the question that the members should be elected for three years, Mr. Randolph moved to amend by substituting "two years."

Mr. Wilson preferred annual elections, as likely to make the representative feel his dependence upon his constituents.

Mr. Madison thought annual elections, or even biennial, would be too great a burden upon the people, and attended with much inconvenience.

Col. Hamilton was for three years, and on the question, the amendment for two years was agreed to.

June 22. The question of compensation of members, their age, and eligibility, was discussed this and the day following.

June 25. The fourth resolution, "that the members of

the second branch (Senate) ought to be chosen by the State Legislatures and hold their office seven years," was taken up.

Mr. Pinckney advocated the resolution. He thought there should be one branch removed from the influences to be apprehended from the fluctuations of the popular passions. The States, too, should be guaranteed some protection for their sovereignty, otherwise the State governments would be overborne by the national government.

Mr. Wilson opposed election by the legislatures as likely to foster local pride and prejudices.

On the question to elect by the State legislatures, it was agreed to, Pennsylvania and Virginia only voting No.

It was then agreed that no person should be eligible for senator till he had arrived at the age of thirty years.

June 26. The term of office for senators being under consideration,

Mr. Gorham moved six years. Mr. Pinckney was in favor of four years. Mr. Read favored nine years.

Mr. Madison said that we are now digesting a plan which in its operations will decide forever the fate of republican government. We ought therefore to provide every possible guard and check to liberty. Those charged with the public happiness may betray their trust. Prudence would dictate that we should so organize that one body might watch and check the other. We should select a limited number of enlightened citizens, whose firmness might be interposed against impetuous counsels.

Mr. Hamilton concurred with Mr. Madison. On the question for nine years it was lost; and on the question for six years it was agreed to.

On the question of compensation, Mr. Pinckney proposed that the senators should receive no pay, as that branch was designed to represent the wealth of the country, and it should be so ordered that none but the wealthy could take that office. Dr. Franklin seconded the motion. The motion was lost. Ayes 5, Noes 6.

It was then moved that the senators be paid by their respective States. Lost. And on the question that they be paid out of the national treasury, it was lost.

June 27. On the seventh resolution, that the right of suffrage in the first branch should be according to an equitable ratio.

Mr. Martin contended with great zeal that the general government was meant to preserve the State governments merely, and not to govern individuals; and that its powers ought, therefore, to be kept in very narrow limits. That to give representation according to population would place it in the power of the large States to crush out the small ones. The vote should be by States and then all would stand upon the same platform of equality.

June, 28. Mr. Madison replied to Mr. Martin's speech on representation, and in a lengthy argument advocated representation in the first branch (House) according to the population. The debate lasted two days during which much angry feeling was manifested. The small States were determined that no provision should pass that did not give them an equal vote with the large States. Some idea of the difficulties encountered at this time may be gathered from a speech of Dr. Franklin near the close of the second day's proceedings. We copy it entire:

Dr. Franklin.—Mr. President: The small progress we have made after four or five weeks' close attendance and continued reasonings with each other—our different sentiments on almost every question, several of the last producing as many noes as ayes—is, methinks, a melancholy proof of the imperfection of the human understanding. We, indeed, seem to feel our own want of political wisdom, since we have been running about in search of it. We have gone back to ancient history for models of government, and examined the different forms of those republics which, having been formed with the seeds of their own dissolution, now no longer exist. And we have viewed modern States all round Europe, but find none of their constitutions suitable to our circumstances.

In this situation of this assembly, groping as it were in the dark to find political truth, and scarce able to perceive it when presented to us, how has it happened, sir, that we have not hitherto once thought of humbly applying to the Father of lights to illuminate our understandings? In the beginning of the contest with Great Britain, when we were sensible of danger, we had daily prayer in this room for the Divine protection. Our prayers, sir, were heard, and they were graciously answered. All of us who were engaged in the struggle must have observed frequent instances of a superintending Providence in our favor.

To that kind Providence we owe this happy opportunity of consulting in peace on the means of establishing our future national felicity. And have we now forgotten that powerful friend? Or do we imagine that we no longer need his assistance? I have lived, sir, a long time, and the longer I live the more convincing proofs I see of this truth—*that God governs in the affairs of man.* And if a sparrow cannot fall to the ground without his notice, is it probable that an empire can rise without his aid? We have been answered, sir, in the sacred writings, that "except the Lord build the house, they labor in vain that build it." I firmly believe this; and I also firmly believe this, that without his concurring aid we shall succeed, in this political building, no better than the builders of Babel. We shall be divided by our little partial local interests; our projects will be confounded; and we shall ourselves become a reproach and by-word down to future ages. And, what is worse, mankind may hereafter, from this unfortunate instance, despair of establishing governments by human wisdom, and leave it to chance, war, and conquest.

I therefore beg leave to move that henceforth prayers, imploring the assistance of Heaven and its blessings on our deliberations, be held in this assembly every morning before we proceed to business, and that one or more of the clergy of this city be requested to officiate in that service.

Mr. Sherman seconded the motion.

Mr. Hamilton was fearful that if the motion should be adopted it would alarm the people, who would think that some extraordinary emergency had arisen in the Convention. It would have been well to have adopted such a motion at the beginning of the session.

Mr. Randolph proposed that a sermon be preached on the fourth of July, and after that prayers. An adjournment was finally carried without a vote by ayes and nays.

June 29.—Dr. Johnson said this controversy seemed endless. On the one side the States were considered as districts of *people*, and hence entitled to representation according to their numbers; on the other side it was contended that they were political *societies*, and hence each should be represented equally. He suggested that each side was partially right, and that therefore the true ground was a compromise; let one branch represent exclusively the people and the other (the Senate) represent the States.

Mr. Madison agreed with Dr. Johnson, that the mixed nature of the government ought to be kept in view. He made a lengthy speech in favor of this proposition. The debate was continued through the day, and it was finally agreed that the representation should be according to the ratio of inhabitants.

June 30.—Mr. Brearly moved that the President write to the Executive of New Hampshire requesting the immediate attendance of the delegates from that State, as the difficulties of the Convention are such, that they wanted all the aid possible. Not agreed to.

Mr. Ellsworth moved that each State be allowed an equal vote in the second branch, and supported his motion by a lengthy argument.

Mr. Wilson opposed the motion. He said we were forming a government for *men*, not for imaginary States.

Mr. Madison thought the difficulty was not between the large and small States, but really between the States having slaves and those not having, or expecting soon not to have slaves. He thought a fair compromise would be to have one branch represented according to the number of free inhabitants only, and the other represented by the whole, counting the slaves as freemen, instead of counting them as five to three. By this arrangement the southern scale would have the advantage in one House and the northern in the other.

Dr. Franklin thought "both sides must part with some of their demands."

The discussion was continued through the day without arriving at any conclusion.

July 2.—On the question allowing each State one vote in the second branch it was lost. Ayes 5. Noes 5.

General Pinckney proposed that a committee of one from each State should be appointed to devise and report a compromise.

Mr. Morris favored a committee. He said the object of the second branch was to check the excesses of the first branch. He thought it must be a branch of property interest, and must also be permanent in order to give stability to the government. Without it the country would have no confidence in the plan. Loaves and fishes would bribe demagogues. Give us a senate for life, without pay, and we will have an honest and conservative branch.

Mr. Madison opposed the committee. It was discussed at length, and on the question, nine States voted Aye. New Jersey and Delaware voted No.

The committee was elected by ballot, and was composed of Messrs. Gerry, Ellsworth, Yates, Patterson, Dr. Franklin, Bedford, Martin, Mason, Davie, Rutledge and Baldwin. To give the committee time to deliberate, the Convention adjourned till Thursday the 5th.

July 5. Mr. Gerry, from the committee appointed on Monday last, made the following report:

1. That in the first branch each State shall be allowed one member for every forty thousand inhabitants, counting all free persons and three-fifths of the slaves, and that all money bills, or bills fixing salaries of public officers, shall originate in the first branch, and shall not be altered or amended by the second branch.

2. That in the second branch each State shall have an equal vote.

[*Note.*—This report was considered as a compromise between the large and small States. The large States were apprehensive that by allowing the small ones an equal representation in the Senate, they might, by combination, vote undue burdens upon them in the way of appropriations of the public money. Hence, the arrangement that money bills shall originate in the House where the representation is in accordance with the ratio of inhabitants, thus protecting the large States in that branch, while the small States find their protection in the Senate, where they have an equal representation. How admirable the arrangement! How beautifully ordered by our fathers for the protection of the rights of the whole Union, is this model constitution—the perfection of governmental excellence—the sum total of the wisdom of ages in the science of self-government!

This report was founded on a motion made, in the committee, by Dr. Franklin.]

Mr. Madison did not consider the concession of the small States that the House should originate all money bills as of much moment. He said the senators could get the members of the House to adopt their notions by handing them amendments, and thus avoid the check that this clause was designed to afford. He thought we should form a government on just principles, and the small States would find it to their interest to adopt it.

A long debate ensued, participated in by Messrs. Morris, Bedford, Ellsworth, Mason, Rutledge and others, and without the question the Convention adjourned.

July 6. Mr. Morris moved to commit so much of the report as relates to one member to every forty thousand inhabitants to a committee of five, which was agreed to.

The clause relating to an equality of votes in the Senate being under consideration, it was postponed, and the clause relating to money bills taken up. After some discussion it was agreed to.

July 7. The clause allowing each State one vote in the Senate being up, after a long and zealous discussion, it was postponed until the committee of five, on the number of members in the first branch, should report.

July 9. Daniel Carroll, of Maryland, took his seat.

Mr. Morris, from the committee of five, reported that the House should at first consist of forty-six members. New Hampshire, two; Massachusetts, seven; Rhode Island, one; Connecticut, four; New York, five; New Jersey, three; Pennsylvania, eight; Delaware, one; Maryland, four; Virginia, nine; North Carolina, five; South Carolina, five; Georgia, two; and that Congress should alter the number from time to time, as it should think proper.

Mr. Patterson thought the proposed estimate for the future too vague. He could regard negro slaves in no light but property. They were not represented in the State governments, and hence should not be in the national government.

Mr. Madison suggested as a compromise, that in the House the representation should be according to the number of free inhabitants; that the Senate was designed, in one respect, to be the guardian of property, and that branch should represent slaves and all. After some further discussion, the first clause of the report was referred to a committee of one from each State.

July 10. Mr. King, from the committee appointed yesterday, reported that the House should consist of sixty-five members. After a long and animated discussion the report was adopted. South Carolina and Georgia alone voting No.

July 11. Mr. Randolph's motion, requiring a census to be taken in order to correct inequalities in representation, was taken up.

Mr. Butler and Gen. Pinckney insisted that blacks should have an equal representation with the whites, and therefore moved that "three-fifths" be struck out.

Mr. Gerry, and Mr. Gorham, favored three-fifths.

Mr. Butler, said the labor of a slave in South Carolina, was as valuable as that of a freeman in Massachussets. Free negroes in the North, have an equal representation with the whites. So should the slaves of the South have.

Mr. Williamson, said that the Eastern States contended for the equality of blacks where taxation was in view, they ought then to be willing to allow an equal representation.

On the question, Mr. Butler's motion was lost, only Delaware, South Carolina, and Georgia, voting Aye.

Mr. Morris, said that if slaves were to be considered as inhabitants, not as wealth, then there would be no use for a census, so far as they were concerned; if simply as wealth, then why not other wealth be included?

Mr. Sherman, was in favor of leaving the whole matter to the discretion of the legislature.

Mr. Morris, said that the people of Pennsylvania would revolt at the idea of being placed on a level with slaves in representation. They would reject any plan in which slaves were included in the census.

On the question of taking a census of *free* inhabitants, it passed in the affirmative.

The next clause, as to three-fifths of the negroes, being considered, Mr. King opposed the clause. He thought the admission of blacks in the representation would excite great discontents among the people.

Mr. Gorham, of Massachusetts, favored the three-fifths rule.

Mr. Wilson, of Pennsylvania, said if negroes were property, why not represent other property?—if they were citizens, why not let them be represented as such?

Mr. Morris, thought that representation for blacks would encourage the slave trade.

On the question for including "three-fifths" of the blacks, it was lost. All the Northern States, except Connecticut, voted No.

July 12. Mr. Morris, moved "that taxation be in proportion to representation."

Dr. Johnson thought population the best measure of wealth, and therefore, would include the blacks equally with the whites.

Mr. Morris, thought the people of Pennsylvania could never agree to a representation of negroes.

Gen. Pinckney, desired that property in slaves should be protected and not left exposed to danger.

Mr. Ellsworth, moved that the rule of taxation shall be

according to the whole number of white inhabitants and three-fifths of every other description, until some other rule, by which the wealth of the States can be ascertained, shall be adopted by the legislature.

Mr. Randolph opposed this amendment. He urged that express security ought to be provided for including slaves in representation. He lamented that such property existed; but as it did exist, the holders of it should require this security in the Constitution and not leave it to the caprice of the legislative body.

Mr. Wilson thought there would be less umbrage taken by the people by adopting the rule of representation according to taxation. The slaves would be taxed and thus indirectly represented.

Mr. Pinckney moved to amend so as to make blacks equal to whites in representation. He said the blacks would be all numbered in the representation of the North, and they were as productive in material resources to the country in the South as in the North. He thought this no more than justice.

On Mr. Pinckney's motion, only South Carolina and Georgia voted Aye.

On the question apportioning representation to direct taxation, to the whole of the white and three-fifths of the black population, Connecticut, Pennsylvania, Maryland, Virginia, North Carolina, and Georgia voted Aye; New Jersey and Delaware voted No; Massachusetts and South Carolina divided.

July 14. From this date till the 17th, the Convention was engaged in an animated discussion on the equality of votes in the Senate from each State. On the 16th a motion was made to adjourn *sine die*, on the ground that the Convention could never agree to the exactions of the smaller States. An equality vote was, however, agreed to. North Carolina and Massachusetts divided; 5 Ayes, 4 Noes.

July 17. The Convention proceeded to the consideration of a resolution concerning the two branches of the legislature, and from this date till the 26th was engaged in discussing the executive, legislative, and judicial branches of the government. Nothing, however, was elicited that would properly come within the scope of this work, or that would be particularly interesting to the general reader.

On the 26th, the resolutions of Mr. Randolph having been a second time gone through with, they, together with those of Messrs. Patterson and Pinckney, were referred to the Committee of Detail, and the Convention adjourned till August 6th, to give the Committee time to prepare and report a Constitution.

The resolutions as committed, expressing the sense of the Convention upon the principles of a Constitution, were as follows:

1. *Resolved,* That the government of the United States ought to consist of a supreme legislative, judiciary, and executive.

2. *Resolved,* That the legislature consist of two branches.

3. *Resolved,* That the members of the first branch of the legislature ought to be elected by the people of the several States for the term of two years; to be paid out of the public treasury; to receive an adequate compensation for their services; to be of the age of twenty-five years at least; to be ineligible to, and incapable of holding, any office under the authority of the United States (except those peculiarly belonging to the functions of the first branch) during the term of service of the first branch.

4. *Resolved,* That the members of the second branch of the legislature of the United States ought to be chosen by the individual legislatures; to be of the age of thirty years at least; to hold their offices for six years, one third to go out biennially; to receive a compensation for the devotion of their time to the public service; to be ineligible to, and

incapable of holding, any office under the authority of the United States (except those peculiarly belonging to the functions of the second branch) during the term for which they are elected, and for one year thereafter.

5. *Resolved,* That each branch ought to possess the right of originating acts.

6. *Resolved,* That the national legislature ought to possess the legislative rights vested in Congress by the Confederation; and, moreover, to legislate in all cases for the general interests of the Union, and also in those to which the States are separately incompetent, or in which the harmony of the United States may be interrupted by the exercise of individual legislation.

7. *Resolved,* That the legislative acts of the United States, made by virtue and in pursuance of the articles of union, and all treaties made and ratified under the authority of the United States, shall be the supreme law of the respective States, as far as those acts or treaties shall relate to the said States, or their citizens and inhabitants; and that the judiciaries of the several States shall be bound thereby in their decisions, any thing in the respective laws of the individual States to the contrary notwithstanding.

8. *Resolved,* That in the general formation of the legislature of the United States, the first branch thereof shall consist of sixty-five members; of which number, New Hampshire shall send 3; Massachusetts, 8; Rhode Island, 1; Connecticut, 5; New York, 6; New Jersey, 4; Pennsylvania, 8; Delaware, 1; Maryland, 6; Virginia, 10; North Carolina, 5; South Carolina, 5; Georgia, 3.

But, as the present situation of the States may probably alter in the number of their inhabitants, the legislature of the United States shall be authorized, from time to time, to apportion the number of representatives; and in case any of the States shall hereafter be divided, or enlarged by addition of territory, or any two or more States united, or any new States created within the limits of the United States, the legislature of the United States shall possess authority to regulate the number of representatives, in any of the foregoing cases, upon the principle of their number of inhabitants, according to the provisions hereafter mentioned, namely—Provided always, that representation ought to be proportioned to direct taxation. And, in order to ascertain the alteration in the direct taxation which may be required from time to time, by the changes in the relative circumstances of the States,—

9. *Resolved*, That a census be taken within six years from the first meeting of the legislature of the United States, and once within the term of every ten years afterwards, of all the inhabitants of the United States, in the manner and according to the ratio recommended by Congress in their resolution of the 18th of April, 1783; and that the legislature of the United States shall proportion the direct taxation accordingly.

10. *Resolved*, That all bills for raising or appropriating money, and for fixing the salaries of the officers of the government of the United States, shall originate in the first branch of the legislature of the United States, and shall not be altered or amended by the second branch; and that no money shall be drawn from the public treasury, but in pursuance of appropriations to be originated by the first branch.

11. *Resolved*, That, in the second branch of the legislature of the United States, each State shall have an equal vote.

12. *Resolved*, That a national executive be instituted, to consist of a single person; to be chosen by the national legislature for the term of seven years; to be ineligible a second time; with power to carry into execution the national laws; to appoint to offices in cases not otherwise provided for; to be removable on impeachment, and con-

viction of malpractice or neglect of duty; to receive a fixed compensation for the devotion of his time to the public service, to be paid out of the public treasury.

13. *Resolved,* That the national executive shall have a right to negative any legislative act; which shall not be afterwards passed, unless by two-thirds of each branch of the national legislature.

14. *Resolved,* That a national judiciary be established, to consist of one supreme tribunal, the judges of which shall be appointed by the second branch of the national legislature; to hold their offices during good behavior; to receive punctually, at stated times, a fixed compensation for their services, in which no diminution, shall be made so as to affect the persons actually in office at the time of such diminution.

15. *Resolved,* That the national legislature be empowered to appoint inferior tribunals.

16. *Resolved,* That the jurisdiction of the national judiciary shall extend to cases arising under laws passed by the general legislature, and to such other questions as involve the national peace and harmony.

17. *Resolved,* That provision ought to be made for the admission of States lawfully arising within the limits of the United States, whether from a voluntary junction of government and territory, or otherwise, with the consent of a number of voices in the national legislature less than the whole.

18. *Resolved,* That a republican form of government shall be guaranteed to each State; and that each State shall be protected against foreign and domestic violence.

19. *Resolved,* That provision ought to be made for the amendment of the articles of union, whensoever it shall seem necessary.

20. *Resolved,* That the legislative, executive, and judiciary powers, within the several States, and of the national

government, ought to be bound, by oath, to support the articles of union.

21. *Resolved*, That the amendments which shall be offered to the Confederation by the Convention ought, at a proper time or times, after the approbation of Congress, to be submitted to an assembly, or assemblies, of representatives, recommended by the several legislatures, to be expressly chosen by the people to consider and decide thereon.

22. *Resolved*, That the representation in the second branch of the legislature of the United States shall consist of two members from each State, who shall vote *per capita*.

23. *Resolved*, That it be an instruction to the committee to whom were referred the proceedings of the Convention for the establishment of a national government, to receive a clause, or clauses, requiring certain qualifications of property and citizenship in the United States, for the executive, the judiciary, and the members of both branches of the legislature of the United States.

August 6. Mr. Rutledge delivered the report of the committee of detail, reporting a constitution at large. [This report was so nearly like the constitution as finally adopted, and as we shall give that at the close of this chapter, it is not thought necessary to occupy space by copying it here.]

August 7. The report of the committee of detail being taken up, Mr. Morris moved that that the right of suffrage be restrained to freeholders. A long debate ensued. Col. Mason opposed it as leading to an aristocracy.

Mr. Madison was for leaving this matter to the States. Some States required it, and others did not. His own opinion was that freeholders would be the safest depositaries of liberty. Those without property might become the tools of the rich and ambitious, hence there would be just the same danger as from the property qualification.

Dr. Franklin opposed the views of Mr. Madison. He

thought the restriction wrong in principle, and had no doubt it would create dissatisfaction with the people.

On the question of Mr. Morris, only Delaware voted Aye. Maryland divided.

August 8. Article 4th, section 2d, being under consideration, declaring that a member of the House shall have been a citizen of the United States at least three years before his election.

Mr. Mason was for opening a wide door to emigrants, but thought three years too short. Foreign nations might impose upon us their tools, and get them into the legislature for insidious purposes. He moved seven years, which was agreed to, only Connecticut voting No.

Section 4th, allowing the legislatures to apportion the representatives according to the number of inhabitants, was taken up.

Mr. Morris moved to insert "free inhabitants." He said he would not agree to a constitution that upheld slavery. It was the curse of Heaven. He proceeded at length to demonstrate the evils of the institution.

Mr. Sherman said he did not regard the admission of negroes in the ratio of representation as a great objection. In fact, it was only the freemen of the South who would be represented, because it was only them who paid the taxes.

On the question to insert "free inhabitants," it was lost, only New Jersey voting Aye.

August 9. From this date to the 18th, the Convention was occupied in discussing questions of naturalization, revenue, &c.

August 18. Mr. Madison submitted to be referred to the committee of detail the following propositions, to be incorporated in the powers of Congress:

"To dispose of the unappropriated lands of the United States.

"To institute temporary governments for new States arising therein.

"To regulate affairs with the Indians, &c"

Mr. Pinckney also submitted several propositions, relating to the seat of government, public debt, post-offices, &c. From this till the 22d, nothing important by way of discussion transpired.

August 22. Article 7, section 4, was resumed.

Mr. Sherman was for leaving the clause as it stands. He disapproved of the slave trade; yet, as the States were now possessed of the right to import slaves, as the public good did not require it to be taken from them, and as it was expedient to have as few objections as possible to the proposed scheme of government, he thought it best to leave the matter as we find it. He observed that the abolition of slavery seemed to be going on in the United States, and that the good sense of the several States would probably, by degrees, complete it. He urged on the Convention the necessity of dispatching its business.

Col. Mason. This infernal traffic originated in the avarice of British merchants. The British government constantly checked the attempts of Virginia to put a stop to it. The present question concerns not the importing States alone, but the whole Union. The evil of having slaves was experienced during the late war. Had slaves been treated as they might have been by the enemy, they would have proved dangerous instruments in their hands. But their folly dealt by the slaves as it did by the tories. He mentioned the dangerous insurrections of slaves in Greece and Sicily; and the instructions given by Cromwell, to the commissioners sent to Virginia, to arm the servants and slaves in case other means of obtaining its submission might fail. Maryland and Virginia, he said, had already prohibited the importation of slaves expressly; North Carolina had done the same in substance. All this would be vain, if South

Carolina and Georgia be at liberty to import. The western people are already calling out for slaves for their new lands, and will fill that country with slaves, if they can be got through South Carolina and Georgia. Slavery discourages arts and manufactures. The poor despise labor when performed by slaves. They prevent the emigration of whites, who really enrich and strengthen a country. They produce the most pernicious effect on manners. Every master of slaves is born a petty tyrant. They bring the judgment of HEAVEN on a country. As nations cannot be rewarded or punished in the next world, they must be in this. By an inevitable chain of causes and effects, Providence punishes national sins by national calamities. He lamented that some of our Eastern brethren had, from a lust of gain, embarked in this nefarious traffic. As to the States being in possession of the right to import, this was the case with many other rights, now to be properly given up. He held it essential, in every point of view, that the general government should have power to prevent the increase of slavery.

Mr. Ellsworth, as he had never owned a slave, could not judge of the effects of slavery on character. He said, however, that if it was to be considered in a moral light, we ought to go further, and free those already in the country. As slaves also multiply so fast in Virginia and Maryland, that it is cheaper to raise than import them, whilst in the sickly rice-swamps foreign supplies are necessary, if we go no further than is urged, we shall be unjust toward South Carolina and Georgia. Let us not intermeddle. As population increases, poor laborers will be so plenty as to render slaves useless. Slavery, in time, will not be a speck in our country. Provision is already made in Connecticut for abolishing it. And the abolition has already taken place in Massachusetts. As to the danger of insurrections from foreign influence, that will become a motive to kind treatment of the slaves.

Mr. Pinckney. If slavery be wrong, it is justified by the example of all the world. He cited the case of Greece, Rome, and other ancient states; the sanction given by France, England, Holland, and other modern states. In all ages, one-half of mankind have been slaves. If the Southern States were let alone, they will probably of themselves stop importations. He would himself, as a citizen of South Carolina, vote for it. An attempt to take away the right, as proposed, will produce serious objections to the constitution which he wished to see adopted.

Gen. Pinckney declared it to be his firm opinion, that if himself and all his colleagues were to sign the constitution, and use their personal influence, it would be of no avail towards obtaining the assent of their constituents. South Carolina and Georgia cannot do without slaves. As to Virginia, she will gain by stopping the importations. Her slaves will rise in value, and she has more than she wants. It would be unequal to require South Carolina and Georgia to confederate on such unequal terms. He said the royal assent, before the Revolution, had never been refused to South Carolina and Virginia. He contended that the importation of slaves would be for the interest of the whole Union. The more slaves, the more produce to employ the carrying trade; the more consumption also; and the more of this, the more revenue for the common treasury. He admitted it to be reasonable that slaves should be treated like other imports, but should consider a rejection of the clause as an exclusion of South Carolina from the Union.

Mr. Baldwin had conceived national objects alone to be before the Convention, not such as, like the present, were of a local nature. Georgia was decided on this point. That State has always hitherto supposed a general government to be the pursuit of the central States, who wished to have a vortex for every thing; that her distance would preclude her from equal advantage; and that she could not prudently purchase it by yielding national powers. From this it might be understood in what light she would view an attempt to abridge one of her favorite prerogatives. If left to herself she may probably put a stop to the evil. As one ground for this conjecture, he took notice of the sect of ———, which was, he said, a respectable class of people, who carried ethics beyond the mere *equality of men*, extending their humanity to the claims of the whole animal creation.

Mr. Wilson observed that, if South Carolina and Georgia were themselves disposed to get rid of the importation of slaves in a short time, as had been suggested, they would never refuse to unite because the importation might be prohibited. As the section now stands, all articles imported are to be taxed. Slaves alone are exempt. This is, in fact, a bounty on that article.

Mr. Gerry thought we had nothing to do with the conduct of the States as to slaves, but ought to be careful not to give any sanction to it.

Mr. Dickinson considered it as indispensable, on every principle of honor and safety, that the importation of slaves should be authorized to the States by the Constitution. The true question was, whether the national happiness would be promoted or impaired by the importation—and this question ought to be left to the national government—not to the States particularly interested. If England and France permit slavery, slaves are, at the same time, excluded from both those kingdoms. Greece and Rome were made unhappy by their slaves. He could not believe that the Southern States would refuse to confederate on the account apprehended; especially as the power was not likely to be immediately exercised by the general government.

General Pinckney thought himself bound to say, that he

did not think South Carolina would stop her importations of slaves in any short time; but only stop them occasionally, as she now does. He moved to commit the clause, that slaves might be made liable to an equal tax with other imports; which he thought right, and which would remove one difficulty that had been stated.

Mr. Rutledge. If the Convention thinks that North Carolina, South Carolina, and Georgia, will ever agree to the plan, unless their right to import slaves be untouched, the expectation is vain. The people of those States will never be such fools as to give up so important an interest. He was against striking out the section, and seconded the motion of General Pinckney for a commitment.

Mr. Gouverneur Morris wished the whole subject to be committed, including the clauses relating to taxes on exports and to a navigation act. These things may form a bargain among the Northern and Southern States.

Mr. Butler declared, that he never would agree to the power of taxing exports.

Mr. Sherman said it was better to let the Southern States import slaves than to part with them, if they made that a *sine qua non*. He was opposed to a tax on slaves imported as making the matter worse, because it implied they were *property*. He acknowledged that, if the power of prohibiting the importation should be given to the general government, it would be exercised. He thought it would be its duty to exercise the power.

Mr. Read was for the commitment, provided the clause concerning taxes on exports could also be committed.

Mr. Sherman observed, that that clause had been agreed to, and therefore could not be committed.

Mr. Randolph was for committing, in order that some middle ground might, if possible, be found. He could never agree to the clause as it stands. He would sooner risk the constitution. He dwelt on the dilemma to which the Convention was exposed. By agreeing to the clause, it would revolt the Quakers, the Methodists, and many others in the States having no slaves. On the other hand, two States might be lost to the union. Let us then, he said, try the chances of a commitment.

On the question for committing the remaining part of sections 4 and 5 of article 7,—Connecticut, New Jersey, Maryland, Virginia, North Carolina, South Carolina, Georgia, Aye, 7; New Hampshire, Pennsylvania, Delaware, No, 3; Massachusetts absent.

Mr. Williamson stated the law of North Carolina on the subject, to wit, that it did not directly prohibit the importation of slaves. It imposed a duty of five pounds on each slave imported from Africa; ten pounds on each from elsewhere, and fifty pounds on each from a State licensing manumission. He thought the Southern States could not be members of the union, if the clause should be rejected, and that it was wrong to force any thing down not absolutely necessary, and which any State must disagree to.

Mr. King thought the subject should be considered in a political light only. If two States will not agree to the constitution, as stated on one side, he could affirm with equal belief, on the other, that great and equal opposition would be experienced from the other States. He remarked that the exemption of slaves from duty, whilst every other import was subject to it, was an inequality that could not fail to strike the commercial sagacity of the Northern and Middle States.

Mr. Langdon was strenuous for giving the power to the general government. He could not, with a good conscience, leave it with the States, who could then go on with the traffic without being restrained by the opinions here given, that they will themselves cease to import slaves.

Mr. Rutledge, from the committee to whom was referred the propositions of Mr. Madison and Mr. Pinckney on the

18th and 20th, made a report embodying the general views of the propositions as committed, but striking out the following propositions of Mr. Madison,

"To dispose of the unappropriated lands of the United States."

"To institute temporary governments for new States arising therein."

[*Note.*—If, as is claimed, the framers of the constitution intended to invest Congress with the power of government over territories, why was this proposition of Mr. Madison struck out which conferred that power in express terms? It is difficult to explain this action upon any other hypothesis than that they intended no such power to be lodged in the federal government; for it cannot be supposed that the sages of that Convention were so fond of *implications*, as to strike from the frame of government, which they were preparing, *express words*, for the sake of having powers inferred.]

August 23. The convention was engaged in the discussion of the subject of the militia, treaty-making power, etc.

August 24. Gov. Livingston, from the committee of eleven to whom was referred the clause of the fourth section of the seventh article, relating to the importation of slaves, made the following report.

"Strike out so much of the fourth section as was referred to the committee and insert:—'The migration or importation of such persons as the several States now existing shall think proper to admit, shall not be prohibited by the legislatures prior to the year 1800, but a tax or duty may be imposed on such immigration or importation, not exceeding the average duties laid on imports.'"

August 25. The above report was taken up. Gen. Pinckney moved to strike out the year 1800 as the year limiting the importing of slaves, and insert 1808. Mr. Madison opposed it on the ground that so long a period would be more dishonorable than though nothing was said about it in the constitution.

On the motion of Gen. Pinckney to extend the importation of slaves till 1808.

New Hampshire, Massachusetts, Connecticut, Maryland, North Carolina, South Carolina, and Georgia voted Aye; New Jersey, Pennsylvania, Delaware, and Virginia voted No. So it was agreed to.

Some further amendments were proposed and rejected. The report as amended was then agreed to by the same vote as on Gen. Pinckney's amendment.

August 27. The 27th and 28th were occupied in discussing the judicial branch of the government, and the subject of commerce.

August 29. Mr. Butler moved to insert after Article 15,—

" If any person bound to service or labor in any of the United States shall escape into another State, he or she shall not be discharged from such service or labor in consequence of any regulations subsisting in the State to which they escape, but shall be delivered up to the person justly claiming their service or labor;" which was agreed to unanimously without debate.

Mr. Morris, of Pennsylvania, moved the following:

" The legislature shall have power to dispose of, and make all needful rules and regulations respecting the territory or other property belonging to the United States; and nothing in this constitution contained shall be so construed as to prejudice any claims, either of the United States, or of any particular States." This section was agreed to, Maryland alone dissenting.

[*Note*—If, as is claimed, the above section was intended to give Congress the right of government over the *people* of the territories, how could it have passed so nearly unanimous, and without debate, when the proposition of Mr.

Madison, only seven days before, giving that power in express language, was rejected? The subject-matter before the Convention at the time was the *property* of the United States, and only with reference to that subject was this section adopted.]

August 31. From this date till the 12th of September the Convention was occupied in settling the details of the constitution, in the way of amendments and modifications to the various articles. Very little debate occurred,—none that would come within the purpose of this book. On the latter day the committee on revision reported the following draft of a constitution, which with some slight amendments, on the 16th was agreed to by the unanimous vote of all the States. On the 17th the instrument, having been engrossed, was signed by the members, with two or three exceptions, and the Convention adjourned *sine die.*

CONSTITUTION OF THE UNITED STATES OF AMERICA.

WE, the People of the United States, in order to form a more perfect union, establish justice, insure domestic tranquillity, provide for the common defense, promote the general welfare, and secure the blessings of liberty to ourselves and our posterity, do ordain and establish this Constitution for the United States of America.

ARTICLE 1. *Section* 1. All legislative powers herein granted shall be vested in a Congress of the United States, which shall consist of a Senate and House of Representatives.

Section 2. The House of Representatives shall be composed of members chosen every second year by the people of the several States, and the electors in each State shall have the qualifications requisite for electors of the most numerous branch of the State legislature.

No person shall be a representative who shall not have

attained to the age of twenty-five years, and been seven years a citizen of the United States, and who shall not, when elected, be an inhabitant of that State in which he shall be chosen.

Representatives and direct taxes shall be apportioned among the several States which may be included within this Union, according to their respective numbers, which shall be determined by adding to the whole number of free persons, including those bound to service for a term of years, and excluding Indians not taxed, three-fifths of all other persons. The actual enumeration shall be made within three years after the first meeting of the Congress of the United States, and within every subsequent term of ten years, in such manner as they shall by law direct. The number of representatives shall not exceed one for every thirty thousand, but each State shall have at least one representative; and until such enumeration shall be made, the State of New Hampshire shall be entitled to choose three, Massachusetts eight, Rhode Island and Providence plantations one, Connecticut five, New York six, New Jersey four, Pennsylvania eight, Delaware one, Maryland six, Virginia ten, North Carolina five, South Carolina five, and Georgia three.

When vacancies happen in the representation from any State, the executive authority thereof shall issue writs of election to fill such vacancies.

The House of Representatives shall choose their speaker and other officers; and shall have the sole power of impeachment.

Section 3. The Senate of the United States shall be composed of two senators from each State, chosen by the legislature thereof, for six years; and each senator shall have one vote.

Immediately after they shall be assembled in consequence of the first election, they shall be divided as equally as may be into three classes. The seats of the senators of the first class shall be vacated at the expiration of the second year, of the second class at the expiration of the fourth year, and of the third class at the expiration of the sixth year, so that one-third may be chosen every second year; and if vacancies happen by resignation, or otherwise, during the recess of the legislature of any State, the executive thereof may make temporary appointments until the next meeting of the legislature, which shall then fill such vacancies.

No person shall be a senator who shall not have attained to the age of thirty years, and been nine years a citizen of the United States, and who shall not, when elected, be an inhabitant of that State for which he shall be chosen.

The Vice-President of the United States shall be President of the Senate, but shall have no vote, unless they be equally divided.

The Senate shall choose their other officers, and also a president pro tempore, in the absence of the Vice-President, or when he shall exercise the office of President of the United States.

The Senate shall have the sole power to try all impeachments. When sitting for that purpose, they shall be on oath or affirmation. When the President of the United States is tried, the Chief Justice shall preside: and no person shall be convicted without the concurrence of two-thirds of the members present.

Judgment in cases of impeachment shall not extend further than to removal from office, and disqualification to hold and enjoy any office of honor, trust, or profit under the United States: but the party convicted shall nevertheless be liable and subject to indictment, trial, judgment and punishment, according to law.

Section 4. The times, places, and manner of holding elections for senators and representatives, shall be prescribed in each State by the legislature thereof, but the

Congress may at any time, by law, make or alter such regulations, except as to the places of choosing senators.

Congress shall assemble at least once in every year, and such meeting shall be on the first Monday in December, unless they shall, by law, appoint a different day.

Section 5. Each House shall be the judge of the election returns and qualifications of its own members, and a majority of each shall constitute a quorum to do business, but a smaller number may adjourn from day to day, and may be authorized to compel the attendance of the absent members, in such manner, and under such penalties, as each House may provide.

Each House may determine the rules of its proceedings. punish its members for disorderly behavior, and, with the concurrence of two-thirds, expel a member.

Each House shall keep a journal of its proceedings, and from time to time publish the same, excepting such parts as may in their judgment require secrecy; and the yeas and nays of the members of either House on any question, shall, at the desire of one-fifth of those present, be entered on the journal.

Neither House, during the session of Congress, shall, without the consent of the other, adjourn for more than three days, nor to any other place than that in which the two Houses shall be sitting.

Section 6. The senators and representatives shall receive a compensation for their services, to be ascertained by law, and paid out of the treasury of the United States. They shall in all cases, except treason, felony, and breach of the peace, be privileged from arrest during their attendance at the session of their respective Houses, and in going to, and returning from the same; and for any speech or debate in either House, they shall not be questioned in any other place.

No senator or representative shall, during the time for

which he was elected, be appointed to any civil office under the authority of the United States, which shall have been created, or the emoluments whereof shall have been increased, during such time; and no person holding any office under the United States, shall be a member of either House, during his continuance in office.

Section 7. All bills for raising revenue shall originate in the House of Representatives; but the Senate may propose or concur with amendments as on other bills.

Every bill which shall have passed the House of Representatives and the Senate shall, before it become a law, be presented to the President of the United States; if he approve, he shall sign it, but if not, he shall return it, with his objections, to that House in which it shall have originated, who shall enter the objections at large on their journal, and proceed to reconsider it. If, after such reconsideration, two-thirds of that House shall agree to pass the bill, it shall be sent, together with the objections, to the other House, by which it shall likewise be reconsidered, and if approved by two-thirds of that House, it shall become a law. But in all such cases the votes of both Houses shall be determined by yeas and nays, and the names of the persons voting for and against the bill shall be entered on the journal of each House respectively. If any bill shall not be returned by the President within ten days (Sundays excepted) after it shall have been presented to him, the same shall be a law, in like manner as if he had signed it, unless the Congress by their adjournment prevent its return, in which case it shall not be a law.

Every order, resolution, or vote, to which the concurrence of the Senate and House of Representatives may be necessary, (except on a question of adjournment,) shall be presented to the President of the United States; and before the same shall take effect, shall be approved by him, or being disapproved by him, shall be repassed by two-thirds of the

Senate and House of Representatives, according to the rules and limitations prescribed in the case of a bill.

Section 8. The Congress shall have power—

To lay and collect taxes, duties, imposts, and excises, to pay the debts and provide for the common defense and general welfare of the United States; but all duties, imposts, and excises shall be uniform throughout the United States;

To borrow money on the credit of the United States;

To regulate commerce with foreign nations, and among the several States, and with the Indian tribes;

To establish a uniform rule of naturalization, and uniform laws on the subject of bankruptcies throughout the United States;

To coin money, regulate the value thereof, and of foreign coin, and fix the standard of weights and measures;

To provide for the punishment of counterfeiting the securities and current coin of the United States;

To establish post-offices and post roads;

To promote the progress of science and useful arts, by securing for limited times to authors and inventors the exclusive right to their respective writings and discoveries;

To constitute tribunals inferior to the Supreme Court;

To define and punish piracies and felonies committed on the high seas, and offences against the law of nations;

To declare war, grant letters of marque and reprisal, and make rules concerning captures on land and water;

To raise and support armies, but no appropriation of money to that use shall be for a longer term than two years;

To provide and maintain a navy;

To make rules for the government and regulation of the land and naval forces;

To provide for calling forth the militia to execute the laws of the Union, suppress insurrections and repel invasions;

To provide for organizing, arming, and disciplining, the militia, and for governing such part of them as may be employed in the service of the United States, reserving to the States respectively, the appointment of the officers, and the authority of training the militia according to the discipline prescribed by Congress;

To exercise exclusive legislation in all cases whatsoever, over such district (not exceeding ten miles square) as may, by cession of particular States and the acceptance of Congress, become the seat of the government of the United States, and to exercise like authority over all places purchased by the consent of the legislature of the State in which the same shall be, for the erection of forts, magazines, arsenals, dock-yards, and other needful buildings;—and

To make all laws which shall be necessary and proper for carrying into execution the foregoing powers, and all other powers vested by this Constitution in the government of the United States, or in any department or officer thereof.

Section 9. The migration or importation of such persons as any of the States now existing shall think proper to admit, shall not be prohibited by the Congress prior to the year one thousand eight hundred and eight, but a tax or duty may be imposed on such importation, not exceeding ten dollars for each person.

The privilege of the writ of habeas corpus shall not be suspended, unless when in cases of rebellion or invasion the public safety may require it.

No bill of attainder or ex post facto law shall be passed.

No capitation, or other direct, tax shall be laid, unless in proportion to the census or enumeration herein before directed to be taken.

No tax or duty shall be laid on articles exported from any State.

No preference shall be given by any regulation of commerce or revenue to the ports of one State over those of another: nor shall vessels bound to, or from, one State, be obliged to enter, clear, or pay duties in another.

No money shall be drawn from the treasury, but in consequence of appropriations made by law; and a regular statement and account of the receipts and expenditures of all public money shall be published from time to time.

No title of nobility shall be granted by the United States: and no person holding any office of profit or trust under them, shall, without the consent of the Congress, accept of any present, emolument, office, or title, of any kind whatever, from any king, prince, or foreign State.

Section 10. No State shall enter into any treaty, alliance, or confederation; grant letters of marque and reprisal; coin money; emit bills of credit; make any thing but gold and silver coin a tender in payment of debts; pass any bill of attainder, ex post facto law, or law impairing the obligation of contracts, or grant any title of nobility.

No State shall, without the consent of the Congress, lay any imposts or duties on imports or exports, except what may be absolutely necessary for executing its inspection laws: and the net produce of all duties and imposts, laid by any State on imports or exports, shall be for the use of the treasury of the United States; and all such laws shall be subject to the revision and control of the Congress.

No State shall, without the consent of Congress, lay any duty of tonnage, keep troops, or ships of war in time of peace, enter into any agreement or compact with another State, or with a foreign power, or engage in war, unless actually invaded, or in such imminent danger as will not admit of delay.

ARTICLE 2. *Section* 1. The executive power shall be vested in a President of the United States of America. He shall hold his office during the term of four years, and, together with the Vice-President, chosen for the same term, be elected as follows:

Each State shall appoint, in such manner as the legislature thereof may direct, a number of Electors, equal to the whole number of senators and representatives to which the State may be entitled in the Congress; but no senator or representative, or person holding an office of trust or profit under the United States, shall be appointed an Elector.

The Congress may determine the time of choosing the Electors, and the day on which they shall give their votes; which day shall be the same throughout the United States.

No person except a natural-born citizen, or a citizen of the United States, at the time of the adoption of this Constitution, shall be eligible to the office of President; neither shall any person be eligible to that office who shall not have attained to the age of thirty-five years, and been fourteen years a resident within the United States.

In case of the removal of the President from office, or of his death, resignation, or inability to discharge the powers and duties of the said office, the same shall devolve on the Vice-President, and Congress may by law provide for the case of removal, death, resignation, or inability, both of the President and Vice-President, declaring what officer shall then act as President, and such officer shall act accordingly, until the disability be removed, or a President shall be elected.

The President shall, at stated times, receive for his services a compensation, which shall neither be increased nor diminished during the period for which he shall have been elected, and he shall not receive within that period any other emolument from the United States or any of them.

Before he enter on the execution of his office, he shall take the following oath or affirmation:

"I do solemnly swear (or affirm) that I will faithfully

execute the office of President of the United States, and will, to the best of my ability, preserve, protect, and defend the Constitution of the United States."

Section 2. The President shall be commander-in-chief of the army and navy of the United States, and of the militia of the several States, when called into the actual service of the United States; he may require the opinion, in writing, of the principal officer in each of the executive departments, upon any subject relating to the duties of their respective offices, and he shall have power to grant reprieves and pardons for offenses against the United States, except in cases of impeachment.

He shall have **power**, by and with the advice and consent of the Senate, to make treaties, provided two-thirds of the senators present concur; and he shall nominate, and by and with the advice and consent of the Senate, shall appoint ambassadors, other public ministers and consuls, judges of the Supreme Court, and all other officers of the United States, whose appointments are not herein otherwise provided for, and which shall be established by law: but the Congress may by law vest the appointment of such inferior officers, as they think proper, in the President alone, in the courts of law, or in the heads of departments.

The President shall have power to fill up all vacancies that may happen during the recess of the Senate, by granting commissions which shall expire at the end of their next session.

Section 3. He shall, from time to time, give to the Congress information of the state of the Union, and recommend to their consideration such measures as he shall judge necessary and expedient; he may, on extraordinary occasions, convene both Houses, or either of them, and in case of disagreement between them, with respect to the time of adjournment, he may adjourn them to such time as he shall think proper; he shall receive ambassadors and other public ministers; he shall take care that the laws be faithfully executed, and shall commission all the officers of the United States.

Section 4. The President, Vice President, and all civil officers of the United States, shall be removed from office on impeachment for and conviction of treason, bribery, or other high crimes and misdemeanors.

ARTICLE 3. *Section* 1. The judicial power of the United States shall be vested in one Supreme Court, and in such inferior courts as the Congress may from time to time ordain and establish. The judges both of the supreme and inferior courts, shall hold their offices during good behavior, and shall, at stated times, receive for their services a compensation, which shall not be diminished during their continuance in office.

Section 2. The judicial power shall extend to all cases, in law and equity, arising under this Constitution, the laws of the United States, and treaties made, or which shall be made, under their authority;—to all cases affecting ambassadors, other public ministers and consuls;—to all cases of admiralty and maritime jurisdiction;—to controversies to which the United States shall be a party;—to controversies between two or more States;—between a State and citizens of another State;—between citizens of different States;—between citizens of the same State claiming lands under grants of different States, and between a State or the citizens thereof, and foreign states, citizens or subjects.

In all cases affecting ambassadors, other public ministers and consuls, and those in which a State shall be party, the Supreme Court shall have original jurisdiction. In all the other cases before mentioned, the Supreme Court shall have appellate jurisdiction, both as to law and fact, with such exceptions and under such regulations as the Congress shall make.

The trial of all crimes, except in cases of impeachment,

shall be by jury; and such trial shall be held in the State where the said crimes shall have been committed; but when not committed within any State, the trial shall be at such place or places as the Congress may by law have directed.

Section 3. Treason against the United States shall consist only in levying war against them, or in adhering to their enemies, giving them aid and comfort. No person shall be convicted of treason unless on the testimony of two witnesses to the same overt act, or on confession in open court.

The Congress shall have power to declare the punishment of treason, but no attainder of treason shall work corruption of blood or forfeiture, except during the life of the person attainted.

ARTICLE 4. *Section* 1. Full faith and credit shall be given in each State to the public acts, records, and judicial proceedings of every other State. And the Congress may, by general laws, prescribe the manner in which such acts, records, and proceedings shall be proved, and the effect thereof.

Section 2. The citizens of each State shall be entitled to all the privileges and immunities of citizens in the several States.

A person charged in any State with treason, felony, or other crime, who shall flee from justice, and be found in another State, shall, on demand of the executive authority of the State from which he fled, be delivered up, to be removed to the State having jurisdiction of the crime.

No person held to service or labor in one State, under the laws thereof, escaping into another, shall, in consequence of any law or regulation therein, be discharged from such service or labor, but shall be delivered up on claim of the party to whom such service or labor may be due.

Section 3. New States may be admitted by the Congress into this Union; but no new State shall be formed or erected within the jurisdiction of any other State; nor any State be formed by the junction of two or more States, or parts of States, without the consent of the legislatures of the States concerned as well as of the Congress.

The Congress shall have power to dispose of and make all needful rules and regulations respecting the territory or other property belonging to the United States; and nothing in this Constitution shall be so construed as to prejudice any claims of the United States, or of any particular State.

Section 4. The United States shall guarantee to every State in this Union a republican form of government, and shall protect each of them against invasion, and on application of the legislature, or of the executive (when the legislature cannot be convened) against domestic violence.

ARTICLE 5. The Congress, whenever two-thirds of both Houses shall deem it necessary, shall propose amendments to this Constitution, or, on the application of the legislatures of two-thirds of the several States, shall call a convention for proposing amendments, which, in either case, shall be valid to all intents and purposes, as part of this Constitution, when ratified by the legislatures of three-fourths of the several States, or by conventions in three-fourths thereof, as the one or the other mode of ratification may be proposed by the Congress; Provided that no amendment which may be made prior to the year one thousand eight hundred and eight shall in any manner affect the first and fourth clauses in the ninth section of the first article; and that no State, without its consent, shall be deprived of its equal suffrage in the Senate.

ARTICLE 6. All debts contracted and engagements entered into, before the adoption of this Constitution, shall be as valid against the United States under this Constitution, as under the Confederation.

This Constitution, and the laws of the United States which shall be made in pursuance thereof; and all treaties made, or which shall be made, under the authority of the United States, shall be the supreme law of the land; and the judges in every State shall be bound thereby, anything in the Constitution or laws of any State to the contrary notwithstanding.

The senators and representatives before mentioned, and the members of the several State legislatures, and all executive and judicial officers, both of the United States and of the several States, shall be be bound by oath or affirmation, to support this Constitution; but no religious Test shall ever be required as a qualification to any office or public trust under the United States.

ARTICLE 7. The ratification of the Conventions of nine States, shall be sufficient for the establishment of this Constitution between the States so ratifying the same.

Done in Convention by the unanimous consent of the States present the seventeenth day of September in the year of our Lord, one thousand seven hundred and eighty seven and of the Independence of the United States of America the twelfth. In witness whereof, We have hereunto subscribed our names.

GEORGE WASHINGTON,
President, and Deputy from Virginia.

The Constitution was ratified by the Conventions of the several States, as follows. viz.: Delaware, 7th December, 1787; Pennsylvania, 12th December, 1787; New Jersey, 18th December, 1787; Georgia, 2d January, 1788; Connecticut, 9th January, 1788; Massachusetts, 6th February, 1788; Maryland, 28th April, 1788; South Carolina, 23d May, 1788; New Hampshire, 21st June, 1788; Virginia, 26th June, 1788; New York, 26th July, 1788; North Carolina, 21st November, 1789; Rhode Island, 29th May,

OFFICIAL LETTER

Adopted by the Convention, and addressed to Congress, with a copy of the Constitution.

" We have now the honor to submit to the consideration of the United States in Congress assembled, that Constitution which has appeared to us the most advisable.

" The friends of our country have long seen and desired, that the power of making war, peace, and treaties; that of levying money and regulating commerce; and the correspondent executive and judicial authorities, should be fully and effectually vested in the general government of the Union. But the impropriety of delegating such extensive trust to one body of men is evident. Thence results the necessity of a different organzation. It is obviously impracticable in the federal government of these States, to secure all rights of independent sovereignty to each, and yet provide for the interest and safety of all. Individuals entering into society must give up a share of liberty to preserve the rest.

The magnitude of the sacrifice must depend as well on situation and circumstances, as on the object to be obtained. It is at all times difficult to draw with precision the line between those rights which must be surrendered and those which may be reserved. And on the present occasion this difficulty was increased by a difference among the several States as to their situation, extent, habits, and particular interests.

In all our deliberations on this subject, we kept steadily in our view that which appeared to us the greatest interest of every true American,—the consolidation of our Union, in which is involved our prosperity, felicity, safety, perhaps our national existence. This important consideration, seriously and deeply impressed on our minds, led each State in the Convention to be less rigid in points of inferior magnitude than might have been otherwise expected. And thus the Constitution which we now present is the result of a spirit of amity, and of that mutual deference and concession, which the peculiarity of our political situation rendered indispensable.

"That it will meet the full and entire approbation of every State is not, perhaps, to be expected. But each will doubtless consider that, had her interest alone been consulted, the consequence might have been particularly disagreeable and injurious to others. That it is liable to as few exceptions as could reasonably have been expected, we hope and believe; that it will promote the lasting welfare of that country so dear to us all, and secure our freedom and happiness, is our most ardent wish."

ARTICLES

In addition to, and amendment of, the Constitution of the United States of America, proposed by Congress, and ratified by the Legislatures of the several States, pursuant to the fifth article of the original Constitution.

ARTICLE 1. Congress shall make no law respecting an establishment of religion, or prohibiting the free exercise thereof; or abridging the freedom of speech, or of the press; or the right of the people peaceably to assemble, and to petition the government for a redress of grievances.

ARTICLE 2. A well regulated militia being necessary to the security of a free State, the right of the people to keep and bear arms, shall not be infringed.

ARTICLE 3. No soldier shall, in time of peace, be quartered in any house, without the consent of the owner, nor in time of war, but in a manner to be prescribed by law.

ARTICLE 4. The right of the people to be secure in their persons, houses, papers, and effects, against unreasonable searches and seizures, shall not be violated, and no warrants shall issue, but upon probable cause, supported by oath or affirmation, and particularly describing the place to be searched, and the persons or things to be seized.

Article 5. No person shall be held to answer for a capital, or otherwise infamous crime, unless on a presentment or indictment of a grand jury, except in cases arising in the land or naval forces, or in the militia, when in actual service in time of war or public danger; nor shall any person be subject for the same offense to be twice put in jeopardy of life or limb; nor shall be compelled in any criminal case to be a witness against himself, nor be deprived of life, liberty, or property, without due process of law; nor shall private property be taken for public use, without just compensation.

Article 6. In all criminal prosecutions, the accused shall enjoy the right to a speedy and public trial, by an impartial jury of the State and district wherein the crime shall have been been committed, which district shall have been previously ascertained by law, and to be informed of the nature and cause of the accusation; to be confronted with the witnesses against him; to have compulsory process for obtaining witnesses in his favor, and to have the assistance of counsel for his defense.

Article 7. In suits at common law, where the value in controversy shall exceed twenty dollars, the right of trial by jury shall be preserved, and no fact tried by a jury shall be otherwise re-examined in any court of the United States, than according to the rules of the common law.

Article 8. Excessive bail shall not be required, nor excessive fines imposed, nor cruel and unusual punishments inflicted.

Article 9. The enumeration in the Constitution, of certain rights, shall not be construed to deny or disparage others retained by the people.

ARTICLE 10. The powers not delegated to the United States by the Constitution, nor prohibited by it to the States, are reserved to the States respectively, or to the people.

ARTICLE 11. The judicial power of the United States shall not be construed to extend to any suit in law or equity, commenced or prosecuted against one of the United States by citizens of another State, or by citizens or subjects of any foreign State.

ARTICLE 12. The Electors shall meet in their respective States, and vote by ballot for President and Vice-President, one of whom, at least, shall not be an inhabitant of the same State with themselves; they shall name in their ballots the person voted for as President, and in distinct ballots the person voted for as Vice-President, and they shall make distinct lists of all persons voted for as President, and of all persons voted for as Vice-President, and of the number of votes for each, which lists they shall sign and certify, and transmit sealed to the seat of the government of the United States, directed to the President of the Senate;— the President of the Senate shall, in presence of the Senate and House of Representatives, open all the certificates and the votes shall then be counted;—The person having the greatest number of votes for President, shall be the President, if such number be a majority of the whole number of Electors appointed; and if no person have such majority, then from the persons having the highest numbers not exceeding three on the list of those voted for as President, the House of Representatives shall choose immediately, by ballot, the President. But in choosing the President, the votes shall be taken by States, the representation from each State having one vote; a quorum for this purpose shall consist of a member or members from two-thirds of the States, and a majority of all the States shall be necessary to a choice. And if the House of Representatives shall not choose a President whenever the right of choice shall devolve upon them, before the fourth day of March next following, then the Vice-President shall act as President, as in the case of the death or other constitutional disability of the President. The person having the greatest number of votes as Vice-President, shall be the Vice-President, if such number be a majority of the whole number of Electors appointed, and if no person have a majority, then from the two highest numbers on the list, the Senate shall choose the Vice-President; a quorum for the purpose shall consist of two-thirds of the whole number of senators, and a majority of the whole number shall be necessary to a choice. But no person constitutionally ineligible to the office of President shall be eligible to that of Vice-President of the United States.

The first ten of the preceding amendments were proposed at the first session of the first Congress of the United States, 25th September, 1789, and were finally ratified by the constitutional number of States, on the 15th day of December, 1791.

The eleventh amendment was proposed at the first session of the third Congress, 5th March, 1794, and was declared in a message from the President of the United States to both houses of Congress, dated 8th January, 1798, to have been adopted by the constitutional number of States.

The twelfth amendment was proposed at the first session of the eighth Congress, 12th December, 1803, and was adopted by the Constitutional number of States in 1804, according to a public notice thereof by the Secretary of State, dated 25th September, of the same year.

CHAPTER III.

THE STATE CONVENTIONS.

THE following chapter contains all the debates on the subject of slavery, in the Conventions of the several States to ratify the Constitution, that have been preserved. Of the Conventions of Vermont, Delaware, Maryland, and Georgia, none were reported, or, if reported, have never been published. In Pennsylvania, the only speeches preserved are those of James Wilson, a member of the Federal Convention, and Thomas McKean. The only allusion in these speeches to the question of slavery was by Mr. Wilson, expressing his gratification that, after twenty years, Congress would have power to prohibit the slave trade, and that thus slavery would finally die out of itself. No debates were preserved of the New Hampshire Convention, save a mere fragment of a speech by Joshua Atherton, reprobating the slave trade. It does not appear, however, whether he opposed the Constitution on that ground, or supported it because it provided a way for its final extinction. We therefore do not copy it.

In some States the debates are voluminous, and yet very little, comparatively, on the subject of slavery. We have aimed to give *all* that was said, *pro* and *con*, leaving the reader to form his own opinions.

EXTRACTS FROM THE DEBATES IN THE CONVENTION OF MASSACHUSETTS.

February 4, 1788. Rev. Mr. Backus said—Mr. President, I have said very little in this honorable Convention; but I now beg leave to offer a few thoughts upon some points in the Constitution proposed to us, and I shall begin with the exclusion of the religious test. Many appear to be much concerned about it; but nothing is more evident, both in reason and the Holy Scriptures, than that religion is ever a matter between God and individuals; and therefore no man or men can impose any religious test, without invading the essential prerogatives of our Lord Jesus Christ. Ministers first assumed this power under the Christian name; and then Constantine approved of the practice, when he adopted the profession of Christianity, as an engine of State policy. And let the history of all nations be searched from that day to this, and it will appear that the imposing of religious tests hath been the greatest engine of tyranny in the world. And I rejoice to see so many gentlemen who are now giving in their rights of conscience in this great and important matter. Some serious minds discover a concern lest, if all religious tests should be excluded, the Congress would hereafter establish Popery, or some other tyrannical way of worship. But it is most certain that no such way of worship can be established without any religious test.

Much, sir, hath been said about the importation of *slaves* into this country.

I believe that, according to my capacity, no man abhors that wicked practice more than I do; I would gladly make use of all lawful means toward the abolition of slavery in all parts of the land.

But let us consider where we are and what we are doing. In the Articles of Confederation, no provision was made to hinder the importation of slaves into any of these States; but a door is now open hereafter to do it, and each State is at liberty now to abolish slavery as soon as they please. And let us remember our former connection with Great Britain, from whom many in our own land think we ought not to have revolted. How did they carry on the slave trade? I know that the Bishop of Gloucester, in an annual sermon in London, in February, 1776, endeavored to justify their tyrannical claims of power over us by casting the reproach of the slave trade upon the Americans.

But at the close of the war, the Bishop of Chester, in an annual sermon, in February, 1783, ingenuously owned that their nation is the most deeply involved in the guilt of that trade of any nation in the world; and, also, that they have treated their slaves in the West Indies worse than the French or Spaniards have done theirs.

Thus slavery grows more odious through the world; and as an honorable gentleman said, some days ago, "Though we cannot say that slavery is struck with an apoplexy, yet we may hope it will die with consumption."

Mr. Dawes said he was sorry to hear so many objections raised against the paragraph under consideration. He thought them wholly unfounded; that the *black inhabitants* of the Southern States must be considered either as slaves, and as so much *property*, or in the character of so many freemen; if the former, why should they not be wholly represented? Our own State laws and Constitutions would lead us to consider these blacks as freemen, and so indeed, would our own ideas of natural justice. If, then, they are freemen, they might form an equal basis for representation as though they were all white inhabitants.

In either view, therefore, he could not see that the Northern States would suffer, but directly to the contrary. He thought, however, that gentlemen would do well to connect the passage in dispute with another article in the Constitution, that permits Congress, in the year 1808, wholly to prohibit the importation of slaves, and in the mean time to impose a duty of ten dollars a head on such blacks as should be imported before that period. Besides, by the new Constitution, every particular State is left to its own option totally to prohibit the introduction of slaves into its own territories. What could the Convention do more? The members of the Southern States, like ourselves, have *their* prejudices. It would not do to abolish slavery, by an Act of Congress, in a moment, and so destroy what our Southern brethren consider as property.

But we may say, that although slavery is not smitten by apoplexy, yet it has received a mortal wound, and will die of consumption.

Gen. Heath said, the paragraph respecting the migration or importation of such persons as any of the States now existing shall think proper to admit, &c., is one of those considered during my absence, and I have heard nothing on the subject, save what has been mentioned this morning; but I think the gentlemen who have spoken have carried the matter rather too far on both sides.

I apprehend that it is not in our power to do any thing for or against those who are in slavery in the Southern States.

No gentleman within these walls detests every idea of slavery more than I do: it is generally detested by the people of this commonwealth; and I ardently hope that the time will soon come when our brethren in the Southern States will view it as we do, and put a stop to it; but to this we have no right to compel them. Two questions naturally arise. If we ratify the Constitution, shall we do anything by our act to hold the blacks in slavery? Or shall we become partakers of other men's sins? I think, neither of them. Each State is sovereign and independent to a certain degree, and the States have a right, and they will regulate their own internal affairs as to themselves appears proper; and shall we refuse to eat, or to drink, or to be united, with those who do not think, or act, just as we do? Surely not. We are not, in this case, partakers of other men's sins; for in nothing do we voluntarily encourage the slavery of our fellow man.

* * * * *

Mr. President: After a long and painful investigation of the Federal Constitution, by paragraphs, this honorable Convention is drawing nigh to the ultimate question—a question as momentous as ever invited the attention of man.

We are soon to decide on a system of government, digested, not for the people of the commonwealth of Massachusetts only—not for the present people of the United States only—but, in addition to these, for all those States which may hereafter rise into existence within the jurisdiction of the United States, and for millions of people yet unborn; a system of government, not for a nation of slaves, but for a people as free and virtuous as any on earth; not for a conquered nation, subdued to our will, but for a people who have fought, who have bled, and who have conquered; who under the smiles of Heaven, have established their independence and sovereignty, and have taken equal rank among the nations of the earth.

In short, sir, it is a system of government for ourselves and for our children, for all that is near and dear to us in life; and on the decision of the question is suspended our political prosperity or infelicity, perhaps our existence as a nation. What can be more solemn? What can be more interesting? Everything depends on our union. I know that some have supposed, that although the union should be broken, particular States may retain their importance; but this cannot be.

The strongest nerved State, even the right arm, if separated from the body, must wither. If the great union be broken, our country, as a nation, perishes; and if our country so perishes, it will be as impossible to save a particular State as to preserve one of the fingers of a mortified hand.

By one of the paragraphs of the system, it is declared that the ratifications of the Conventions of nine States shall be sufficient for the establishment of the Constitution between the States so ratifying the same. But, sir, how happy will it be if, not only nine, but even all the States should ratify it.

It will be a happy circumstance if only a small majority of this Convention should ratify the federal system; but how much more happy if we could be unanimous! And if there are any means whereby they may be united, every exertion should be made to effect it. I presume, sir, that there is not a single gentleman within these walls who does not wish for a federal government—for an efficient federal government; and that this government should be possessed of every power necessary to enable it to shed on the people the benign influence of a good government.

The third paragraph of the 2d section being read, Mr. King, a member of the Federal Convention, rose to explain it. There has, says he, been much misconception of this section. It is a principle of this Constitution that representation and taxation should go hand in hand. This paragraph states that to the number of free persons, including those bound to service for a term of years, and excluding Indians not taxed, three-fifths of all other persons shall be added. These persons are the slaves. By this rule are representation and taxation to be apportioned; and it was adopted, because it was the language of all America. According to the Confederation, ratified in 1781, the sums for the general welfare and defense should be apportioned according to the surveyed lands, and improvements thereon, in the several States; but that it hath never been in the power of Congress to follow that rule, the returns from the several States being so very imperfect.

EXTRACTS FROM THE DEBATES IN THE CONVENTION OF THE STATE OF NEW YORK.

June 20, 1788. *Mr. Hamilton said: In order that the committee may understand clearly the principle on which the general Convention acted, I think it necessary to explain some preliminary circumstances. Sir, the natural situation of this country seems to divide its interests into different classes. There are navigating and non-navigating States. The Northern are properly navigating States; the Southern appear to possess neither the means nor the spirit of navigation. This difference or situation naturally produces a dissimilarity of interests and views respecting foreign commerce. It was the interest of the Northern States that there should be no restraints on their navigation, and that they should have full power, by a majority in Congress, to make commercial regulations in favor of their own, and in restraint of the navigation of foreigners. The Southern States wished to impose a restraint on the Northern, by requiring that two-thirds in Congress should be requisite to pass an act in regulation of commerce. They were apprehensive that the restraints of a navigation law would discourage foreigners, and, by obliging them to employ the shipping of the Northern States, would probably enhance their freight. This being the case, they insisted strenuously on having this provision engrafted in the Constitution; and the Northern States were as anxious in opposing it. On the other hand, the small States, seeing themselves embraced by the Confederation upon equal terms, wished to retain the advantages which they already possessed. The large States, on the contrary, thought it improper that Rhode Island and Delaware should enjoy an equal suffrage with themselves.

---

* Mr. Hamilton was the only delegate in the New York Convention that discussed, or expressed an opinion on the subject of slavery.

From these sources a delicate and difficult contest arose. It became necessary, therefore, to compromise, or the Convention must have dissolved without effecting anything. Would it have been wise and prudent in that body, in this critical situation, to have deserted their country? No! Every man who hears me, every wise man in the United States would have condemned them.

The Convention were obliged to appoint a committee for accommodation. In this committee the arrangement was formed as it now stands, and their report was accepted. It was a delicate point, and it was necessary that all parties should be indulged.

Gentlemen will see that, if there had been no unanimity, nothing could have been done; for the Convention had no power to establish, but only to recommend, a government. Any other system would have been impracticable.

Let a convention be called to-morrow. Let them meet twenty times,—nay, twenty thousand times; they will have the same difficulties to encounter, the same clashing interests to reconcile.

But, dismissing these reflections, let us consider how far the arrangement is in itself entitled to the approbation of this body. We will examine it upon its own merits.

The first thing objected to is that clause which allows a representation for three-fifths of the *negroes*. Much has been said of the impropriety of representing men who have no will of their own. Whether this be reasoning or declamation I will not presume to say. It is the unfortunate situation of the Southern States to have a great part of their population, as well as property, in blacks. The regulation complained of was one result of the spirit of accommodation which governed the Convention, and without this indulgence no union could possibly have been formed.

But, sir, considering some peculiar advantages which we

derive from them, it is entirely just that they should be granted.

The Southern States possess certain staples—tobacco, rice, indigo, &c.—which must be capital objects in treaties of commerce with foreign nations; and the advantages which they necessarily procure in those treaties will be felt throughout all the States. But the justice of this plan will appear in another view. The best writers on government have held that representation should be compounded of persons and property. This rule has been adopted, as far as it could be, in the Constitution of New York. It will, however, by no means be admitted that the slaves are considered altogether as property. They are men, though degraded to the condition of slavery.

They are persons known to the municipal laws of the States which they inhabit, as well as to the laws of nature. But representation and taxation go together, and one uniform rule ought to apply to both.

Would it be just to compute these slaves in the assessment of taxes, and discard them from the estimate in the apportionment of representatives?

Would it be just to impose a singular burden, without conferring some adequate advantage?

Another circumstance ought to be considered. The rule we have been speaking of is a general rule, and applies to all the States. Now, you have a great number of people in your State which are not represented at all, and have no voice in your government.

These will be included in the enumeration—not two-fifths, nor three-fifths, but the whole.

This proves that the advantages of the plan are not confined to the Southern States, but extend to other parts of the Union.

EXTRACTS FROM THE DEBATES IN THE CONVENTION OF CONNECTICUT.

January 4, 1788.—Oliver Ellsworth. Mr. President: It is observable that there is no preface to the proposed Constitution; but it evidently pre-supposes two things; one is, the necessity of a federal government, the other is the inefficiency of the old Articles of Confederation.

A union is necessary for the purposes of national defense. United we are strong, divided we are weak. It is easy for hostile nations to sweep off a number of separate states, one after another. Witness the states in the neighborhood of ancient Rome. They were successively subdued by that ambitious city, which they might have conquered with the utmost ease if they had been united.

Witness the Canaanitish nations, whose divided situation rendered them an easy prey. Witness England, which, when divided into separate states, was twice conquered by an inferior force. Thus it always happens to small states, and to great ones if divided. Or if, to avoid this, they connect themselves with some powerful state, their situation is not much better. This shows us the necessity of combining our whole force, and, as to national purposes, becoming one state.

A *union*, sir, is likewise necessary, considered with relation to economy.

They must provide for their defense.

The expense of it, which would be moderate for a large kingdom, would be intolerable to a petty state. The Dutch are wealthy, but they are one of the smallest of the European nations, and their taxes are higher than in any other country of Europe. Their taxes amount to forty shillings per head, when those of England do not exceed half that sum.

We must unite in order to preserve peace among ourselves. If we be divided, what is to prevent wars from breaking out among the States? States, as well as individuals, are subject to ambition, to avarice, to those jarring passions which disturb the peace of society. What is to check these? If there be a parental hand over the whole, this, and nothing else, can restrain the unruly conduct of the members.

Union is necessary to preserve commutative justice between the States.

If divided what is to prevent the large States from oppressing the small? What is to defend us from the ambition and rapacity of New York, when she has spread over that vast territory which she claims and holds? Do we not already see in her the seeds of an overbearing ambition? On our other side there is a large and powerful State. Have we not already begun to be tributaries? If we do not improve the present critical time—if we do not unite—shall we not be like Issachar of old, a strong ass crouching down between two burdens. New Jersey and Delaware have seen this, and have adopted the Constitution unanimously.

A more energetic system is necessary.

The present is merely advisory. It has no coercive power. Without this, government is ineffectual, or rather is no government at all. But it is said, "Such a power is not necessary. States will not do wrong. They need only to be told their duty and they will do it." I ask, sir, what warrant is there for this assertion? Do not States do wrong? Whence come wars? One of two hostile nations must be in the wrong.

But it is said, "Among sister States this can never be presumed." But do we not know that when friends become enemies, their enmity is the most virulent?

The seventeen provinces of the Netherlands were once confederated: they fought under the same banner. Antwerp, hard pressed by Philip, applied to the other states for relief. Holland, a rival in trade, opposed and prevented the needy succors.

Antwerp was made a sacrifice. I wish I could say there were no seeds of similar injustice springing up among us. Is there not in one of our States injustice too barefaced for Eastern despotism? That State is small. It does little hurt to any but itself.

But it has a spirit which would make a Tophet of the universe. But some will say, "We formerly did well without any union."

I answer, our situation is materially changed. While Great Britain held her authority, she awed us. She appointed governors and councils for the American provinces. She had a negative upon our laws. But now, our circumstances are so altered, that there is no arguing what we shall be, from what we have been.*

EXTRACTS FROM THE DEBATES OF THE COMMONWEALTH OF VIRGINIA.

June 2, 1788. Mr. George Nicholas. Mr. Chairman: I feel apprehensions lest the subject of our debates should be misunderstood. Every one wishes to know the true meaning of the system; but I fear those who hear us will think we are captiously quibbling on words. We have been told, in the course of this business, that the government will operate like a *screw*. Give me leave to say that the exertions of the opposition are like that instrument. They catch at every thing, and take it into their vortex.

---

* The report of the debates in the Connecticut Convention is very meagre, occupying but a few pages. In none of the speeches reported is the slavery question debated at all. We copy the foregoing from Mr. Ellsworth, as containing healthy Union sentiments, peculiarly applicable to a large class of people at the present time.

The worthy member says that this government is defective, because it comes from the people.

Its greatest recommendation with me, is putting the power in the hands of the people.

He disapproves of it because it does not say in what particular instances the militia shall be called out to execute the laws.

This is a power of the Constitution, and particular instances must be defined by the legislature. But, says the worthy member, those laws which have been read are arguments against the Constitution, because they show that the States are now in possession of the power, and competent to its execution.

Would you leave this power in the States, and by that means deprive the general government of a power which will be necessary for its existence? If the State governments find this power necessary, ought not the general government to have a similar power? But, sir, there is no State check in this business. The gentleman near me has shown that there is a very important check.

Another worthy member says there is no power in the States to quell an insurrection of slaves. Have they it now? If they have, does the Constitution take it away? If it does, it must be one of the three clauses which have been mentioned by the worthy member. The first clause gives the general government power to call them out when necessary. Does this take it away from the States? No. But it gives an additional security; for, beside the power in the State governments to use their own militia, it will be the duty of the general government to aid them with the strength of the Union when called for.

No part of this Constitution can show that this power is taken away.

But an argument is drawn from that clause which says "that no State shall engage in war, unless actually invaded, or in such imminent danger as will not admit of delay." What does this prohibition amount to? It must be a war with a foreign enemy that the States are prohibited from making; for the exception to the restriction proves it. The restriction includes only offensive hostility, as they are at liberty to engage in war when invaded, or in imminent danger. They are, therefore, not restrained from quelling domestic insurrections, which are totally different from making war with a foreign power. But the great thing to be dreaded is that, during an insurrection, the militia will be called out from the State.

This is his kind of argument. Is it possible that, at such a time, the general government would order the militia to be called! It is a groundless objection to work on gentlemen's apprehensions within these walls. As to the 4th article, it was introduced wholly for the particular aid of the States. A republican form of government is guaranteed, and protection is secured against invasion and domestic violence on application. Is not this a guard as strong as possible? Does it not exclude the unnecessary interference of Congress in business of this sort.

The gentlemen over the way cannot tell who will be the militia at a future day, and enumerates dangers of select militia. Let me attend to the nature of gentlemen's objections. One objects because there will be a select militia; another objects because there will be no select militia; and yet both oppose it on these contradictory principles.

If you deny the general government the power of calling out the militia, there must be a recurrence to a standing army.

If you are really jealous of your liberties confide in Congress.

Mr. George Mason. Mr. Chairman: This is a fatal section, which has created more dangers than any other. The first clause allows the importation of slaves for twenty years.

Under the royal government, this evil was looked upon as a great oppression, and many attempts were made to prevent it; but the interest of the African merchants prevented its prohibition. No sooner did the Revolution take place than it was thought of. It was one of the great causes of our separation from Great Britain. Its exclusion has been a principal object of this State, and most of the States of the Union.

The augmentation of slaves weakens the States; and such a trade is diabolical in itself, and disgraceful to mankind; yet, by this Constitution, it is continued for twenty years. As much as I value a union of all the States, I would not admit the Southern States into the Union unless they agree to the discontinuance of this disgraceful trade, because it would bring weakness, and not strength, to the Union.

And, though this infamous traffic be continued, we have no security for the property of that kind which we have already. There is no clause in this Constitution to secure it; for they may lay such a tax as will amount to manumission. And should the government be amended, still this detestable kind of commerce will be continued till after the expiration of twenty years; for the 5th article which provides for amendments, expressly excepts this clause. I have ever looked upon this as a most disgraceful thing to America.

I cannot express my detestation of it. Yet they have not secured us the property of the slaves we have already.

So that "they have done what they ought not to have done, and have left undone what they ought to have done."

Mr. Madison. Mr. Chairman: I should conceive this clause to be impolitic, if it were one of those things which could be excluded without encountering greater evils.

The Southern States would not have entered into the

Union of America without the temporary permission of that trade; and if they were excluded from the Union, the consequences might be dreadful to them and to us. We are not in a worse situation than before. The traffic is prohibited by our laws, and we may continue the prohibition. The Union in general is not in a worse situation.

Under the Articles of Confederation, it might be continued forever; but, by this clause, an end may be put to it after twenty years. There is, therefore, an amelioration of our circumstances.

A tax may be laid in the mean time; but it is limited; otherwise Congress might lay such a tax as would amount to a prohibition. From the mode of representation and taxation, Congress cannot lay such a tax on slaves as will amount to manumission.

Another clause secures us that property which we now possess.

At present, if any slave elopes to any of those States where slaves are free, he becomes emancipated by their laws; for the laws of the States are uncharitable to one another in this respect. But in this Constitution, " no person held to service or labor in one state, under the laws thereof, escaping into another, shall, in consequence of any law or regulation therein, be discharged from such service or labor; but shall be delivered up on claim of the party to whom such service or labor shall be due." This clause was expressly inserted, to enable owners of slaves to reclaim them.

This is a better security than any that now exists. No power is given to the general government to interpose with respect to the property in slaves now held by the States. The taxation of this State being equal only to its representation, such a tax cannot be laid as he supposes.

They cannot prevent the importation of slaves for twenty years; but after that period they can. The gentlemen from South Carolina and Georgia argued in this manner: "We have now liberty to import this species of property, and much of the property now possessed had been purchased, or otherwise acquired, in contemplation of improving it by the assistance of imported slaves. What would be the consesequence of hindering us from it? The slaves of Virginia would rise in value, and we should be obliged to go to your markets."

I need not expatiate on this subject. Great as the evil is, a dismemberment of the Union would be worse. If those States should disunite from the other States for not indulging them in the temporary continuance of this traffic, they might solicit and obtain aid from foreign powers.

Mr. Tyler warmly enlarged on the impolicy, iniquity, and disgracefulness of this wicked traffic. He thought the reasons urged by gentlemen in defense of it were inconclusive and ill founded.

It was one cause of the complaints against British tyranny, that this trade was permitted. The Revolution had put a period to it; but now it was to be revived. He thought nothing could justify it.

This temporary restriction on Congress militated, in his opinion, against the arguments of gentlemen on the other side, that what was not given up was retained to the States; for that, if this restriction had not been inserted, Congress could have prohibited the African trade. The power of prohibiting it was not expressly delegated to them; yet they would have had it by implication, if this restraint had not been provided. This seemed to him to demonstrate most clearly the necessity of restraining them, by a bill of rights, from infringing our unalienable rights. It was immaterial whether the bill of rights was by itself, or included in the Constitution.

But he contended for it one way or the other. It would be justified by our own example and that of England.

His earnest desire was, that it should be handed down to posterity that he had opposed this wicked clause.

Mr. Madison was surprised that any gentleman should return to the clauses which had already been discussed.

He begged the gentleman to read the clauses which gave the power of exclusive legislation, and he might see that nothing could be done without the consent of the States.

With respect to the supposed operation of what was denominated the sweeping clause, the gentleman, he said, was mistaken; for it only extended to the enumerated powers.

Should Congress attempt to extend it to any power not enumerated, it would not be warranted by the clause.

As to the restriction in the clause under consideration, it was a restraint on the exercise of a power expressly delegated to Congress; namely, that of regulating commerce with foreign nations.

Patrick Henry insisted that the insertion of these restrictions on Congress was a plain demonstration that Congress could exercise powers by implication. The gentleman had admitted that Congress could have interdicted the African trade, were it not for this restriction. If so, the power, not having been expressly delegated, must be obtained by implication. He demanded where, then, was their doctrine of reserved rights. He wished for negative clauses to prevent them from assuming any powers but those expressly given. He asked why it was omitted to secure us that property in slaves which we held now. He feared its omission was done with design. They might lay such taxes on slaves as would amount to emancipation; and then the Southern States would be the only sufferers.

His opinion was confirmed by the mode of levying money. Congress, he observed, had power to lay and collect taxes, imposts, and excises. Imposts (or duties) and excises were to be uniform; but this uniformity did not extend to taxes. This might compel the Southern States to liberate their negroes. He wished this property, therefore, to be guarded. He considered the clause, which had been adduced by the gentleman as a security for this property, as no security at all. It was no more than this—that a runaway negro could be taken up in Maryland or New York.

This could not prevent Congress from interfering with that property by laying a grievous and enormous tax on it, so as to compel owners to emancipate their slaves rather than pay the tax.

He apprehended it would be productive of much stock-jobbing, and that they would play into one another's hands in such a manner as that this property would be lost to the country.

Mr. George Nicholas wondered that gentlemen who were against slavery should be opposed to this clause; as, after that period, the slave trade would be done away.

He asked if gentlemen do not see the inconsistency of their arguments.

They object, says he, to the Constitution, because the slave trade is laid open for twenty odd years; and yet they tell you that, by some latent operation of it, the slaves who are so now will be manumitted.

At the same moment it is opposed for being promotive and destructive of slavery. He contended that it was advantageous to Virginia that it should be in the power of Congress to prevent the importation of slaves after twenty years, as it would then put a period to the evil complained of.

As the Southern States would not confederate without this clause, he asked if gentlemen would rather dissolve the confederacy than to suffer this temporary inconvenience, admitting it to be such.

Virginia might continue the prohibition of such importation during the intermediate period, and would be benefited by it, as a tax of ten dollars on each slave might be laid, of which she would receive a share.

He endeavored to obviate the objection of gentlemen, that the restriction on Congress was a proof that they would have powers not given them, by remarking, that they would only have had a general superintendency of trade, if the restriction had not been inserted.

But the Southern States insisted on this exception to that general superintendency for twenty years. It could not, therefore, have been a power by implication, as the restriction was an exception from a delegated power. The taxes could not, as had been suggested, be laid so high on negroes as to amount to emancipation; because taxation and representation were fixed according to the census established in the Constitution. The exception of taxes from the uniformity annexed to duties and excises could not have the operation contended for by the gentleman, because other clauses had clearly and positively fixed the census.

Had taxes been uniform, it would have been universally objected to; for no one object could be selected without involving great inconveniences and oppressions.

But, says, Mr. Nicholas, is it from the general government we are to fear emancipation? Gentlemen will recollect what I said in another house, and what other gentlemen have said, that advocated emancipation. Give me leave to say, that clause is a great security for our slave tax. I can tell the committee that the people of our own country are reduced to beggary by the taxes on negroes.

Had this Constitution been adopted, it would not have been the case. The taxes were laid on all our negroes. By this system two-fifths are exempted.

He then added, that he had not imagined gentlemen would support here what they had opposed in another place.

Mr. Henry replied that, though the proportion of each was to be fixed by the census, and three-fifths of the slaves only were included in the enumeration, yet the proportion of Virginia, being once fixed, might be laid on blacks and blacks only; for the mode of raising the proportion of each State being to be directed by Congress, they might make slaves the sole object to raise it.

Personalities he wished to take leave of; they had nothing to do with the question, which was solely whether that paper was wrong or not.

Mr. Nicholas replied, that negroes must be considered as persons or property. If as property, the proportion of taxes to be laid on them was fixed in the Constitution.

If he apprehended a poll tax on negroes, the Constitution had prevented it; for, by the census, where a white man paid ten shillings, a negro paid but six shillings; for the exemption of two fifths of them reduced it to that proportion.

Mr. George Mason said, that gentlemen might think themselves secured by the restriction, in the fourth clause, that no capitation or other direct tax should be laid but in proportion to the census before directed to be taken; but that, when maturely considered, it would be found to be no security whatsoever. It was nothing but a direct assertion, or mere confirmation of the clause which fixed the ratio of taxes and representation. It only meant that the quantum to be received of each State should be in proportion to their numbers, in the manner therein directed. But the general government was not precluded from laying the proportion of any particular State on any one species of property they might think proper.

For instance, if five hundred thousand dollars were to be raised, they might lay the whole of the proportion of the Southern States on the blacks, or any one species of property; so that by laying taxes too heavily on slaves, they might totally annihilate that kind of property. No real security could arise from the clause which provides that persons held to labor in one state, escaping into another, shall be delivered up. This only meant that runaway slaves should not be protected in other States. As to the exclusion of *ex post facto* laws, it could not be said to create any security in this case; for laying a tax on slaves would not be *ex post facto*.

Mr Madison replied, that even the Southern States, which were most affected, were perfectly satisfied with this provision, and dreaded no danger to the property they now hold. It appeared to him that the general government would not intermeddle with that property for twenty years, but to lay a tax on every slave imported, not exceeding ten dollars; and that, after the expiration of that period, they might prohibit the traffic altogether. The census in the Constitution was intended to introduce equality in the burdens to be laid on the community.

No gentleman objected to laying duties, imposts, and excises uniformly. But uniformity of taxes would be subversive of the principles of equality; for it was not possible to select any article which would be easy for one State but what would be heavy for another; that the proportion of each State being ascertained, it would be raised by the general government in the most convenient manner for the people, and not by the selection of any one particular object; that there must be some degree of confidence put in agents, or else we must reject a state of civil society altogether.

Another great security to this property, which he mentioned, was, that five States were greatly interested in that species of property, and there were other States which had some slaves, and had made no attempt, or taken any step, to take them from the people.

There were a few slaves in New York, New Jersey, and Connecticut; these States would, probably, oppose any attempts to annihilate this species of property.

He concluded by observing that he should be glad to eave the decision of this to the committee.

Mr. Henry. As much as I deplore slavery, I see that prudence forbids its abolition. I deny that the general government ought to set them free, because a decided majority of the States have not the ties of sympathy and fellow-feeling for those whose interest would be affected by their emancipation. The majority of Congress is to the North, and the slaves are to the South.

In this situation, I see a great deal of the property of the people of Virginia in jeopardy, and their peace and tranquillity gone. I repeat it again, that it would rejoice my very soul that every one of my fellow-beings were emancipated.

As we ought with gratitude to admire that decree of Heaven which has numbered us among the free, we ought to lament and deplore the necessity of holding our fellowmen in bondage.

But is it practicable, by any human means, to liberate them without producing the most dreadful and ruinous consequences? We ought to possess them in the manner we inherited them from our ancestors, as their manumission is incompatible with the felicity of our country.

But we ought to soften, as much as possible, the rigor of their unhappy fate. I know, that in a variety of particular instances, the legislature, listening to complaints, have admitted their emancipation. Let me not dwell on this subject.

I will only add, that this, as well as every other property of the people of Virginia, is in jeopardy, and put in the hands of those who have no similarity of situation with us.

This is a local matter, and I can see no propriety in subjecting it to Congress.

Gov. Randolph. Mr. Chairman: Once more, sir, I address you, and perhaps it will be the last time I shall speak concerning this Constitution, unless I be urged by the observations of some gentlemen.

Although this is not the first time that my mind has been brought to contemplate this awful period, yet I acknowledge it is not rendered less awful by familiarity with it.

Did I persuade myself that those fair days were present which the honorable gentlemen described—could I bring my mind to believe that there were peace and tranquillity in this land, and that there was no storm gathering which would burst, and that previous amendments could be retained—I would concur with the honorable gentleman; for nothing but the fear of inevitable destruction would lead me to vote for the Constitution in spite of the objections I have to it.

But, sir, what have I heard to-day? I sympathized most warmly with what other gentlemen said yesterday, that, let the contest be what it may, the minority should submit to the majority. With satisfaction and joy I heard what he then said—that he would submit, and that there should be peace if his power could preserve it.

What a sad reverse to-day! Are we not told, by way of counterpart to language that did him honor, that he would secede? I hope he will pardon, and correct me if I misrecite him; but if not corrected, my interpretation is, that secession by him will be the consequence of adoption without previous amendments.

[Here Mr. Henry explained himself, and denied having said any thing of secession; but that he said, he would have no hand in subsequent amendments; that he would remain and vote, and afterward he would have no business here.]

I see, continued His Excellency, that I am not mistaken in my thoughts.

The honorable gentleman says, he will remain and vote on the question, but after that he has no business here, and that he will go home. I beg to make a few remarks on the subject of secession.

If there be in this house members who have in contemplation to secede from the majority, let me conjure them, by all the ties of honor and duty, to consider what they are about to do.

Some of them have more property than I have, and all of them are equal to me in personal rights. Such an idea of refusing to submit to the decision of the majority is destructive of every republican principle.

It will kindle a civil war, and reduce every thing to anarchy and confusion. To avoid a calamity so lamentable, I would submit to it, if it contained greater evils than it does.

What are they to say to their constituents when they go home? "We come here to tell you that liberty is in danger, and, though the majority is in favor of it, you ought not to submit." Can any man consider, without shuddering with horror, the awful consequences of such desperate conduct? I entreat men to consider and ponder what good citizenship requires of them.

I conjure them to contemplate the consequences as to themselves as well as others. They themselves will be overwhelmed in the general disorder.

I did not think that the proposition of the honorable gentleman near me (Mr. White) could have met with the treatment it has. The honorable gentleman says there are only three rights stipulated in it. I thought this error might have been accounted for at first; but after he read it, the continuance of the mistake has astonished me.

He has wandered from the point. [Here he read Mr. White's proposition.] Where in this paper do you discover that the people of Virginia are tenacious of three rights only? It declares that all power comes from the people, and whatever is not granted by them remains with them; that among other things remaining with them are liberty of the press, right of conscience, and some other essential rights. Could you devise any express form of words by which the rights contained in the bill of rights of Virginia could be better secured or more fully comprehended? What is the paper which he offers in the form of a bill of rights? Will that better secure our rights than a declaration like this? All rights are therein declared to be completely vested in the people, unless expressly given away. Can there be a more pointed or positive reservation?

That honorable gentleman, and some others, have insisted that the abolition of slavery will result from it, and at the same time have complained that it encourages its continuation.

The inconsistency proves, in some degree, the futility of their arguments.

But if it be not conclusive, to satisfy the committee that there is no danger of enfranchisement taking place, I beg leave to refer them to the paper itself.

I hope that there is none here who, considering the subject in the calm light of philosophy, will advance an objection dishonorable to Virginia—that, at the moment they are securing the the rights of their citizens, an objection is started that there is a spark of hope that those unfortunate men now held in *bondage* may, by the operation of the general government, be made free. But if any gentleman be terrified by this apprehension, let him read the system.

I ask, and I will ask again and again, till I be answered (not by declamation), Where is the part that has a tendency to the *abolition of slavery?* Is it the clause which says that "the migration or importation of such persons as any of the States now existing shall think proper to admit shall be prohibited by Congress prior to the year 1808"?

This is an exception from the power of regulating commerce, and the restriction is only to continue till 1808.

Then Congress can, by the exercise of that power, prevent future importations; but does it affect the existing state of slavery? Were it right here to mention what passed in Convention on the occasion, I might tell you *that the Southern States, even South Carolina herself, conceived this property to be secure by these words.*

I believe, whatever we may think here, that there was not a member of the Virginia delegation who had *the smallest suspicion of the abolition of slavery.* Go to their meaning. Point out the clause where this formidable power of emancipation is inserted.

But another clause of the Constitution proves the absurdity of the supposition. The words of the clause are, "No persons held to service or labor in one State, under the laws thereof, escaping into another, shall, in consequence of any law or regulation therein, be discharged from such service or labor, but shall be delivered up on claim of the party to whom such service or labor may be due." Every one knows that *slaves* are held to service and labor. And when authority is given to owners of slaves to vindicate their property, *can* it be supposed they can be *deprived* of it?

If a citizen of this State, in consequence of this clause, can take his runaway slave in Maryland, can it be seriously thought that, after taking him and bringing him home, he could be made free? I observed that the honorable gentleman's proposition comes in a truly questionable shape, and is still more extraordinary and unaccountable for another consideration—that although we went, article by article, through the Constitution, and although we did not expect a general review of the subject (as a most comprehensive view had been taken of it before it was regularly debated), yet we are carried back to the clause giving that dreadful power, for the general welfare.

Pardon me, if I remind you of the true state of that business. I appeal to the candor of the honorable gentleman, and if he thinks it an improper appeal, I ask the gentlemen here, *whether* there be a *general, indefinite* power of providing for the general welfare? The power is, "to lay and collect taxes, duties, imposts, and excise, to pay the debts, and provide for the common defense and general welfare;" so that they can only raise money by these means, in order to provide for the general welfare.

No man who reads it can say it is general, as the honorable gentleman represents it. You must violate every rule of construction and common sense, if you sever it from the power of raising money, and annex it to any thing else, in order to make it that formidable power which it is represented to be.

EXTRACTS FROM THE DEBATES IN THE CONVENTION OF NORTH CAROLINA.

July 24, 1788. Mr. Goudy. Mr. Chairman: This clause of taxation will give an advantage to some States over the others. It will be oppressive to the Southern States. Taxes are equal to our representation. To augment our taxes, and increase our burdens, our negroes are to be represented. If a State has fifty thousand *negroes*, she is to send one representative for them. I wish not to be represented with negroes, especially if it increases my burdens.

Mr. Davie. Mr. Chairman: I will endeavor to obviate what the gentleman last up said. I wonder to see gentlemen so precipitate and hasty on a subject of awful importance. It ought to be considered, that some of us are slow of apprehension, or not having those quick conceptions and luminous understandings, of which other gentlemen may be possessed.

The gentleman "does not wish to be represented with

negroes." This, sir, is an unhappy species of population; but we cannot at present alter their situation.

The Eastern States had great jealousies on this subject. They insisted that their cows and horses were equally entitled to representation; *that the one was property as well as the other.*

It became our duty, on the other hand, to acquire as much weight as possible in the legislation of the Union; and, as the Northern States were more populous in whites, this only could be done by insisting that a certain proportion of our slaves should make a part of the computed population. It was attempted to form a rule of representation from a compound ratio of wealth and population; but, on consideration, it was found impracticable to determine the comparative value of lands, and other property, in so extensive a territory, with any degree of accuracy; and population alone was adopted as the only practicable rule or criterion of representation.

It was urged by the deputies of the Eastern States, that a representation of two-fifths would be of little utility, and that their entire representation would be unequal and burdensome—that, in a time of war, slaves rendered a country more vulnerable, while its defense devolved upon its free inhabitants. On the other hand, we insisted that, in time of peace, they contributed, by their labor, to the general wealth, as well as other members of the community—that, as rational beings, they had a right of representation, and, in some instances, might be highly useful in war.

On these principles, the Eastern States gave the matter up, and consented to the regulation as it has been read.

I hope these reasons will appear satisfactory. It is the same rule or principle which was proposed some years ago by Congress, and assented to by twelve of the States. It may wound the delicacy of the gentleman from Guilford, (Mr. Goudy,) but I hope he will endeavor to accommodate his feelings to the interest and circumstances of his country. [1st clause of the 9th section read.]

Mr. J. McDowall, wished to hear the reasons of this restriction.

Mr. Spaight answered, that there was a contest between the Northern and Southern States; that the Southern States, whose principal support depended on the labor of slaves, would not consent to the desire of the Northern States to exclude the importation of slaves absolutely; that South Carolina and Georgia insisted on this clause, as they were now in want of hands to cultivate their lands; that in the course of twenty years they would be fully supplied; that the trade would be abolished then, and that, in the mean time, some tax or duty might be laid on it.

Mr. M'Dowall replied, that the explanation was just such as he expected, and by no means satisfactory to him, and that he looked upon it as a very objectionable part of the system.

Mr. Iredell. Mr. Chairman: I rise to express sentiments similar to those of the gentleman from Craven. For my part, were it practicable to put an end to the importation of slaves immediately, it would give me the greatest pleasure; for it is a trade inconsistent with the rights of humanity, and under which great cruelties have been exercised.

When the entire abolition of slavery takes place, it will be an event which must be pleasing to every generous mind, and every friend of human nature; but we often wish for things which are not attainable. It was the wish of a great majority of the Convention to put an end to the trade immediately; but the States of South Carolina and Georgia would not agree to it. Consider, then, what would be the difference between our present situation in this respect, if we do not agree to the Constitution, and what it will be if we do agree to it.

If we do not agree to it, do we remedy the evil? No, sir, we do not. For if the Constitution be not adopted, it will be in the power of every State to continue it forever.

They may or may not abolish it, at their discretion. But if we adopt the Constitution, the trade must cease after twenty years, if Congress declare so, whether particular States please so or not; surely, then, we can gain by it.

This was the utmost that could be obtained. I heartily wish more could have been done. But, as it is, this government is nobly distinguished above others by that very provision.

Where is there another country in which such a restriction prevails? We, therefore, sir, set an example of humanity, by providing for the abolition of this inhuman traffic, though at a distant period.

I hope, therefore, that this part of the Constitution will not be condemned because it has not stipulated for what was impracticable to obtain.

Mr. Spaight further explained the clause. That the limitation of this trade to the term of twenty years was a compromise between the Eastern States and the Southern States. South Carolina and Georgia wished to extend the term.

The Eastern States insisted on the entire abolition of the trade. That the State of North Carolina had not thought proper to pass any law prohibiting the importation of slaves, and therefore its delegation in the Convention did not think themselves authorized to contend for an immediate prohibition of it.

Mr. Iredell added to what he had said before, that the States of Georgia and South Carolina had lost a great many slaves during the war, and that they wished to supply the loss.

Mr. Galloway. Mr. Chairman: The explanation given to

this clause does not satisfy my mind. I wish to see this abominable trade put an end to.

But in case it be thought proper to continue this abominable traffic for twenty years, yet I do not wish to see the tax on the importation extended to all persons whatsoever. Our situation is different from the people of the North. We want citizens; they do not.

Instead of laying a tax, we ought to give a bounty to encourage foreigners to come among us. With respect to the abolition of slavery, it requires the utmost consideration. The property of the Southern States consists principally of slaves. If they mean to do away slavery altogether, this property will be destroyed. I apprehend it means to bring forward manumission. If we must manumit our slaves, what country shall we send them to? It is impossible for us to be happy if, after manumission, they are to stay among us.

Mr. Iredell. Mr. Chairman: The worthy gentleman, I believe, has misunderstood this clause, which runs in the following words: "The migration or importation of such persons as any of the States now existing shall think proper to admit, shall not be prohibited by the Congress prior to the year 1808; but a tax or duty may be imposed on such importation, not exceeding ten dollars for each person." Now, sir, observe that the Eastern States, who long ago have abolished slaves, did not approve of the expression *slaves;* they therefore used another, that answered the same purpose.

The committee will observe the distinction between the words *migration* and *importation*. The first part of the clause will extend to persons who come into this country as free people, or are brought as slaves. But the last part extends to slaves only. The word *migration* refers to free persons; but the word *importation* refers to slaves, because free people cannot be said to be imported. The tax, therefore, is only to be laid on slaves who are imported, and not on free persons who migrate.

I further beg leave to say that the gentleman is mistaken in another thing. He seems to say that this extends to the abolition of slavery. Is there anything in this Constitution which says that Congress shall have it in their power to abolish the slavery of those slaves who are now in the country? Is it not the plain meaning of it, that after twenty years they may prevent the future importation of slaves? It does not extend to those now in the country.

There is another circumstance to be observed. There is no authority vested in Congress to restrain the States, in the interval of twenty years, from doing what they please. If they wish to prohibit such importation, they may do so. Our next assembly may put an entire end to the importation of slaves.

Article 4. The first section and two first clauses of the second section read without observation. The last clause read.

Mr. Iredell begged leave to explain the reason of this clause. In some of the Northern States they have emancipated all their *slaves*. If any of our slaves, said he, go there, and remain there a certain time, they would, by the present laws, be entitled to their freedom, so that their masters could not get them again. This would be extremely prejudicial to the inhabitants of the Southern States; and to prevent it, this clause is inserted in the Constitution. Though the word *slave* is not mentioned, this is the meaning of it.

The Northern delegates, owing to their particular scruples on the subject of slavery, did not choose the word *slave* to be mentioned.

Mr. Iredell, upon Art. 5th, said—Mr. Chairman: This is a very important clause. In every other constitution of government that I have ever heard or read of, no provision is made for necessary amendments.

The misfortune attending most constitutions which have been deliberately formed, has been, that those who formed them thought their wisdom equal to all possible contingencies, and that there could be no error in what they did.

The gentlemen who framed this Constitution thought with much more diffidence of their capacities; and, undoubtedly, without a provision for amendment, it would have been justly liable to objection, and the characters of its framers would have appeared much less meritorious.

This, indeed, is one of the greatest beauties of the system, and should strongly recommend it to every candid mind.

The constitution of any government which cannot be regularly amended when its defects are experienced, reduces the people to this dilemma—they must either submit to its oppressions, or bring about amendments, more or less, by a civil war. Happy this, the country we live in!

The Constitution before us, if it be adopted, can be altered with as much regularity, and as little confusion, as any act of Assembly; not, indeed, quite so easily, which would be extremely impolitic; but it is a most happy circumstance, that there is a remedy in the system itself for its own fallibility, so that alterations can without difficulty be made, agreeable to the general sense of the people. Let us attend to the manner in which amendments may be made. The proposition for amendments may arise from Congress itself, when two-thirds of both Houses shall deem it necessary.

If they should not, and yet amendments be generally wished for by the people, two-thirds of the legislatures of the different States may require a general convention for the purpose, in which case Congress are under the necessity of convening one

Any amendments which either Congress shall propose, or which shall be proposed by such general convention, are afterwards to be submitted to the legislatures of the different States, or conventions called for that purpose, as Congress shall think proper, and upon the ratification of three-fourths of the States, will become a part of the Constitution. By referring this business to legislatures, expense would be saved; and in general, it may be presumed, they would speak the genuine sense of the people. It may, however, on some occasions, be better to consult an immediate delegation for that special purpose. This is therefore left discretionary. It is highly probable that amendments agreed to in either of these methods would be conducive to the public welfare, when so large a majority of the States consented to them.

And in one of these modes, amendments that are now wished for may, in a short time, be made to this Constitution by the States adopting it.

It is, however, to be observed, that the 1st and 4th clauses in the 9th section of the 1st article are protected from any alteration till the year 1808; and in order that no consolidation should take place, it is provided that no State shall, by any amendment or alteration, be ever deprived of an equal suffrage in the Senate without its own consent.

The first two prohibitions are with respect to the census, (according to which direct taxes are imposed,) and with respect to the importation of slaves. As to the first, it must be observed, that there is a material difference between the Northern and Southern States. The Northern States have been much longer settled, and are much fuller of people, than the Southern, but have not land in equal proportion, nor scarcely any slaves. The subject of this article was regulated with great difficulty, and by a spirit of concession which it would not be prudent to disturb for a good many years.

In twenty years, there will probably be a great alteration, and then the subject may be reconsidered with less difficulty and greater coolness.

In the mean time, the compromise was upon the best footing that could be obtained. A compromise likewise took place in regard to the importation of slaves. It is probable that all the members reprobated this inhuman traffic; but those of South Carolina and Georgia would not consent to an immediate prohibition of it—one reason of which was, that, during the last war, they lost a vast number of negroes, which loss they wish to supply.

In the mean time, it is left to the States to admit or prohibit the importation, and Congress may impose a limited duty upon it.

EXTRACTS FROM THE DEBATES, IN THE CONVENTION OF SOUTH CAROLINA.

January 16, 1788. Hon. Rawlins Lowndes. It has been said that this new government was to be considered as an experiment. He really was afraid it would prove a fatal one to our peace and happiness. An experiment!

What! risk the loss of political existence on experiments? No, sir; if we are to make experiments, rather let them be such as may do good, but which cannot possibly do any injury to us or our posterity.

So far from having any expectation of success from such experiments, he sincerely believed that, when this new Constitution should be adopted, the sun of the Southern States would set, never to rise again.

To prove this, he observed, that six of the Eastern States formed a majority in the House of Representatives. In the enumeration he passed Rhode Island, and included Pennsylvania.

Now, was it consonant with reason, with wisdom, with

policy, to suppose, in a legislature where a majority of persons sat whose interests were greatly different from ours, that we had the smallest chance of receiving adequate advantages? Certainly not. He believed the gentlemen that went from this State, to represent us in Convention, possessed as much integrity, and stood as high in point of character, as any gentlemen that could have been selected; and he also believed that they had done everything in their power to procure for us a proportionate share in this new government; but the very little they had gained proved what we may expect in future—that the interest of the Northern States would so predominate as to divest us of any pretensions to the title of a republic.

In the first place, what cause was there for jealousy of our importing negroes? Why confine us to twenty years, or, rather, why limit us at all? For his part, he thought this trade could be justified on the principles of religion, humanity, and justice; for certainly to translate a set of human beings from a bad country to a better, was fulfilling every part of these principles.

But they don't like our slaves, because they have none themselves and therefore want to exclude us from this great advantage. Why should the Southern States allow of this, without the consent of nine States.

Judge Pendleton observed, that only three States, Georgia, South Carolina, and North Carolina, allowed the importation of negroes. Virginia had a clause in her Constitution for this purpose, and Maryland, he believed, even before the war prohibited them.

Mr. Lowndes continued, that we had a law prohibiting the importation of negroes for three years, a law he greatly approved of; but there was no reason offered why the Southern States might not find it necessary to alter their conduct, and open their ports.

Without negroes, this State would degenerate into one

of the most contemptible in the Union; and he cited an expression that fell from General Pinckney, on a former debate, that whilst there remained one acre of swamp-land in South Carolina, he should raise his voice against restricting the importation of negroes. Even in granting the importation for twenty years, care had been taken to make us pay for this indulgence, each negro being liable, on importation, to pay a duty not exceeding ten dollars, and in addition to this they were liable to a capitation tax. Negroes were our wealth, our only natural resource; yet behold how our kind friends in the North were determined soon to tie up our hands, and drain us of what we had! The Eastern States drew their means of subsistence, in a great measure, from their shipping; and, on that head, they had been particularly careful not to allow of any burdens; they were not to pay tonnage or duties; no, not even the form of clearing out; all ports were free and open to them. Why then call this a reciprocal bargain, which took all from one party to bestow it on the other.

Hon. E. Rutledge. In the Northern States the labor is performed by white people, in the Southern by black. All the free people (and there are few others) in the Northern States are to be taxed by the new Constitution; whereas only the free people and two-fifths of the slaves, in the Southern States, are to be rated in the apportioning of taxes. But the principal objection is, that no duties are laid on shipping; that, in fact, the carrying trade was to be vested, in a great measure, in the Americans; that the ship-building business was principally carried on in the Northern States.

When this subject is duly considered, the Southern States should be the last to object to it.

Gen. Charles Cotesworth Pinckney said he would make a few observation on the objections which the gentleman had thrown out on the restriction that might be laid on the African trade after the year 1808.

On this point your delegates had to contend with the religious and political prejudices of the Eastern and Middle States,, and with the interested and inconsistent opinion of Virginia, who was warmly opposed to our importing more slaves.

I am of the same opinion now as I was two years ago, when I used the expressions the gentleman has quoted— that while there remained one acre of swamp-land uncleared in South Carolina, I would raise my voice against restricting the importation of negroes.

I am as thoroughly convinced as that gentleman is, that the nature of our climate, and the flat, swampy situation of our country, obliges us to cultivate our lands with negroes, and that without them South Carolina would soon be a desert waste.

You have so frequently heard my sentiments on this subject, that I need not now repeat them. It was alleged, by some of the members who opposed an unlimited importation, that slaves increased the weakness of any State who admitted them; that they were a dangerous species of property, which an invading enemy could easily turn against ourselves and the neighboring States; and that, as we were allowed a representation for them in the House of Representatives, our influence in government would be increased in proportion as we were less able to defend ourselves.

"Show some period," said the members from the Eastern States, "when it may be in our power to put a stop, if we please, to the importation of this weakness, and we will endeavor, for your convenience, to restrain the religious and political prejudices of our people on this subject."

The Middle States and Virginia made us no such proposition; they were for an immediate and total prohibition.

We endeavored to obviate the objections that were made

in the best manner we could, and assigned reasons for our insisting on the importation, which there is no occasion to repeat, as they must occur to every gentleman in the house; a committee of the States was appointed, in order to accommodate this matter, and, after a great deal of difficulty, it was settled on the footing recited in the Constitution.

By this settlement we have secured an unlimited importation of negroes for twenty years. Nor is it declared that the importation shall then be stopped; it may be continued.

We have a security that the general government can never emancipate them, for no such authority is granted; and it is admitted, on all hands, that the general government has no powers but what are expressly granted by the Constitution, and that all rights not expressed were reserved by the several States.

We have obtained a right to recover our slaves, in whatever part of America they may take refuge, which is a right we had not before.

In short, considering all circumstances, we have made the best terms for the security of this species of property it was in our power to make.

We would have made better if we could; but on the whole, I do not think them bad.

CHAPTER IV.

THE ORDINANCE OF 1787.

THE following authentic history of the Ordinance of 1787 was prepared for the *National Intelligencer* in 1847. The author has kindly permitted us to use it in this volume. It is unquestionably the only perfect history of that Ordinance ever given to the American people. We copy it with the remarks of that journal.

"A discussion having arisen in the public prints as to the authorship of certain important provisions embraced in the Ordinance of 1787 for the government of the Western Territory, now constituting several States of the Union, and especially in regard to that celebrated provision which forever excluded slavery from that vast and fertile region; our fellow-townsman, PETER FORCE, ESQ., has prepared from authentic materials the article which appears on the preceding page. From this careful exposition, it seems clear that Mr. Webster was right when, in his celebrated speech on Foote's resolution, he ascribed the authorship (if not the original conception) of the clause above specified to NATHAN DANE, of Massachusetts.

"It happens that, in seeking among the archives of all the old States, and among numerous private collections, for materials for his voluminous work, 'American Archives,' Mr. Force became possessed of the original projects and reports submitted to Congress respecting a plan of government for the Northwestern Territory, from this step in 1784 to 1787, when the Ordinance was finally adopted. He has the copy of the Ordinance of 1787, with all its alterations marked on it, while under consideration, just as it was amended at the President's table, among which the clause respecting slavery remains attached to it as an amendment in Mr. Dane's hand-writing, in the exact words in which it now stands in the Ordinance. From these materials, together with the official journals of the body, Mr. Force has compiled the narrative which we now insert; and, his materials being thus authentic, we must receive it as settling the question. He has taken this trouble for the sake of historic truth, and the same motive, together with the intrinsic interest of the subject, and the further reason that we have given currency to versions of the transaction which do injustice to the dead, have induced us cheerfully to yield to it the large share of our space which it occupies."

NOTES ON THE ORDINANCE OF 1787.

In the history of the Ordinance of 1787, published in the National Intelligencer on the 6th of the present month, there are several errors, which, before they become "fixed facts" should be corrected. These notes furnish material for the correction of some of them.

On the 1st of March 1784, a committee, consisting of Mr. Jefferson, of Virginia, Mr. Chase, of Maryland, and Mr. Howell, of Rhode Island, submitted to Congress the following plan for the temporary government of the Western Territory:

The committee appointed to prepare a plan for the temporary government of the Western Territory have agreed to the following resolutions,—

Resolved, That the Territory ceded or to be ceded by individual States to the United States, whensoever the same shall have been purchased of the Indian inhabitants and offered for sale by the United States, shall be formed into additional States, bounded in the following manner, as nearly as such cessions will admit; that is to say North-

THE ORDINANCE OF 1787. 157

wardly and Southwardly by parallels of latitude, so that each State shall comprehend, from South to North, two degrees of latitude, beginning to count from the completion of thirty-one degrees north of the equator: but any territory northwardly of the 47th degree shall make part of the State next below. And eastwardly and westwardly they shall be bounded, those on the Mississippi, by that river on one side and the meridian of the lowest point of the rapids of the Ohio on the other; and those adjoining on the east, by the same meridian on their western side, and on their eastern by the meridian of the western cape of the mouth of the Great Kanawha. And the territory eastward of this last meridian, between the Ohio, Lake Erie and Pennsylvania shall be one State.

That the settlers within the territory so to be purchased and offered for sale, shall, either on their own petition, or the order of Congress, receive authority from them, with appointments of time and place, for their free males, of full age, to meet together, for the purpose of establishing a temporary government, to adopt the constitution and laws of any one of these States, so that such laws nevertheless shall be subject to alteration by their ordinary legislature, and to erect, subject to a like alteration, counties or townships for the election of members for their legislature.

That such temporary government shall only continue in force in any State until it shall have acquired 20,000 free inhabitants, when, giving due proof thereof to Congress, they shall receive from them authority, with appointments of time and place, to call a convention of representatives to establish a permanent constitution and government for themselves.

Provided, That both the temporary and permanent government be established on these principles as their basis:

1. That they shall forever remain a part of the United States of America

2. That in their persons, property, and territory they shall be subject to the government of the United States in Congress assembled, and to the Articles of Confederation in all those cases in which the original States shall be so subject.

3. That they shall be subject to pay a part of the federal debts contracted or to be contracted, to be apportioned on them by Congress according to the same common rule and measure by which apportionments thereof shall be made on other States.

4. That their respective governments shall be in republican forms, and shall admit no person to be a citizen who holds any hereditary title.

5. That after the year 1800 of the Christian era there shall be neither slavery nor involuntary servitude in any of the said States otherwise than in punishment of crimes, whereof the party shall have been duly convicted to have been personally guilty.

That whensoever any of the said States shall have of free inhabitants as many as shall then be in any one of the least numerous of the thirteen original States, such State shall be admitted by its delegates into the Congress of the United States, on an equal footing with the said original States, after which the assent of two-thirds of the United States, in Congress assembled, shall be requisite in all those cases wherein, by the confederation, the assent of nine States is now required; provided the consent of nine States to such admission may be obtained according to the 11th of the Articles of Confederation. Until such admission by their delegates into Congress, any of the said States, after the establishment of their temporary government, shall have authority to keep a sitting member in Congress, with a right of debating, but not voting.

That the territory northward of the 45th degree, that is to say, of the completion of 45 degrees from the equator, and extending to the Lake of the Woods, shall be called *Sylvania;* that of the territory under the 45th and 44th degrees, that which lies westward of Lake Michigan shall be called *Michigania;* and that which is eastward thereof, within the peninsula formed by the Lakes and waters of Michigan, Huron, St. Clair, and Erie shall be called *Cherronesus,* and shall include any part of the peninsula which may extend above the 45th degree. Of the territory under the 43d and 45th degrees, that to the westward, through which the Assenippi or Rock river runs, shall be called *Assenisipia;* and that to the eastward, in which are the the fountains of the Muskingum, the two Miamies of Ohio, the Wabash, the Illinois, the Miami of the Lake, and the Sandusky rivers, shall be called *Metropotamia.* Of the territory which lies under the 39th and 38th degrees, to which shall be added so much of the point of land within the fork of the Ohio and Mississippi as lies under the 37th degree, that to the westward within and adjacent to which are the confluences of the rivers Wabash, Shawnee, Tamsee, Ohio, Illinois, Mississippi and Missouri, shall be called *Polypotamia;* and that to the eastward farther up the Ohio, shall be called *Polisipia.*

This report was recommitted to the same committee on the 17th of March and a new one was submitted on the 22d of the same month. The second report agreed in substance with the first. The principal difference was the omission of the paragraph giving names to the States to be formed out of the Western Territory. It was taken up for consideration by Congress on the 19th of April, on which day, on the motion of Mr. Spaight, of North Carolina, the following clause was struck out:

That after the year 1800 of the Christian era there shall be neither slavery nor involuntary servitude in any of the said States, otherwise than in the punishment of crimes whereof the party shall have been duly convicted to have been personally guilty.

The report was further considered and amended on the 20th and 21st. On the 23d it was agreed to (ten States voting *Aye*, and one *No*), without the clause prohibiting slavery and involuntary servitude after the year 1800. On the question to agree to the report, after the prohibitory clause was struck out, the yeas and nays were required by Mr. Beresford. The vote was:

Ayes—New Hampshire, Mr. Foster, Mr. Blanchard; Massachusetts, Mr. Gerry, Mr. Partridge; Rhode Island, Mr. Ellery, Mr. Howell; Connecticut, Mr. Sherman, Mr. Wadsworth; New York, Mr. Dewitt, Mr. Payne; New Jersey, Mr. Beatty, Mr. Dick; Pennsylvania, Mr. Mifflin, Mr. Montgomery, Mr. Hand; Maryland, Mr. Stone, Mr. Chase; Virginia, Mr. Jefferson, Mr. Mercer, Mr. Monroe; North Carolina, Mr. Williamson, Mr. Spaight.

Nays—South Carolina, Mr. Read, Mr. Beresford.

A*bsent*—Delaware, Georgia.

Thus the report of Mr. Jefferson for the temporary government of the Western Territory, without any restriction as to slavery, received the vote of every State present except South Carolina. It did not lie on the table of Congress during the three years from 1784 to 1787. During these three years it was the law of the land. It was repealed in 1787.

Nearly a year after the first plan was adopted, the clause originally offered by Mr. Jefferson, as a part of the *charter of compact and fundamental constitutions* between the thirteen original States and the new States to be formed in the Western Territory prohibiting slavery and involuntary servitude, was again submitted to Congress, omitting the time named, "after the year 1800 of the Christian era."

On the 16th March, 1785—"A motion was made by Mr. King, seconded by Mr. Ellery, that the following proposition be committed:

THE ORDINANCE OF 1787. 161

"That there shall be neither slavery nor involuntary servitude in any of the States described in the resolve of Congress of the 23d of April, 1784, otherwise than in the punishment of crimes, whereof the party shall have been personally guilty; and that this regulation shall be an article of compact, and remain a fundamental principle of the constitutions between the thirteen original States, and each of the States described in the said resolve of the 23d of April, 1784."

The motion was, "that the following proposition be committed"—that is, committed to a committee of the whole House: it was not "in the nature of an instruction to the Committee on the Western Territory." At that time there was no such committee. It was a separate, independent proposition. The very terms of it show that it was offered as an addition to the resolve of April 23d, 1784, with the intention of restoring to that resolve a clause that had originally formed part of it.

Mr. King's motion to commit was agreed to; eight States (New Hampshire, Massachusetts, Rhode Island, Connecticut, New York, New Jersey, Pennsylvania, and Maryland) voted in the affirmative, and three States (Virginia, North Carolina, and South Carolina) in the negative. Neither Delaware nor Georgia was represented.

After the commitment of this proposition, it was neither called up in Congress nor noticed by any of the committees who subsequently reported plans for the government of the Western Territory.

The subject was not laid over from this time till September, 1786. It is noticed as being before Congress on the 24th of March, the 10th of May, the 13th of July, and the 24th of August, of that year.

On the 24th of March, 1786, a report was made by the grand committee of the House, to whom had been referred a motion of Mr. Monroe upon the subject of the Western Territory.

On the 10th of May, 1786, a report was made by another committee, consisting of Mr. Monroe of Virginia, Mr. Johnson of Connecticut, Mr. King of Massachusetts, Mr. Kean of South Carolina, and Mr. Pinckney of South Carolina, to whom a motion of Mr. Dane, for considering and reporting the form of a temporary government for the Western Territory, was referred. This report, after amendments, was recommitted on the 13th of July following.

On the 24th of August, 1786, the Secretary of Congress was directed to inform the inhabitants of Kaskaskia "that Congress have under their consideration the plan of a temporary government for the said district, and that its adoption will be no longer protracted than the importance of the subject and a due regard to their interest may require."

On the 19th of September, 1786, a committee, consisting of Mr. Johnson of Connecticut, Mr. Pinckney of South Carolina, Mr. Smith of New York, Mr. Dane of Massachusetts, and Mr. Henry of Maryland, appointed to prepare a "plan of temporary government for such Districts or New States as shall be laid out by the United States upon the principles of the acts of cession from individual States, and admitted into the confederacy," made a report, which was taken up for consideration on the 29th, and, after some discussion and several motions to amend, the further consideration was postponed.

On the 26th of April, 1787, the same committee (Mr. Johnson, Mr. Pinckney, Mr. Smith, Mr. Dane, and Mr. Henry) reported "An Ordinance for the government of the Western Territory." It was read a second time, and amended on the 9th of May, when the next day was assigned for the third reading. On the 10th the order of the day for the third reading was called for by the State of Massachusetts, and was postponed. On the 9th and 10th of May, Massachusetts was represented by Mr. Gorham, Mr. King, and Mr. Dane. The proposition which, on Mr. King's motion, was "committed" on the 16th of March of the preceding year, was not in the Ordinance as reported by the committee, nor was any motion made in the Congress to insert it as an amendment.

The following is a copy of the Ordinance, as amended, and ordered to a third reading:

AN ORDINANCE
For the Government of the Western Territory.

It is hereby ordained by the United States, in Congress assembled, That there shall be appointed from time to time, a Governor, whose commission shall continue in force for the term of three years, unless sooner revoked by Congress.

There shall be appointed by Congress from time to time, a secretary, whose commission shall continue in force for four years, unless sooner revoked by Congress. It shall be his duty to keep and preserve the acts and laws passed by the General Assembly, and public records of the district, and of the proceedings of the Governor in his executive department, and transmit authentic copies of such acts and proceedings every six months to the Secretary of Congress.

There shall also be appointed a court, to consist of three judges, any two of whom shall form a court, who shall have a common law jurisdiction, whose commissions shall continue in force during good behavior.

And to secure the rights of personal liberty and property to the inhabitants and others, purchasers in the said district. it is hereby ordained that the inhabitants of such districts shall always be entitled to the benefits of the act of habeas corpus, and of the trial by jury.

The Governor and judges, or a majority of them, shall

adopt, and publish in the district, such laws of the original States, criminal and civil, as may be necessary and best suited to the circumstances of the district, and report them to Congress from time to time, which shall prevail in said district until the organization of the General Assembly, unless disapproved of by Congress; but afterwards the General Assembly shall have authority to alter them as they shall think fit, provided, however, that said Assembly shall have no power to create perpetuities.

The Governor for the time being shall be commander-in-chief of the militia, and appoint and commission all officers in the same below the rank of general officer. All officers of that rank shall be appointed and commissioned by Congress.

Previous to the organization of the General Assembly, the Governor shall appoint such magistrates and other civil officers in each county or township, as he shall find necessary for the preservation of peace and good order in the same. After the General Assembly shall be organized, the powers and duties of magistrates and other civil officers shall be regulated and defined by the said Assembly; but all magistrates and other civil officers not herein otherwise directed, shall, during the continuance of this temporary government, be appointed by the Governor.

The Governor shall, as soon as may be, proceed to lay out the district into counties and townships, subject, however, to such alterations as may thereafter be made by the legislature, as soon as there shall be five thousand free male inhabitants of full age within the said district. Upon giving due proof thereof to the Governor, they shall receive authority, with time and place to elect representatives from their counties or townships as aforesaid, to represent them in General Assembly, provided that for every five hundred free male inhabitants there shall be one representative, and so on progressively with the number of free male inhabitants shall the right of representation increase, until the number of representatives amount to twenty-five; after which the number and proportion of representatives shall be regulated by the legislature, provided that no person shall be eligible or qualified to act as a representative, unless he shall be a citizen of one of the United States, or have resided within the district three years, and shall likewise hold, in his own right in fee simple, two hundred acres of land within the same; provided also, that a freehold or life estate in fifty acres of land, in the said district, of a citizen of any of the United States, and two years' residence, if a foreigner, in addition shall be necessary to qualify a man as elector for said representatives.

The representatives thus elected shall serve for the term of two years; and in the case of the death of a representative or removal from office, the Governor shall issue a writ to the county or township for which he was a member, to elect another in his stead, to serve during the residue of the time.

The General Assembly shall consist of the Governor, a Legislative Council—to consist of five members, to be appointed by the United States, in Congress assembled, to continue in office during pleasure, any three of whom to be a quorum—and a House of Representatives, who shall have a legislative authority, complete in all cases for the good government of said district; provided that no act of the said General Assembly shall be construed to affect any lands the property of the United States; and provided further, that the lands of the non-resident proprietors shall in no instance be taxed higher than the lands of residents.

All bills shall originate indifferently either in the Council or House of Representatives, and having been passed by a majority in both Houses, shall be referred to the Governor for his assent, after obtaining which, they shall be complete and valid; but no bill or legislative act, whatever, shall be valid, or of any force, without his assent.

The Governor shall have power to convene, prorogue, and dissolve the General Assembly, when in his opinion it shall be expedient.

The said inhabitants or settlers shall be subject to pay a part of the federal debts contracted, or to be contracted, and to bear a proportional share of the burdens of the government, to be apportioned on them by Congress, according to the same common rule and measure by which apportionments thereof shall be made on the other States.

The Governor, Judges, Legislative Council, Secretary, and such other officers as Congress shall at any time think proper to appoint in such district, shall take an oath or affirmation of fidelity; the Governor before the President of Congress, and all other officers before the Governor, prescribed on the 27th day of January, 1785, to the Secretary of War, *mutatis mutandis*.

Whensoever any of the said States shall have of free inhabitants as many as are equal in number to the one-thirteenth part of the citizens of the original States, to be computed from the last enumeration, such State shall be admitted by its delegates into the Congress of the United States on an equal footing with the said original States, provided the consent of so many States in Congress is first obtained as may at that time be competent to such admission.

Resolved, That the resolutions of the 23d of April, 1784, be, and the same are hereby annulled and repealed.

Such was the Ordinance for the government of the Western Territory, when it was ordered to a third reading on the 10th of May, 1787. It had then made no further progress in the development of those great principles for which it has since been distinguished as one of the greatest monuments of civil jurisprudence. It made no provision for the equal distribution of estates. It said nothing of extending the fundamental principles of civil and religious liberty; nothing of the rights of conscience, knowledge, or education. It did not contain the articles of compact which were to remain unaltered forever unless by common consent.

We now come to the time when these great principles were first brought forward.

On the 9th of July, 1787, ordinances were again referred. The committee now consisted of Mr. Carrington of Virginia, Mr. Dane of Massachusetts, Mr. R. H. Lee of Virginia, Mr. Kean of South Carolina, and Mr. Smith of New York. Mr. Carrington, Mr. Lee, and Mr. Kean, the new members, were a majority.

This Committee did not merely revise the Ordinance, they prepared and reported the great BILL OF RIGHTS for the territory northwest of the Ohio.

The question is here presented, why was Mr. Carrington, a new member of the committee, placed at the head of it, to the exclusion of Mr. Dane and Mr. Smith, who had served previously? In the absence of positive evidence, there appears to be but one answer to this question, the opinions of all the members were known in Congress. In the course of debate new views had been presented which must have been received with general approbation. A majority of the committee were the advocates of these views, and the member by whom they were presented to the House, was selected as the chairman. There is nothing improbable or out of the usual course in this. Indeed the prompt action of the committee and of the Congress goes far to confirm it.

On the 11th of July (two days after the reference), Mr. Carrington reported the ordinance for the government of the Territory of the United States northwest of the Ohio. This ordinance was read a second time on the 12th, (and amended as stated below,) and on the 13th it was read a third time, and passed by the unanimous vote of the eight States present in the Congress.

On the passage the Yeas and Nays (being required by Mr. Yates,) were as follows:

Ayes—Massachusetts, Mr. Holten, Mr. Dane; New York, Mr. Smith, Mr. Harney, Mr. Yates; New Jersey, Mr. Clark, Mr. Schureman; Delaware, Mr. Kearney; Mr. Mitchell; Virginia, Mr. Grayson, Mr. R. H. Lee, Mr. Carrington; North Carolina, Mr. Blount, Mr. Hawkins; South Carolina, Mr. Kean, Mr. Huger; Georgia, Mr. Few, Mr. Pierce.

Nays—None.

Absent—New Hampshire, Rhode Island, Connecticut, Pennsylvania, Maryland.

It appears then that, instead of having "this ordinance under deliberation and revision for three years and six months," in FIVE DAYS it was passed through all the forms of legislation—the reference, the action of the committee, the report, the three several readings, the discussion and amendment by Congress, and the final passage.

On the 12th of July (as above stated), Mr. Dane offered the following amendment, which was adopted as the sixth of the articles of the compact:

"Article the sixth. There shall be neither slavery nor involuntary servitude in the said territory, otherwise than in the punishment of crimes whereof the party shall have been duly convicted. *Provided always*, That any person escaping into the same, from whom labor or service is claimed in any of the original States, such fugitive may be lawfully reclaimed and conveyed to the person claiming his or her labor or service as aforesaid."

This had in part been presented by Mr. Jefferson, in 1784, and again by Mr. King, in 1785. The assertion that this clause, "as it now exists in the ordinance," was "proposed and carried by Mr. King, when neither Jefferson nor Dane was present," is singularly incorrect. In the proposition submitted by Mr. King in 1785 (which was never afterwards called up in Congress) there was no provision for reclaiming fugitives; and without such a provision it could not have been carried at all: besides, the clause, "as it now exists in the ordinance," was proposed by Mr. Dane on the 12th of July, 1787, and carried by the unanimous vote of Congress when Mr. King was not present.

Mr. King was a member of the Convention for framing the federal Constitution. He was present and voted in the Convention on the 12th of July, 1787. The whole of that day was occupied in settling the proportion of representation and direct taxation, which was then determined as it now stands in the Constitution, viz., "by adding to the whole number of free persons, including those bound to service for a term of years, and excluding Indians not taxed, *three-fifths of all other persons.*

The Congress and the Convention were both in session at the same time in Philadelphia; there was of course free intercourse and interchange of opinion between the members of the two bodies. To this may be attributed the adoption on the same day, of the clause in the Ordinance and the clause in the Constitution.*

The accompanying copy of the Ordinance shows the

* An additional reason for the agreement of the Southern States to this restriction of slavery, may be found in the fact that the institution would not be likely to flourish to any considerable extent in that climate. They therefore gave up little and gained what was far more important to them, a recognition, in the article itself, of their right to capture their fugitive slaves in that territory—a right they had not before possessed. This all occurred prior to the adoption of the present Constitution, and seems to have been a compromise of sectional interests.

amendments made in Congress, on the 12th of July to Mr. Carrington's report of the 11th. All that was struck out is printed in *italic*, what was inserted is in SMALL CAPITALS. The reader, on comparing this with the plans previously reported by Mr. Jefferson, and by Mr. Johnson, will see that most of the principles on which its wisdom and fame rest, were first presented by Mr. Carrington.

Washington, August 20th, 1847. P. F.

AN ORDINANCE

For the Government of the Territory of the United States Northwest of the river Ohio.

Be it ordained by the United States in Congress assembled, That the said Territory, for the purposes of temporary government, be one district; subject, however to be divided into two districts, as circumstances may in the opinion of Congress make it expedient.

Be it ordained by the authority aforesaid, That the estates both of resident and non-resident proprietors in the said territory dying intestate, shall descend to and be distributed among their children and the descendants of a deceased child in equal parts; the descendants of a deceased child or grandchild to take the share of their deceased parent in equal parts among them; and where there shall be no children or descendants, then in equal parts to the next of kin in equal degree; and among collaterals, the children of a deceased brother or sister of the intestate shall have in equal parts among them their deceased parents' share; AND THERE SHALL IN NO CASE BE A DISTINCTION BETWEEN KINDRED OF THE WHOLE AND HALF BLOOD; saving in all cases to the widow of the intestate her third part of the real estate for life, and [*where there shall be no children of the intestate*] one-third part of the personal estate; and this law relative to descent and dower shall remain in full force until altered by the legislature of the district. And until the

THE ORDINANCE OF 1787.

Governor and Judges shall adopt laws as hereinafter mentioned, estates in the said territory may be devised or bequeathed by wills in writing, signed and sealed by him or her, in whom the estate may be (being of full age) and attested by three witnesses; and real estates may be conveyed by lease and release, or bargain and sale, signed sealed and delivered by the person, being of full age, in whom the estate may be, and attested by two witnesses, provided such wills be duly proved, and such conveyances be acknowledged, or the execution thereof duly proved, and be recorded within one year after proper magistrates, courts, and registers shall be appointed for that purpose; and personal property may be transferred by delivery, saving, however, to the [*inhabitants of Kaskaskies and Post Vincent.*] FRENCH AND CANADIAN INHABITANTS, AND OTHER SETTLERS OF THE KASKASKIES, SAINT VINCENT'S, AND THE NEIGHBORING VILLAGES, WHO HAVE HERETOFORE PROFESSED THEMSELVES CITIZENS OF VIRGINIA, their laws and customs now in force among them relative to the descent and conveyance of property.

Be it ordained by the authority aforesaid, That there shall be appointed from time to time by Congress, a Governor, whose commission shall continue in force for the term of three years unless sooner revoked by Congress; he shall reside in the district, and have a freehold estate therein, in one thousand acres of land, while in the exercise of his office.

There shall be appointed from time to time, by Congress, a Secretary, whose commission shall continue in force for four years unless sooner revoked; he shall reside in the district, and have a freehold estate therein, in five hundred acres of land, while in the exercise of his office. It shall be his duty to keep and preserve the acts and laws passed by the legislature, and the public records of the district, and the proceedings of the Governor in his executive department, and transmit authentic copies of such acts and proceedings every six months to the Secretary of Congress. There shall also be appointed a court to consist of three judges, any two of whom to form a court, who shall have a common-law jurisdiction, and reside in the district, and have each therein a freehold estate, in five hundred acres of land while in the exercise of their offices; and their commissions shall continue in force during good behavor.

The Governor and Judges, or a majority of them, shall adopt and publish in the district such laws of the original States, criminal and civil, as may be necessary and best suited to the circumstances of the district, and report them to Congress from time to time, which laws shall be in force in the district until the organization of the General Assembly therein, unless disapproved of by Congress; but afterwards the legislature shall have authority to alter them as they shall see fit.

The Governor for the time being, shall be commander in chief of the militia, appoint and commission all officers in the same below the rank of general officers; all general officers [*above that rank*] shall be appointed and commissioned by Congress.

Previous to the organization of the General Assembly, the Governor shall appoint such magistrates and other civil officers, in each county and township as he shall find necessary for the preservation of the peace and good order in the same. After the General Assembly shall be organized, the powers and duties of magistrates and other civil officers, shall be regulated and defined by the said Assembly; but all magistrates and other civil officers not herein otherwise directed, shall, during the continuance of this temporary government, be appointed by the Governor.

For the prevention of crime and injuries, the laws, to be adopted or made, shall have force in all parts of the district, and for the execution of process, criminal and civil, the

THE ORDINANCE OF 1787.   173

Governor shall make proper division thereof; and he shall proceed from time to time as circumstances may require to lay out the parts of the district in which the Indian titles shall have been extinguished into counties and townships, subject, however, to such alterations as may thereafter be made by the legislature.

So soon as there shall be five thousand free male inhabitants of full age, in the district, upon giving proof thereof to the governor, they shall receive authority, with time and place to elect Representatives from their counties and townships to represent them in the General Assembly; provided that, for every five hundred free male inhabitants there shall be one representative, and so on progressively with the number of free male inhabitants shall the right of representation increase until the number of representatives shall amount to twenty-five, after which the number and proportion of representatives shall be regulated by the legislature; provided that no person be eligible or qualified to act as a representative unless he shall have been a citizen of one of the United States three years and be a resident in the district, or unless he shall have resided in the district three years, and in either case shall likewise hold in his own right, in fee simple, two hundred acres of land within the same. Provided also, that a freehold in fifty acres of land in the district, having been a citizen of one of the States, and being resident in the district, or the like freehold and two years' residence in the district, shall be necessary to qualify a man as an elector of a representative.

The representatives thus elected shall serve for the term of two years, and in case of the death of the representative, or removal from office, the Governor shall issue a writ to the county or township for which he was a member, to elect another in his stead, to serve for the residue of the term.

The General Assembly or Legislature, shall consist of the Governor, Legislative Council and a House of Representatives. The Legislative Council shall consist of five members to continue in office five years, unless sooner removed by Congress, and three of whom to be a quorum, and the members of the Council shall be nominated and appointed in the following manner, to wit: As soon as representatives shall be elected, the Governor shall appoint a time and place for them to meet together, and when met, they shall nominate ten persons, residents in the district, and each possessed of a freehold in five hundred acres of land, and return their names to Congress; five of whom Congress shall appoint and commission to serve as aforesaid, and whenever a vacancy shall happened in the Council, by death or removal from office, the House of Representatives shall nominate two persons, qualified as aforesaid, for each vacancy, and return their names to Congress; one of whom Congress shall appoint and commission for the residue of the term; and every five years, four months at least before the expiration of the time of service of the members of Council the said House shall nominate ten persons, qualified as aforesaid, and return their names to Congress, five of whom Congress shall appoint and commission to serve as members of the Council five years, unless sooner removed. And the Governor, Legislative Council and House of Representatives, shall have authority to make laws in all cases for the good government of the district, not repugnant to the principles and articles in this Ordinance established and declared. And all bills having passed by a majority in the House and by a majority in the Council, shall be referred to the Governor for his assent; but no bill or legislative act whatever shall be of any force without his assent. The Governor shall have power to convene, prorogue, and dissolve the General Assembly, when in his opinion it shall be expedient.

The Governor, Judges, Legislative Council, Secretary, and such other officers as Congress shall appoint in the district, shall take an oath or affirmation of fidelity and of office, the Governor before the President of Congress, and all other officers before the Governor. As soon as a Legislature shall be formed in the district, the Council and House, assembled in one room, shall have authority, by joint ballot, to elect a delegate to Congress, who shall have a seat in Congress, with a right of debating, but not of voting, during this temporary government.

And for extending [*to all parts of the Confederacy*] the fundamental principles of civil and religious liberty, which form the basis whereon these republics, their laws and constitutions, are erected; to fix and establish those principles as the basis of all laws, constitutions, and governments, which forever hereafter shall be formed in the said territory; to provide also for the establishment of States and permanent government therein, and for their admission to a share in the federal councils, on an equal footing with the original States, at as early periods as may be consistent with the general interest:

It is hereby ordained and declared by the authority aforesaid, That the following articles shall be considered as articles of compact between the original States and the people and States in the said territory, and forever remain unalterable, unless by common consent, to-wit:

ARTICLE 1. No person, demeaning himself in a peaceable and orderly manner, shall ever be molested on account of his mode of worship or religious sentiments in the said territory.

ARTICLE 2. The inhabitants of the said territory shall always be entitled to the benefits of the writ of habeas corpus and of the trial by jury; of a proportionate representation of the people in the Legislature, and of judicial proceedings according to the course of the common law; all persons shall be bailable, unless for capital offenses, where the proof shall be evident or the presumption great; all fines shall be moderate, and no cruel or unusual punishments shall be inflicted; no man shall be deprived of his liberty or property but by the judgment of his peers, or the law of the land; and should the public exigencies make it necessary, for the common preservation, to take any person's property, or to demand his particular services, full compensation shall be made for the same; and, in the just preservation of rights and property, it is understood and declared that no law ought ever to be made or have force in the said territory, that shall in any manner whatever interfere with or affect private contracts or engagements, bona fide and without fraud previously formed.

ARTICLE 3. [*Institutions for the promotion of*] religion [*and*] morality, AND KNOWLEDGE, BEING NECESSARY TO GOOD GOVERNMENT AND THE HAPPINESS OF MANKIND, schools and the means of education shall forever be encouraged, [*and all persons while young shall be taught some useful occupation.*] The utmost good faith shall always be observed towards the Indians; their lands and property shall never be taken from them without their consent; and in their property, rights, and liberty, they never shall be invaded or disturbed, unless in just and lawful wars authorized by Congress; but laws founded in justice and humanity shall from time to time be made, for preventing wrongs being done to them, and for preserving peace and friendship with them.

ARTICLE 4. The said territory and the States which may be formed therein, shall forever remain a part of this confederacy of the United States of America, subject to the Articles of Confederation, and to such alterations therein as shall be constitutionally made; and to all the acts and ordinances of the United States in Congress assembled. The Legislature of those districts, or new States, shall never interfere with the primary disposal of the soil by the United States in Congress assembled, nor with any regulations Congress may find necessary for securing the title in such soil to bona fide purchasers. No tax shall be imposed on lands the property of the United States; and in no case shall non-resident proprietors be taxed higher than residents. The navigable waters leading into the Mississippi and St. Lawrence, and the carrying places between the same, shall be common highways, and forever free, as well to the inhabitants of the said territory as to the citizens of the United States, and those of any other States that may be admitted into the confederacy, without any tax, impost, or duty therefor.

ARTICLE 5. There shall be formed in the said territory not less than three, nor more than five States; and the boundaries of the States, as soon as Virginia shall alter her act of cession and [*authorize*] CONSENT TO the same, shall become fixed and established as follows, to wit: The western State in THE said territory shall be bounded by the Mississippi, the Ohio, and Wabash rivers; a direct line drawn from the Wabash and Post Vincent's, due north to the territorial line between the United States and Canada, and by THE said territorial line to the Lake of the Woods and Mississippi. The middle State shall be bounded by the said direct line, the Wabash from Post Vincent's to the Ohio; by the Ohio, by a direct line drawn due north from the mouth of the Great Miami to THE said territorial line, and by THE said territorial line. The eastern State shall be bounded by the last-mentioned direct line, the Ohio, Pennsylvania and the said territorial line: Provided, however, and it is further understood and declared, that the boundaries of these three States, shall be subject so far to be altered, that if Congress shall hereafter find it expedient, they shall have authority to form one or two States in that part of the said territory which lies north of an east and west line drawn through the southerly bend or extreme of Lake Michigan; and whenever any of the said States shall have sixty thousand free inhabitants therein, such State shall be admitted by its delegates into the Congress of the United States, on an equal footing with the original States in all respects whatever; and shall be at liberty to form a permanent constitution and State government: Provided the constitution and government so to be formed shall be republican, and in conformity to the principles contained in these articles; and, so far as it can be consistent with the general interest of the confederacy, such admission shall be allowed at an earlier period, and when there may be a less number of free inhabitants in the State than sixty thousand.

ARTICLE 6. There shall be neither slavery nor involuntary servitude in the said territory, otherwise than in punishment of crimes whereof the party shall have been duly convicted: Provided always, that any person escaping into the same, from whom labor or service is lawfully claimed in any one of the original States, such fugitive may be lawfully reclaimed and conveyed to the person claiming his or her labor or service as aforesaid.

Be it ordained by the authority aforesaid, That the resolutions of the 23d of April, 1784, relative to the subject of this ordinance, be and the same are hereby repealed, and declared null and void.

Done by the United States in Congress assembled the thirteenth day of July, in the year of our Lord 1787, and of the sovereignty and independence the twelfth.

CHAS. THOMPSON,
Secretary.

CHAPTER V.

THE SLAVE TRADE.

IN Congress, Friday, Feb. 12, 1790, the following memorial of the Pennsylvania Society for promoting the abolition of slavery, the relief of free negroes unlawfully held in bondage, and the improvement of the condition of the African race, was presented and read.*

This memorial respectfully showeth, that from a regard for the happiness of mankind, an association was formed several years since in this State, by a number of her citizens of various religious denominations, for promoting the abolition of slavery, and for the relief of those unlawfully held in bondage. A just and acute conception of the true principles of liberty as it spread through the land, produced accessions to their numbers, many friends of their cause, and a legislative co-operation with their views, which by the blessing of Divine Providence, have been successfully directed to the relieving from bondage a large number of their fellow-creatures of the African race. They have also the satisfaction to observe, that—in consequence of that spirit of philanthropy and genuine liberty which is generally diffusing its beneficial influence,—similar institutions are forming at home and abroad.

That mankind are all formed by the same Almighty Being, alike objects of his care, and equally assigned for the

* It will be noticed that this was the first Congress assembled under the Constitution, and was the first action taken by that body on the subject.

enjoyment of happiness, the Christian religion teaches us to believe; and the political creed of Americans fully coincides with the position. Your memorialists, particularly engaged in attending to the distresses arising from slavery, believe it their indispensable duty to present this subject to your notice. They have observed, with real satisfaction, that many important and salutary powers are vested in you for " promoting the welfare, and securing the blessings of liberty to the people of the United States;" and as they conceive that these blessings ought rightfully to be administered, without distinction of color, to all descriptions of people, so they indulge themselves in the pleasing expectation that nothing which can be done for the relief of the unhappy objects of their care will be either omitted or delayed.

From a persuasion that equal liberty was originally the portion, and is still the birthright of all men, and influenced by the strong ties of humanity, and the principles of their institution, your memorialists conceive themselves bound to use all justifiable endeavors to loosen the bands of slavery; and promote a general enjoyment of the blessings of freedom. Under these impressions, they earnestly entreat your serious attention to the subject of slavery. That you will be pleased to countenance the restoration of liberty to those unhappy men who alone in this land of freedom are degraded into perpetual bondage, and who, amidst the general joy of surrounding freemen, are groaning in servile subjection; that you will devise means for removing this inconsistency from the character of the American people; that you will promote mercy and justice toward this distressed race, and that you will step to the very verge of the power invested in you for discouraging every species of traffic in the persons of our fellow-men.

The memorial was referred to a special committee.

REPORT OF THE SPECIAL COMMITTEE.

The Committee to whom were referred sundry memorials from the people called Quakers; and also a memorial from the Pennsylvania Society for promoting the Abolition of Slavery, submit the following report:

That, from the nature of the matters contained in these memorials, they were induced to examine the powers vested in Congress under the present Constitution, relating to the abolition of Slavery, and are clearly of opinion—

Firstly. That the General Government is expressly restrained from prohibiting the importation of such persons " as any of the other States now existing shall think proper to admit until the year one thousand eight hundred and eight."

Secondly. That Congress, by a fair construction of the Constitution, is equally restrained from interfering in the emancipation of slaves, who already are, or who may, within the period mentioned, be imported into, or born within, any of the said States.

Thirdly. That Congress has no authority to interfere in the internal regulations of particular States, relative to the instruction of slaves in the principles of morality and religion; to their comfortable clothing, accommodations, and subsistence; to the regulation of their marriages, and the violation of the rights thereof, or the separation of children from their parents; to a comfortable provision in case of sickness, age, or infirmity; or to the seizure, transportation, or sale of free negroes; but have the fullest confidence in the wisdom and humanity of the legislatures of the several States; that they will revise their laws from time to time, when necessary, and promote the objects mentioned in the memorials, and every other measure that may tend to the happiness of slaves.

Fourthly. That, nevertheless, Congress have authority,

if they shall think it necessary, to lay at any time a tax or duty, not exceeding ten dollars for each person of any description, the importation of whom shall be by any of the States admitted as aforesaid.

Fifthly. That Congress have authority to interdict, or (so far as it is or may be carried on by citizens of the United States for supplying foreigners,) to regulate the African trade, and to make provision for the humane treatment of slaves in all instances while on their passage to the United States, or to foreign ports, so far as it respects the citizens of the United States.

Sixthly. That Congress have also authority to prohibit foreigners from fitting out vessels in any port of the United States, for transporting persons from Africa to any foreign port.

Seventhly. That the memorialists be informed that, in all cases in which the authority of Congress extends, they will exercise it for the humane object of the memorialists, so far as they can be promoted on the principles of justice, humanity, and good policy.

REPORT OF THE COMMITTEE OF THE WHOLE HOUSE,

On the Report of the Special Committee preceding.

March 25, 1790. The Committee of the whole House, to whom was committed the report of the committee on the memorials of the people called Quakers, and of the Pennsylvania Society for promoting the Abolition of Slavery, report the following amendments.

Strike out the first clause, together with the recital thereto, and in lieu thereof, insert, "That the migration or importation of such persons as any of the States now existing shall think proper to admit, cannot be prohibited by Congress, prior to the year one thousand eight hundred and eight."

Strike out the second and third clauses, and in lieu thereof, insert "That Congress have no authority to interfere in the emancipation of slaves or in the treatment of them within any of the States; it remaining with the several States alone to provide any regulations therein, which humanity and true policy may require."

Strike out the fourth and fifth clauses, and in lieu thereof, insert, "That Congress have authority to restrain the citizens of the United States from carrying on the African trade, for the purpose of supplying foreigners with slaves; and of providing, by proper regulations, for the humane treatment during their passage, of slaves imported by the said citizens into the States admitting such importation."

Strike out the seventh clause.

CHAPTER VI.

VIRGINIA RESOLUTIONS OF 1798,

Pronouncing the Alien and Sedition Laws to be unconstitutional, and defining the rights of the States. (Drawn by Mr. Madison.)

Resolved, That the General Assembly of Virginia, doth unequivocally express a firm resolution to maintain and defend the Constitution of the United States, and the Constitution of this State, against every aggression, either foreign or domestic, and that they will support the government of the United States in all measures warranted by the former.

That this Assembly most solemnly declares a warm attachment to the union of the States, to maintain which it pledges its power; and that for this end, it is their duty to watch over and oppose every infraction of those principles which constitute the only basis of that union, because a faithful observance of them can alone secure its existence and the public happiness.

That this Assembly doth explicitly and peremptorily declare, that it views the powers of the federal government as resulting from the compact to which the States are parties, as limited by the plain sense and intention of the instrument constituting that compact, as no further valid than they are authorized by the grant enumerated in that compact; and that, in case of a deliberate, palpable, and dangerous exercise of other powers, not granted by the said compact, the States who are parties thereto, have the right, and are in duty bound to interpose, for arresting the progress of the evil, and for maintaining within their respective limits, the authorities, rights, and liberties, appertaining to them.

That the General Assembly doth also express its deepest regret, that a spirit has, in sundry instances, been manifested by the federal government to enlarge its powers by forced constructions of the constitutional charter which defines them: and that indications have appeared of a design to expound certain general phrases (which, having been copied from the very limited grant of powers in the former Articles of Confederation, were the less liable to be misconstrued) so as to destroy the meaning and effect of the particular enumeration which necessarily explains and limits the general phrases, and so as to consolidate the States, by degrees, into one sovereignty, the obvious tendency and inevitable result of which would be, to transform the present republican system of the United States into an absolute, or, at best, a mixed monarchy.

That the General Assembly doth particularly protest against the palpable and alarming infractions of the Constitution, in the two late cases of the "Alien and Sedition Acts," passed at the late session of Congress: the first of which exercises a power nowhere delegated to the federal government, and which, by uniting legislative and judicial powers to those of executive subverts the general principle of free government, as well as the particular organization and positive provisions of the federal Constitution: and the other of which acts exercises, in like manner, a power not delegated by the Constitution, but, on the contrary, expressly and positively forbidden by one of the amendments thereto—a power, which, more than any other, ought to produce universal alarm, because it is leveled against the right of freely examining public characters and measures, and of free communication among the people thereon, which has ever been justly deemed the only effectual guardian of every other right.

That this State having, by its Convention, which ratified the federal Constitution, expressly declared that, among other essential rights, "the liberty of conscience and the press cannot be concealed, abridged, restrained, or modified by any authority of the United States," and from its extreme anxiety to guard these rights from every possible attack of sophistry and ambition, having, with other States, recommended an amendment for that purpose, which amendment was, in due time, annexed to the Constitution,—it would mark a reproachful inconsistency, and criminal degeneracy, if an indifference were now shown to the most palpable violation of one of the rights thus declared and secured, and to the establishment of a precedent which may be fatal to the other.

That the good people of this commonwealth, having ever felt, and continuing to feel, the most sincere affection for their brethren of the other States; the truest anxiety for establishing and perpetuating the union of all, and the most scrupulous fidelity to that Constitution, which is the pledge of mutual friendship, and the instrument of mutual happiness, the General Assembly doth solemnly appeal to the like dispositions in the other States, in confidence that they will concur with this commonwealth in declaring, as it does hereby declare, that the acts aforesaid are unconstitutional, and that the necessary and proper measures will be taken *by each* for co-operating with this State in maintaining unimpaired the authorities, rights, and liberties, reserved to the States respectively or to the people.

That the Governor be desired to transmit a copy of the foregoing resolutions to the executive of each of the other States, with a request that the same may be communicated to the legislature thereof, and that a copy be furnished to each of the senators and representatives representing this State in the Congress of the United States.

KENTUCKY RESOLUTIONS OF 1798 AND 1799.
(Drawn by Mr. Jefferson.)

1. *Resolved,* That the several States composing the United States of America are not united on the principle of unlimited submission to their general government; but that by compact, under the style and title of a Constitution for the United States, and of amendments thereto, they constituted a general government for special purposes, delegated to that government certain power, reserving, each State to itself, the residuary mass of rights to their own self-government, and that whensoever the general government assumes undelegated powers, its acts are unauthoritative, void, of no force; that to this compact each State acceded as a State, and is an integral party; that this government, created by this compact, was not made the exclusive or final judge of the extent of the powers delegated to itself, since that would have made its discretion, and not the Constitution, the measure of its powers; but that, as in all other cases of compact among parties having no common judge, *each party has an equal right to judge for itself, as well of infractions as of the mode and measure of redress.*

2. *Resolved,* That the Constitution of the United States having delegated to Congress a power to punish treason, counterfeiting the securities and current coin of the United States, piracies and felonies committed on the high seas, and offenses against the laws of nations, and no other crimes whatever, and it being true, as a general principle, and one of the amendments to the Constitution having also declared, "that the powers not delegated to the United States by the Constitution, nor prohibited by it to the States, are reserved to the States respectively or to the people," therefore, also, the same act of Congress, passed on the 14th day of July, 1798, and entitled "An Act in addition to the Act entitled an Act for the punishment of certain crimes against the

United States;" as also the act passed by them on the 27th day of June, 1798, entitled an Act to punish frauds committed on the Bank of the United States, (and all other their acts which assume to create, define, or punish crimes other than those enumerated in the Constitution,) are altogether void, and of no force; and that the power to create, define, and punish such other crimes is reserved, and of right appertains, solely and exclusively to the respective States, each within its own territory.

3. *Resolved*, That it is true, as a general principle, and is also expressly declared by one of the amendments of the Constitution, that "the powers not delegated to the United States by the Constitution, nor prohibited by it to the States, are reserved to the States respectively, or to the people;" and that, no power over the freedom of religion, freedom of speech, or freedom of the press, being delegated to the United States by the Constitution, nor prohibited by it to the States, all lawful powers respecting the same did of right remain, and were reserved to the States, or to the people; that thus was manifested their determination, to retain to themselves the right of judging how far the licentiousness of speech, and of the press, may be abridged without lessening their useful freedom, and how far those abuses which cannot be separated from their use, should be tolerated rather than the use be destroyed; and thus also they guarded against all abridgment, by the United States, of the freedom of all religious principles and exercises, and retained to themselves the right of protecting the same, as thus stated, by a law passed on the general demand of its citizens, had already protected them from all human restraint or interference, and that, in addition to this general principle, and express determination, another and more special provision has been made by one of the amendments to the Constitution, which expressly declares, that "Congress shall make no laws respecting an establishment of re-

ligion, or prohibiting the free exercise thereof, or abridging the freedom of speech or the press," thereby guarding in the same sentence and under the same words, the freedom of religion, of speech, and of the press, insomuch that whatever violates either throws down the sanctuary which covers the others,—and that libels, falsehood and defamation, equally with heresy and false religion, are withheld from the cognizance of federal tribunals. That, therefore, the act of the Congress of the United States, passed on the 14th of July, 1798, entitled, An Act in addition to the Act entitled an Act for the punishment of certain crimes against the United States," which does abridge the freedom of the press, is not law, but is altogether void, and of no force.

4. *Resolved*, That alien friends are under the jurisdiction and protection of the laws of the State wherein they are; that no power over them has been delegated to the United States, nor prohibited to the individual States, distinct from their power over citizens; and it being true as a general principle, and one of the amendments to the Constitution having also declared, that "the powers not delegated to the United States by the Constitution, nor prohibited to the States, are reserved to the States, respectively, or to the people," the Act of the Congress of the United States, passed the 22nd day of June, 1798, entitled, "An Act concerning Aliens," which assumes power over alien friends not delegated by the Constitution, is not law, but is altogether void and of no force.

5. *Resolved*, That, in addition to the general principle, as well as the express declaration, that powers not delegated are reserved, another and more special provision, inserted in the Constitution from abundant caution, has declared, "that the migration or importation of such persons as any of the States now existing shall think proper to admit, shall not be prohibited by the Congress prior to the year 1808." That this commonwealth does admit the

migration of alien friends described as the subject of the said act concerning aliens, that a provision against prohibiting their migration is a provision against all acts equivalent thereto, or it would be nugatory; that to remove them when migrated, is equivalent to a prohibition of their migration, and is, therefore, contrary to the said provision of the Constitution, and *void*.

6. *Resolved*. That the imprisonment of a person under the protection of the laws of this Commonwealth, on his failure to obey the simple order of the President to depart out of the United States, as is undertaken by the said act, entitled, "An Act concerning Aliens," is contrary to the Constitution, one amendment in which has provided that "no person shall be deprived of liberty without due process of law;" and that another having provided, "that, in all criminal prosecutions, the accused shall enjoy the right of a public trial by an impartial jury, to be informed as to the nature and cause of the accusation, to be confronted with the witnesses against him, to have compulsory process for obtaining witnesses in his favor, and to have assistance of counsel for his defense," the same act undertaking to authorize the President to remove a person out of the United States who is under the protection of the law, on his own suspicion, without jury, without public trial, without confrontation of the witnesses against him, without having witnesses in his favor, without defense, without counsel,— contrary to these provisions also of the Constitution—is therefore not law, but utterly void, and of no force.

That transferring the power of judging any person who is under the protection of the laws, from the courts to the President of the United States, as is undertaken by the same act concerning aliens, is against the article of the Constitution which provides "that the judicial power of the United States shall be vested in the courts, the judges of which shall hold their office during their good behavior," and that the said act is void for that reason also; and it is further to be noted that this transfer of judiciary power is to that magistrate of the general government who already possesses all the executive and a qualified negative on all the legislation.

7. *Resolved,* That the construction applied by the general government (as is evident by sundry of their proceedings) to those parts of the Constitution of the United States which delegate to Congress power to lay and collect taxes, duties, imposts, excises, to pay the debts, and provide for the common defense and general welfare, of the United States, and to make all laws which shall be necessary and proper for carrying into execution the powers vested by the Constitution in the Government of the United States, or any department thereof, goes to the destruction of all the limits prescribed to their power by the Constitution; that words meant by that instrument to be subsidiary only to the execution of the limited powers, ought not to be so construed as themselves to give unlimited powers, nor a part so to be taken as to destroy the whole residue of the instrument; that the proceedings of the general government under color of these articles, will be a fit and necessary subject for revisal and correction at a time of greater tranquillity, while those specified in the preceding resolutions call for immediate redress.

8. *Resolved,* That the preceding resolutions be transmitted to the senators and representatives in Congress from this commonwealth, who are enjoined to present the same to their respective houses, and to use their best endeavors to procure, at the next session of Congress, a repeal of the aforesaid unconstitutional and obnoxious acts.

9. *Resolved,* lastly, That the governor of this commonwealth be, and is, authorized and requested to communicate the preceding resolutions to the legislatures of the several States, to assure them that this commonwealth considers

union for special national purposes, and particularly for those specified in their late federal compact, to be friendly to the peace, happiness, and prosperity of all the States; that, faithful to that compact, according to the plain intent and meaning in which it was understood and acceded to by the several parties, it is sincerely anxious for its preservation; that it does also believe that, to take from the States all the powers of self-government, and transfer them to a general and consolidated government, without regard to the special government and reservations solemnly agreed to in that compact, is not for the peace, happiness, or prosperity of these States; and that, therefore, this commonwealth is determined, as it doubts not its co-States are, to submit to undelegated and consequently unlimited powers in no man, or body of men, on earth; that, if the acts before specified should stand, these conclusions would flow from them,—that the general government may place any act they think proper on the list of crimes, and punish it themselves, whether enumerated or not enumerated by the Constitution as recognized by them; that they may transfer its cognizance to the President, or any other person, who may himself be the accuser, counsel, judge, and jury, whose suspicions may be evidence, his order the sentence, his officer the executioner, and his breast the sole record of the transaction; that a very numerous and valuable description of the inhabitants of these States, being by this precedent reduced, as outlaws, to the absolute dominion of one man, and the barriers of the Constitution thus swept from us all, no rampart now remains against the passion and the power of a majority of Congress to protect from a like exportation, or other grievous punishment, the minority of the same body, the legislatures, judges, governors, and counsellors of the State, nor their peaceable inhabitants, who may venture to reclaim the constitutional rights and liberties of the States and people, or who, for other causes, good or bad, may be obnoxious to the view, or marked by the suspicions, of the President, or thought dangerous to his elections, or other interests, public or personal; that the friendless alien has been selected as the safest subject of a first experiment; but the citizen will soon follow, or rather has already followed; for already has a Sedition Act marked him as a prey; that these and successive acts of the same character, unless arrested on the threshold, may tend to drive these States into revolution and blood, and will furnish new calumnies against republican governments, and new pretexts for those who wish it to be believed that man cannot be governed but by a rod of iron; that it would be a dangerous delusion were a confidence in the men of our choice to silence our fears for the safety of our rights; that confidence is everywhere the parent of despotism; free government is founded in jealousy, and not in confidence; it is jealousy, not confidence, which prescribes limited constitutions to bind down those whom we are obliged to trust with power; that our Constitution has accordingly fixed the limits to which, and no farther, our confidence may go; and let the honest advocate of confidence read the Alien and Sedition Acts, and say if the Constitution has not been wise in fixing limits to the government it created, and whether we should be wise in destroying those limits; let him say what the government is, if it be not a tyranny, which the men of our choice have conferred on the President, and the President of our choice has assented to and accepted, over the friendly strangers to whom the mild spirit of our country and its laws had pledged hospitality and protection; that the men of our choice have more respected the base suspicions of the President, than the solid rights of ignorance, the claims of justification, the sacred force of truth, and the forms and substance of law and justice.

In questions of power, then, let no more be said of confidence in man, but bind him down from mischief by the chains of the Constitution. That this commonwealth does therefore call on its co-States for an expression of their sentiments on the acts concerning aliens, and for the punishment of certain crimes herein before specified, plainly declaring whether these acts are or are not authorized by the federal compact. And it doubts not that their sense will be so announced as to prove their attachment to limited government, whether general or particular, and that the rights and liberties of their co-States will be exposed to no dangers by remaining embarked on a common bottom with their own; but they will concur with this commonwealth in considering the said acts as so palpably against the Constitution as to amount to an undisguised declaration, that the compact is not meant to be the measure of the powers of the general government, but that it will proceed in the exercise over these States of all powers whatever; that they will view this as seizing the rights of the States, and consolidating them in the hands of the general government, with a power assumed to bind the States, not merely in cases made federal, but in all cases whatsoever, by laws made, not with their consent, but by others against their consent; that this would be to surrender the form of government we have chosen, and live under one deriving its powers from its own will, and not from our authority; and that the co-States, recurring to their natural rights not made federal, will concur in declaring them void and of no force, and will each unite with this commonwealth in requesting their repeal at the next session of Congress.

CHAPTER VII.

THE MISSOURI QUESTION.

IN December, 1818, Congress received a petition from the legislature of the territory asking admission into the Union. On the 19th February, 1819, while the bill was under discussion for the admission, an amendment was offered "providing that the further introduction of slavery, or involuntary servitude be prohibited in said State." Adopted, 87 to 76 votes in the House. Another amendment, "That all children born in said State, after admission thereof, shall be free after the age of twenty-five years." Adopted, 79 to 67. The Senate struck out this amendment, 22 to 16. Each House adhered obstinately to its position and the bill was lost.

At the next session Mr. Taylor of New York offered a resolution raising a committee to report "a bill prohibiting the further admission of slaves into the territory west of the Mississippi." This proposition was postponed. In the mean time, a bill was introduced for the admission of Maine into the Union, which passed the House. The Senate tacked a section admitting Missouri to the Maine bill. On the 18th January, 1820, Mr. Thomas of Illinois introduced in the Senate the celebrated slavery restriction, excluding slavery forever from all territory north of 36° 30' north latitude. After an exciting debate it was referred to a select committee. The motion to exclude slavery from Missouri was lost in the Senate, 16 to 27.

On the 17th February, Mr. Thomas's amendment, excluding slavery from the territory north of 36° 30' passed the Senate, Ayes 34; Noes 10. It was moved in the House by Mr. Storrs of New York. The bill for the admission of both Maine and Missouri, with the restriction of slavery in territories West, in lieu of applying it to the State, then passed the Senate. Mr. Macon of North Carolina, and Mr. Smith of South Carolina, being the only Southern Senators that voted against it. The House subsequently agreed to the Senate bill by a vote of 134 to 42, and thus ended the agitation for that session. The restriction thus engrafted upon the territorial law was repealed in the Kansas-Nebraska Act of 1854; but was not, as will be seen, and as has been generally understood by the people, a part of Mr. Clay's Compromise, by which Missouri was finally admitted into the Union.

At the session of 1821, Missouri presented her Constitution to Congress. It contained a clause excluding free colored people from the State. The question was at once raised, that her Constitution was not republican in form, as required by the Constitution of the United States. The Senate voted to admit and the House refused. Committees of conference were appointed, of which Mr. Clay was chairman in the House, and Mr. Holmes of Maine, in the Senate. On the 26th of February, 1821, Mr. Clay, from the Joint Committee, reported a resolution for the admission of Missouri, upon condition that the clause in her Constitution prohibiting free negroes from coming into or remaining in the State, should never be construed to authorize the passage of any law by which any citizen of any other State should be excluded from any privileges to which such citizen is entitled under the Constitution of the United States. This resolution passed the House the same day by a vote of 87 to 31.

The resolution was called up in the Senate on the 27th, and finally passed in that body on the 28th of February, 1821, by a vote of 28 to 14. Missouri accepted the condition imposed by the resolution of Mr. Clay, and on the 10th of August, 1821, President Monroe issued his proclamation declaring the admission of Missouri complete according to law. This resolution of Mr. Clay was, properly speaking, *the* Missouri Compromise, and of itself had nothing to do, whatever, with the question of slavery in the territories. That question had been settled nearly a year prior to the passage of this resolution, under which that State became a member of the confederacy.

For the purpose of showing what the doctrine of the Southern States, and of that party in the North that acted with the South in that struggle, was upon the subject of the power of Congress to restrict slavery in the territories, we make the following extracts from the speeches of those most prominent in that debate, North and South. The reader will of course understand, that those who advocated the power of restriction in Congress, used, necessarily, the same arguments that are used at the present time upon that subject. It is only in reference to what was, at that time, claimed as *the national* view of the slavery question, that we compile this chapter; and, in compiling it, we have sought to give the opinion of those who, from their position and talents, may be fairly supposed to have reflected that view at that day. Some of the extracts refer to the State restriction, which was abandoned, but most are upon the amendment of Mr. Thomas, of the Senate, introduced in the House by Mr. Storrs, of New York, involving the constitutional power of Congress to prohibit slavery in the territories. This was the first debate ever had in Congress upon the subject.

January 26, 1821. The Bill for the admission of Missouri into the Union being under consideration, Mr. Storrs, of New York, offered the following proviso:

"*And provided further, and it is hereby enacted*, That, forever hereafter, neither slavery nor involuntary servitude, (except in the punishment of crimes, whereof the party shall have been duly convicted,) shall exist in the territory of the United States, lying north of the 38th degree of north latitude, and west of the river Mississippi, and the boundaries of the State of Missouri, as established by this act: *Provided*, That any person escaping into the said territory, from whom labor or service is lawfully claimed, in any of the States, such fugitive may be lawfully reclaimed, and conveyed, according to the laws of the United States in such case provided, to the person claiming his or her labor or service as aforesaid."

Mr. Meigs, of New York, said :—It is now at least twenty years, that I have, with some pain and apprehension, remarked the increasing spirit of local and sectional envy and dislike between the North and South. A continued series of sarcasms upon each other's circumstances, modes of living, and manners, so foolishly persevered in, has produced at length that keen controversy which now enlists us in masses against each other on the opposite sides of the line of latitude.

Gentlemen may dignify it by whatever titles they please. They may flatter themselves that all is logic, reason, pure reason. But certain I am, that it is neither more nor less than sectional feeling.

Feeling, sir, however gravely dignified, has brought us in hostility to this singular line of combat, and we, who are, you know sir, "but children of a larger growth," are now most aptly comparable to those celebrated and eternal factions of "*Up-Town* and *Down-Town Boys.*" I put this observation to every one who hears me, with the wish that he may apply his own recollections and reflections to it.

Gentlemen may exhaust all their arguments, all their eloquence upon the question before us; they may pour out every flower of rhetoric upon it; but, sir, I view their labors as wholly vain, and I fear that their flowers will be found to be the most deleterious and the most poisonous in the whole range of botany. They poison the national affection.

Reason divided by parallels of latitude! Why, sir, it is easy for prejudice and malevolence, by aid of ingenuity, to erect an eternal, impenetrable wall of brass between the North and South, at the latitude of thirty-nine degrees! But, in the view of reason, there is no other line between them than that celestial arc of thirty-nine degrees which offers no barrier to the march of liberal and rational men.

It is forgotten that the enlightened high priest, the archbishop of one belligerent, goes to the temple of the Almighty and chants " *Te Deum laudamus*," for the victory obtained by his country, with carnage and devastation, over the enemy; while the archbishop of another belligerent is at the same time entering the house of God, and singing also, " *Te Deum laudamus pro victoria*," upon the other side of the line, the creek, or the river? We, who know these things, should profit by our knowledge, learn liberality, and practice it. It is true, and I glory in the knowledge of the truth, that in matters of religion, this country has, in its constitutions, attained a high point of reason and liberality.

Men, after forty or sixty years of religious intolerance, here, at last, may worship the Creator in their own way. What a privilege! how dearly acquired! how much to be prized! It fills us with astonishment, when we reflect how hard it is for us to refrain from forcing by power our opinions upon our brother men! how readily each individual imagines that the light is alone in his own breast, and how enthusiastically he engages in propagating it among mankind by all possible means, fancying, dreaming that he is a prophet, a vicegerent of Almighty God.

January 27, 1830. Mr. Holmes, of Massachusetts, rose and spoke as follows:—Mr. Chairman: When a man is fallen into distress, his neighbors surround him to offer relief. Some, by an attempt at condolence, increase the grief which they would assuage; others, by administering remedies, inflame the disorder; while others, affecting all the solicitude of both, actually wish him dead. It is so with liberty. Always in danger—often in distress—she not only suffers from open and secret foes, but officious and unskillful friends. And among the thousands and millions that throng her temple from curiosity or policy, how few—very few—there are, who are her sincere, faithful, and intelligent worshipers? Among these few, I trust, are to be found all the advocates for restriction in this House. And I readily admit, that most of those out of doors, whose zeal is excited on this occasion, are of the same description.

But is it not probable that there are some jugglers behind the screen who are playing a deeper game—who are combining to rally under this standard, as the last resort, the forlorn hope of an expiring party. But while we admit this in behalf of the respectable gentlemen who advocate the restriction of slavery in Missouri, we ask, may we demand of them the same liberality. We are not the advocates or the abettors of slavery.

For one, sir, I would rejoice if there was not a slave on earth. Liberty is the object of my love—my adoration. I would extend its blessings to every human being. But, though my feelings are strong for the abolition of slavery, they are yet *stronger* for the *Constitution* of my country. And, if I am reduced to the sad alternative to tolerate the holding of slaves in Missouri or violate the Constitution of my country, I will not admit a doubt to cloud my choice.

Sir, of what benefit would be abolition, if at a sacrifice of your Constitution? Where would be the guarantee of the liberty which you grant? Liberty has a temple here, and it is the only one which remains. Destroy this, and she must flee—she must retire among the brutes of the wilderness—to mourn and lament the misery and folly of man.

The proposition for the consideration of the committee is, to abolish slavery in Missouri, as a condition of her admission into the Union.

This Constitution, which I hold in my hand, I am sworn to support, not according to legislative or judicial exposition, but as I shall understand it; not as private interest or public zeal may urge, but as I shall believe; not as I may wish it, but as it is.

I have carefully examined this Constitution, and I can find no such power. I have looked it through, and I am certain it is not in the book.

This power is not express, and if given at all, it must be constructive.

This amplifying power by construction is dangerous, and will, not improbably, effect the eventual destruction of the Constitution.

That there are resulting or implied powers, I am not disposed to deny; but they are only where the powers are subordinate and the implication necessary.

All powers not granted are prohibited, is a maxim to which we cannot too religiously adhere.

*   *   *   *   *   *

How comes it that Congress can prohibit a transfer of a slave from one State to another, and under this power to regulate commerce, when they are expressly forbidden to compel a vessel bound from one State to enter, clear, nor pay duties, in that of another? If Congress has this power under this clause in the Constitution, then slaves are to be prohibited as commerce.

And, sir, where is the authority to prohibit the transfer of an article of commerce from State to State? A man leaves a State to go into another with his family, slaves, cattle, and implements of husbandry, to clear up and culti vate a farm or plantation. His object is exclusively agricultural. He is met at the line by a law of Congress, and his slaves are stopped under the authority to regulate commerce!

When under this power, you shall have succeeded in proving the extravagant and untenable position that Congress can prohibit this transfer, how do you arrive at the conclusion, that you can pass this act of abolition which the amendment proposes?

There are two powers grown out of that to regulate commerce. And preserve your gravity while I repeat, one of them is to prohibit a transfer of slaves from State to State, and the other to abolish slavery in Missouri, as a condition of her admission into the Union.

*   *   *   *   *   *

Sir, I trust enough has been said to prove that this clause gives no authority to prohibit a transfer of slaves from one State to another; and if it did, it has nothing to do with the question. Sir, it is a new doctrine, and allow me to add, it is an alarming doctrine. Let me ask the gentleman from New York a question, and I will do it with that confidence which friendship inspires. With the suggestion that the Declaration of Independence is an act of general emancipation, and with this doctrine, that Congress may confine the slaves within the limits of the respective States, let the four hundred thousand slaves of Virginia be transferred to New York, and what would be his feelings? [Here Mr. Taylor rose, and disclaimed having advanced that the Declaration of Independence had any effect to emancipate the slaves.]

Sir, I have not said that that gentleman did advance such a doctrine.

I stated that such an opinion had been advanced, and from high authority.

And I again appeal to the candor of that gentleman,

and ask him, whether he should feel entirely easy if the slaves of Virginia were shut up in New York, under this power which he advocates, and if it had come to their ears from any respectable source that they were all free?

Would he not be inclined to doubt the constitutionality or policy of such a law?

Confine the slaves in the old slaveholding States, where they are most numerous; the constant emigration of the whites will soon bring them to an equality with their slaves. Emigration will increase with the danger, and murder and massacre will succeed.

And yet, we can look on and see this storm gathering—hear its thunders, and witness its lightnings, with great composure, with wonderful philosophy!

We are aware, gentlemen, that we are diffusing sentiments which endanger your safety, happiness, and lives; nay, more, the safety, happiness, and lives of those whom you value more than your own.

But it is a constitutional question.

Keep cool. We are conscious that we are inculcating doctrines that will result in spilling the best of your blood, but as this blood will be spilled in the cause of humanity, keep cool.

We have no doubt that the promulgating of these principles will be the means of cutting your throats; but, as it will be done in the most unexceptionable manner possible, by your slaves, who will no doubt perform the task in great style and dexterity, and with much delicacy and humanity, too, therefore keep cool.

Sir, speak to the wind, command the waves, expostulate with the tempest, rebuke the thunder, but never ask an honorable man thus circumstanced to suppress his feelings.

But, sir, I beg pardon for this digression; it is aside from my purpose.

My object is not declamation, but reason.

January 28.—Mr. Smyth, of Virginia, addressed the Chair. He said that the constitutionality of the measure proposed was the subject which he intended first to consider. The legislative power of every State is originally co-extensive. Each State, by the Constitution, commits an equal portion of its legislative powers to Congress, and all the residue is reserved to the States, unless prohibited to them or to the people. The only powers of this government are given by the Constitution.

The powers granted are to be exercised over every State; and the powers reserved are retained by every State.

In Pennsylvania and in Virginia, the power to legislate respecting slavery is in the legislature. In Ohio and Indiana that power is in the people, who have denied it to their legislatures. No power has been delegated to Congress to legislate on that subject.

The Constitution provides that, "the powers not delegated to the United States by the Constitution, nor prohibited by it to the States, are reserved to the States respectively, or to the people." The powers not delegated being reserved to the States, respectively, are reserved to each of the States, whether new or old.

Has the power to legislate over slavery been delegated to the United States? It has not.

Has it been prohibited to the States? It has not.

Then it is reserved to the States respectively, or to the people. Consequently, it is reserved to the State of Missouri, or to the people of that State. And any attempt by Congress to deprive them of this reserved power, will be unjust, tyrannical, unconstitutional, and void.

The only condition that may constitutionally be annexed to the admission of a new State into this Union is that its constitution shall be republican.

This the Constitution authorizes us to require, and it is the only condition that is necessary. We possess power to make all needful regulations respecting the territorial property of the United States.

Our acts in pursuance of the Constitution are paramount to the laws of any State.

When we pursue our constitutional authority, we need no aid from stipulations; and when we exceed it, our acts are acts of usurpation, and void.

It has been questioned by some, whether a constitution can be said to be republican which does not exclude slavery.

But we must understand the phrase "republican form of government," as the people understood it when they adopted the Constitution. We are bound by the construction which was put upon the Constitution by the people. It would be perfidious toward them to put on the Constitution a different construction from that which induced them to adopt it.

The people of each of the States who adopted the Constitution, except Massachusetts, owned slaves, yet they certainly considered their own constitutions to be republican.

And the federal government has not, by virtue of its power to guarantee a republican constitution to each State in the union, required a change of the constitution of any one of those States.

The Constitution recognizes the right to the slave property, and it thereby appears that it was intended by the Convention and by the people that that property should be secure.

The representation of each State in this House is proportioned by the whole number of free persons and three-fifths of the number of the slaves. In forming the Constitution, the Southern States, Virginia excepted, insisted on and obtained a provision, authorizing them to import slaves for twenty years.

And the Constitution provides that slaves running away

from their masters in one State and going into another, shall be delivered up to their masters.

* * * * * *

To render this right, with other rights, still more secure, Virginia, in adopting the Constitution, declared that "no right of any denomination can be canceled, abridged, restrained, or modified, except in those instances in which power is given by the Constitution for those purposes;" and New York declared that "every power, jurisdiction, and right, which is not by the said Constitution clearly delegated to the Congress of the United States, remains to the people of the several States, or to their respective State governments." Several of the other States made similar declarations.

But the States were not content to declare their rights. An amendment to the Constitution declares that, "The powers not delegated to the United States by the Constitution, nor prohibited by it to the States, are reserved to the States respectively, or to the people." The right to own slaves being acknowledged and secured by the Constitution, can you proscribe what the Constitution guarantees? Can you touch a right reserved to the States or the people? You cannot!

* * * * * *

If you possessed power to legislate concerning slavery, the adoption of the proposition on your table, which goes to emancipate all children of slaves hereafter born in Missouri, would be a direct violation of the Constitution, which provides that "no person shall be deprived of property without due process of law; nor shall private property be taken for public use, without just compensation."

If you cannot take property even for public use, without just compensation, you certainly have not power to take it away for the purpose of annihilation, without compensation. And if you cannot take away that which is in existence, you cannot take away that which will come into existence hereafter. If you cannot take away the land, you cannot take the future crops; and if you cannot take the slaves, you cannot take their issue, who, by the laws of slavery, will be also slaves. You cannot force the people to give up their property. You cannot force a portion of the people to emancipate their slaves.

*   *   *   *   *   *

All legitimate power proceeds from the people. And although an illegitimate power may be imposed by force and submitted to from necessity, it cannot bind the people longer than the force and necessity are present. Such was the power which the British Parliament exercised before the Revolution over these then colonies; and such was the power asserted by the Congress of 1787 over the Northwestern territory.

But, as the declaration of the British Parliament, that they had power to bind the colonies in all cases whatsoever, does not bind the people of these States; so the Ordinance of 1787 does not bind the people of Ohio any longer than they please to submit to it.

It was an act of illegitimate power; and it cannot bind those who are the source of all legitimate power.

It is even doubtful whether the Ordinance was duly passed. By the Articles of Confederation, the concurrence of nine States was necessary to important transactions. The power exercised was not given; and of the powers which were given, those of making appropriations and treaties most resemble the power exercised. It was necessary that nine States should concur in exercising either of these powers. Only eight States were present and concurring in passing this Ordinance.

It has been said that the restriction on the introduction of slavery northwest of the Ohio river was proposed by Virginia, and that the Southern States unanimously agreed to it. This is said to fix the character of inconsistency on Virginia. The fact is, that Virginia and the Southern States voted for the whole ordinance, when completed; but it is also true that those States had repeatedly voted against the clause excluding slavery. In April, 1784, a vote was taken on this clause, when Maryland, Virginia, and South Carolina voted against it; North Carolina divided, and Georgia absent. And although seven States voted for the clause, it was rejected; a proof that Congress then conceived that the concurrence of nine States was necessary to every clause of this Ordinance; which they called a "compact."

In March, 1785, Mr. King proposed a similar clause; Virginia, North Carolina, South Carolina, and Georgia, voted against it; eight States voted for the commitment of it, and it was committed. The member from Virginia, (Mr. Grayson,) to whom the measure is ascribed, was not a member of Congress in 1784.

My honorable friend from Massachusetts (Mr. Holmes) was mistaken, when he supposed that Congress of 1787, was bound by the Ordinance of 1784, which did not exclude slavery from the Northwestern Territory.

They would have been bound, had any part of the land in Ohio been sold, not to change the Ordinance of 1784, without the consent of Ohio. But no point of the land was sold, previous to the passage of the Ordinance on the 13th July, 1787.

I have examined that matter carefully, and am unwilling that the committee should be under any erroneous impressions that I can remove.

*   *   *   *   *   *   *   *

It has been said that the Constitution vests in Congress a power to make all needful regulations respecting the territory of the United States; and this power, it is supposed authorizes us to exclude slaves from the territories of the

United States, and also to demand from any of those territories about to become States, a stipulation for the exclusion of slaves.

The clause of the Constitution referred to, reads thus: "The Congress shall have power to dispose of, and make all needful rules and regulations respecting, the territory or other property belonging to the United States." It has been contended that this gives a power of legislation over persons and private property within the territories of the United States.

The clause obviously relates to the territory belonging to the United States, as property only. The power given is to dispose of, and make all needful regulations respecting, the territorial property, or other property of the United States; and Congress has power to pass all laws necessary and proper to the exercise of that power. This clause speaks of the territory as property, as a subject of sale. It speaks not of the jurisdiction.

This clause, as first proposed in Convention, read thus: "To dispose of the unappropriated lands of the United States; to institute temporary governments for new States arising therein." The latter power was not granted. (See Journal Convention, page 260.)

That the Convention considered as being provided for by the Ordinance of Congress. This clause contains no grant of power to legislate over persons and private property within a territory.

A power to dispose of, and make all needful regulations respecting the property of the United States, is very different from a power to legislate over the persons and the property of the people. When it was the intention of the Convention that the Constitution should convey to Congress power to legislate over persons and private property, they expressed themselves in terms not doubtful.

Thus they said, "Congress shall have power to exercise exclusive legislation in all cases whatsoever," within the ten miles square.

But no such power to legislate over the territories is granted.

The power is, to dispose of, and make all needful regulations respecting the property of the United States.

When that is sold and conveyed, it ceases to be an object of the power to make regulations respecting the property of United States; and if the construction contended for by our opponents be correct, and Congress possesses power to legislate for a territory, that would not authorize them to make regulations which shall continue in force when the territory became a State, and the United States ceased to own property therein.

*   *   *   *   *   *   *

Suppose that a general emancipation was to take place, and the two people were to co-mingle, what would be the effect on the character of your country throughout the civilized world? Would you be willing that your nation should become a nation of mulattoes, and be considered on a level with Hayti? Are the two races equal? If so, how is it that that the race of whites has produced so many civilized nations in ancient and modern times, and the race of African negroes not one.

*   *   *   *   *   *   *

As the emancipation of the present race of blacks in this country cannot be effected, the tendency of the popular meetings, resolutions, pamphlets, and newspaper publications, respecting this question, merit notice and exposition. The philosophers, the abolition societies, and societies of friends to the negroes, in Europe, who were not at all interested in negro slavery themselves, produced the catastrophe of St. Domingo. The philanthropists, societies, and popular meetings of the North, are pursuing a similar course.

Like causes produce like effects.

Our philanthropists may acquire as good a title to the execrations of the Southern people as Robespierre and Gregoire acquired to the execrations of the French people of St. Domingo.

February 1. Mr. Reid, of Georgia, said: Sir, the slaves of the South are held to a service which, unlike that of the ancient villain, is certain and moderate.

They are well supplied with food and raiment.

They are "content and careless of to-morrow's fare."

The lights of our religion shine as well for them as for their masters; and their rights of personal security, guaranteed by the Constitution and the laws, are vigilantly protected by the courts. It is true, they are often made subject to wanton acts of tyranny; but this is not their peculiar misfortune! For, search the catalogue of crimes, and you will find that man—the tyrant—is continually preying upon his fellow-men; there are as many white as black victims to the vengeful passion and the lust of power! Believe me, sir, I am not the panegyrist of slavery. It is an unnatural state; a dark cloud which obscures half the lustre of our free institutions! But it is a fixed evil, which we can only alleviate.

Are we called upon to emancipate our slaves? I answer, their welfare, the safety of our citizens, forbid it. Can we incorporate them with us, and make them and us one people? The prejudices of the North and of the South rise up in equal strength against such a measure; and even those who clamor most loudly for the sublime doctrines of your Declaration of Independence, who shout in your ears "all men are by nature equal," would turn with abhorrence and disgust from a parti-colored progeny! Shall we then be blamed for a state of things to which we are obliged to submit? Would it be fair, would it be manly, would it be generous, would it be just, to offer contumely and contempt to the unfortunate man who wears a cancer in his bosom, because he will not submit to cautery at the hazard of his existence? For my own part, surrounded by slavery from my cradle to the present moment, I yet

> "Hate the touch of servile hands;
> I loathe the slaves who cringe around;"

and I would hail that day as the most glorious in its dawning which should behold, with safety to themselves and our citizens, the black population of the United States placed upon the high eminence of equal rights, and clothed in the privileges and immunities of American citizens! But this is a dream of philanthropy which can never be fulfilled; and whoever shall act in this country upon such wild theories, shall cease to be a benefactor, and become a destroyer of the human family.

It is said, however, to be high time to check the progress of this evil, and that this may be best done by inhibiting slavery beyond the Mississippi, and in Missouri, which prays to be admitted as a State into the Union. It is important to consider if this project be consistent with the Constitution of the United States.

The States formed the Constitution in the capacity of sovereign and independent States, and the Constitution is the instrument by which they conveyed certain power to the general government. This is evident, not only from the nature of the government formed, and in every line of the Constitution, but it is a doctrine distinctly asserted in the ninth and tenth articles of the amendments. "The enumeration, in the Constitution, of certain rights shall not be construed to deny or disparage others retained by the people; and the powers not delegated to the United States by the Constitution, nor prohibited by it to the States, are reserved to the States respectively, or to the people." Hence it will follow, that the several States retain every power not delegated by the Constitution to the general government; or, in other words, that in all enumerated cases, the several States are left in the full enjoyment of their sovereign and independent jurisdictions.

* * * * * * * *

But it is argued that Congress has ever imposed restrictions upon new States, and no objection has been urged until this moment.

If it be true, that only one condition can constitutionally be imposed, it would seem that any other is null and void, and may be thrown off by the State at pleasure.

And then this argument, the strength of which is in precedent, cannot avail.

Uniformity of decision for hundreds of years cannot make that right which at first was wrong.

If it were otherwise, in vain would science and the arts pursue their march toward perfection; in vain the constant progress of truth; in vain the new and bright lights which are daily finding their way to the human mind, like the rays of the distant stars, which, passing onward from the creation of time, are said to be continually reaching our sphere.

Malus usus abolendus est. When error appears, let her be detected and exposed, and let evil precedents be abolished.

It is true that the old Confederation, by the 6th section of the Ordinance of 1787, inhibited slavery in the territory northwest of the Ohio, and that the States of Illinois, Ohio, and Indiana, have been introduced into the Union under this restriction.

Sir, the Ordinance of 1787 had an origin perfectly worthy of the end it seems destined to accomplish. It had no authority in the Articles of Confederation, which did not contemplate, with the exception of Canada, the acquisition of territory.

It was in contradiction of the resolution of 1780, by which the States were allured to cede their unlocated lands to the General Government, upon the condition that these should constitute several States, to be admitted into the Union upon an equal footing with the original States.

It is in fraud of the acts of cession by which the States conveyed territory in faith of the resolution of 1780. And, when recognized by acts of Congress, and applied to the States formed from the territory beyond the Ohio, it is in violation of the Constitution of the United States.

So much for the efficacy of the precedent which, although binding here, is not, it would seem, of obligation upon Ohio, Indiana, or Illinois, or, if you impose it, upon Missouri. It is not the force of your legal provisions which attaches the restrictive 6th article of the ordinance to the States I have mentioned.

It is the moral sentiment of the inhabitants. Impose it upon Missouri, and she will indignantly throw off the yoke and laugh you to scorn! You will then discover that you have assumed a weapon that you cannot wield—the bow of Ulysses, which all your efforts cannot bend.

The open and voluntary exposure of your weakness will make you not only the object of derision at home, but a by-word among nations. Can there be a power in Congress to do that which the object of the power may rightfully destroy? Are the rights of Missouri and of the Union in opposition to each other? Can it be possible that Congress has authority to impose a restriction which Missouri, by an alteration of her Constitution, may abolish? Sir, the course we are pursuing reminds me of the urchin who, with great care and anxiety, constructs his card edifice, which the slightest touch may demolish, the gentlest breath dissolve.

But let us stand together upon the basis of precedent;

and upon that ground you cannot extend this restriction to Missouri.

You have imposed it upon the territory beyond the Ohio, but you have never applied it elsewhere. Tennessee, Vermont, Kentucky, Louisiana, Mississippi, and Alabama, have come into the Union without being required to submit to the condition inhibiting slavery; nay, whenever the Ordinance of 1787 has been applied to any of these States, the operation of the 6th article has been suspended or destroyed.

According, then, to the uniform tenor of the precedent, let the States to be formed of the territory without the boundaries of the territory northwest of Ohio remain unrestricted, and in the enjoyment of the fullness of their rights.

Thus, it appears to me, the power you seek to assume is not found in the Constitution, or to be derived from precedent.

Shall, it, then, without any known process of generation, spring spontaneously from your councils, like the armed Minerva from the brain of Jupiter? The goddess, sir, although of wisdom, was also the inventress of war—and the power of your creation, although extensive in its dimensions, and ingenious in its organization, may produce the most terrible and deplorable effects.

Assure yourselves you have not authority to bind a State coming into the Union, with a single hair! If you have, you may rivet a chain upon every limb, a fetter upon every joint.

Where, then, I ask is the independence of your State governments? Do they not fall prostrate, debased, covered with sackloth and crowned with ashes, before the gigantic power of the Union? They will no longer, sir, resemble planets, moving in order around a solar centre, receiving and imparting lustre. They will dwindle to mere satellites, or, thrown from their orbits, they will wander "like stars condemned, the wrecks of worlds demolished!"

* * * * * *

But, let gentlemen beware! Assume the Mississippi as the boundary. Say, that to the smiling Canaan beyond its waters no slave shall approach, and you give a new character to its inhabitants, totally distinct from that which shall belong to the people thronging on the east of your limits.

You implant diversity of pursuits, hostility of feeling, envy, hatred, and bitter reproaches, which

> "Shall grow to clubs and naked swords,
> To murder and to death."

If you remain inexorable; if you persist in refusing the humble, the decent, the reasonable prayer of Missouri, is there no danger that her resistance will rise in proportion to your oppression? Sir, the firebrand, which is even now cast into your society, will require blood—ay, and the blood of freemen—for its quenching. Your Union shall tremble, as under the force of an earthquake! While you incautiously pull down a constitutional barrier, you make way for the dark, and tumultuous, and overwhelming waters of desolation! If you "sow the wind, must you not reap the whirlwind?"

February 25. Mr. Scott, of Missouri, said: The powers given to Congress by the Constitution were few, express, limited, positive, and defined; the majority of them were to be found in the eighth section of that instrument, and consisted in the authority to levy taxes, borrow money, and regulate commerce; establish a uniform system of bankruptcy; to regulate the coin, punish counterfeiting, establish post-offices and post-roads, constitute courts, declare war, raise armies, maintain a navy, call forth the militia, organize and regulate them; to have exclusive jurisdiction over the District of Columbia, and their forts, magazines, arsenals, dock-yards, and to make all laws which should be necessary and proper to carry into effect the enumerated powers. Mr. S. could not discover that the authority to impose restrictions on States could be derived from any latitude of construction growing out of this section.

But the powers of Congress were not only enumerated and expressed in the Constitution; the tenth section was equally explicit in declaring of what attributes of sovereignty the States should be deprived; no State was to enter into any treaty of alliance, grant letters of marque and reprisal, coin money, emit bills of credit, make anything but gold and silver a tender, pass any bill of attainder, ex post facto law, impair contracts, or grant titles of nobility; nor, without consent of Congress, lay imposts or duties on imports or exports, lay any duty on tonnage, keep troops or ships of war in time of peace, or make any agreement with any foreign power, or even with a sister State, or engage in war, unless actually invaded.

The States, then, were divested by the Constitution of no portion of sovereignty but those actually named and voluntarily surrendered; all other powers, and the residue of sovereignty, were inherent in, and expressly reserved to, the States and the people.

*   *   *   *   *   *   *   *

The second clause of the third section of the fourth article provided that "Congress shall have power to dispose of, and make all needful rules and regulations respecting the territory or other property of the United States."

The whole context of this article showed that it was as property, and not otherwise, that Congress were to make rules and regulations. Certainly the boldest advocate for restriction would not contend that Congress had any property in the persons of the citizens of Missouri, because they were circumstantially connected with a territory over which they had a limited control. Surely gentlemen would not undertake to advance the doctrine that Congress had any property in the confirmed lands of individuals, or in the lands purchased of the government and patented to the purchaser, and still less had Congress any property in the rights of the people.

And if Congress ever had the power contended for, while they owned the land, it would surely cease to exist so soon as they parted with the soil.

The sovereignty of Congress over the territory, as the lords paramount, was but temporary, and could only endure so long as they retained the soil; when that was disposed of, their sovereignty ceased also.

Yet, by virtue of this brief and temporary authority, limited in its extent, and short in its duration, Congress were about to fix on Missouri a never-ending condition, that was to continue long after the authority on which it rested for existence, had passed away.

If, in consequence of owning the land, Congress possessed that description of sovereignty that would authorize them to legislate in regard to the property of the citizens of a Territory or a State, or to dictate what kind of property the citizens should introduce and hold, then might they at this day undertake to regulate the affairs of the States of Ohio, Indiana, Illinois, Louisiana, Mississippi, and Alabama; and their right to impose restrictions on each of them, similar to that contemplated in regard to Missouri, would be equally as unquestionable.

The whole amount of the authority Congress could claim under this clause of the Constitution, was, to make rules and regulations for the surveying and disposing of the public lands, to regulate the quantities in which it should be sold, the price, and the credit.

But this power was limited in its operation to the property alone, and by no construction could be extended to the rights of the citizens inhabiting the territory. Congress had no power over the right or property of the citizen, but, in certain cases, to levy taxes; and this authority was one of those expressly conferred by the Constitution, and was not alone supported by inference.

* * * * * *

To ascertain what powers Congress had under the Constitution, which was ratified on the 17th of September 1787, resort was made to an ordinance of the 13th of July, 1787, several months, in date, prior to the Constitution of the United States.

The ordinance was passed by the old Congress, under the Articles of Confederation.

The adoption of the federal Constitution was the formation of a new government, and an abolition of the old; and yet, an ordinance passed by the former government was brought up in judgment to define and expound the powers of Congress under a new and totally different government—under a new Constitution, and new organization.

Gentlemen had contended that Congress had revived and ratified the ordinance in the act of 1802, relating to Ohio; the act of 1816, relating to Indiana; and the act of 1818, in reference to Illinois; these being the acts by which Congress authorized those States to form a Constitution and State government.

But, were he to surrender this part of the argument to gentlemen, could it possibly be deduced, that, because Congress had revived the ordinance in reference to any one or all those States, that, by that revival, it would have any operation beyond the State actually named, and to which it was applied. Nor, had the question ever been made, by any of those States, which Missouri now made, how far Congress had the power to impose the provisions of that ordinance over a State; they had taken it as a matter of course because it comported with their wishes and their will.

Missouri did not intend so to take it, because it neither promoted her interest, nor complied with her wishes or her will; nor did he believe that either of those States would now acknowledge that they had not the equal right with any other State of the Union to call a convention, and so alter their constitution as to admit slavery; and if they had this right, the operation of the ordinance upon them as a State was void and of no avail.

The Ordinance of 1787, then, was a dead letter, so far as it had been resorted to as furnishing any explanation of the powers of Congress under the federal Constitution, and it was equally inapplicable, as precedent, in relation to Missouri, because, at no period of the territorial government, had any portion of its provisions been extended to that territory, save only those principles that had been incorporated into the act of the 4th of June, 1802, when the second grade of government had been conferred upon Missouri.

*　*　*　*　*　*

A member from Ohio (Mr. Brush) had contended that, under the 8th section of the Constitution that gave Congress the power "to provide for the common defense and general welfare," they could impose the restriction on Missouri, because he had assumed it for granted, that, to limit the negroes to certain latitudes, and to confine them within certain limits, would be promoting the common defense and general welfare.

Now, what would contribute to the common defense and general welfare was mere matter of opinion, and it was not always that the means used produced the end; a mistake in the one was sure to defeat the other, and it appeared to Mr. S. much more reasonable to suppose that the common defense was weakened, and the general welfare much more endangered, by confining the slaves within certain districts, condensing their population, and enabling them to act in concert, than to spread them over a vast extent of territory, distributing them in small proportions among the whites,

THE MISSOURI QUESTION. 221

and thus prevent the probability of insurrection, from a want of capacity to concentrate their forces.

If, then, an occasional majority of Congress had the right, under this or any other clause of the Constitution, to say that, in their opinion, it promoted the common defense and general welfare, that slavery should not exist in certain States of the Union; a counter majority, at any other time, under the same clause of the Constitution, would have the power to declare that it comported with their views of common defense and general welfare that it should exist in all the States, and that the non-slaveholding States should admit slaves within their borders, under pain of suspension or expulsion from the Union.

How would gentlemen then stand affected?

Would they not then declare against this mighty power, exercised upon mere speculation, whether this or that measure promoted the common defense and general welfare of the nation! In point of fact there was little, if any, difference between the taking away, or forcing upon, any person or people that which they did or did not want; each was equally a violation of their rights.

Mr. Tucker, of Virginia, said: Putting aside the feelings of the people of Missouri, is it not a solid objection to this restriction, that your power to impose it is doubtful and contested? However thoroughly gentlemen on the other side may be persuaded that Congress possesses this power, they must know that a large portion of the United States are as thoroughly persuaded that it does not; that, on this question there is entire unanimity in the slaveholding States; and that, with all the motives to an opposite unanimity in the other States, there is among them, as well as among their representatives in this House, considerable diversity of opinion.

They must also recollect, that, though these circumstances do not produce conviction, they must produce some doubt, awaken some distrust in the infallibility of human reason in every ingenuous mind.

And, Mr. Chairman, when we consider the influence of public opinion on the harmony and stability of this Union, it must always be a matter of regret that the government should exercise powers that are doubtful, or even disputed. Until habit and custom have had their wonted effect in cementing the Union, its strength and permanency must rest on the affections, the undivided affections, of the people, and nothing is more likely to weaken their attachment than a want of confidence in this House, the natural guardian of the people's rights, and their immediate representatives.

March 2. Mr. Stevens, of Connecticut, said: In this question of compromise now to be decided, I am more fortunate, I now have the floor, and must avail myself of this first opportunity to state, explicitly, that I have listened with pain to the very long, protracted debate that has been had on this unfortunate question; I call it unfortunate, sir, because it has drawn forth the worst passions of man in the course of the discussion. I have heard gentlemen, and I must in candor say, gentlemen on both sides of the question, boast of *sectional powers*, and *sectional achievements;* and remind gentlemen from opposite sections of the Union that they had not so fought and so conquered; or left such conclusion irresistibly to follow.

I want, and the manifest public good requires that the reverse of this language should be holden.

Let each gentleman boast the valor of the inhabitants of an opposite section of the Union, then all get the praise due them, and in a way infinitely more acceptable to gentlemen of becoming modesty; and surely if any people ever merited all the praise that has been arrogated instead of being bestowed, the American people do. But it is not the inhabitants of any section of America that exclusively merit all their exalted praise ; but the Union collectively. In casting my eye over the map of my country, I scarcely discover a spot on it but is rendered memorable as the birth-place of some sage, hero, or philosopher; if these occur most frequently in Connecticut it is very well—if most frequently in some other State, very well—it is still my country. Shall I forego every joy of my life because the immortal Washington was not born in the State, of very circumscribed limits, in which I was born ? Preposterous thought ! He was born in America.

That is enough for me. His glory reaches us, bottomed on merit, and scorns the proffered aid of mouldering marble to perpetuate it. If the deadliest enemy this country has, or ever had, could dictate language the most likely to destroy your glory, prosperity, and happiness, would it not be precisely what has been so profusely used in this debate—sectional vaunting ? Most undoubtedly it would. If the fell Spirit of Discord, the prime mover of sedition and rebellion in the heavenly realms, should rack his hellish invention for the same malicious purpose, he would undoubtedly pull the cord of sectional prowess ; he would magnify the valorous deeds of each particular State or party division, and distort or obliterate all the rest. The arch planner of the first sedition and rebellion must for ever despair of improving on the sad invention. But, sir, gentlemen start at the mention—Why do this ? You hold your seats by the tenure of compromise. The Constitution is a creature of compromise ; it originated in a compromise ; and has existed ever since by a perpetual extension and exercise of that principle ; and must continue to do so, as long as it lasts. When your Convention met for its formation, they immediately discovered that the general welfare, the object of their solicitude, could not be secured and perpetuated, without giving up something like particular rights ; and this giving up of particular rights, to secure the great end and object of their meeting was called a compromise What did they do? They debated some months and then came to the obviously necessary result—compromise. It was plainly seen then as now—that, to obtain the object sought, it was necessary to make some sacrifices and to assume some evils. They thus thought the good sought was worth the sacrifices necessary to obtain it; and now after thirty years' successful experience, who dare arraign their wisdom or their patriotism? Rashness itself must forever remain dumb to this demand. If gentlemen are in favor of any compromise, it is a fit time to discuss that subject, and see if any can be hit on that will give general satisfaction. I am in favor of a compromise, but have strong objections to that now under consideration. I greatly fear it would tend to perpetuate the evil we seek to remedy. The south line of Pennsylvania State and the Ohio waters now form the boundary line between the two parties. If you continue that line, by the 36° 30' of north latitude, to the Pacific Ocean, I fear it will not prove a pacific measure. This would be to place on your records a perpetual sallying place for party. It is devoutly to be wished that such compromise might be hit on as would forever put an end to the unhappy existence of parties in their present shape. I should prefer a prohibition of the admission of slaves into that State, as a measure most likely to effect that desirable object. The number already there is not so great now as to be a subject of any great uneasiness to those most opposed to the continuance of slavery.

Few gentlemen have risen in debate on this question, without deeply lamenting (and I think with great reason) the existence of parties, designated by geographical lines and boundaries.

I also deprecate it, as being a division of the Union into parties so equal in number, wealth, intelligence, and extent of territory. Indeed, sir, there is no view of this unhappy division of our country, but must be sickening to the patriot, and in direct violation of the dictate of wisdom and the last, though not least, important advice of the father and friend of his country. He forbids the use of the words Northern and Southern, Atlantic and Western, as descriptive of the various parts of your country.

And will you forget so important an injunction from that man in so short a time? Was there no political wisdom in the command? If none, why has it been so long venerated? I should prefer a compromise forbidding the importation of any more slaves into the State of Missouri.

This, I think, would allay party feeling, drive into forgetfulness present feuds, and satisfy my friends to the north and east, with whom I have acted, and delight to act. In common with them, I have an hereditary dislike to slavery, strengthened by a residence all my life, to the present time, in a country where it does not exist. I honor their dislike of slavery, and firmly believe there is not a gentleman in this House but deprecates its existence. Agreeing in this all-important point, let us not separate because we cannot think precisely alike of the means best calculated to eradicate it.

Was it ever known that a body so numerous thought exactly alike throughout any one grand, all-important measure for public good, in all the detail? And is it not the circumstance of a division in sentiment in so large a body, so equal in point of number, a thing that should lead both to suspect they may be wrong? Gentlemen who have much property of this sort, I agree, are deeply interested; but candor must at the same time admit they have, from the fact of being slaveholders, much practical and useful knowledge on this subject that cannot be claimed by non-slaveholders. And this knowledge is extremely useful, not to say indispensable, especially as to the extent of the evil to the slaves, and to the community generally. This knowledge is indispensable when it is sought to effect emancipation on terms the best calculated to insure infallible success, and to effect it in a way the least likely to hazard any destructive revolution that might, in unskillful hands, insure more evil than the good intended. If we admit slaveholders to have more knowledge on this subject than, from the nature of the case, we can have, their voice in council should not be entirely unheeded.

But, sir, we have now arrived at a point at which every gentleman agrees something must be done. A precipice lies before us, at which perdition is inevitable. Gentlemen on both sides of this question, and in both Houses, in doors and out of doors, have evinced a determination that augurs ill of the high destinies of this country? And who does not tremble for the consequences?

I do not here speak of that feeling which results from an apprehension of personal danger. No, sir! I speak of that feeling which agitates the soul of every patriot when his country is in danger.

I speak of that feeling, without a susceptibility of which a man is no ornament to any country. I wish not to be misunderstood, sir. I don't pretend to say that in just five calendar months your union will be at an end; your constitution destroyed; your proud trophies, won in the most valiant combat, profaned; glories of half a century, gained by yourselves and your departed friends, and unequaled in the history of any country or people on the face of the earth, made the sport of an envying world; and all this in a sacrilegious contest, at the end of which no wise man would give a pea-straw for his choice on which side to be found, as the victors would have lost all, and the vanquished have nothing left to excite envy.

February, 1820. Mr. Richard M. Johnson, of Kentucky, addressed the Senate as follows:

Mr. President: It appears to me, sir, that in the course of this debate we have unhappily misunderstood each other. Expressions have been used, on both sides, conveying different sentiments from what were intended. Those who have advocated the measure of restriction, have used language which would indicate a disposition to proceed to universal emancipation, alike regardless of the means by which they would accomplish it, and of the sovereignty of the States in which it is tolerated; at the same time charging upon the present proprietors of this species of property all the odium of that perfidy and cruelty by which slavery was first introduced into the country. Those, on the other hand, who have contended for the sovereignty of the States, and opposed the measure of restriction as an assumption of power unknown in the Constitution, have given a latitude to their expressions which has been construed into a justification of the abstract principle of slavery. Misconceptions, and misconstructions of language, producing crimination and recrimination, should ever be avoided in this body, especially upon this delicate subject.

On reviewing the scope of argument, on both sides, I am satisfied that the one cannot be justly charged with advocating the sentiments which their language would seem to indicate; nor the other, with an attempt to justify the abstract principle of slavery as either religiously, morally, or politically, correct. None will pretend, that Congress can interfere with the subject of slavery in the several States; and no member of the Senate could advocate the slave trade without exciting the indignation of the whole nation. The tree is known by its fruit. And let me entreat you, sir, to recollect what has been the conduct of the representatives of States, where this property is recognized, from the commencement of 1808, the moment in which the general government was authorized by the Constitution to put an end to this merciless traffic. Not a solitary voice has been raised in favor of the African slave trade. A universal disposition has ever been evinced to annihilate forever this cruel branch of commerce, which swells every bosom with sorrow; which fills every heart with indignation. If all the States, in which slavery exist, can furnish one exception— if the slave trade has ever had one advocate within these walls, let it be proclaimed to the world! No such exception does exist—no such advocate can be found. For my own part, in verity I protest, that no person in existence more detest this abominable traffic in human beings than myself; and I am confident that every man whom I represent has the same abhorrent feelings in relation to the subject. But, sir, the right of Congress to interfere in property of this, and other description, is quite a different question. It was originally imposed upon us by the policy of Great Britain; but now we have acquired in it a legitimate propriety; we have paid for it our money; we hold it under the sanction of law, and have the right to dispose of it as we please. The General Government, if not pledged to guarantee to us the enjoyment of it, certainly have no right, constitutional or moral, to wrest it from us. We hold not ourselves accountable to the nation for the treatment we shall observe, or the disposition we shall make of this, more than any other species of property, nor will any be permitted to dictate our conduct therein. Notwithstanding these sentiments, no person can more sincerely lament, than I do, the existence of involuntary servitude in the United States; and none would make greater personal sacrifices, could I discover a way, in the providence of God, to bring it to an end.

We are not the only people who have had slaves; yes, and slaves of their own complexion. I speak not this to justify the principle, but to remind you of the fact, that slavery has existed from the earliest ages of antiquity to the present day. Nor has its existence been confined to heathen nations; both Jews and Christians, believers as well as unbelievers in divine revelation, from the patriarchs of God's ancient people to the present time, have been the proprietors of slaves, without one admonition from Heaven in the whole book of inspiration against it. The law of Moses, delivered by the Almighty himself for the government of his own chosen race, recognized a complete property in slaves. "Abraham, the father of the faithful," "the friend of God," had upwards of two hundred born in his own house, whom he trained to war. Isaac, the child of promise, inherited this property; and Jacob, the progenitor of the twelve tribes of Israel, had bond-men and bond-maids of his own. We even find the same custom to have prevailed with them, which continues to the present day; that when a daughter was given in marriage, she received, as a gift from her father, a maid-servant, and a man-servant was given with a son. Under the benign influence of the gospel dispensation, no change in this respect is found. The Apostle Paul, in his letters to the churches of Ephesus and Colosse, and in his instruction to Timothy, designed for all Christians, and in all ages, speaking of the relative and reciprocal duties of parents and children, of husbands and wives, never fails to exhort servants or slaves to be obedient to their masters, and masters to deal gently with their slaves. Fidelity, on the part of the slave, and kindness, on the part of the master, are thus made Christian duties; but emancipation is not even hinted at, as the right of the one, or the obligation of the other. Before I leave this part of the subject it may not be improper to advert to the story of Onesimus; he was the slave of Philemon, a distinguished Christian minister. Onesimus fled from his master and went to Rome, where, by the instruction of Paul, he was converted to the Christian faith. Paul found him useful in the cause, and desired to retain him in Rome; but recognizing the property of Philemon in him, he had no hesitation to remand Onesimus to his master; and not even to employ him in the cause of God, without first obtaining his master's consent. Now, sir, as it is evident, that, under every dispensation of Heaven, slavery has existed, and that neither patriarchs, prophets, nor apostles, to whom the word of inspiration was committed, ever made the subject a test of piety, or matter of animadversion, I know of no principle, either human or divine, by which slaveholders in America can be justly reprobated as the most odious of mankind.

Do I attempt to justify the principle of slavery by thus adverting to sacred history to prove its existence among good men? No. But the allusion is made to prove this fact: that there may be a state of things in which slavery becomes a necessary evil, and which its existence is not incompatible with true religion. Such a state of things, the gentlemen on the opposite side must acknowledge to have existed among themselves; for in the abolition of slavery in those States where it is abolished, though the number was small, yet the wisdom of their legislatures, in almost every instance, prevented the evils which they expected to result from a sudden change, by providing for its gradual abolition. Yes, sir, those who are now most censorious in their declamations against slavery, have, by their own acts, in their own States, sanctioned, every principle which the slaveholder in other States, either sanctions or avows; because, in the gradual instead of sudden abolition, they have acknowledged the existence of that state of things among themselves, which justified the holding of some in a state of involuntary servitude for life, and of others for a term of years. If such has been the policy of States, where the numbers of slaves, owing originally to the coldness of their climate rather than to any moral cause, bore but a very small proportion to their whole population, it is but reasonable to conclude that they would have justified the same policy which has governed their sister States, had it been their lot to have embosomed as great a proportion of slaves.

But *humanity* is the plea. And can gentlemen sincerely believe that the cause of humanity will be promoted by still confining this population within such limits as that their relative numbers will oppose everlasting obstacles to their emancipation? Upon the most extensive principle of philanthropy, I say, let them spread forth with the growing extent of our nation. I am sure I plead the cause of humanity. I advocate the best interests of the sons of bondage, when I entreat you to give them room to be happy; and so disperse them as that, under the auspices of Providence, they may one day enjoy the rights of man, without convulsing the empire or endangering society. We must now take the world as we find it—not as we would have it—and adapt our measures to the actual state of things. The cruelties which are passed cannot be retracted; and upon the slave trade we can now only look back with emotions of regret, which have but one balm of consolation to mitigate our sorrows. It is this: that outrages upon humanity may be tolerated in civilized society, which are overruled by Divine Providence, for the ultimate good of those who were the victims of cruelty. Such has been the consequence of the slave trade; and let it now be our object to make them feel the benefit, since they have not been exempted from the misery.

There is no just cause for irritation on this subject. We should suppress our feelings, when they threaten to transport us beyond the bounds of reason. Early habits beget strong prejudices; and under a heavy burden of them we all labor. But it becomes us to bring them to one common altar, and consume them together. Before we compel our brother to pluck the mote from his eye, it will be wise to take the beam from our own. On this occasion I cannot omit to mention my own feelings on a former occurrence. When I first came to Congress, it was with mingled emotions of horror and surprise that I saw citizens from the non-slaveholding States, as they are called—yes, and both branches of our National Legislature—riding in a coach and four, with a white servant seated before, managing the reins, another standing behind the coach, and both of these white servants in livery. Is this, said I to myself, the degraded condition of the citizen, on whose voice the liberties of a nation may depend? I could not reconcile it with my ideas of freedom; because, in the State where I received my first impressions, slaves alone were servile. All white men there are on an equality, and every citizen feels his independence. We have no classes—no patrician or plebeian rank. Honesty and honor form all the distinctions that are felt or known. Whatever may be the condition of a citizen with us, you must treat him as an equal. This, I find, is not so in every part of the non-slaveholding States, especially in your populous cities, where ranks and distinctions, the precursors of aristocracy, already begin to exist. They whose business it is to perform menial offices in other States, are as servile as our slaves in the West. Where is the great difference betwixt the condition of him who keeps your stable, who blacks your boots, who holds your stirrups, or mounts behind your coach when you ride, and the slave who obeys the command of his master? There may be a nominal difference; but it would be difficult to describe its reality. In the one case it is called voluntary, because it is imposed by its own necessity, and in the other involuntary, because imposed by the will of another. Whatever difference there may be in the principle, the effects upon society are the same. The condition, in some respects, is in favor of the slave. He is supplied with food and clothing; and in the hour of sickness he finds relief. No anxious cares in relation to age and infirmity, invade his breast. He fears no duns: careless of the pressure of the times, he dreads not the coercion of payment, nor feels the cruelty of that code which confines the white servant in prison, because the iron hand of poverty has wrested from him the means of support for his family. Though slavery still must be confessed a bitter draught, yet where the stamp of nature marks the distinction, and when the mind, from early habit, is moulded to the condition, the slave often finds less bitterness in the cup of life than most white servants. What is the condition of many, who are continually saluting our ears with cries of want, even in this city? Men, women, boys, girls, from infancy to old age, craving relief from every passenger. Are they slaves? No. Among the slaves are no beggars; no vagrants; none idle for want of employ, or crying for want of bread. Every condition of life has its evils; and most evils have some palliative; though perhaps none less than those of white menials. Yet, sir, none are more lavish of their censures against slavery than those lordlings with livery servants of their own complexion. For my own part, I have hitherto been fortunate in my public course, in having retained the confidence of my fellow citizens. I have not only triumphed over the most troubled elements—I have even braved the storm produced by the famous compensation law; but I never could stand having white servants dressed in livery. No, sir, when the honest laborer, the mechanic, however poor, or whatever his employment, visits my house, it matters not what company is there, he must sit with me at my board, and receive the same treatment as the most distinguished guest; because in him I recognize a fellow citizen and an equal.

The condition of the slave is but little understood by those who are not the eye-witnesses of his treatment. His sufferings are greatly aggravated in their apprehension. The general character of the slaveholding community can no more be determined, nor should they be any more stigmatized, by a particular instance of cruelty to a slave, than the character of the non-slaveholding community by a particular instance of cruelty in a parent toward his child, a guardian to his ward, or a master to his apprentice. No man among us can be cruel to his slave without incurring the execration of the whole community. The slave is trained to industry; and he is recompensed by kindness and humanity, which lighten his burden. His master is his guardian. He enjoys the rights of conscience, and worships God as he chooses. The Gospel sheds as bright a lustre on his path as on that of the white man; and quite as great a proportion of them become believers in the Saviour, and are admitted into the communion of the Christian Church.

Except on the sugar, the rice, and the cotton plantations, at the South, the slave is not a profit to his master. Upon a fair calculation of debtor and creditor, the majority of them would fall in debt; and the holding of them is more a matter of convenience than profit.

A solemn appeal has been made to the Declaration of Independence, as if that instrument had a bearing upon this question; though, at that day, and long since, slavery existed in every State of the Union. That sentiment has been quoted, that all men are created equal; that they are endowed by their Creator with certain equal, inalienable rights; among which are life, liberty, and the pursuit of happiness. This sacred truth should be engraven upon every heart, for it is the foundation of all civil rights, and the palladium of our liberties. The meaning of this sentence is defined in its application; that all communities stand upon an equality; that Americans are equal with Englishmen, and have the right to organize such government for themselves as they shall choose, whenever it is their pleasure to dissolve the bonds which unite them to another people. The same principle applied to Missouri will defeat the object of gentlemen who advocate this restriction.

Could this principle be reduced to practice in relation to every human being, it would be happy; but such is the character, and such the condition of man, that it is perpetually violated by every individual, and by every body politic; often wantonly, sometimes through necessity. Every State in this Confederacy, not even excepting the great and unambitious State of Pennsylvania, violates this principle, if it be understood according to the application given it by gentlemen, in the most important political rights—the elective franchise and the qualification for office. The organization of every department, both of the general government and the State governments, infringes upon this principle. Different qualifications are required in different States; in some, a freehold inheritance; and the least, in the most democratic States, are age and residence. And shall we reject a State for this violation of principle? However unfortunate it may be, this great principle of equality, so delightful in theory, is but very partially regarded in practice; and I will not deny the allegation, when it is asserted that necessity often justifies the measure. Then, sir, let imperious necessity, in this case, also prefer its claim to consideration.

*   *   *   *   *   *   *

There is a mystery in this anxiety, this excitement of popular commotion on the one hand, and this utter indifference on the other, which it requires a casuist to divine. Is your object the emancipation of slaves? No one pretends that this measure will diminish the number of slaves, unless, by this very singular kind of humanity, you diminish their comfort to such a degree as to prevent the increase of that species of population. Nor is it pretended that the failure of this favorite motion for restriction will enslave a solitary individual of the human race; though we have witnessed that strange kind of sympathy for their sufferings which would so confirm their misery as to deprive them of a posterity. For my own part, Mr. President, I do not well comprehend this humanity. I would prefer a different exercise of this noble principle. Miserable as the condition of the slave may be, his condition is yet preferred to that of annihilation. He finds in life sufficient charms to induce him still to cleave to it; and in his rising progeny he has the same kind of satisfaction that the free man feels. He will never court your sympathies, if they are to be elicited in adding confinement to servitude, and to ultimate in annihilation. Humanity has a head as well as heart; and as the citizens of Missouri have the same right in nature to govern themselves that any others enjoy, the legitimate exercise of this principle will be, to leave them to the enjoyment of that right, and they will decide for themselves the most humane policy to be pursued.

But, sir, this is not a question of slavery. The simple question involved is this; whether I shall have an equal right with my worthy friend from Pennsylvania (Mr. Roberts) to remove with my property (slaves and all) to Missouri — a common property, purchased by the common treasure of the whole Union; and whether my constituents, the citizens of Kentucky, shall enjoy the same right with the citizens of Maine to inherit this common property, with all their effects. I am aware, sir, that, by some means, this question has been made to assume the appearance of a question for freedom, on the one hand, and slavery on the other. From the popular excitement which has manifested itself in many communities at the North, I am warranted in this conclusion. The mass of society in every section of our country is righteous; and I am certain the expression of their sentiments upon this subject, by such worthy and honorable citizens, in so many popular meetings, has been upon this mistaken view. It has not been the clamor of intriguing politicians, striving for an ascendancy of power, provoking local animosities for ambitious purposes, but from a misapprehension of the main question for that of slavery. I am ready to acknowledge that they have shown a zeal in the cause of liberty which does honor to their hearts. I will mention a case in point: A very worthy friend of mine, who was always an enemy to slavery, and had made personal sacrifices in the cause of emancipation, was of the opinion that Congress had no constitutional right to impose this restriction. He received a letter from an intimate friend of his, expressing much surprise on learning that he had become an advocate for slavery. In his reply, he denied the charge of having changed his sentiments; but stated his reasons for the opinion which he held in a manner which would have done honor both to the head and heart of a legislator. He conceived the government to be pledged, by the solemn stipulation of the treaty of cession by which that territory was acquired, to admit them into the Union; which pledge could not be honorably redeemed, if conditions were imposed which did not exist in relation to the original States. As slavery therein had been sanctioned by law while it remained a territory; and as citizens of the States, holding slaves, had purchased lands from the Government, in that territory, under the expectation of removing to it, and improving it with their slaves, he conceived it to be an act of injustice in that Government to require a condition which would deprive them of these benefits. The power of Congress to admit new States into the Union, he conceived to be no other than that of the principle of the Constitution; whereby every State so admitted must retain the same sovereignty as that retained by the States which formed the Federal compact; and as those States had reserved to themselves the power of sanctioning or abolishing slavery, so Missouri, on becoming a State, could not be constitutionally deprived of that power. This reasoning, sir, appears to me conclusive. The stipulations of the treaty; the sanctions under which the lands have been sold, and the nature of the Constitution itself, in regard to State sovereignties, oppose irresistible obstacles to the restriction proposed. But these misunderstandings of the real question at issue are unfortunate, as they produce a false alarm in the community. Prejudices thus riveted upon the minds of a virtuous people are calculated to array one part of the great American family against the other, without the hope of one solitary benefit for the result. Ambitious men may gladly seize the occasion to court popularity and confidence; but rest assured the people are to be the victims of their wiles.

The division which this subject produces is the more to be deprecated as it is marked by geographical lines. The mischievous consequences of thus provoking jealousies and animosities have not been sufficiently contemplated by the patriot and statesman. The inevitable result must be this: you will look for *residence*, and overlook *merit*. Public services and private virtues will be forgotten. A demon or a saint will equally suit your purpose, till the favorite object is accomplished. Prejudice will blind your eyes to the danger of bad principles; and while laboring in vain to break the manacles of others, who do not thank you for the effort, you are forging chains for yourselves that will one day hold you in bondage. Heretofore we have divided upon the principle of measures equally affecting every part of the nation. In 1798, when measures tending to consolidation, threatening the liberty of speech and the press, were pursued, no geographical lines, marking the division between slaveholding and non-slaveholding States, produced the sentiments of either party. The strife was betwixt honest and patriotic members of every community and every village. The consequences were often unhappy for a moment, but not dangerous to the whole family. The enmities which it occasioned were temporary, and would soon die a natural death. But when local residence becomes the occasion of deep-rooted animosities, the consequences are always dangerous, and often fatal. Why, then, attempt a dangerous course when necessity does not demand it? There is nothing in the legitimate exercise of the powers of the general government, touching any of the objects of the confederacy, which requires a single allusion to the subject of slavery in the States. Once in ten years it may possibly have its influence in fixing the ratio of representation; and I believe, at the last census, the slaveholding States lost several representatives, by the superior management of the other States, in leaving the greatest fraction upon them. But, this being accidental and temporary, was no subject of contention.

On the present occasion, sir, you attempt impossibilities. You may injure, but you cannot benefit, the black population. If ever they enjoy freedom their emancipation must be gradual; and it must be preceded by a progressive amelioration of their condition, to prepare them for liberty. The more you suffer them to disperse, the more rapidly you will accelerate this desirable state of things. The energies of the Christian world are now combined in the diffusion of evangelical light, and the principles which it inculcates are every day relaxing the bonds of slavery.

Providence, all wise and inscrutable in its ways, is gradually effecting the ultimate object of our wishes, which your ill-timed interposition is calculated only to retard. Individual exertion, acting in concert, can alone prepare the way. Encourage Sunday-schools; multiply Bible societies; increase missionary exertions; animate to deeds of benevolence abolition societies, and perfect the system of colonization. Then trust the kind providence of God for the result, and you will perform the duties of Christians and patriots, in the service of God and his creatures. But till you can change the spots of the leopard, you cannot change the condition of the slaves by the illegitimate measures now proposed. You may violate the Constitution—you may impair the social compact by encroaching upon the sovereignty of the States, which is the palladium of our liberties—you may touch the right of property under the pretext of letting the captive go free; you may essay to bind the people of Missouri, by prescribing to them conditions of legislation; but your effort will be fruitless. You risk much and gain nothing. The people of Missouri are Americans. They have the right of self-government, and they will govern themselves. You may prepare chains for them, but, like Samson's cords, they will be as tow, and fall asunder like ropes of sand. These people are descendants of freemen. They are of the old stock who achieved your independence, and they will be free. Do you hope to abridge their sovereignty? Their character is a pledge that they will not yield their rights.

Whatever may be our anxiety for universal freedom, it is very certain that no sudden change can be effected. To attempt impossibilities will only expose our folly. God himself has taught us to wait patiently the operations of time, by his own example, in six days' employment in the formation of the world; and while we find sufficient evil to awaken all our sensibilities, we should remember that man cannot renovate the world in one day. In the moral world, we see vices and crimes; in the religious world, persecutions and martyrdoms; in the political world, despotism and convulsions; in the physical world, earthquakes and tornadoes. Who can renovate the heart of the vicious, and chasten the thoughts of the wicked? Who can sustain the martyr upon the cross? Who can hush the tempest in the political world, or control the destinies of nature? He only, who holds the winds in the hollow of his hand. I charge you, then, to let patience have its perfect work;

and do not rashly disturb the balance of this harmonious political system. If you do, the blood will be upon your own heads. I have unshaken confidence in the providence of God, that he will, in his goodness, provide the ways and means of deliverance from this great evil, and that he will do it without violence or compulsion. But we are to choose the time, and effect in a day what cannot be accomplished in years, without a miracle; and this is to be done without respect to either the sentiments or rights of our neighbors. Instead of satisfying ourselves with the happy condition in which a kind Providence has placed us, we are to aspire, like our first parents in Eden, to become as gods; and, for the sake of giving law to others, independent as ourselves, we are to set the whole nation in a state of commotion. Beware, lest, like them, you should experience a sad reverse, and entail the curse upon posterity. We are to become constitution-makers, and give both the text and commentary. I was taught to believe in the doctrine of the Revolutionary patriots, *vox populi vox Dei*, but now the maxim is too antiquated to be regarded. I have been a disciple of the old school, which taught us to believe that all power belonged to the people; and have ever admired the beautiful fabric of this Western empire, because it was calculated to secure the exercise of this power to each State, while it delegated to the federal government a sufficient portion, to provide for the common safety, and secure the harmony of its several parts; but this harmony is now to be disturbed; this *magna charta* of our rights is to be broken; this fair fabric is to be shaken, to gratify the lust of power; and Congress, deriving all its authority from the States, is to prescribe to the States the limits of their constitutional prerogative. I would not impeach the political sagacity of this body; but such is my confidence in the virtue and talents of the community, that, in my opinion, every ten miles square in the United States is as competent as the whole collected wisdom of the nation to frame a constitution. Competent or not, the people of Missouri have the right, and they must exercise it without any restriction which is not common to all the States. If you begin to prescribe restrictions, you may pursue the course without limitation or control. You may prescribe the qualifications of electors and candidates; the powers and organization of every branch of their government, till self-government is lost, and their liberty is but an empty name. The doctrine, sir, is alarming. But one security from its baleful influence is in the independence of the people. They will not submit. It is not the question whether the thing required is right or wrong in itself, but whether you have the right to impose it. The principle of taxation, or the amount levied, had no influence in bringing on the American Revolution; but the right of Parliament, in which the colonies had no representation, to impose the tax. They persisted, and a bloody war ensued; and the decision was in favor of that side where justice was.

I exhort to moderation and justice. Look at the starving poor in England. Hear the clanking chains of despotism throughout Europe, Asia, and Africa. The cries of oppression are heard in every region, and the cause of injured humanity rends every American bosom. But will our commiseration justify our interference? Shall we become a nation of knight-errants, and involve the country in war with all the rest of the world to establish free government in other quarters of the globe? We may pity other nations, but we have no right to intermeddle with their policies; and to attempt it would be the extreme of madness. Still more cautious should we be about intermeddling with the right of property and self-government in Missouri. In so doing, you will jeopardize the harmony of the Union, which may possibly ultimate in a civil war. Recollect, Greece was destroyed by division, and Rome by consolidation. Then let us be content with our inheritance, and profit by their example; lest, in our zeal to perform what we cannot accomplish, we one day become what Greece and Rome now are.

I will readily admit, sir, that the non-slaveholding States are composed of brave and virtuous citizens, but merit does not exclusively attach to them. We will not shrink from the comparison, whether we look at periods or principles— the Revolution, the late war; internal policy, republican principles, moral character, or religious practice. The authors of this discussion are welcome to all the advantages they can derive from the comparison. There is no essential difference of character among all the different sections of this community. A general coincidence of sentiment strengthens their mutual attachments, which I trust the demon of discord will never be able to dissolve. Yes, sir, the Union is founded in the affections of the people, cemented by the blood of our fathers, endeared by common suffering, and secured by common interest. Future generations, remembering that their fathers mingled their blood in one common cause, and their ashes in one common urn, will still feel like brothers, when ambition shall have wasted its efforts; and the blessings of the confederacy shall be long enjoyed after oblivion shall have drawn a vail over the disturbers of its peace. The history of other nations is before us, and they should be marked as beacons of warning. Remember the unhappy record of the ten tribes of Israel, and the miserable consequences, whenever you contemplate the effects of local jealousies. Before we are aware, we are too apt to excite our own passions as well as others, and rush precipitately into measures which will leave us to regret our folly when it shall be too late to retract.

But another cause of complaint is recently brought to light. In the ratio of representation and direct taxation, three-fifths of the slaves are enumerated. The Constitution was framed by patriots of the Revolution; and the principles of that event were too deeply engraven upon their minds to suffer them to separate the ratio of representation from that of taxation; and, by mutual compromise, the ratio was settled by all the States as we now have it. But, in the organization of this branch of the legislature, there is a total departure from this rule. Upon what principle does the little State of Delaware send two members to this body, and the great State of New York send no more? This also was settled upon a principle of compromise. It is, that State sovereignties may be here represented, and, in the confederacy the States, are all equal. The federal character is here preserved; and, in the other House, the representative character. In one house every State is equal, in the other every individual; and none would wish it otherwise.

In what way, I would ask, is the just principle of representation violated, by taking three-fifths of the slaves into the calculation? The answer is given, because slaves have no political rights. And what political rights have the female and the minor? And how many free persons of full age are excluded from the exercise of the elective franchise in the different States? Yet all are taken into the enumeration as the basis for representation. Why? Because they are also taken into the enumeration for taxation; so are three-fifths of the slaves taken into the enumeration as the basis for taxation, and of course for representation. In the one case no complaint is made, but in the other injustice is urged. Every argument, true or false, must be brought to bear upon the subject; which, in the end, will effect nothing, and is, in fact, worse than nothing.

There is another article of the Constitution, which is thought to have some relation to this intended restriction. "Congress shall guarantee to each State a republican form of government;" and here we have a controlling powe. Suppose, then, you erect your standard of republicanism, and revise the constitutions of the different States. Virginia requires a freehold qualification in the voter. Dictate to her better principles. Most of the other States require some property qualifications. Change their constitutions, and proclaim annual elections and universal suffrage, such as we have in Kentucky, where every person is equal; and the beggar (if such a being can be found there) has as good a vote as the man of wealth. Attempt these things, and you will have enough to do; but you may accomplish it as easily, and upon as fair Constitutional ground, as the restriction upon Missouri. The fact is, we shall be better employed in confining ourselves to the great objects of the confederacy, and leave every State to manage its own concerns.

Philosophers have said much upon the theory of colors, and especially upon the variety of complexion in the human species. It is contended by some that the black man, the red man, and the white man, originally sprang from different ancestors; by others that all sprang from one common stock; and the last theory is supported by revelation. It is further believed, that the difference of color, from the slightest shade to the deepest black, is owing principally to climate, and the different degrees of heat to which they have been for many ages exposed. To whatever cause it may be owing, the difference does now exist; and it is as well known that a universal prejudice also exists as to the color of the African, which in a great measure deprives him of the blessings of freedom when emancipated. Till this prejudice is eradicated, or till the Ethiopian shall change his skin, his freedom is nominal in every part of the United States. If not, where is the black man of the north? Like the red man, he is nearly extinct. If your humanity has conquered your prejudice, till you know no color, where are your magistrates, your governors, your representatives, of the black population? You proclaim them equal, but you are still their lawgivers; we see none of them in the national legislature, nor hear of them in your State governments. The prejudices which these distinctions of color create cannot be overcome in a moment, and we should contentedly wait that gradual change in the moral world—that slow but certain progress of improvement, which will one day give universal liberty to the race of Adam.

One insurmountable, I may say omnipotent barrier with us, against this sudden revolution, is, the number of our slaves. It would produce convulsions and derangements, destructive to the morals and safety of the whole community. But liberty has charms, and so has music; but was there anything captivating in Nero's harp while Rome was enveloped in flames? Let the safety of the commonwealth be first secured, and then extend the blessings of freedom as time shall prepare them to enjoy it, with advantage to themselves and tranquillity to the State.

The sages of our Revolution were not so conscientious as to make emancipation a *sine qua non* to a Union against British encroachments; nor did they ever think of interfering in the subject of slavery with the States. That was left with God and the consciences of those interested. Slaveholders and others could march under one standard in the common cause. Washington and Greene could move in perfect concert of action; Hancock and Jefferson could act in harmony of council, without one discordant passion on this account. Nor did the wise framers of the Constitution essay to give it the slightest touch. Even a part of the New England States voted against the power of Congress to check the importation of slaves for twenty years. But now, when all political animosities are subsiding, and every angry passion is sinking to rest, the golden apple must be thrown. Political power and personal aggrandizement must arise, and light the torch of discord among this happy, this virtuous, this affectionate people. Keep in mind the theory of our general government. We have no original powers. We act as an agent would under a special power of attorney; and the Constitution is the charter by which we act. The powers delegated are there defined. Those not expressly delegated are reserved to the States, or to the people. To transcend the powers prescribed by the Constitution, is to violate the rights of the States and of the people. Congress have no power delegated to them by the Constitution to impose a restriction like this upon any of the States; nor can it be pretended, unless by that kind of legerdemain construction which would make Congress omnipotent, and render the sovereignties a mere shadow, that this text book of the American statesman contains a single clause even hinting at the delegation of this power. The imposition of this restriction upon Missouri, then, would be a violation of the Constitution; and, however plausible the pretext, the principle is equally dangerous to the Union.

I have entertained doubts as to the wisdom of the organization of this body in the tenure of office. Six years I have thought too long; that the member did not feel sufficient responsibility to the elective principle. But, on this interesting occasion, I can see great evils, which we have it in our power more effectually to prevent, and thus give proof to the world that we are worthy of this trust. The examples of Greece, of Carthage, and of Rome show us the danger of being moved by a momentary excitement of popular passion; but, when time for sober reasoning shall have elapsed, the popular sentiment, the result of dispassionate deliberation, must prevail. This body is peculiarly formed for that deliberation; and when I behold around me those who have gone through the gradation of every office of honor and of trust—who have withstood every trial, and now bear upon their hoary heads the crown of honor—elected by their fellow-citizens to this station, I feel a confidence that they will sustain the cause of the Union. Then, when this excitement shall subside, the deliberate, settled sentiment of the people will justify your decision. But, should your determination to effect this restriction so completely overcome every consideration of right, that you deem it paramount to all constitution and compact, you will pay dearly for the object. Victory will be worse than a defeat. You will violate the plighted faith of the nation, under the sacred sanction of your own laws, which have heretofore held out an invitation to the citizens of every section of the country to embrace the advantages which this newly-acquired wilderness promised. You will violate the solemn stipulations of the treaty by which this territory was gained. You will violate the Constitution of the United States, that sacred instrument which once had power to compose the jarring interests and passions of the nation; the offspring of our former suffering; the pledge of our future harmony; and the standing bulwark of our liberty and independence. You will alarm the fears and destroy the confidence of the States, by abridging their prerogatives and usurping their rights. You will check the progress of humanity, and strengthen the chains of the captive. You will prolong the time of slavery, and augment its evils. You will divide the sentiments and affections by hills and dales, by rivers and mountains, and by imaginary lines, drawn only for convenience, and not for hostility. You will excite to action every discordant passion of the soul; produce jargon, animosity, and strife, which may eventuate in murder and devastation. And shall I proceed to enumerate the crimes which belong to this black catalogue? The heart sickens, the tongue falters, and I forbear. Ponder well your doings; let wisdom and justice direct you; confine your measures to the legitimate object of the confederacy, and we are still a united and happy people.

Mr. Pinckney, of South Carolina, the only member of Congress who was a member of the Federal Convention, addressed the chair as follows:

Mr. Chairman: It was not my intention at first, and it is not now my wish, to rise on this important question; one that has been so much and so ably discussed in both branches of Congress; one that has been the object of so many meetings of the people of the different States, and of so many resolutions of the legislatures, and instructions to their members: but I am so particularly circumstanced that it is impossible to avoid it. Coming from one of the most important of the Southern States, whose interests are deeply involved, and representing here a city and district which, I believe, export more of our native products than any other in the Union; having been also a member of the Old Congress, some important acts of which are brought into question on this occasion, and, above all, *being the only member of the General Convention which formed the Constitution of the United States, now on this floor, and on whose acts rest the great question in controversy,* how far you are or are not authorized to adopt this measure, it will, from all these circumstances, be seen that it is impossible for me to avoid requesting your permission to state some observations in support of the vote I shall give on a question, certainly, the most important that can come before Congress; one, to say the least of it, on which may depend, not only the peace, the happiness, and the best interests, but, not improbably, the existence of that Union which has been, since its formation, the admiration of the world, and the pride, the glory, and the boast of every American bosom that beats within it.

In performing this solemn duty, I trust I shall do it with that deference to the opinions of others which it is always my duty to show on this respectable floor, and that I shall be as short as the nature of the subject will permit, and completely moderate. Indeed, in questions of this importance, moderation appears to me to be indispensable to the discovery of truth. I, therefore, lament extremely that so much warmth has been unnecessarily excited, and shall, in the remarks I may make, studiously do, what I conceive the decorum of debate ought to enjoin upon every member.

At the time I left, or sailed from the city I here represent, scarcely a word was said of the Missouri question; no man there ever supposed that one of such magnitude was before you. I, therefore, have, since the serious aspect this subject has assumed, received numerous inquiries on it, and wishes to know my opinion as to the extent and consequences of it. I have candidly replied, that, so far as respects the regaining an ascendency on both the floors of Congress; of regaining the possession of the honors and offices of our government; and of, through this measure, laying the foundation of forever securing their ascendency, and the powers of the government, the Eastern and Northern States had a high and deep interest. That, so far as respects the retaining the honors and offices and the powers of the government, and the preventing the establishment of principles to interfere with them, the Southern and Western States had equal interest with the Northern. But that, when we consider to what lengths the right of Congress to touch the question of slavery at all might reach, it became one, indeed, of tremendous import.

Among the reasons which have induced me to rise, one is to express my surprise. Surprise, did I say? I ought rather to have said, my extreme astonishment, at the assertion I heard made on both floors of Congress, that, in forming the Constitution of the United States, and particularly that part of it which respects the representation on this floor, the Northern and Eastern States, or, as they are now called, the non-slaveholding States, have made a great concession to the Southern, in granting them a representation of three-fifths of their slaves; that they saw the concession was a very great and important one at the time, but that they had no idea it would so soon have proved itself of such consequence; that it would so soon have proved itself to be by far the most important concession that had been made. They say, that it was wrung from from them by their affection to the Union, and their wish to preserve it from dissolution or disunion; that they had, for a long time, lamented they had made it; and that if it was to do over, no earthly consideration should again tempt them to agree to so unequal and so ruinous a compromise. By this, I suppose, Mr. Chairman, is meant that they could have had no idea that the Western and Southern States would have grown with the rapidity they have, and filled so many of the seats in this House: in other words, that they would so soon have torn the sceptre from the East.

It was, sir, for the purpose of correcting this great and unpardonable error; unpardonable, because it is a wilful one, and the error of it is well-known to the ablest of those who make it; of denying the assertion, and proving that the contrary is the fact, and that the concession, on that occasion, was from the Southern and not the Northern States, that, among others, I have risen.

It is of the greatest consequence that the proof I am about to give should be laid before this nation; for, as the inequality of representation is the great ground on which the Northern and Eastern States have always, and now more particularly and forcibly than ever, raised all their complaints on this subject, if I can show and prove that they have not even a shadow of right to make pretenses or complaints; that they are as fully represented as they ought to be; while we, the Southern members, are unjustly deprived of any representation for a large and important part of our population, more valuable to the Union, as can be shown, than any equal number of inhabitants in the Northern and Eastern States can, from their situation, climate, and productions, possibly be. If I can prove this, I think I shall be able to show most clearly the true motives which have given rise to this measure; to strip the thin, the cobweb veil from it, as well as the pretended ones of religion, humanity, and love of liberty; and to show, to use the soft terms the decorum of debate obliges me to use, the extreme want of modesty in those who are already as fully represented here as they can be, to go the great lengths they do in endeavoring, by every effort in their power, public and private, to take from the Southern and Western States, which are already so greatly and unjustly deprived of an important part of the representation, a still greater share; to endeavor to establish the first precedent, which extreme rashness and temerity have ever presumed, that Congress has a right to touch the question and legislate on slavery; thereby shaking the property in them, in the Southern and Western States, to its very foundation, and making an attack which, if successful, must convince them that the Northern and Eastern States are their greatest enemies; that they are preparing measures for them which even Great Britain, in the heat of the Revolutionary war, and when all her passions were roused by hatred and revenge to the highest pitch, never ventured to inflict upon them. Instead of a course like this, they ought, in my judgment, sir, to be highly pleased with their present situation; that they are fully represented, while we have lost so great a share of our representation; they ought, sir, to be highly pleased at the dexterity and managament of their members in the Convention, who obtained for them this great advantage; and, above all, with the moderation and forbearance with which the Southern and Western States have always borne their bitter provocations on this subject, and now bear the open, avowed, and, by many of the ablest men among them, undisguised attack on our most valuable rights and properties.

At the commencement of our revolutionary struggle with Great Britain, all the States had slaves. The New England States had numbers of them, and treated them in the same manner the Southern did. The Northern and Middle States had still more numerous bodies of them, although not so numerous as the Southern. They all entered into that great contest with similar views, properties, and designs. Like brethren, they contended for the benefit of the whole, leaving to each the right to pursue its happiness in its own way.

They thus nobly toiled and bled together, really like brethren; and it is a most remarkable fact that, notwithstanding in the course of the Revolution the Southern States were continually overrun by the British, and that every negro in them had an opportunity of leaving their owners, few did; proving thereby not only a most remarkable attachment to their owners, but the mildness of the treatment, from which their affection sprang. They then were, as they still are, as valuable a part of our population to the Union as any other equal number of inhabitants. They were, in numerous instances, the pioneers, and in all, the laborers of your armies. To their hands were owing the erection of the greatest part of the fortifications raised for the protection of our country; some of which, particularly Fort Moultrie, gave, at that early period of the inexperience and untried valor of our citizens, immortality to American arms; and in the Northern States numerous bodies of them were enrolled into and fought, by the sides of the whites, the battles of the Revolution.

Things went on in this way until the period of our attempt to form our first national compact, the confederation, in which the equality of vote was preserved, and the first squeamishness on the subject of not using, or even alluding to the word slavery, or making it a part of our political machinery, was shown. In this compact, the value of the lands and improvements was made the rule for apportioning the public burdens and taxes. But the Northern and Eastern States, who are always much more alive to their interests than the Southern, found that their squeamishness was inconsistent with their interest; and, as usual, made the latter prevail. They found it was paying too dear for their qualms to keep their hand from the slaves any longer. At their instance, and on their motion, as will appear by a reference to the journals of the old Congress, the making lands the rule was changed, and people, including the whites and three-fifths of other descriptions, was adopted. It was not until in 1781, that the confederation was adopted by, and became binding on all the States. This miserable, feeble mockery of government crawled on until 1785, when, from New York's refusing to agree with all the States to grant to Congress the impost, (I am not sure, but I believe she stood alone in the refusal,) the States determined no longer to put up with her conduct, and absolutely rebelled against the government. The first State that did so was New Jersey, who, by a solemn act passed in all its proper forms by her legislature and government, most positively and absolutely refused any longer to obey the requisitions of Congress, or to pay another dollar. As there was no doubt other States would soon follow their example—as Pennsylvania shortly did—Congress, aware of the mischiefs which must arise if a dissolution took place of the Union before a new government could be formed, sent a deputation of their own body to address the legislature of New Jersey, of which I was appointed chairman. We did repair there, and addressed them, and I had the honor and happiness to carry back with me to Congress the repeal of her act by

New Jersey—a State, during the whole of the revolutionary war, celebrated for her patriotism, and who, in this noble self-denial, and forgetfulness of injuries inflicted by New York on her and the rest of the Union, exhibited a disinterestedness and love of Union which did her the highest honor.

The revolt of New Jersey and Pennsylvania accelerated the new Constitution. On a motion from Virginia the Convention met at Philadelphia, where as you will find from the journals, we were repeatedly in danger of dissolving without doing any thing; that body being equally divided as to large and small States, and each having a vote, and the small States insisting most pertinaciously, for near six weeks, on equal power in both branches—nothing but the prudence and forbearance of the large States saved the Union. A compromise was made, that the small States and large should be equally represented in the Senate, and proportionally in the House of Representatives. I am now arrived at the reason for which I have, sir, taken the liberty to make these preliminary remarks. For, as the true motive for all this dreadful clamor throughout the Union, this serious and eventful attack on our most sacred and valuable rights and properties, is, to gain a fixed ascendency in the representation in Congress; and, as the only flimsy excuse under which the Northern and Eastern States shelter themselves, is, that they have been hardly treated in the representation in this House, and that they have lost the benefit of the compromise they pretend was made, and which I shall most positively deny, and show that nothing like a compromise was ever intended.

By all the public expenses being borne by indirect taxes, and not direct, as was expected; if I can show that all their pretensions and claims are wholly untrue and unfounded, and that while they are fully represented, they did, by force, or something like it, deprive us of a rightful part of our representation, I shall then be able to take the mask from all their pretended reasons and excuses, and show this unpardonable attack, this monster, in its true and uncovered hideousness.

Long before our present public distresses had convinced even the most ignorant and uninformed politician of the truth of the maxim I am about to mention, all the well-informed statesmen of our Union knew that the only true mode for a large agricultural and commercial country to flourish was, never to import more than they can pay for by the export of their own native products; that, if they do, they will be sure to plunge themselves into the distressing and disgraceful situation this country is in at present.

If, then, this great political truth or maxim, or call it what you please, is most unquestionable, let us now see who supports this government; who raises your armies, equips your navies, pays your public debt, enables you to erect forts, arsenals, and dock-yards. Who nerves the arm of this government, and enables you to lift it for the protection, the honor, and extension of our beloved republic into regions where none but brutes and savages have before roamed? Who are your real sinews in war, and the best—I had almost said, nearly the only—sinews and sources of your commerce in peace? I will presently tell you.

If, as no doubt, you will in future confine your imports to the amount of your exports of native products, and all your revenue is to be, as it is now, raised by taxes or duties on your imports, I ask you who pays the expense, and who, in fact, enables you to go on with your government at all, and prevents its wheels from stopping? I will show you by the papers which I hold in my hand. This, sir, is your Secretary of the Treasury's report, made a few weeks ago, by which it appears that all the exports of native products, from Maine to Pennsylvania inclusive, for the last year, amounted to only about eighteen millions of dollars; while those among the slaveholding States, to the southward of

Pennsylvania, amounted to thirty-two millions or thereabouts, thereby enabling themselves, or acquiring the right, to import double as much as the others, and furnishing the treasury with double the amount the Northern and Eastern States do. And here let me ask, from whence do these exports arise? By whose hands are they made? I answer, entirely by the slaves; and yet these valuable inhabitants, without whom your very government could not go on, and the labor of two or three of whom in the Southern States is more valuable to it than the labor of five of their inhabitants in the Eastern States, the States owning and possessing them are denied a representation but for three-fifths on this floor, while the whole of the comparatively unproductive inhabitants of the Northern and Eastern States are fully represented here. Is it just—is this equal? And yet they have the modesty to complain of the representation, as unjust and unequal; and that they have not the return made them they expected, by taxing the slaves, and making them bear a proportion of the public burdens. Some writers on political economy are of opinion that the representation of a State ought always to be equally founded on population and taxation. It is my duty to believe that these are the true criterions; for my own State (South Carolina) having, in her House of Representatives, 124 members, 62 of them are apportioned by the white population, and 62 on taxation; thus representing the contributions of our citizens in every way, whether arising from services or taxes.

Before I proceed to the other parts of this question, I have thus endeavored to give a new view of the subject of representation in the House; to show how much more the Eastern and Northern States are represented than the Southern and Western; how little right the former have to complain, and how unreasonable it is, that while to continue the balance of representation in the Senate, we consent to give admission to Maine, to make up for Missouri, they most unconscionably require to have both, and thus add four to the number now preparing, most cruelly, to lift the arm of the government against the property of the Southern and Western States.

If I have succeeded, as I hope I have, in proving the unreasonableness of the complaints of the Eastern and Northern States on the subject of representation, it would, I suppose, appear extraordinary to the people of this nation that this attempt should now be made, even if Congress should be found to possess the right to legislate or interfere in it. But if, in addition to this, it should be in my power to show that they have not the most distant right to interfere, or to legislate at all upon the subject of slavery, or to admit a State in any way whatever except on terms of perfect equality; that they have no right to make compacts on the subject, and that the only power they have is to see that the government of the State to be admitted is a republican one, having legislative, executive, and judiciary powers, the rights of conscience, jury, a habeas corpus, and all the great leading principles of our republican systems, well secured, and to guarantee them to it: if I shall be able to do this, of course the attempt must fail, and the amendment be rejected.

The supporters of the amendment contend that Congress have the right to insist on the prevention of involuntary servitude in Missouri; and found the right on the ninth section of the first article, which says, "the migration or importation of such persons as the States now existing may think proper to admit, shall not be prohibited by the Congress prior to the year 1808, but a tax or duty may be imposed on such importation not exceeding ten dollars."

In considering this article, I will detail, as far as at this distant period is possible, what was the intention of the Convention that formed the Constitution in this article. The intention was, to give Congress a power, after the year 1808, to prevent the importation of slaves either by land or water from other countries. The word *import*, includes both, and applies wholly to slaves. Without this limitation, Congress might have stopped it sooner under their general power to regulate commerce; and it was an agreed point, a solemnly understood compact, that, on the Southern States consenting to shut their ports against the importation of Africans, no power was to be delegated to Congress, nor were they ever to be authorized to touch the question of slavery; that the property of the Southern States in slaves was to be as sacredly preserved, and protected to them, as that of land, or any other kind of property in the Eastern States were to be to their citizens.

The term, or word, migration, applies wholly to free whites; in its constitutional sense, as intended by the Convention, it means "voluntary change of servitude," from one country to another. The reasons of its being adopted and used in the Constitution, as far as I can recollect, were these: that the Constitution being a frame of government, consisting wholly of delegated powers, *all power, not expressly delegated, being reserved to the people or the States*, it was supposed, that, without some express grant to them of power on the subject, Congress would not be authorized ever to touch the question of migration hither, or emigration to this country, however pressing or urgent the necessity for such a measure might be; that they could derive no such power from the usages of nations, or even the laws of war; that the latter would only enable them to make prisoners of alien enemies, which would not be sufficient, as spies or other dangerous emigrants, who were not alien enemies, might enter the country for treasonable purposes, and do great injury; that, as all governments possessed this power, it was necessary to give it to our own, which could alone exercise it, and where, on other and much greater points, we had placed unlimited confidence; it was, therefore, agreed that, in the same article, the word migration should be placed; and that, from the year 1808, Congress should possess the complete power to stop either or both, as they might suppose the public interest required; the article, therefore, is a *negative pregnant*, restraining for twenty years, and giving the power after.

The reasons for restraining the power to prevent migration hither for twenty years, were, to the best of my recollection, these: That as, at this time, we had immense and almost immeasurable territory, peopled by not more than two millions and a half of inhabitants, it was of very great consequence to encourage the emigration of able, skillful, and industrious Europeans. The wise conduct of William Penn, and the unexampled growth of Pennsylvania, were cited. It was said, that the portals of the only temple of true freedom now existing on earth should be thrown open to all mankind; that all foreigners of industrious habits should be welcome, and none more so than men of science, and such as may bring to us arts we are unacquainted with, or the means of perfecting those in which we are not yet sufficiently skilled—capitalists whose wealth may add to our commerce or domestic improvements; let the door be ever and most affectionately open to illustrious exiles and sufferers in the cause of liberty; in short, open it liberally to science, to merit, and talents, wherever found, and receive and make them your own. That the safest mode would be to pursue the course for twenty years, and not, before that period, put it at all into the power of Congress to shut it; that, by that time, the Union would be so settled, and our population would be so much increased, we could proceed on our own stock, without the farther accession of foreigners; that as Congress were to be prohibited from stopping the importation of slaves to settle the Southern States, as no obstacle was to be thrown in the way of their increase and settlement for that period, let it be so with the Northern and Eastern, to which, particularly New York and Philadelphia, it was expected most of the emigrants would go from Europe: and it so happened, for, previous to the year 1808, more than double as many Europeans emigrated to these States, as of Africans were imported into the Southern States.

I have, sir, smiled at the idea of some gentlemen, in supposing that Congress possessed the power to insert this amendment, from that which is given in the Constitution to regulate commerce between the several States; and some have asserted, that under it, they not only have the power to inhibit slavery in Missouri, but even to prevent the migration of slaves from one State to another—from Maryland to Virginia. The true and peculiarly ludicrous manner in which a gentleman from that State lately treated this part of the subject, will, no doubt, induce an abandonment of this pretended right; nor shall I stop to answer it until gentlemen can convince me that migration does not mean change of residence from one country or climate to another, and that the United States are not one country, one nation, or one people. If the word does mean as I contend, and we are one people, I will then ask how it is possible to migrate from one part of a country to another part of the same country? Surely, sir, when such straws as these are caught at to support a right, the hopes of doing so must be slender indeed. I will only mention here, as it is perfectly within my recollection, that the power was given to Congress to regulate the commerce by water between the States; and it being feared, by the Southern, that the Eastern would, whenever they could, do so to the disadvantage of the Southern States, you will find, in the 6th section of the 1st article, Congress are prevented from taxing exports, or giving preference to the ports of one State over another, or obliging vessels bound from one State to clear, enter, or pay duties in another; which restrictions, more clearly than anything else, prove what the power to regulate commerce among the several States means.

The gentlemen, being driven from these grounds, come then to what they call their great and impregnable right—that, under the third section of the fourth article, it is declared, new States may be admitted into this Union by the Congress; and that, by the latter clause of the same section, the Congress shall have power to dispose of, and make all needful rules and regulations, respecting the territory or other property belonging to the United States.

By the first clause they contend, that Congress has an ample and unlimited command over the whole subject; that they can reject the admission of a State altogether, or can admit one, and impose such conditions, or make such compacts with a State as they may please; and that, unless a State accepts the offers they may make, they may refuse her admission. Let us first inquire what the laws of nations call a State. Vattel says, "Nations or States are bodies politic: societies of men united together to procure their mutual safety and advantage by means of their union. Such a society has its affairs and interests; it deliberates and resolves in common, and thus becomes a moral person, having an understanding and a will peculiar to itself, and is susceptible of obligations and laws." This is what he calls a State. What do we call one? A territory inhabited by a people living under a government formed by themselves, which government possesses, in a republican form, all the legislative, executive, and judiciary powers necessary to the protection of the lives, liberties, characters and properties of their citizens, or which they can exercise for their benefit, and have not delegated to the general government, for the common defense and general welfare of a union, composed of a number of States, whose rights and political powers are all perfectly equal; that, among these, one of the most important is, that of deciding for themselves what kind of persons shall inhabit their country, no others being either so capable or fit to judge on this very important point as respects their private happiness as themselves, as they alone are either to suffer or benefit from the injudicious or wise choice they may make; that as the other States possess completely this power, Missouri has the same right; that, if she was inclined, she could not give to Congress the right to decide for her, nor could the latter accept it; that all the inhabitants of Missouri being against the prohibition, to insist on it, is to entirely put it out of her power to enter the Union, and to keep her in a state of colonial tyranny; that, if you can exercise this right, where will you stop? May you not dictate to her the nature of the government she shall have? may you not give her a plural executive, a legislature for six and judges for one year? If you say there shall be no slavery, may you not say there shall be no marriage? may you not insist on her being different in every respect from the others? Sir, if you are determined to break the Constitution in this important point, you may even proceed to do so in the essences of the very form you are bound to guarantee to them. Instead of endeavoring to lessen or injure the force and spirit of the State governments, every true friend of his country ought to endeavor, as far as he can, to strengthen them; for, be assured, it will be to the strength and increase of our State governments, more than any other, that the American Republic will owe its firmness and duration.

The people of Europe, from their total ignorance of our country and government, have always augured that its great extent, when it came to be thickly peopled, would occasion its separation; this is still the opinion of all, and the hope of many there; whereas, nothing can be more true in our politics than that, in proportion to the increase of the State governments, the strength and solidity of the federal Government are augmented; so that with twenty or twenty-two governments, we shall be much more secure from disunion than with twelve, and ten times more so than if we were a single or consolidated one. By the individual States exercising, as they do, all the powers necessary for municipal or individual purposes—trying all questions of property, and punishing all crimes not belonging, in either case, to the federal courts, and leaving the general government at leisure and in a situation solely to devote itself to the exercise of the great powers of war and peace, commerce, and our connections with foreigners, and all the natural authorities delegated by the Constitution, it eases them of a vast quantity of business that would very much disturb the exercise of their general powers. Nor is it clear that any single government, in a country so extensive, could transmit the full influence of the laws necessary to local purposes through all its parts; whereas, the State governments, having all a convenient surrounding territory, exercise these powers with ease, and are always at hand to give aid to the federal tribunals and officers placed among them to execute their laws, should assistance be necessary. Another great advantage is, the almost utter impossibility of erecting among them the standard of faction, to any alarming degree, against the Union, so as to threaten its dissolution, or produce changes in any but a constitutional way. It is well known that faction is always much more easy and dangerous in small than large countries; and, when we consider that, to the security afforded by the extent of our territory are to be added, the guards of the State legislatures, which being selected as they are, and always the most proper organs of their citizens' opinions as to the measures of the general government, stand as alert and faithful sentinels to disapprove, as they did in the times that are past, such acts as appear impolitic or unconstitutional, or to approve and support, as they have frequently done since, such as were patriotic or praiseworthy. With such guards it is impossible for

THE MISSOURI QUESTION. 265

any serious opposition to be made to the federal government on slight or trivial grounds; nor, through such an extent of territory or number of States, would any but the most tyrannical or corrupt acts claim serious attention; and, whenever they occur, we can always safely trust to a sufficient number of the States arraying themselves in a manner to produce by their influence the necessary reforms in a peaceable and legal mode. With twenty-four or more States it will be impossible, sir, for four or five States, or any comparatively small number, ever to threaten the existence of the Union. They will be easily seen through by the other eighteen or twenty, and frowned into insignificancy and submission to the general will, in all cases where the proceedings of the federal government are approved by them. And, even in cases where doubts may arise as to the wisdom or policy of their measures, all factious measures will be made to wait constitutional redress in the peaceable manner prescribed by the Constitution.

Without the instrumentality of the States, in a country so large and free, and with their government at a great distance from its extremities, there would be considerable danger of faction; but at present there is very little, and, as the States increase, the danger will lessen; and it is this admirable expanding principle or system, if I may use the term, which, while it carries new States and governments into our forests, and increases the population and resources of the Union, must unquestionably, at the same time, add to its means to resist and repress with ease all attacks of foreign hostility or domestic faction. It is this system, which is not at all understood in Europe and too little among ourselves, that will long keep us a strong and united people; nor do I see any question, but the one which respects slavery, that can ever divide us.

The question being the admission of a new State, I hope these remarks will be considered as in point, as they go to show the importance of the State governments, and how really and indeed indispensably they are the pillars of the federal government, and how anxious we should be to strengthen and not to impair them, to make them all the strong and *equal* supporters of the federal system.

With respect to Louisiana, Congress have already, by their acts, solemnly ratified the treaty which extends to all the States, created out of that purchase, the benefits of an admission into the Union on equal terms with the old States; they gave to Louisiana first, and afterwards to Missouri and Arkansas, territorial governments, in all of which they agreed to the admission of slaves. Louisiana was incorporated into the Union, allowing their admission; Missouri was advanced to the second grade of territorial government, without the prohibition of slavery: thus, for more than sixteen years, Missouri considered herself precisely in the situation of her sister Louisiana, and many thousands of slaves have been carried by settlers there. To deny it then, now, will operate as a snare, unworthy the faith of this government. What is to be done? Are the slaves now there to be manumitted, or their masters obliged to carry them away, break up all their settlements, and, in this unjust and unexpected manner, to be hurled into ruin? If we are to pay no respect to the Constitution, or to treaties, are we to pay no respect to our own laws, by which the faith of the nation has, for sixteen years, been solemnly pledged, that no prohibition would take place, as to slavery, in those States? I have said so much, to show how important it is to the firmness and duration of the American Union, to preserve the States and their government in the full possession of all the rights secured by the Constitution.

* * * * * *

as. Having thus, I trust, proved clearly that you have no port, " to adopt this inhibition of slavery, but are forbid to otic or prai͡͡͡e Constitution, as well as by the treaty, I ought 'op here; but there are some other points which I ought not to pass unnoticed. One of these is the ordinance of July, 1787, passed by the old Congress, at the period of the sitting of the Convention in Philadelphia, for forming the Constitution, by which that body (the old Congress) undertook to form a code for the future settlement, government, and admission into the Union, of all the Territory northwest of the river Ohio, ceded by Virginia to the United States in 1785; which cession has so often been read to the House in this discussion. On this subject, I beg leave to remark that, by the confederation of the United States, the old Congress had no power whatever but that of admitting new States, provided nine States assented. By this, it is most unquestionable, that no number of States under nine had any right to admit new States. Of course, it was the intention of the confederation that, on so important a measure as the establishment of governments for, and the admission of, new States, Congress should never possess the power to act, unless nine States were represented in that body at the time of their doing so. This ordinance, therefore, in prescribing the forms of government, as they respected legislative, executive, and judiciary powers, in establishing bills of rights, and times and terms of their admission into the Union, and inhibiting servitude therein, is chargeable with ingratitude and usurpation. It is chargeable with ingratitude, when we reflect that the cession of the great tract of country—this rising empire of freemen—was gratuitously, and with noble disinterestedness and patriotism, made by Virginia, that the passing of an ordinance which contained a provision which could not but go to prevent the admission of Virginians there, as they could not move there with their slaves, was a most ungracious and ungrateful return to that State for her liberality, and could not but meet with the disapprobation of this nation.

I have already mentioned the reasons to show, that nuless they had nine States present, the old Congress had no power to admit new States, and of course no power to prescribe the forms of government, bills of rights, or terms or times of admissions, benefits, or exclusions, with a less number than nine.

If there were not other strong reasons attending the passing this ordinance, those already mentioned are sufficient to show that it is a nullity; that it never had or could have had a binding force; that the present Congress has not any constitutional right to confirm that part of it which respects the exclusion of involuntary servitude from that Territory; and that the States of Ohio and Indiana, add Illinois, having by their constitutions voluntarily excluded it, possess the power whenever they please to alter their constitutions, and admit servitude in any way they think proper.

Let us, sir, recollect the circumstances the old Congress were in at the time they passed this ordinance: they had dwindled almost to nothing; the Convention had then been three months in session; it was universally known a Constitution was in its essentials agreed to: and the public were daily expecting (what soon happened) the promulgation of a new form of government for the Union. I ask, sir, was it, under these circumstance, proper for a feeble, dwindled body, that had wholly lost the confidence of the nation, and which was then waiting its suppression by the people—a feeble, inefficient body, in which only seven or eight States were represented, the whole of which consisted of but seventeen or eighteen men—a number smaller than your large committees; a body literally in the very agonies of political death;—was it, sir, even decent in them (not to say lawful or constitutional) to have passed an ordinance of such importance? I do not know or recollect the names of the members who voted for it, but it is to be fairly presumed they could not have been among the men who possessed the greatest confidence of the Union, or at that very time they would have been members of the Convention sitting at Philadelphia. But I am perhaps taking up your time unnecessarily on this subject, and I shall proceed to others.

A great deal has been said on the subject of slavery—that it is an infamous stain and blot on the States that hold them; not only degrading the slave, but the master, and making him unfit for republican government; that it is contrary to religion and the law of God; and that Congress ought to do every thing in their power to prevent its extension among the new States.

Now, sir, I should be glad to know how any man is acquainted with what is the will or the law of God on this subject. Has it ever been imparted either to the old or new world? Is there a single line in the Old or New Testament, either censuring or forbidding it? I answer without hesitation, no. But there are hundreds speaking of and recognizing it. Hagar, from whom millions sprang, was an African slave, bought out of Egypt by Abraham, the father of the faithful and the beloved servant of the Most High; and he had, besides, three hundred and eighteen male slaves. The Jews in the time of the theocracy, and the Greeks and Romans, had all slaves; at that time there was no nation without them. If we are to believe that this world was formed by a great and omnipotent Being; that nothing is permitted to exist here but by his will, and then throw our eyes throughout the whole of it, we should form an opinion very different indeed from that asserted, that slavery was against the law of God.

Let those acquainted with the situation of the people of Asia and Africa, where not one man in ten can be called a freeman, or whose situation can be compared with the comforts of our slaves, throw their eyes over them, and carry them to Russia, and from the north to the south of Europe, where, except Great Britain, nothing like liberty exists.

Let them view the lower classes of their inhabitants, by far the most numerous of the whole; the thousands of beggars that infest their streets, more than half starved, half naked, and in the most wretched state of human degradation. Let him then go to England; the comforts, if they have any, of the lower classes of whose inhabitants are far inferior to those of our slaves. Let him, when there, ask of their economists, what are the numbers of millions daily fed by the hand of charity; and, when satisfied there, then let him come nearer home, and examine into the situation of the free negroes now resident in New York and Philadelphia, and compare them with the situation of our slaves, and he will tell you that, perhaps, the most miserable and degraded state of human nature is to be found among the free negroes of New York and Philadelphia, most of whom are fugitives from the Southern States, received and sheltered in those States. I did not go to New York, but I did to Philadelphia, and particularly examined this subject while there. I saw their streets crowded with idle, drunken negroes, at every corner; and, on visiting their penitentiary, found, to my astonishment, that, out of five hundred convicts there confined, more than one-half were blacks; and, as all the convicts throughout that State are sent to that penitentiary, and, if Pennsylvania contains eight hundred thousand white inhabitants, and only twenty-six thousand blacks, of course the crimes and vices of the blacks in those States are, comparatively, twenty times greater than those of the whites in the same States, and clearly proves that a state of freedom is one of the greatest curses you can inflict on them.

From the opinions expressed respecting the Southern States and the slaves there, it appears to me most clear, that the members on the opposite side know nothing of the Southern States, their lands, products, or slaves. Those who visit us, or go to the southward, find so great a difference that many of them remain and settle there. I perfectly recollect when, in 1791, General Washington visited South Carolina, he was so surprised at the richness, order, and soil of our country, that he expressed his great astonishment at the state of agricultural improvement and excellence our tide-lands exhibited. He said, he had no idea the United States possessed it. Had I then seen as much of Europe as I have since, I would have replied to him, that he would not see its equal in Europe. Sir, when we recollect that our former parent State was the original cause of introducing slavery into America, and that neither ourselves nor ancestors are chargeable with it; that it cannot be got rid of without ruining the country, certainly the present mild treatment of our slaves is most honorable to that part of the country where slavery exists. Every slave has a comfortable house, is well fed, clothed, and taken care of; he has his family about him, and in sickness has the same medical aid as his master, and has a sure and comfortable retreat in old age, to protect him against its infirmities and weakness. During the whole of his life he is free from care, that canker of the human heart, which destroys at least one-half of the thinking part of mankind, and from which a favored few, very few, if indeed any, can be said to be free. Being without education, and born to obey, to persons of that description moderate labor and discipline are essential. The discipline ought to be mild, but still, while slavery is to exist, there must be discipline. In this state they are happier than they can possibly be if free. A free black can only be happy where he has some share of education, and has been bred to a trade, or some kind of business. The great body of slaves are happier in their present situation than they could be in any other, and the man or men who would attempt to give them freedom would be their greatest enemies.

All the writers who contend that the slaves increase faster than the free blacks, if they assert what is true, prove that the black, when in the condition of a slave, is happier than when free, as, in proportion to the comfort and happiness of any kind of people, such will be the increase; and the next census will show what has been the increase of both descriptions, free and slave, and will, I think, prove the truth of these opinions.

In this discussion the question as to the purchase of Louisiana has been introduced, and gives me an opportunity to state my opinion on the subject. So far as my knowledge of the facts, preceding that purchase, enable me to form an opinion, I pronounce that Mr. Jefferson, in planning the purchase, and the gentlemen who were employed in negotiating it, covered themselves with glory. The facts that preceded that purchase were these: In the year 1786, Spain despatched a Minister, named Gardoqui, to this country, instructed to offer to form with us a treaty of commerce, which she said was an advantageous one, if we would, in the same treaty, consent to give up the navigation of that part of the river Mississippi which ran through the Spanish dominions. This, sir, I asserted on this floor some days ago, and now repeat, that, on this treaty being, according to the then routine of business, referred to Mr. Jay, then Secretary for Foreign Affairs, he did, to the best of my recollection, report that it would, in his opinion, be expedient to adopt it; that seven, all of the Eastern and Northern States, did vote for it, but that, owing to the Confederation requiring that nine States should be necessary to form a treaty, it was at length defeated. If any part of the public business in this country, in which I have been engaged, ever gave me more pleasure than others, it was the agency I had, in association with an honorable gentleman, now high in office, and in Washington, in preventing it. I believe I may venture to say, that it was owing to us the whole of the Western country now belongs to us, and that the Mississippi now flows through American lands, and that the American flag now waves alone on her waters. I, therefore, have always felt more than a fraternal—I have felt, sir, a paternal love for this country. Nor, sir, is this the only important agency I have had in the affairs of this very valuable part of our Union. It will be remembered that, in the year 1802, the Intendant of New Orleans issued a proclamation, shutting that port to the further reception and deposit of American produce, under the treaty of 1795, and that, on his doing so, a ferment was excited throughout the Union, of the most alarming nature; that war was called for, both in the Senate and out of doors, which it was difficult for all the prudence and love of peace of the President to repress. Being, at that time, the Minister of the United States in Spain, I received instructions from our government to use every exertion in my power, consistent with its dignity, to get the deposit restored, which I fortunately did, and this affair led to the acquisition of both the river and whole country in the manner you know. At the time I went to Europe, I was alone commissioned and authorized to treat for, and purchase, all the part of Louisiana, including New Orleans, to the east of the Mississippi and the Floridas; but, on arriving in Europe, I found Louisiana had been previously secretly sold to Bonaparte, of which I informed Mr. Jefferson, and he took the measures which accomplished the purpose.

In pursuing the arguments of some gentlemen on this subject, I have omitted to notice one of their arguments springing from that part of the third section of the fourth article, which says, "the Congress shall have the power to make all needful rules and regulations respecting the territory, or other property belonging to the United States," because this article certainly refers only to the territorial state, to which I have already referred, and in which, I do not hesitate to aver, that, in making such regulations for the government of the territory, they are no more authorized to inhibit slavery in the territory, than they are in the State—for, if they should have the power, it would indirectly effect the same thing; it not being difficult to see, that, when a territory has been, like Missouri, for sixteen years in a strict state of territorial discipline, prohibiting slavery, when the period arrives for her admission as a State, she will be peopled entirely by inhabitants not having slaves, and who will, of course, insert the prohibition in their constitution.

It ought to be remembered, Mr. Chairman, that the greatest part of the debt due for Louisiana is still unpaid, and that, if the mode I have asserted, by which your treasury is now furnished, and must be in future, is true, then the slaveholding States will have more than half of the purchase to pay; but, suppose we have only one-half of it to pay, is it not fair, is it not just, that the use of this purchase should be as open to the inhabitants of the slaveholding, as to the inhabitants of the non-slaveholding States? And how can this happen, if you say to the inhabitants of the Northern States, you may go there with your families, and all your properties; but, if you, from the Southern or slaveholding States, choose to go there, it must be without your slaves, these shall not go? thus denying to these the instruments of their agriculture, and the means of their comfort, and completely preventing the possibility of their removing. From this, sir, will arise another evil, that of the fall of the value of all the lands the United States may have to sell in the Territories or States from which slavery is excluded, at least one-half, which, if the computations of the number of acres come any thing near the mark, must amount to at least six hundreds of millions of dollars to the common treasury.

I have not condescended to notice the remark, that one of the evils of slavery is, the lessening and depreciating the character of the whites in the slaveholding States, and rendering it less manly and republican, and less worthy, than in the non-slaveholding States, because it is not less decorous than true; it is refuted in a moment by a review of the revolutionary, and particularly the last war. Look into your histories, compare the conduct of the heroes and statesmen of the North and South, in both those wars, in the field and in the Senate; see the monuments of valor, of wisdom, and patriotism, they have left behind them, and then ask an impartial world, on which side the Delaware lies the preponderance: they will answer in a moment, to the South.

It will not be a matter of surprise to any one, that so much anxiety should be shown by the slaveholding States, when it is known that the alarm, given by this attempt to legislate on slavery, has led to the opinion that the very foundations of that kind of property are shaken; that the establishment of the precedent is a measure of the most alarming nature; for, should succeeding Congresses continue to push it, there is no knowing to what length it may be carried.

Have the Northern States any idea of the value of our slaves? At least, sir, six hundred millions of dollars. If we lose them, the value of the lands they cultivate will be diminished in all cases one-half, and, in many, they will become wholly useless, and an annual income of at least forty millions of dollars will be lost to your citizens; the loss of which will not alone be felt by the non-slaveholding States, but by the whole Union; for, to whom, at present, do the Eastern States most particularly, and the Eastern and Northern generally, look for the employment of their shipping, in transporting our bulky and valuable products, and bringing us the manufactures and merchandises of Europe? Another thing, in case of these losses being brought on us, and our being forced into a division, what becomes of your public debt? Who are to pay this, and how will it be paid? In a pecuniary view of this subject, therefore, it must ever be the policy of the Eastern and Northern States to continue connected with us. But, sir, there is an infinitely greater call upon them, and this is the call of justice, of affection, and humanity. Reposing at a great distance, in safety, in the full enjoyment of all their federal and State rights, unattacked in either, or in their individual rights, can they, with indifference, or ought they to risk, in the remotest degree, the consequences which this measure may produce. These may be the division of this Union, and a civil war. Knowing that whatever is said here, must get into the public prints, I am unwilling, for obvious reasons, to go into the description of the horrors which such a war must produce, and ardently pray that none of us may ever live to witness such an event.

If you refuse to admit Missouri without this prohibition, and she refuses it, and proceeds to form a constitution for herself, and then applies to you for admission, what will you do? Will you compel them by force? By whom, or by what force can this be effected? Will the States in her neighborhood join in this crusade? Will they who, to a man, think Missouri is right, and you are wrong, arm in such a cause? Can you send a force from the eastward of the Delaware? The very distance forbids it; and distance is a powerful auxiliary to a country attacked. If, in the days of James II., English soldiers, under military discipline, when ordered to march against their countrymen, contending in the cause of liberty, disobeyed the order, and laid down their arms, do you think our free brethren on the Mississippi will not do the same? Yes, sir, they will refuse, and you will at last be obliged to retreat from this measure, and in a manner that will not add much to the dignity of your government.

I cannot, on any ground, think of agreeing to a compromise on this subject. However we all may wish to see Missouri admitted, as she ought, on equal terms with the other States, this is a very unimportant object to her, compared with keeping the Constitution inviolate—with keeping the hands of Congress from touching the question of slavery. On the subject of the Constitution, no compromise ought ever to be made. Neither can any be made on the national faith, so seriously involved in the treaty which gives to all Louisiana, to every part of it, a right to be incorporated into the Union on equal terms with the other States.

Surely, sir, when we consider the public distress of this country, and the necessity of union and good humor to repair our finances, and place our commerce in that improved situation which will give us some hope of the rise of our products, such as may have a tendency to relieve our public and private embarrassments, if we had no other motives for it, certainly this should be sufficient. But, sir, there is one of infinitely higher moment. Do we recollect, that we are the only free republic now in existence, and that, probably, such existence can only depend upon our distance from Europe, and our union with our present numbers? It may safely be calculated we have two millions of men, the greatest part of whom are able to bear arms.

In case of our continuing a united people, no attack from Europe, a distance of four thousand miles, could ever be made with the least hope of success. From the distance, all Europe could not furnish either the men or the means sufficient to divide or destroy this Union. If we continue united, as we have been, in such an event, the States would so second the general government, and so nerve its arm, as to put all attack at defiance. But, if on this, or any other occasion, this Union should unhappily divide, and from friends become bitter and implacable enemies to each other, who shall say what Europe may attempt? Mark what they have done among themselves, to subjugate France, and destroy, in that part of the world, everything that has the semblance of republicanism. View the league they have formed, in which, for the first time, all Europe is seen united as a single government, to maintain their monarchical forms. Such is, no doubt, their detestation of everything like republicanism, that, were the United States in Europe, where they could be reached by land, I have not the smallest doubt, they would long since have been attacked, and every attempt made to reduce them to a monarchy. We are considered, sir, as an evil example to the monarchical world. We are considered as the only repository of those principles which have lately appeared and flourished for a time in Europe, and which it has cost them so much blood and treasure to suppress; and should our divisions, from friends to enemies, ever afford them an opportunity of striking at us, with the least probability of success, no doubt they will do so.

I will not trespass further on your patience, but thank the committee for the honor they have done me by their attention. I hope the great importance of the subject will be my excuse; and that, considering the relation in which I have stood to the Western country and the Mississippi, for the salvation of which, so far as means the keeping it annexed to this Union, as I have already said, I think I may claim to a gentleman, now high in office, and myself, as much as any other two can claim, the happiness of being the instruments, and having thus, in the early part of my life, labored with success for the parent, I cannot but think it a little extraordinary that I should, at this distant period, be called upon to defend the right of her children. My fervent wish is, that I may be able to do it with the same success.

Extract from the speech of Mr. Whitman, of Massachusetts, on the Missouri bill, which may be found in the sixteenth volume of Niles's Register. It was delivered upon the occasion of a motion to apply the slavery restriction in the Arkansas territorial bill:

"We should consider that we have, by our common and joint funds, acquired a large tract of vacant territory west of the Mississippi : that it is valuable to our country, as furnishing a fertile region for the citizens of our country to resort to for the purpose of bettering their condition, acquiring property, and providing for their children. The two great sections of the Union—to wit, the slaveholding and non-slaveholding sections—have an equal right to its enjoyment. By permitting slavery in every part of it, the non-slaveholding portion will be deprived of it; if not entirely, certainly in a very great degree. On the other hand, if the people of the South cannot carry their slaves with them when they emigrate, the benefit will be equally lost to them."

Extract from the speech of Mr. Shaw, of Massachusetts, on the Missouri bill, in 1820.

"The opinion of mutual interest, is the chain which binds these States together. Change this opinion, for one, that a section of this country is hostile to the interest of another, and distrust and jealousy ensue: make that hostility palpable, and the Union would not last a day. The slaveholding States, like the non-slaveholding States, are alive to all questions that touch their property: and, however humiliating it may be to speak of human beings as property, the Constitution and laws of our country consider the slaves of the South as such. Any question calculated to affect the value, or the right to this species of population, could not but be regarded by our countrymen of the south with the utmost jealousy. The country west of the Mississippi was purchased with the joint funds of the nation; all, therefore, had a joint interest in it. But the amendment proposed, by excluding slaves, absolutely excluded the population of all the southern and a part of the western States from that fertile domain. This furnished another ground of distrust: besides, it exhibited a spirit of monopoly altogether incompatible with that harmony and good will so essential in preserving the Union of the States; it created a distinction between slaveholding and non-slaveholding States—a distinction that loses none of its mischievous quality from the ability to trace it on the map of our country. Who that regards the union of the States, can contemplate the feelings which the agitation of this question excited, without emotion? And who, in reflecting upon it, is not strongly reminded of the admonition of the Father of his Country, to 'frown with indignation upon the first dawnings of an attempt to array one portion of the inhabitants of this country against another'?

"And, after all, what has this question to do with the principle of slavery? Our ancestors brought this unfortunate race of beings into our country; they have multiplied to an alarming extent; they are the property of our fellow citizens, secured to them by the Constitution and laws of the United States. Their number forbids the idea of general emancipation. What, then, does policy require in relation to them? That we should prevent the increase by importation, by the most rigid execution of the severest penalties. This we are attempting; and I had the pleasure of voting for a law at the late session, inflicting the penalty of death on any one convicted of importing a slave into the United States. What does humanity demand? That we should confine them forever within the present limits of the slaveholding States, or suffer the master to emigrate with his slaves into western America, where, from the extent, the fertility and productions of the country, they must be more tenderly treated, better fed, and in all respects their condition ameliorated."

Extract from the speech of Mr. Holmes, of Massachusetts, on the Missouri bill—the same gentleman to whom

Jefferson addressed his celebrated letter on the Missouri question:

"But this division, (upon the question of slave territory,) he says, is singularly unfortunate. It is the only subject in which the slaveholding States could be made to unite against the rest. Are the general interests of Delaware more united with those of Georgia than Pennsylvania? Are the interests of Ohio more coincident with Massachusetts than Kentucky? Sir, the hopes and prospects of the north and east are interwoven with the prosperity of the south and west; and yet we have armed ourselves against them all. It is not with them a question of *policy*, of *political power*, but of SAFETY, PEACE, EXISTENCE. They consider it is hastening and provoking scenes of insurrection and massacre. Their jealousy and their sensibility are roused; and they demand what motive, what inducement, you have to this? They are answered, 'Humanity!' In the name of humanity, desist. She asks no such sacrifices at her altar. Create jealousies, heartburnings, and hatred—set brother against brother—kindle the flames of civil discord—destroy the Union—and your liberties are gone. And then where will your slaves find the freedom which you have proffered them at the expense of your own?"

*　　*　　*　　*　　*　　*

"New States may be admitted, and no difference is authorized. The authority is to admit or not, but not to prescribe conditions. What would be a fair construction of this? Surely not that Congress might hold a territory in a colonial condition as long as they choose, nor that they might admit a new State with less political rights than another, *but that the admission should be as soon as the people needed, and were capable of supporting a State government.*"—*National Intelligencer*, Feb. 19, 1820.

Mr. J. Barbour, at that time a Senator in Congress from the State of Virginia, said:

"What, then, is your power? Simply whether you will admit or refuse. This is the limit of your power. And even this power is subject to control, *whenever a Territory is sufficiently large, and its population sufficiently numerous, your discretion ceases, and the obligation becomes imperious that you forthwith admit; for I hold that, according to the spirit of the Constitution, the people thus circumstanced are entitled to the privilege of self-government.*"—*National Intelligencer, March* 18, 1820.

CHAPTER VIII.

OPINIONS OF MADISON, JEFFERSON AND HARRISON.

Mr. Madison to President Monroe.—Extracts from a letter dated Montpelier, Feb. 23d, 1820.

"I RECEIVED yours of the 19th, on Monday. * * * * The pinch of the difficulty in the case stated, seems to be in words "forever," coupled with the interdict relating to the territory north of latitude 36° 30'. If the necessary import of these words be, that they are to operate as a condition on future States admitted into the Union, and as a restriction on them after admission, they seem to encounter, indirectly, the arguments which prevailed in the Senate for an unconditional admission of Missouri. I must conclude, therefore, from the assent of the Senate to the words, after the strong vote, on constitutional grounds, against the restriction on Missouri, that there is some other mode of explaining them in their actual application.

As to the right of Congress, to apply such a restriction during the *territorial* period, it depends on the clause especially providing for the management of those subordinate establishments.

On one side it naturally occurs, *that the right being given from the necessity of the case,* and in suspension *of the great principle of self-government,* ought not to be extended further, nor continued longer, than the occasion might fairly require.

On the other side, it cannot be denied that the constitutional phrase "to all rules," &c., as expounded by uniform practice, is somewhat of a ductile nature, and leaves much to legislative discretion. The question to be decided seems to be—

"1. Whether a *territorial* restriction be an assumption of illegitimate power; or,

"2. A misuse of legitimate power; and if the latter only, whether the injury threatened to the nation from an acquiescence in the misuse, or from a frustration of it, be the greater.

"On the first point, there is certainly room for difference of opinion; though for myself, I must own that I have always leaned to the belief that *the restriction was not within the true scope of the Constitution.*

In reply to a letter from Mr. Monroe, on the Missouri question he said: "The question to be decided seem to be—

"1. Whether a *territoral* restriction be an assumption of illegitimate power; or,

"2 A misuse of legitimate power; and if the latter only, whether the injury threatened to the nation from an acquiescence in the misuse, or from a frustration of it, be the greater.

"On the first point, there is certainly room for difference of opinion; though, for myself, I must own that I have always leaned in the belief that the restriction was not within the true scope of the Constitution.

"On the alternative presented by the second point, there can be no room, with the cool and candid, for blame in those acquiescing in a conciliatory course, the demand for which was deemed urgent, and the course itself deemed not irreconcilable with the Constitution.

"This is the hasty view I have taken of the subject. I am aware that I may be suspected of being influenced by the habit of a guarded construction of constitutional powers; and I have certainly felt all the influence that could justly flow from a conviction, that an uncontrolled dispersion of the slaves now within the United States, was not only best for the nation, but most favorable for the slaves also, both as to their prospects of emancipation, and as to their condition in the mean time."

As to the reason of the passage of the Ordinance of 1787, under the old Confederation, Mr. Madison says:—

"I have observed, as yet, in none of the views taken of the Ordinance of 1787, interdicting slavery northwest of the river Ohio, an allusion to the circumstance that when it passed, Congress had no authority to prohibit the importation of slaves from abroad; that all the States had, and some were in the full exercise of, the right to import them; and, consequently, that there was no mode in which Congress could check the evil, but the indirect one of narrowing the space open for the reception of slaves.

"Had a federal authority then existed to prohibit, directly and totally, the importation from abroad, can it be doubted that it would have been exerted, and that a regulation having merely the effect of preventing the interior disposition of slaves actually in the United States, and creating a distinction among the States in the degree of their sovereignty, would not have been adopted, or perhaps thought of?"—Mr. Madison to Mr. Monroe, February 10th, 1820.

Rough draught, or notes, of President Monroe's intended Veto Message, rejecting the Missouri Bill, if it had passed Congress with certain restrictions, found in his handwriting, among his papers in possession of S. L. Gouverneur, Esq.

Having fully considered the bill entitled, &c., and disapproved of it, I now return it to the —— in which it originated, with my objections to the same.

That the Constitution, in providing that new States may

be admitted into the Union, as is done by the third section of the fourth article, intended that they should be admitted with all the rights and immunities of the original States, retaining, like them, all the powers as to their local governments, all the powers ceded to it by the Constitution.

That if conditions of a character not applicable to the original States should be imposed on a new State, an inequality would be imposed or created, lessening in degree the right of State sovereignty, which would always be degrading to such new State, and which, operating as a condition of its admission, its incorporation would be incomplete, and would also be annulled, and such new State be severed from the Union, should afterwards assume equality, and exercise a power acknowledged to belong to all the original States.

That the proposed restriction to territories which are to be admitted into the Union, *if not in direct violation of the Constitution*, IS REPUGNANT TO ITS PRINCIPLES, since it is intended to produce an effect on the future policy of the new States, operating unequally in regard to the original States, injuring those affected by it, in an interest protected from such injury by the Constitution, without benefiting any State in the Union; and that, in this sense, it is repugnant to the generous spirit which has ["so long" erased] always existed and been cherished by the several States toward each other.

That the first clause of the ninth section of the first article, which provides that "the migration or importation of such persons as any of the States now existing shall think proper to admit, shall not be prohibited by the Congress prior," &c., in whatever sense the term migration or importation may be understood, whether as applicable to the same description of persons or otherwise, confines the power of Congress exclusively to persons entering the United States, or who might be disposed to enter, FROM ABROAD, and precludes ALL INTERFERENCE *with such persons*, or any other persons, who had previously entered according to the laws of any of the States.

That by the third section of the first article, whereby it is provided that representation and direct taxes shall be apportioned among the several States which may be included within this Union, according to the whole number of free persons, including those bound to service for a number of years, and excluding Indians not taxed, three-fifths of all other persons—[the words "*the persons held in bondage*" erased,] slavery, as existing under the laws of the several States, [the word "*were*" erased] was not only recognized, but [the word "secured" erased] its political existence was secured to the States, which it would be unjust to the States within which such persons are to deprive them of, as it would be inhuman to the persons themselves.

That should the slaves be confined to the States in which slavery exists, as the free people will continue to emigrate, the disproportion between them will in a few years be very great, and at no distant period the whole country will fall into the hands of the blacks. As soon as this disproportion reaches a certain State, the white population would probably abandon those States to avoid insurrection and massacre. What would become of the country without States? Would the general government ["*protect*" erased] support the owners of slaves in their authority over them, after the States individually had lost the power?—or the slaves being in possession of those States, and independent of their owners, would the States be recognized as belonging to them, and their representatives be received in Congress.

That it would be better to compel the whites to remain, and the blacks to move, &c.

That slavery is not the offspring of this Revolution; that it took place in our colonial state; that all further importations have been prohibited since the Revolution, under laws which are vigorously enforced; that in our revolutionary struggle, the States in which slavery existed sustained their share in the common burdens, furnished their equal quotas of troops, and paid their equal share of taxes; that slavery, though a national evil, is felt most sensibly by the States in which it exists; that it would be destructive to the whites to confine it there, and to the *blacks*, as the distribution of them over an extensive territory, and among many owners, will secure them a better treatment; that the extension of it to new States cannot possibly injure the old, as they will claim all their rights, since no attempt can ever be made, or idea entertained, of requiring them to admit slavery; that an attempt to fix on the States having slavery any odium is unmerited, and would be ungenerous.

Mr. Jefferson to President Monroe.—Extract from a letter dated Monticello, March 3d, 1820.

"I am indebted to you for your two letters of February 7th and 19th. This Missouri question, by a geographical line of division, is the most portentous one I have ever contemplated. * * * * is ready to risk the Union for any chance of restoring his party to power and wriggling himself to the head of it; nor is * * * * * * * without his hopes, nor scrupulous as to the means of fulfilling them. I hope I shall be spared the pains of witnessing it, either by the good sense of the people, or by the more certain reliance—the hand of death. On this or that side of the Styx, I am ever and devotedly yours."

In a letter, dated on the 13th of April, 1820, he says;

"The old schism of Federal and Republican threatened nothing, because it existed in every State, and united them together by the fraternism of party; but the coincidence of a marked principle, moral and political, with a geographical line, once conceived, I feared, would never more be obliterated from the mind; that it would be recurring on every occasion, and renewing irritations until it would kindle such mutual and mortal hatred, as to render separation preferable to eternal discord. I have been amongst the most sanguine in believing that our Union would be of long duration. I now doubt it much; and see the event at no great distance, and the direct consequence of this question.

On the 20th of December, 1820, he wrote thus:

"Nothing has ever presented so threatening an aspect as what is called the Missouri question. The Federalists, completely put down, and despairing of ever rising again under the old divisions of Whig and Tory, devised a new one, of slaveholding and non-slaveholding States, which, while it had a semblance of being moral, was at the same time geographical, and calculated to give them ascendency by debauching their old opponents to a coalition with them. Moral, the question certainly is not, because the removal of slaves from one State to another, no more than their removal from one country to another, would never make a slave of one human being who would not be so without it. Indeed, if there be any morality in the question, it is on the other side, because, by spreading them over a larger surface their happiness would be increased, and the burden of their future liberation lightened, by bringing a greater number of shoulders under it. However, it seemed to throw dust into the eyes of the people, and to fanaticize them, while to the knowing ones it gave a geographical and preponderating line of the Potomac and Ohio, throwing fourteen States to the North and East and ten to the South and West. With these, therefore, it is merely a question of power. But with this geographical minority it is a question of existence; for if Congress once goes out of the Constitution to arrogate the right of regulating the condition of the inhabitants of the States, its majority may, and probably will declare, that the condition of all within the United States shall be that of freedom; in which case all the whites south of the Potomac and the Ohio must evacuate their States, and most fortunate those who can do it first."

And in this letter, after speculating on the probable consequence of the threatened disunion, he adds:

"Should the scission take place, one of its most deplorable consequences would be its discouragement of the efforts of European nations, in the regeneration of their oppressive and cannibal governments."

In a letter of the same date (20th of December) to the Marquis de Lafayette, he prophetically shadows forth, what we now see realized, with the same precision as if he were the historian of to-day.

"With us things are going well. The boisterous sea of liberty, indeed, is never without a wave; and that from Missouri is now rolling towards us. But we shall ride over it as we have done over all others. It is not a moral question, but one merely of power. Its object is to raise a geographical principle for the choice of a President, and the noise will be kept up till that is effected. All know that permitting the slaves of the South to spread into the West, will not add one being to that unfortunate condition; that it will increase the happiness of those existing, and by spreading them over a large surface will dilate the evil everywhere, and facilitate the means of getting finally rid of it."

So thought and so wrote Jefferson, on the question which divided and threatened us then, as it divides and threatens us now.

Mr. Jefferson was minister to France whilst the Convention sat which formed the Constitution; and Mr. Mason, at whose relation he recorded this scrap of history, was a member of that Convention, and it is dated at the family seat of the relator, (Gunston Hall,) some four years only after the event.

September 30th, 1792. "Ex relatione G. Mason. The

Constitution, as agreed to, till a fortnight before the Convention rose, was such an one as he would have set his hand and heart to. 1. The President was to be elected for seven years, then ineligible for seven years more. 2. Rotation in the Senate. 3. A vote of two-thirds in the legislature on particular subjects, and expressly on that of navigation. The three New England States were constantly with us in all questions—(Rhode Island not there, and New York seldom.) So that it was these three States, with the five Southern ones, against Pennsylvania, Jersey, and Delaware With respect to the importation of slaves, it was left to Congress. This disturbed the two southernmost States, who knew that Congress would immediately suppress the importation of slaves. These two States, therefore, struck up a bargain with the three New England States: if they would join to admit slaves for some years, the two southernmost States would join in changing the clause which required two-thirds of the legislature in any vote. It was done. These articles were changed accordingly, and from that moment the two Southern States and the three Northern ones joined Pennsylvania, Jersey, and Delaware, and made the majority 8 to 3 against us, instead of 8 to 3 for us, as it had been through the whole Convention. Under this coalition, the great principles of the Constitution were changed in the last days of the Convention."

In a letter to Mr. Adams, dated January 22d, 1821, he says:

"Our anxieties in this quarter are all concentrated in the question, What does the Holy Alliance in and out of Congress mean to do with us on the Missouri question? And this, by the by, is but the name of the case, it is only the John Doe or Richard Roe of the ejectment. The real question, as seen in the States afflicted with this unfortunate population, is, Are our slaves to be presented with freedom and a dagger? For if Congress has the power to regulate the conditions of the inhabitants of the States, within the

States, it will be but another exercise of that power to declare that all shall be free."

Again, in a letter to General Lafayette, dated November 4th, 1823, he uses the following striking language:

"On the eclipse of federalism with us, although not its extinction, its leaders got up the Missouri question, under the false front of lessening the measure of slavery, but with the real view of producing a geographical division of parties, which might insure them the next President. The people of the North went blindfold into the snare, followed their leaders for a while with a zeal truly moral and laudable, until they became sensible that they were injuring instead of aiding the real interests of the slaves; that they had been used merely as tools for electioneering purposes; and that trick of hypocrisy then fell as quickly as it had been got up."

General (afterwards President) Harrison to President Monroe.—Extract of a Letter dated North Bend, June 16, 1823.

"In relation to the Missouri question, I am, and have been for many years, so much opposed to slavery, that I will never live in a State where it exists. But I believe that the Constitution has given no power to the General Government to interfere in this matter, and that to have slaves or no slaves, depends upon the will of the people in each State alone.

"Besides the constitutional objection, I am persuaded that the obvious tendency of such interferences on the part of the States which have no slaves with the property of their fellow citizens of the others, is to produce a state of discord and jealousy that will, in the end, prove fatal to the Union. I believe in no other State are such wild and dangerous sentiments entertained on this subject as in Ohio, and I claim the merit of being the only person of any political standing in the State who publicly oppose them."

CHAPTER IX.

FUGITIVE SLAVES—ORDINANCE OF 1787—THE CONSTITUTION—ACT OF 1793.

(*From Benton's Thirty Years.*)

It is of record proof that the anti-slavery clause in the Ordinance of 1787, could not be passed until the fugitive slave recovery clause was added to it. That anti-slavery clause, first prepared in the Congress of the Confederation by Mr. Jefferson, in 1784, was rejected, and remained rejected for three years, until 1787; when, receiving the additional clause for the recovery of fugitives, it was unanimously passed. This is clear proof that the first clause, that prohibiting slavery in the Northwest Territory, could not be obtained without the second, authorizing the recovery of slaves who should take refuge in that territory. It was a compromise between the slave States and the free States, unanimously agreed upon by both parties, and founded on a valuable consideration, one preventing the spread of slavery over a vast extent of country, the other retaining the right of property in the slaves which might flee to it. Simultaneously with the adoption of this article in the Ordinances, in 1787, was the formation of the Constitution of the United States, both formed at the same time in neighboring cities, and (it may be said) by the same men. The Congress sat in New York, the Federal Convention in Philadelphia; and while the most active members of both were members of each, as Madison and Hamilton, yet, by constant interchange of opinion, the members of both bodies may be assumed to have worked together for a common object. The right to recover fugitive slaves went into the Constitution as it went into the Ordinance, simultaneously and unanimously; and it may be assumed upon the facts of the case, and all the evidence of the day, that the Constitution, no more than the Ordinance, could have been formed without the fugitive slave recovery clause contained in it. A right to recover slaves is not only authorized in the Constitution, but it is a right without which there would have been no Constitution, and also no anti-slavery Ordinance.

One of the early acts of Congress, as early as February, 1793, was a statute to carry into effect the clause in the Constitution for the reclamation of fugitives from justice and fugitives from labor; and that statute made by the men who made the Constitution, as interpreted by men who had a right to know its meaning. That act consisted of four sections, all brief and clear, and the first two applied exclusively to fugitives from justice. The third and fourth applied to fugitives from labor, embracing apprentices as well as slaves, and applying the same rights and remedies in each case: and of these two, the third alone contains the whole provisions for reclaiming the fugitive—the fourth merely containing penalties for the obstruction of that right. The third section, then, is the only one essential to the object of this chapter, and is in these words:

"That when a person held to labor in any of the United States, or in either of the territories on the northwest or south of Ohio, under the laws thereof, shall escape into any other of said States or territories, the person to whom such labor is due, his agent or attorney, is hereby empowered to seize or arrest such fugitive from labor, and to take him or her before any judge of the circuit or district courts of the United States, residing or being within the State, or before any magistrate of a county, city, or town corporate, wherein such seizure or arrest shall be made, and upon proof to the satisfaction of such judge or magistrate, either by oral testimony, or by affidavit taken before and certified by a magistrate, of any such State or territory, that the person so seized and arrested, doth, under the laws of the State or territory from which he or she fled, owe service to the persons claiming him or her, it shall be the duty of such judge or magistrate to give a certificate thereof to such claimant, his agent or attorney, which shall be sufficient warrant for removing the said fugitive from labor to the State or territory from which he or she fled."

This act was passed on the recommendation of President Washington in consequence of a case having arisen between Pennsylvania and Virginia, which showed the want of an act of Congress to carry the clause in the Constitution into effect. It may be held to be a fair interpretation of the Constitution, and by it the party claiming the service of the fugitive in any State or territory had the right to seize his slave whenever he saw him, and to carry him before a judicial authority in the State; and upon affidavit or oral testimony, showing his right, he was to receive a certificate to that effect, by virtue of which he might carry him back to the State from which he had fled. This act, fully recognizing the right of the claimant to seize his slave by mere virtue of ownership, and then to carry him out of the State upon a certificate and without a trial, was passed as good as unanimously by the second Congress which sat under the Constitution—the proceedings of the Senate showing no division, and in the House only seven voting against the bill, there being no separate votes on the two parts of it, and two of these seven from the slave States (Virginia and Maryland). It does not appear to what these seven objected—whether to the fugitive slave sections, or those which applied to fugitives from justice. Such unanimity in its passage by those who helped to make the Constitution was high evidence in its favor; the conduct of the

States, and both judiciaries, State and federal, were to the same effect. The act was continually enforced, and the courts decided that this right of the owner to seize his slave was just as large in the free State to which he had fled as in the slave State from which he had run away— that he might seize, by night as well as by day, on Sunday as well as other days, and also in a house, provided no breach of the peace was committed. The penal section in the bill was clear and heavy, and went upon the ground of the absolute right of the master to seize his slave by his own authority wherever he saw him, and the criminality of any obstruction or resistance in the exercise of that right. It was in these words:

"That any person who shall knowingly and wilfully obstruct or hinder such claimant, his agent or attorney, in so seizing or arresting such fugitive from labor, or shall rescue such fugitive from such claimant, his agent or attorney, when so arrested pursuant to the authority herein given or declared; or shall harbor, or conceal such persons after notice that he or she was a fugitive from labor as aforesaid, shall, for either of the said offenses, forfeit and pay the sum of five hundred dollars, which penalty may be recovered by and for the benefit of such claimant, by action of debt in any court proper to try the same, saving, moreover, to the person claiming such labor or service his right of action for or on account of the said injuries, or either of them."

State officers, the magistrates and judges, though not bound to act under the law of Congress, yet did so; and State jails, though not obligatory under a federal law, were freely used for the recaptured fugitives. This continued till a late day in most of the free States—in all of them until after the Congress of the United States engaged in the slavery agitation—and in the great State of Pennsylvania until the 20th March, 1847; this is to say, until a month after Mr. Calhoun brought into the Senate the slavery resolutions, stigmatized by Mr. Benton as "firebrand" at the moment of their introduction, and which are since involving the Union in conflagration. Then Pennsylvania passed the law forbidding her judicial authorities to take cognizance of any fugitive slave case—granted a habeas corpus remedy to any fugitives arrested—denying the use of her jails to confine any one, and repealing the six months' slave sojourning law of 1780.

Some years before the passage of this harsh act, and before the slavery agitation had commenced in Congress, to wit, 1826 (which was nine years before the commencement of the agitation) Pennsylvania had passed a most liberal law of her own, done upon the request of Maryland, to aid the recovery of fugitive slaves. It was entitled "*An Act to give effect to the Constitution of the United States in reclaiming fugitives from justice.*" Such has been the just and generous conduct of Pennsylvania toward the slave States until up to the passing the harsh act of 1847. Her legal right to pass that act is admitted; her magistrates were not bound to act under the federal law—her jails were not liable to be used for federal purposes. The sojourning law of 1780 was her own, and she had a right to repeal it. But the whole act of 1847 was the exercise of a mere right, against the comity which is due to states united under a common head, against moral and social duty, against high national policy, against the spirit in which the Constitution was made, against her own previous conduct for sixty years, and injurious and irritating to the people of the slave States, and part of it unconstitutional. The denial of the intervention of her judicial officers, and the use of her prisons, though an inconvenience, was not insurmountable, and might be remedied by Congress; the repeal of the act of 1780 was the radical injury, and for which there was no remedy in federal legislation.

That act was passed before the adoption of the Constitution, and while the feelings of cordiality, good-will, and entire justice prevailed among the States, it was allowed to continue in force nearly sixty years after the Constitution was made, and was a proof of good feeling toward all during that time. By the terms of this act, a discrimination was established between sojourners and permanent residents, and the elements of time—the most obvious and easy of all arbiters—was taken for the rule of discrimination. Six months was the time allowed to discriminate a sojourn from a residence; and during that time the rights of the owner remained complete in his slave; after the lapse of that time, his ownership ceased. This six months was equally in favor of all persons. But there was further and indefinite provisions in favor of members of Congress, and of the federal government, all of whom coming from slave States, were allowed to retain their ownership as long as their federal duties required them to remain the States. Such an act was just and wise, and in accordance with the spirit of comity which should prevail among States formed into a Union, having a common general government, and reciprocating the rights of citizenship. It is to be deplored that any event ever arose to occasion a repeal of that act. It is to be wished a spirit would arise to re-enact it, and that other of the free States should follow the example. For there were others, and several which had similar acts, and which repealed them in like manner as Pennsylvania, under the same unhappy influences, and with the same baleful consequences. New York for example—her law of discrimination between the sojourner and resident being the same in principle, and still more liberal in detail than that of Pennsylvania—allowing nine months instead of six to determine that character.

This act of New York, like that of Pennsylvania, continued undisturbed in the State until the slavery agitation took root in Congress, and was even so well established in the good opinion of the people of that State, as late as thirteen years after the commencement of that agitation, as to be boldly sustained by the candidates for the highest office. On this an eminent instance will be given in the canvass for the governorship of the State in the year 1838. In that year Mr. Marcy and Mr. Seward were the opposing candidates, and an anti-slavery meeting, held at Utica, passed a resolve to have them interrogated (among other things) on the point of repealing the slave sojournment act. Messrs. Gerrit Smith and William Jay were nominated a committee for that purpose, and fulfilled their mission so zealously as to rather overstate the terms of the act, using the word "importation" as applied to the coming of these slaves with their owners, thus: "Are you in favor of the repeal of the law which now authorizes the importation of slaves into this State, and their detention as such for the time of nine months?" Objecting to the substitution of the term importation, and stating the act correctly, both the candidates answered fully in the negative, and with reasons for their opinion. The act was first in its own term, as follows:

"Any person not being an inhabitant of this State, who shall be traveling to or from, or passing through this State, may bring with him any person lawfully held by him in slavery, and may take such person with him from this State; but the person so held in slavery shall not reside or continue in the State longer than nine months, and if such residence be continued beyond that time, such person shall be free." Replying to the interrogatory, Mr. Marcy then proceeds to give his opinion and reasons in favor of sustaining the act, which he does unreservedly:

By comparing this law with your interrogatory, you will perceive at once that the latter implies much more than the former expresses. The discrepancy between them is so great, that I suspected, at first, that you had reference to some other enactment which had escaped general notice. As none, however, can be found but the foregoing, to which the question is in any respect applicable, there will be no mistake, I presume, in assuming it to be the one you had in view. The deviation, in putting the question, from what would seem to be the plain and obvious course of directing the attention to the particular law under consideration, by referring to it in the very terms in which it is expressed or at least in language showing its objects and limitations, I do not impute to an intention to create an erroneous impression as to the law, or to ascribe to it a character of odiousness which it does not deserve; yet I think that it must be conceded that your question will induce those who are not particularly acquainted with the section of the statute to which it refers, to believe that there is a law of this State which allows a free importation of slaves into it, without restriction as to object, and without limitation as to the persons who may do so, yet this is very far from being true. This law does not permit any inhabitant of this State to bring into it any person held in slavery, under any pretense, or for any object whatsoever: nor does it allow any person of any other State or country to do so, except such person is actually passing to or from, or passing through this State. This law, in its operation and effect, only allows persons belonging to States or nations where domestic slavery exists, who happen to be traveling in this State, to be attended by their servants, whom they lawfully hold in slavery when at home, provided they do not remain within our territories longer than nine months. The difference between it and the one implied by 'your interrogatory is so manifest, that it is perhaps fair to presume, that if those by whose appointment you act in this matter had not misapprehended its character, they would not have instructed you to make it the subject of one of your questions. It is so restricted in its object, and that is so unexceptionable that it can scarcely be regarded as obnoxious to well-founded objections when viewed in its true light. Its repeal would, I apprehend, have an injurious effect upon our intercourse with some of the other States, and particularly upon their business connection with our commercial emporium. In addition to this, the repeal would have a tendency to disturb the political harmony among the members of the confederacy, without producing any beneficial result to compensate for these evils. I am not therefore in favor of it."

This is an explicit answer, meeting the interrogatory with a full negative, and implicitly rebuking the phrase, "importation," by supposing it would not have been used if the Utica convention had understood the act. Mr. Seward answered in the same spirit, and to the same effect, only giving a little more amplitude to his excellent reason. He says:

"Does not your inquiry give too broad a meaning to the section? It certainly does not confer upon any citizen of a State, or of any other country, or any citizen from any other State, except the owner of slaves in another State by virtue of the laws thereof, the right to bring slaves into this State or detain them here under any circumstances as such. I understand your inquiry, therefore, to mean, whether I am in favor of a repeal of the law which declares, in substance, that any person from the Southern or southwestern States, who may be traveling to or from or passing through the State, may bring with him and take with him any person lawfully held by him in slavery in the State from whence he came, provided such slaves do not remain here more than nine months. The article of the Constitution of the United States which bears upon the present question, declares that no person held to service or labor in one State under the laws thereof, escaping to another State, shall, in consequence of any law or regulation therein, be discharged from such service or labor, but such person shall be delivered up on claim of the party to whom such service or labor may be due. I understand that, in the State of Massachusetts, this provision of the Constitution has been decided by the courts not to include the case of a slave brought by his master into the State and escaping thence. But the courts of law in this State have uniformly given a different construction to the same article of the Constitution, and have always decided that it does embrace the case of a slave brought by his master into this State, and escaping from him here. Consequently, under this judicial construction of the Constitution, and without, and in defiance of any law or regulation of this State, if the slave escape from his master in this State, he must be restored to him, when claimed at any time during his master's temporary sojournment, within the State, whether that sojournment be six months, nine months, or longer. It is not for me to say that this decision is erroneous, nor is it for our legislature. Acting under its authority, they passed the law to which you object, for the purpose not of conferring new powers or privileges on the slave-owner, but to prevent his abuse of that which the Constitution of the United States, thus expounded, secures to him. The law, as I understood it, was intended to fix a period of time as a test of transient passage through, or temporary residence in the State, within the provisions of the Constitution. The duration of nine months is not material in the question, and if it be unnecessarily long, may and ought to be abridged. But, if no such law existed, the right of the master (under the construction of the Constitution before mentioned) would be indefinite, and the slave must be surrendered to him in all cases of traveling through or passage to or from the State. If I have correctly apprehended the subject, this law is one not conferring a right upon any person to import slaves into the State, and hold them here as such, but is an attempt at restriction upon the constitutional right of the master: a qualification, or at least a definition of it, and is in favor of the slave. Its repeal, therefore, would have the effect to put in greater jeopardy the class of persons you propose to benefit by it.

"While the construction of the Constitution adopted here is maintained, the law it would seem ought to remain upon our statute book, not as an encroachment upon the rights of man but a protection for them.

"But, gentlemen, being desirous to be entirely candid in this communication, it is proper I should add, that I am not convinced it would be either wise, expedient or humane to declare to our fellow citizens of the Southern and Southwestern States, that if they travel to or from or pass through the State of New York, they shall not bring with them the attendants whom custom, or education, or habit may have rendered necessary to them. I have not been able to discover any good object to be attained by such an act of inhospitality. It certainly can work no injury to us, nor can it be injurious to the unfortunate beings held in bondage to permit them, once perhaps in their lives, and at most on occasions few and far between, to visit a country where slavery is unknown, I can even conceive of benefits to the great cause of human liberty, from the cultivation of this intercourse with the South. I can imagine but one ground of objection, which is, that it may be regarded as an implication that this State sanctioned slavery. If this objection, were well grounded, I should at once condemn the law. But, in truth the law does not imply any such sanction. The same statute which, in necessary obedience to the Constitution of the United States as expounded, declares the exception, condemns, in the most clear and definite terms, all human bondages. I will not press the consideration flowing from the nature of our Union, and the mutual concessions on which it was founded, against the propriety of such an exclusion as your question contemplates, apparently for the purpose only of avoiding an implication not founded in fact, and which the history of our State so nobly contradicts. It is sufficient to say that such an exclusion could have no good effect practically, and would accomplish nothing in the great cause of human liberty."

These answers do not seem to have affected the election in any way. Mr. Seward was elected, each candidate receiving the full vote of his party. Since that time the act has been repealed, and no voice has been raised to restore it. Just and meritorious as were the answers of Messrs. Marcy and Seward in favor of sustaining the sojourning act, their voices in favor of its restoration would be still more so now. It was a measure in the very spirit of the Constitution, and in the very nature of a union, and in full harmony with the spirit of concession, deference, and good will in which the Constitution was founded. Several other States had acts to the same effect, and the temper of the people in all the free States was accordant. It was not until after the slavery question became a subject of *political* agitation, in the national legislature, that these acts were repealed, and this spirit destroyed. Political agitation has done all the mischief.

The act of Pennsylvania, of March 3d, 1847, beside repealing the slave sojournment act of 1780—(an act made in the time of Dr. Franklin, and which had been on her statute book near seventy years)—beside repealing her recent act of 1826, and beside forbidding the use of her prisons and the intervention of her officers in the recovery of fugitive slaves—beside all this, went on to make positive enactment to prevent the exercise of the rights of forcible recaption of fugitive slaves, as regulated by the act of Congress, under the clause in the Constitution; and for that purpose contained this section.

"That if any person or persons, claiming any negro or mulatto, as fugitive from servitude or labor, shall, under any pretense of authority whatever, violently and tumultuously seize upon and carry away in a riotous, violent, and tumultuous manner, and so as to disturb and endanger the public peace, any negro or mulatto within this commonwealth, either with or without the intention of taking such negro or mulatto before any district or circuit judge, the person or persons so offending against the peace of this commonwealth shall be deemed guilty of a misdemeanor; and, on conviction thereof, shall be sentenced to pay a fine of not less than one hundred nor more than two thousand dollars; and, further, be confined in the county jail for any period not exceeding three months, at the discretion of the court."

The granting of the habeas corpus writ to any fugitive slave, completed the enactment of this statute, which thus carried out, to the full, the ample intimations contained in its title, to-wit: *"An act to prevent kidnapping, preserve the public peace, prohibit the exercise of certain powers heretofore exercised by judges, justices of the peace, aldermen, and jailors within this commonwealth: and to repeal certain slave laws."* This act made a new starting-point in the anti-slavery movements North, as the resolutions of Mr. Calhoun, of the previous month, made a new starting-point in the pro-slavery movements in the South. The first led to the new fugitive slave recovery act of 1850; the other has led to the abrogation of the Missouri Compromise line; and between the two, the state of things has been produced which now afflicts and distracts the country, and is working a sectional divorce of the States.

A citizen of Maryland, acting under the federal law of 1793, in recapturing his slave in Pennsylvania, was prosecuted under the State act of 1826, convicted, and sentenced to its penalties. The constitutionality of this enactment was in vain pleaded in the Pennsylvania court; but her authorities acted in the spirit of deference and respect to the authorities of the Union, and concurred in an *"agreed case,"* to be carried before the Supreme Court of the United

States, to test the constitutionality of the Pennsylvania law. That court decided, fully and promptly, all the points in the case, and to the full vindication of all the rights of a slaveholder, under the recaption clause in the Constitution. The points decided cover all the ground, and, besides, show precisely in what particular the act of 1793 required to be amended, to make it work out its complete effect under the Constitution, independent of all extrinsic aid. The points were these:

"The provisions of the act of February 12th, 1793, relative to fugitive slaves, is clearly constitutional in all its leading provisions, and, indeed, with the exception of that part which confers authority on State magistrates, is free from reasonable doubt or difficulty. As to the authority so conferred on State magistrates, while a difference of opinion exists, and may exist on this point, in different States, whether State magistrates are bound to act under it, none is entertained by the Court that State magistrates may, if they choose, exercise that authority, unless forbid by State legislation." "The power of legislation in relation to fugitives from labor is exclusively in the national legislature."

"The right to seize and retake fugitive slaves, and the duty to deliver them up, in whatever State of the Union they may be found is, under the Constitution, recognized as an absolute positive right and duty, pervading the whole Union with an equal and supreme force, uncontrolled and uncontrollable by State sovereignty or State legislation. The right and duty are co-extensive and uniform in remedy and operation throughout the whole Union. The owner has the same exemptions from State regulations and control, through however many States he may pass with the fugitive slaves in his possession *in transitu* to his domicile.

"The act of the legislature of Pennsylvania, on which the indictment against Edward Prigg was founded, for carrying away a fugitive slave, is unconstitutional and void. It purports to punish, as a public offense against the State, the very act of seizing and removing a slave by his master, which the Constitution of the United States was designed to justify and uphold." "The constitutionality of the act of Congress (1793) relating to fugitives from labor has been affirmed by the adjudications of the State tribunal, and by those of the courts of the United States."

CHAPTER X.

SLAVERY IN THE DISTRICT OF COLUMBIA.

December 12, 1831. This being the first day of the session for presenting petitions, a great number were presented. Among others,

Mr. Adams, of Massachusetts, (ex-President of the United States) presented fifteen petitions, all numerously subscribed, from sundry inhabitants of Pennsylvania, all of the same purport, praying for the abolition of slavery and the slave trade in the District of Columbia, and moved that the first of them should be read, and it was read accordingly.

Mr. A. then observed that it had doubtless been remarked that these petitions came, not from Massachusetts, a portion of whose people he had the honor to represent, but from the citizens of the State of Pennsylvania. He had received the petitions many months ago, with a request that they should be presented; and, although the petitions were not of his immediate constituents, he had not deemed himself at liberty to decline presenting their petitions, the transmission of which to him manifested a confidence in him for which he was bound to be grateful. From a letter which had accompanied these petitions, he inferred that they came from members of the Society of Friends, a body of men than whom there was no more respectable and worthy class of citizens; none who more strictly made their lives a commentary on their professions; a body of men comprising, in his firm opinion, as much of human virtue, as little of human infirmity, as any other equal number of men of any denomination on the face of the globe.

The petitions, Mr. A. continued, asked for two things:

SLAVERY IN THE DISTRICT OF COLUMBIA. 309

the first was the abolition of slavery; the second, the abolition of the slave trade in the District of Columbia. There was a traffic of slaves carried on in the District, of which he did not know but that it might be a proper subject of legislation by Congress, and he therefore moved that the petition he had the honor of presenting, should be referred to the committee on the affairs of the District of Columbia, who would dispose of them as they, upon examination of their purport, should deem proper, and might report on the expediency of granting so much of the prayer of the petitioners as referred to the abolition of the slave trade in the District.

As to the other prayer of the petitioners, the abolition by Congress of slavery in the District of Columbia, it had occurred to him that the petitions might have been committed to his charge under an expectation that it would receive his countenance and support. He deemed it, therefore, his duty to declare that it would not. Whatever might be his opinion of slavery in the abstract, or of slavery in the District of Columbia, it was a subject which he hoped would not be discussed in the House; if it should be, he might perhaps assign the reasons why he could give it no countenance or support. At present, he would only say to the House, and to the worthy citizens who had committed their petitions to his charge, that the most salutary medicines, unduly administered, became the most deadly of poisons. He concluded by moving to refer the petitions to the committee for the District of Columbia.

December 19, 1831. Mr. Doddridge, from the committee for the District of Columbia, made the following report, which was read and concurred in by the House:

The committee for the District of Columbia have, according to order, had under their consideration the memorials of sundry citizens of the State of Pennsylvania, to them referred, praying the passage of such law or laws by Congress, as may be necessary for the abolition of slavery and the slave trade within the said District, and beg leave to report thereon, in part.

Considering that the District of Columbia is composed of cessions of territory made to the United States by the States of Virginia and Maryland, in both of which States slavery exists, and the territories of which surround the District, your committee are of an opinion, that until the wisdom of State governments shall have devised some practicable means of eradicating or diminishing the evil of slavery, of which the memorialists complain, it would be unwise and impolitic, if not unjust, to the adjoining States, for Congress to interfere in a subject of such delicacy and importance as is the relation between master and slave.

If, under any circumstances, such an interference on the part of Congress would be justified, your committee are satisfied that the present is an inauspicious moment for its consideration. Impressed with these views, your committee offer for the consideration of the House the following [resolution :]

Resolved, That the committee for the District of Columbia be discharged from the further consideration of so much of the prayer of the memorialists—citizens of the State of Pennsylvania asking the passage of such law or laws as may be necessary for the abolition of slavery and the slave trade within said District—as relates to the first of these objects, the abolition of slavery within said District.

December 21, 1835, petitions for the abolition of slavery in the District of Columbia, being under discussion, Hon. John Quincy Adams of Massachusetts,—rose and said he hoped the motion to reconsider this vote would not prevail; and he expressed this hope for the very reason which the gentleman from Virginia [Mr. Patton], had assigned for voting in favor of the motion. It appears to me (said Mr. A)., that the only way of getting the question from the view of the House and of the nation, is to dispose of all petitions on the subject in the same way. This is not a new opinion; I assumed this position in my very first act as a member of this House, from the very time when I first took my seat as a member of 22d Congress. At that time fifteen petitions were transmitted to me, not from my own constituents, but from citizens of the Society of Friends in the State of Pennsylvania, with a request that I should present them to the House. Sir, I did so in homage to the sacred right of petition—a right which, in whatever manner it may be treated by other members of this House, shall never be treated by me other than with respect.

But, sir, not being in favor of the object of the petitions, I then gave notice to the House and to the country, that upon the supposition that these petitions had been transmitted to me under the expectation that I should present them, I felt it my duty to say I should not support them. And, sir, the reason which I gave at that time for declining to support them was precisely the same reason which the gentleman from Virginia now gives for reconsidering this motion—namely, to keep the discussion of the subject out of the House. I said, sir, that I believed this discussion would be altogether unprofitable to the House and to the country; but, in deference to the sacred right of petition, I moved that these fifteen petitions, all of which were numerously signed, should be referred to the committee on the District of Columbia, at the head of which was, at that time, a distinguished citizen of Virginia, now, I regret to say—and the whole country has occasion to regret—no more. These petitions were thus referred, and after a short period of time, the chairman of the committee on the District of Columbia made a report to this House, which report was read, and unanimously accepted; and nothing more has been heard of these petitions from that day to this. In taking the course I then took, I was not sustained by the unanimous voice of my own constituents; there were many among them, persons as respectable and as entitled to consideration as any others, who disapproved of the course I pursued on that occasion.

Attempts were made within the district I then represented to get up meetings of the people to instruct me to pursue a different course, or to multiply petitions of the same character. These efforts were continued during the whole of that long session of Congress; but, I am gratified to add, without any other result than that, from one single town of the district which I had the honor to represent, a solitary petition was forwarded before the close of the session, with a request that I would present it to the House. Sir, I did present it, and it was referred to the same committee on the District of Columbia, and I believe nothing more has been heard of it since. From the experience of this session, I was perfectly satisfied that the true and only method of keeping this subject out of discussion was, to take that course; to refer all petitions of this kind to the committee on the District of Columbia, or some other committee of the House, to receive their report, and to accept it unanimously. This does equal justice to all parties in the country; it avoids the discussion of this agitating question on the one hand, and on the other, it pays due respect to the right of the constituent to petition.

Two years afterwards, similar petitions were presented, and at that time an effort made, without success, to do that which has now been done successfully in one instance. An effort was made to lay these petitions on the table; the House did not accede to the proposition: they referred the petitions as they had been before referred, and with the same result. For, from the moment that these petitions are referred to the committee on the District of Columbia, they all go to the family vault " of all the Capulets," and you will never hear of them afterwards.

Extract from the speech of Hon. Silas Wright, of New York, in the Senate, Jan. 19, 1836, on the subject of abolishing slavery in the District of Columbia.

Mr. Wright said he was not to discuss the subject of slavery in the abstract. He knew it, and the people of the North, as a body, knew it only as it existed under the Constitution of the United States, and was sanctioned by it. They thought of it in that light, and in that light only, so far as its existence in these States is concerned, and so far as the quiet of the country and the preservation of the Union are involved in any agitation of the subject. In that sense, it was not a question for discussion in that body.

Neither was he to debate the question of slavery in the sovereign States of this Union. The sacred and invaluable compact which constitutes us one people, had not given to Congress the jurisdiction over that question. It was left solely and exclusively to those States, and, in his humble judgment, it ought never to be debated here in any manner whatever.

Mr. W. said he would go farther, and say that he did not purpose to trouble the Senate with a discussion upon the propriety of any action on the part of Congress in reference to the abolition of slavery in the District of Columbia, or in regard to the constitutional power of Congress over that subject. He had listened with pleasure and profit to the able argument of the honorable senator from Virginia (Mr. Leigh), upon the powers of Congress, and had marked his concessions of power equal to that possessed by the legislatures of the respective States of Maryland and Virginia over the same subject within those States. He had not studied the question himself, because he was able to mark out his own course, with perfect satisfaction to his own mind, without examining either the constitutional powers of Congress, or the powers of those State legislatures. He was ready to declare his opinion to be, that Congress ought not to act in this matter, but upon the impulse of the two States surrounding the District, and then in a manner precisely graduated by the action of those States upon the same subject. Had the Constitution, in terms, given to Congress all power in the matter, this would, with his present views and feelings, be his opinion of the expedient rule of action, and entertaining this opinion, an examination into the power to act had been unnecessary to determine his vote upon the prayer of these petitions. He was ready promptly to reject their prayer, and he deeply regretted that he was not permitted so to vote without debate.

Extract of a speech delivered in the United States Senate, by Mr. Buchanan, in 1835.

"The Constitution has, in the clearest terms, recognized the right of property in slaves. It prohibits any State into which a slave may have fled from passing any law to discharge him from slavery, and declares that he shall be delivered up by the authorities of such State to his master. Nay, more, it makes the existence of slavery the foundation of political powers, by giving to those States within which it exists representatives in Congress, not only in proportion to the whole number of free persons, but also in proportion to three-fifths of the number of slaves.

"Sir, this question of domestic slavery is a weak point in our institutions. Tariffs may be raised almost to prohibition, and then they may be reduced so as to yield no adequate protection to the manufacturer; our Union is sufficiently strong to endure the shock. Fierce political storms may arise; the moral elements of the country may be convulsed by the struggles of ambitious men for the highest honors of government. The sunshine does not more certainly succeed the storm than that all will again be peace. Touch this question of slavery seriously—let it once be made manifest to the people of the South that they cannot live with us, except in a state of continual apprehension and alarm for their wives and their children, for all that is near and dear to them upon the earth, and the Union is from that moment dissolved. It does not then become a question of expediency, but of self-preservation. It is a question brought home to the fireside, to the domestic circle, of every white man in the Southern States."

OPINIONS OF MR. BENTON.

At the session of 1835, Mr. Buchanan presented to the Senate the memorial of the Society of Friends, adopted at their Caln quarterly meeting, requesting Congress to abolish slavery and the slave trade in the District of Columbia.

Mr. Benton rose to express his concurrence in the suggestion of the Senator from Pennsylvania, [Mr. Buchanan,] that the consideration of this subject be postponed until Monday. It had come up suddenly and unexpectedly to-day, and the postponement would give an opportunity for senators to reflect, and to confer together, and to conclude what was best to be done, where all were united in wishing the same end, namely, to allay, and not to produce excitement. He had risen for this purpose; but, being on his feet, he would say a few words on the general subject, which the presentation of these petitions had so suddenly and unexpectedly brought up.

With respect to the petitioners, and those with whom they acted, he had no doubt but that many of them were good people, aiming at benevolent objects, and endeavoring to ameliorate the condition of one part of the human race, without inflicting calamities on another part; but they were mistaken in their mode of proceeding; and so far from accomplishing any part of their object, the whole effect of their interposition was to aggravate the condition of those in whose behalf they were interfering.

But there was another part, and he meant to speak of the

abolitionists generally, as the body containing the part of which he spoke; there was another part whom he could not qualify as good people, seeking benevolent ends by mistaken means, but as incendiaries and agitators, with diabolical objects in view, to be accomplished by wicked and deplorable means. He did not go into the proofs now to establish the correctness of his opinion of this latter class, but he presumed it would be admitted that every attempt to work upon the passions of the slaves, and to excite them to murder their owners, was a wicked and diabolical attempt, and the work of a midnight incendiary. Pictures of slave degradation and misery, and of the white man's luxury and cruelty, were attempts of this kind; for they were appeals to the vengeance of slaves, and not to the intelligence or reason of those who legislated for them. He [Mr. B.] had had many pictures of this kind, as well as many diabolical publications, sent to him on this subject during the last summer; the whole of which he had cast into the fire, and should not have thought of referring to the circumstance at this time, as displaying the character of the incendiary part of the abolitionists, had he not, within those few days past, and while abolition petitions were pouring into the other end of the Capitol, received one of these pictures, the design of which could be nothing but mischief of the blackest dye. It was a print from an engraving, (and Mr. B. exhibited it, and handed it to senators near him,) representing a large and spreading tree of liberty, beneath whose ample shade a slave owner was at one time luxuriously reposing, with slaves fanning him: at another, carried forth in a palanquin, to view the half-naked laborers in the cotton field, whom drivers, with whips, were scourging to the task. The print was evidently from the abolition mint, and came to him by some other conveyance than that of the mail, for there was no post-mark of any kind to identify its origin, and to indicate its line of march. For what purpose could such a picture be intended, unless to inflame the passions of slaves? And why engrave it, except to multiply copies for extensive distribution? But it was not pictures alone that operated upon the passions of the slaves; but speeches, publications, petitions presented in Congress, and the whole machinery of abolition societies. None of these things went to the understandings of the slaves, but to their passions, all imperfectly understood, and inspiring vague hopes, and stimulating abortive and fatal insurrections. Societies, especially, were the foundation of the greatest mischiefs. Whatever might be their objects, the slaves never did, and never can, understand them but in one way: as allies organized for action, and ready to march to their aid on the first signal of insurrection. It was thus that the massacre of San Domingo was made. The society in Paris, Les Amis des Noirs, friends of the blacks, with its affiliated societies throughout France and in London, made that massacre. And who composed that society? In the beginning, it comprised the extremes of virtue and of vice; it contained the best and the basest of human kind. Lafayette and the Abbe Gregoire, those purest of philanthropists; and Marat, and Anacharsis Cloots, those imps of hell in human shape. In the end, (for all such societies run the same career of degeneration,) the good men, disgusted with their associates, retired from the scene, and the wicked ruled at pleasure. Declamations against slavery, publications in gazettes, pictures, petitions to the constituent assembly, were the mode of proceeding; and the fish women of Paris—he said it with humiliation, because American females had signed the petitions now before us—the fish women of Paris, the very poissardes from the quays of the Seine, became the obstreperous champions of West India emancipation.

The effect upon the French islands is known to the world; but what is not known to the world, or not sufficiently known to it is, that the same societies which wrapt in flames and drenched in blood the beautiful island, which was then a garden and is now a wilderness, were the means of exciting an insurrection upon our continent, in Louisiana.

At the session of 1839, the slavery question being under discussion in the Senate,

Mr. Benton said, I was on the subject of slavery, as connected with the Missouri question, when last on the floor.

The Senator from South Carolina [Mr. Hayne], could see nothing in the question before the senate, nor in any previous part of the debate, to justify the introduction of that topic. Neither could I. He thought he saw the ghost of the Missouri question brought in among us. So did I. He was astonished at the apparition. I was not: for a close observance of the signs in the west had prepared me for this development from the east. I was well prepared for that invective against slavery, and for that amplification of the blessings of exemption from slavery, exemplified in the condition of Ohio, which the Senator from Massachusetts indulged in, and which the object in view required to be derived from the north east. I cut the root of that derivation by reading a passage from the journals of the old Congress; but this will not prevent the invective and encomium from going forth to do their office; nor obliterate the line which was drawn between the free State of Ohio and the slave State of Kentucky. If the only results of this invective and encomium were to exalt still higher the oratorical fame of the speaker, I should spend not a moment in remarking upon them. But it is not to be forgotten that the terrible Missouri agitation took its rise from the "substance of two speeches" delivered on this floor; and since that time, anti-slavery speeches, coming from the same political and geographical quarter, are not to be disregarded here.

What was said upon that topic was certainly intended for

the north side of the Potomac and Ohio; to the people then, of that division of the Union, I wish to address myself and to disabuse them of some erroneous impressions.

To them I can truly say, that slavery, in the abstract, has but few advocates or defenders in the slaveholding States, and that slavery as it is, an hereditary institution descended upon us from our ancestors, would have fewer advocates among us than it has, if those who have nothing to do with the subject would only let us alone. The sentiment in favor of slavery was much weaker before those intermeddlers began their operations than it is at present. The views of leading men in the North and the South were indisputably the same in the earlier periods of our government. Of this our legislative history contains the highest proof. The foreign slave trade was prohibited in Virginia, as soon as the Revolution began.

It was one of her first acts of sovereignty. In the convention of that State which adopted the federal Constitution, it was an objection to that instrument that it tolerated the African slave trade for twenty years. Nothing that has appeared since has surpassed the indignant denunciations of this traffic by Patrick Henry, George Mason, and others in that convention.

Sir, I regard with admiration, that is to say, with wonder, the sublime morality of those who cannot bear the abstract contemplation of slavery, at the distance of five hundred or a thousand miles off. It is entirely above, that is to say, it affects a vast superiority over the morality of the primitive Christians, the Apostles of Christ, and Christ himself.

Christ and the apostles appeared in a province of the Roman empire, when that empire was called the Roman world, and that world was filled with slaves. Forty millions was the estimated number, being one-fourth of the whole population. Single individuals held twenty thousand slaves.

A freed man, one who had himself been a slave, died the

possessor of four thousand—such were the numbers. The rights of the owners over this multitude of human beings was that of life and death, without protection from law or mitigation from public sentiment.

The scourge, the cross, the fish-pond, the den of the wild beast, and the arena of the gladiator, was the lot of the slave, upon the slightest expression of the master's will.

A law of incredible atrocity made all slaves responsible with their own lives for the life of their master; it was the law that condemned the whole household of slaves to death, in case of the assassination of the master—a law under which as many as four hundred have been executed at a time.

And the slaves were the white people of Europe, and of Asia Minor, the Greeks and other nations, from whom the present inhabitants of the world derive the most valuable productions of the human mind.

Christ saw all this—the number of slaves—their helpless condition—and their white color, which was the same with his own; yet he said nothing against slavery; he preached no doctrines which led to insurrection and massacre; none which, in their application to the state of things in our country, would authorize an inferior race of blacks to exterminate that superior race of whites, in whose ranks he himself appeared upon earth.

He preached no such doctrines, but those of a contrary tenor, which inculcated the duty of fidelity and obedience on the part of the slave—humanity and kindness on the part of the master. His apostles did the same.

St. Paul sent back a runaway slave, Onesimus, to his owner, with a letter of apology and supplication.

He was not the man to harbor a runaway, much less to entice him from his master; and least of all, to excite an insurrection.

CHAPTER XI.

SESSION OF CONGRESS OF 1839—THE GAG RULE—SLAVERY AGITATION IN THE HOUSE OF REPRESENTATIVES, AND RETIRING OF SOUTHERN MEMBERS FROM THE HALL.

(*From "Benton's Thirty Years' View."*)

THE most angry and portentous debate which had yet taken place in Congress, occurred at this time, in the House of Representatives. It was brought on by Mr. William Slade, of Vermont, who, besides presenting petitions of the usual abolition character, and moving to refer them to a committee, moved their reference to a select committee, with instructions to report a bill in conformity to their prayer. This motion, inflammatory and irritating in itself, and without practical legislative object, as the great majority of the House was known to be opposed to it, was rendered still more exasperating by the manner of supporting it. The mover entered into a general disquisition on the subject of slavery, all denunciatory, and was proceeding to speak upon it in the State of Virginia, and other States, in the same spirit, when Mr. Legare, of South Carolina, interposed, and hoped the gentleman from Vermont would allow him to make a few remarks before he proceeded further. He sincerely hoped that the gentleman would consider well what he was about, before he ventured on such ground, and that he would take time to consider what might be its probable consequences. He solemnly entreated him to reflect on the possible results of such a course, which involved the interests of a nation and a continent. He would warn him, not in the language of defiance, which all brave and wise men despised, but he would warn him in the language of a solemn sense of duty, that if there was a spirit aroused in the north in relation to this subject, that spirit would encounter another spirit in the south, full as stubborn. He would tell them, that, when this question was forced upon the people of the south, they would be ready to take up the gauntlet. He concluded by urging on the gentleman from Vermont to ponder well on his course before he ventured to proceed.

Mr. Slade continued his remarks, when Mr. Dawson, of Georgia, asked him for the floor, that he might move an adjournment—evidently to carry off the storm which he saw rising. Mr. Slade refused to yield it; so the motion to adjourn could not be made. Mr. Slade continued, and was proceeding to answer his own inquiry, put to himself—*What was slavery?* when Mr. Dawson again asked for the floor to make his motion of adjournment. Mr. Slade refused it. A visible commotion began to pervade the House—members rising, clustering together, and talking with animation.

Mr. Slade continued, and was about reading a judicial opinion in one of the southern States, which defined a slave to be a chattel, when Mr. Wise called him to order for speaking beside the question—the question being upon the abolition of slavery in the District of Columbia, and Mr. Slade's remarks going to its legal character, as property, in a State. The Speaker, Mr. John White, of Kentucky, sustained the call, saying it was not in order to discuss the subject of slavery in any of the States. Mr. Slade denied that he was doing so, and said he was merely quoting a Southern judicial decision, as he might quote a legal opinion delivered in Great Britain.

Mr. Robertson, of Virginia, moved that the House adjourn. The Speaker pronounced the motion (and correctly) out of order, as the member from Vermont was in possession of the floor and addressing the House. He would, however, suggest to the member from Vermont, who could not but observe the state of the House, to confine himself strictly to the subject of his motion.

Mr. Slade went on, at great length, when Mr. Petrikin, of Pennsylvania, called him to order; but the Chair did not sustain the call. Mr. Slade went on, quoting from the Declaration of Independence, and the Constitutions of the several States, and had got to that of Virginia, when Mr. Wise called him to order for reading papers without the leave of the House. The Speaker decided, that no paper, objected to, could be read without the leave of the House.

Mr. Wise then said: That the gentleman had wantonly discussed the abstract question of slavery, going back to the very first day of the creation, instead of slavery as it existed in the District, and the powers and duties of Congress in relation to it. He was now examining the State Constitutions, to show, that as it existed in the States, it was against them, and against the laws of God and man. This was out of order.

Mr. Slade explained, and argued in vindication of his course, and was about to read a memorial of Dr. Franklin, and an opinion of Mr. Madison on the subject of slavery, when the reading was objected to by Mr. Griffin, of South Carolina; and the Speaker decided they could not be read without the permission of the House.

Mr. Slade, without asking the permission of the House, which he knew would not be granted, assumed to understand the prohibition as extending only to himself personally, said—"Then I send them to the clerk: let him read them." The Speaker decided that this was equally against the rule.

Then Mr. Griffin withdrew the objection, and Mr. Slade proceeded to read the papers, and to comment upon them as he went on, and was about to go back to the State, of

Virginia, and show what had been the feeling there on the subject of slavery, previous to the date of Dr. Franklin's memorial.

Mr. Rhett, of South Carolina, inquired of the Chair what the opinions of Virginia fifty years ago had to do with the case?

The Speaker was about to reply, when Mr. Wise rose with warmth, and said—"He has discussed the whole abstract question of slavery: of slavery in Virginia; of slavery in my own district; and I now ask all my colleagues to retire with me from this hall."

Mr. Slade reminded the Speaker that he had not yielded the floor; but his progress was impeded by the condition of the House, and the many exclamations of members, among whom Mr. Halsey, of Georgia, was heard calling on the Georgia delegation to withdraw with him; and Mr. Rhett was heard proclaiming, that the South Carolina members had already consulted together, and agreed to have a meeting at three o'clock, in the committee room of the District of Columbia. Here the Speaker interposed to calm the House, standing up in his place and saying:

"The gentleman from Vermont had been reminded by the Chair that the discussion of slavery, as existing within the States, was not in order; when he was desirous to read a paper and it was objected to, the Chair had stopped him; but the objection had been withdrawn, and Mr. Slade had been suffered to proceed; he was now about to read another paper, and objection was made; the Chair would therefore take the question on permitting it to be read."

Many members rose, all addressing the Chair at the same time, and many members leaving the hall, and a general scene of noise and confusion prevailing.

Mr. Rhett succeeded in raising his voice above the roar of the tempest which raged in the House, and invited the delegations from all the slave States to retire from the hall forthwith, and meet in the committee room of the District of Columbia. The Speaker again essayed to calm the House, and again standing up in his place, he recapitulated his attempts to preserve order, and vindicated the correctness of his own conduct—seemingly impugned by many. "What his personal feelings were on the subject (he was from a slave State) might easily be conjectured. He had endeavored to enforce the rules. Had it been in his power to restrain the discussion, he should promptly have exercised the power; but it was not.

Mr Slade continuing, said the paper which he wished to read was of the Continental Congress of 1774. The Speaker was about to put the question on leave, when Mr. Cost Johnson, of Maryland, inquired whether it would be in order to force the House to vote that the member from Vermont be not permitted to proceed? The Speaker replied it would not. Then Mr. James J. McKay, of North Carolina, a clear, cool-headed, sagacious man—interposed the objection which headed Mr. Slade.

There was a rule of the House, that when a member was called to order, he should take his seat; and if decided to be out of order, he should not be allowed to speak again, except on leave of the House. Mr. McKay judged this to be a proper occasion for the enforcement of that rule; and stood up and said:

"That the gentleman had been pronounced out of order in discussing slavery in the States; and the rule declared that when a member was so pronounced by the chair, he should take his seat, and if any one objected to his proceeding again, he should not do so, unless by leave of the House. Mr. McKay did now object to the gentleman from Vermont proceeding any further."

Redoubled noise and confusion ensued—a crowd of members rising and speaking at once—who eventually yielded to the resounding blows of the speaker's hammer upon the lid of his desk, and his apparent desire to read something to the House, as he held a book (recognized to be that of the rules) in his hand. Obtaining quiet, so as to enable himself to be heard, he read the rule referred to by Mr. McKay; and said, that as objection had now for the first time been made under that rule to the gentleman's resuming his speech, the Chair decided that he could not do so without the leave of the House. Mr. Slade attempted to go on; the Speaker directed him to take his seat until the question of leave should be put. Then, Mr. Slade still keeping his feet, asked leave to proceed as in order, saying he would not discuss slavery in Virginia. On that question Mr. Allen, of Vermont, asked the yeas and nays.

Mr. Rencher, of North Carolina, moved an adjournment. Mr. Adams, and many others, demanded the yeas and nays on this motion, which were ordered, and resulted in 106 yeas and 63 nays—some fifty or sixty members having withdrawn. This opposition to adjournment was one of the worst features of that unhappy day's work—the only effect of keeping the House together being to increase irritation, and multiply the chances for an outbreak.

From the beginning Southern members had been in favor of it, and essayed to accomplish it, but were prevented by the tenacity with which Mr. Slade kept possession of the floor: and now, at last, when it was time to adjourn any way—when the House was in a condition in which no good could be expected, and great harm might be apprehended, there were sixty-three members—being nearly one-third of the House—willing to continue it in session.

The House then stood adjourned; and as the adjournment was being pronounced, Mr. Campbell, of South Carolina, stood upon a chair, and calling for the attention of members, said:

"He had been appointed as one of the Southern delegation, to announce that all those gentlemen who represented slaveholding States, were invited to attend the meeting now being held in the district committee room."

Members from the slaveholding States had repaired in large numbers to the room in the basement, where they were invited to meet. Various passions agitated them—some violent. Extreme propositions were suggested, of which Mr. Rhett, of South Carolina, in a letter to his constituents, gave a full account of his own—thus:

"In a private and friendly letter to the Editor of the Charleston Mercury, amongst other events accompanying the memorable secession of the Southern members from the Hall of the House of Representatives, I stated to him, that I had prepared two resolutions, drawn as amendments to the motion of the member from Vermont, whilst he was discussing the institution of slavery in the South declaring, that the Constitution having failed to protect the South in the peaceable possession and enjoyment of their rights and peculiar institutions, it was expedient that the Union should be dissolved; and the other, appointing a committee of two members from each State, to report upon the best means of peaceably dissolving it! They were intended as amendments to a motion to refer with instructions to report a bill abolishing slavery in the District of Columbia. I expected them to share the fate, which inevitably awaited the original motion, so soon as the floor could have been obtained, viz., to be laid upon the table. My design in presenting them, was to place before Congress and the people, what in my opinion, was the true issue upon this great and vital question; and to point out the course of policy by which it should be met by the Southern States."

But extreme counsels did not prevail. There were members present, who well considered that, although the provocation was great, and the number voting for such a firebrand motion was deplorably large, yet it was but little more than one-fourth of the House, and decidedly less than one-half of the members from the free States : so that, even if left to the free State vote alone, the motion would have been rejected.

But the motion itself, and the manner in which it was supported, was most reprehensible—necessarily leading to disorder in the House, the destruction of its harmony and capacity for useful legislation, tending to a sectional segregation of the members, the alienation of feeling between the North and South ; and alarm to all the slave holding States. The evil required a remedy, but not the remedy of breaking up the Union ; but one which might prevent the like in future, while administering a rebuke upon the past. That remedy was found in adopting a proposition to be offered to the House, which if agreed to, would close the door against any discussion upon abolition petitions in future, and assimilate the proceedings of the House, in that particular, to those of the Senate. This proposition was put into the hands of Mr. Patton of Virginia, to be offered as an amendment to the rules at the opening of the House the next morning.

It was in these words:

"Resolved, That all petitions, memorials and papers, touching the abolition of slavery or the buying, selling or transferring of slaves, in any State, District or Territory, of the United States, be laid on the table, without being debated, printed, read or referred, and that no further action whatever shall be had thereon."

Accordingly, at the opening of the House, Mr. Patton asked leave to submit the resolution—which was read for information.

Mr. Adams objected to the grant of leave.

Mr. Patton then moved a suspension of the rules—which motion required two-thirds to sustain it; and unless obtained, this salutary remedy for an alarming evil (which was already in force in the Senate), could not be offered. It was a test

SLAVERY AGITATION. 329

motion, and on which the opponents of abolition agitation in the House required all their strength: for unless two to one, they were defeated.

Happily the two to one were ready, and on taking the yeas and nays, demanded by an abolition member (to keep his friends to the track, and to hold the free State anti-abolitionists to their responsibility at home), the result stood one hundred and thirty-five yeas to sixty nays—the full two-thirds, and fifteen over. The yeas on this important motion, were:

Messrs. Hugh J. Anderson, John J. Andrews, Charles G. Atherton, William Beatty, Andrew Beirne, John Bell, Bennet Bicknell, Richard Biddle, Samuel Birdsall, Ratliff Boon, James W. Bouldin, John C. Brodhead, Isaac H. Bronson, Andrew D. W. Bruyn, Andrew Buchanan, John Calhoun, C. C. Cambreleng, Wm. B. Campbell, John Campbell, Timothy J. Carter, Wm. B. Carter, Zadok Casey, John Chambers, John Chaney, Reuben Chapman, Richard Cheatham, Jonathan Cilley, John F. H. Claiborne, Jesse F. Cleaveland, Wm. K. Clowney, Walter Coles, Thomas Corwin, Robert Craig, John W. Crockett, Samuel Cushman, Edmund Deberry, John J. DeGraff, John Dennis, George C. Dromgoole, John Edwards, James Farrington, John Fairfield, Jacob Fry, Jr., James Garland, James Graham, Seaton Grantland, Abr'm. P. Grant, William J. Graves, Robert H. Hammond, Thomas L. Hamar, James Harlan, Albert G. Harrison, Richard Hawes, Micajah T. Hawkins, Charles E. Haynes, Hopkins Holsey, Orrin Holt, George W. Hopkins, Benjamin C. Howard, Edward B. Hubly, Jabez Jackson, Joseph Johnson, Wm Cost Johnson, John W. Jones, Gouverneur Kemble, Daniel Kilgore, John Klingensmith Jr., Jacob Lawler, Hugh S. Legare, Henry Logan, Francis S. Lyon, Francis Mallory, James M. Mason, Joshua L. Martin, Abram P. Maury, Wm. S. May, James J. McKay, Robert McClellan,

Abraham McClelland, Charles McClure, Isaac McKim, Richard H. Menefee, Charles F. Mercer, William Montgomery, Ely Moore, Wm. S. Morgan, Samuel W. Morris, Henry A. Muhlenberg, John L. Murray, Wm. H. Noble, John Palmer, Amasa I. Parker, John M. Patton, Lemuel Paynter, Isaac S. Pennybacker, David Petrikin, Lancelot Phelps, Arnold Plumer, Zadock Pratt, John H. Prentiss, Luther Reily, Abraham Rencher, John Robertson, Samuel T. Sawyer, Augustine H. Shepperd, Charles Shepard, Ebenezer J. Shields, Matthias Sheplor, Francis O. J. Smith, Adam W. Snyder, Wm. W. Southgate, James B. Spencer, Edward Stanly, Archibald Stuart, Wm. Stone, John Taliaferro, Wm. Taylor, Obadiah Titus, Isaac Toucey, Hopkins L. Turney, Joseph R. Underwood, Henry Vail, David D. Wagner, Taylor Webster, Joseph Weeks, Albert S. White, John White, Thomas J. Whittlesey, Lewis Williams, Sherrod Williams, Jared W. Williams, Joseph L. Williams, Christ'r H. Williams, Henry A. Wise, Archibald Yell.

The Nays were:

Messrs. John Quincy Adams, James Alexander, Jr., Heman Allen, John W. Allen, J. Banker Aycrigg, Wm. Key Bond, Nathaniel B. Borden, George N. Briggs, Wm. B. Calhoun, Charles D. Coffin, Robert B. Crauston, Caleb Cushing, Edward Darlington, Thomas Davee, Edward Davies, Alexander Duncan, George H. Dunn, George Evans, Horace Everett, John Ewing, Isaac Fletcher, Millard Fillmore, Henry A. Foster, Patrick G. Goods, George Grennell, Jr., Elisha Haley, Hiland Hall, Alexander Harper, Wm. S. Hastings, Thomas Henry, Wm. Herod, Samuel Ingham, Levi Lincoln, Richard P. Marvin, Samson Mason, John P. B. Maxwell, Thos. M. T. McKennan, Matthias Morris, Calvary Morris, Charles Naylor, Joseph C. Noyes, Charles Ogle, Wm. Parmenter, Wm. Patterson, Luther C. Peck, Stephen C, Phillips, David Potts, Jr., James Rariden, Joseph F. Randolph, John Reed, Joseph

Ridgway, David Russell, Daniel Sheffer, Mark H. Sibley. Wm. Slade, Charles C. Stratton, Joseph L. Tillinghast, Geo. W. Toland, Elisha Whittlesey, Thomas Jones Yorke.

This was one of the most important votes ever delivered in the House. Upon its issue depended the quiet of the House on one hand, or on the other, the renewal, and perpetuation of the scenes of the day before—ending in breaking up all deliberation, and all national legislation.

It was successful, and that critical step being safely over, the passage of the resolution was secured—the free State friendly vote being itself sufficient to carry it: but although the passage of the resolution was secured, yet resistance to it continued.

Thus was stifled, and in future prevented in the House, the inflammatory debates on these disturbing petitions. It was the great session of their presentation—being offered by hundreds, and signed by hundreds of thousands of persons—many of them women, who forgot their sex and their duties, to mingle in such inflammatory work; some of them clergymen, who forgot their mission of peace, to stir up strife among those who should be brethren. Of the pertinacious 63, who backed Mr. Slade throughout, the most notable were Mr. Adams, who had been President of the United States—Mr. Fillmore, who became so—and Mr. Caleb Cushing, who eventually became as ready to abolish all impediments to the general diffusion of slavery, as he then was to abolish slavery in the District of Columbia. It was a portentous contest.

The motion of Mr. Slade was not for an inquiry into the expediency of abolishing slavery in the District of Columbia (a motion in itself sufficiently inflammatory), but to get the command of the House to bring in a bill for that purpose—which would be a decision of the question.

His motion failed. The storm subsided; and very few of the free State members who had staked themselves on the issue, lost anything among their constituents for the devotion which they had shown to the Union,*

From Mr. Clay's great speech in the U. S. Senate, February 7th, 1839.

"It is well known to the Senate," said Mr. Clay, "that I have thought that the most judicious course with abolition petitions has not of late been pursued by Congress.

"I have believed that it would have been wisest to have received and referred them, without opposition, and to have reported against their object in a calm and dispassionate and argumentative appeal to the good sense of the whole community. It has been supposed, however, by a majority of Congress, that it was most expedient either not to receive the petitions at all, or, if formally received, not to act definitively upon them. There is no substantial difference between these opposite opinions, since both look to an absolute rejection of the prayers of the petitioners. But there is a great difference in the form of proceeding; and, Mr. President, some experience in the conduct of human affairs has taught me to believe that a neglect to observe established forms is often attended with more mischievous consequences than the infliction of a positive injury. We all know that, even in private life, a violation of the existing usages and ceremonies of society cannot take place without serious prejudice. I fear, sir, that the abolitionists have acquired a considerable apparent force by blending with the object which they have in view a collateral and totally different question arising out of an alleged violation of the right of petition. I know full well, and take great

---

* This resolution afterward became notorious, from the stigma cast upon it by the abolitionists, as the "Gag Rule." Hon. David Wilmot, of Pennsylvania, among others, voted against its repeal in the Congress of '46—7. It has since, however, been repealed.

pleasure in testifying, that nothing was remoter from the intention of the majority of the Senate, from which I differed, than to violate the right of petition in any case in which, according to its judgment, that right could be constitutionally exercised, or where the object of the petition could be safely or properly granted. Still, it must be owned that the abolitionists have seized hold of the fact of the treatment which their petitions have received in Congress, and made injurious impressions upon the minds of a large portion of the community. This, I think, might have been avoided by the course which I should have been glad to have seen pursued.

And I desire now, Mr. President, to advert to some of those topics which I think might have been usefully embodied in a report by a committee of the Senate, and which, I am persuaded, would have checked the progress, if it had not altogether arrested the efforts of abolition. I am sensible, sir, that this work would have been accomplished with much greater ability, and with much happier effect, under the auspices of a committee, than it can be by me. But, anxious as I always am to contribute whatever is in my power to the harmony, concord, and happiness of this great people, I feel myself irresistibly impelled to do whatever is in my power, incompetent as I feel myself to be, to dissuade the public from continuing to agitate a subject fraught with the most direful consequences.

There are three classes of persons opposed, or apparently opposed, to the continued existence of slavery in the United States. The first are those who, from sentiments of philanthropy and humanity, are conscientiously opposed to the existence of slavery, but who are no less opposed at the same time to any disturbance of the peace and tranquillity of the Union, or the infringement of the powers of the States composing the confederacy. In this class may be comprehended that peaceful and exemplary society of

"Friends," one of whose established maxims is an abhorrence of war in all its forms, and the cultivation of peace and good-will amongst mankind. The next class consists of apparent abolitionists—that is, those who, having been persuaded that the right of petition has been violated by Congress, co-operate with the abolitionist for the sole purpose of asserting and vindicating that right. And the third class are the real ultra-abolitionists, who are resolved to persevere in the pursuit of their object at all hazards, and without regard to any consequences, however calamitous they may be. With them the rights of property are nothing; the deficiency of the powers of the general government is nothing; the acknowledged and incontestable powers of the States are nothing; civil war, a dissolution of the Union, and the overthrow of a government in which are concentrated the fondest hopes of the civilized world, are nothing. A single idea has taken possession of their minds, and onward they pursue it, overlooking all barriers, reckless and regardless of all consequences. With this class, the immediate abolition of slavery in the District of Columbia, and in the Territory of Florida, the prohibition of the removal of slaves from State to State, and the refusal to admit any new State comprising within its limits the institution of domestic slavery, are but so many means conducing to the accomplishment of the ultimate but perilous end at which they avowedly and boldly aim, are but so many short stages in the long and bloody road to the distant goal at which they would finally arrive. Their purpose is abolition, universal abolition, peaceably if it can, forcibly if it must. Their object is no longer concealed by the thinnest veil; it is avowed and proclaimed. Utterly destitute of constitutional or other rightful power, living in totally distinct communities, as alien to the communities in which the subject on which they would operate resides, so far as concerns political power over that subject, as if they lived in Africa or Asia; they nevertheless promulgate to the world their purpose to be to manumit forthwith, and without compensation, and without moral preparation, three millions of negro slaves, under jurisdictions altogether separated from those under which they live.

I have said that immediate abolition of slavery in the District of Columbia and in the Territory of Florida, and the exclusion of new States, were only means towards the attainment of a much more important end. Unfortunately, they are not the only means. Another, and much more lamentable one, is that which this class is endeavoring to employ, of arraying one portion against another portion of the Union. With that view, in all their leading prints and publications, the alleged horrors of slavery are depicted in the most glowing and exaggerated colors, to excite the imaginations and stimulate the rage of the people in the free States against the people in the slave States. The slaveholder is held up and represented as the most atrocious of human beings. Advertisements of fugitive slaves to be sold are carefully collected and blazoned forth, to infuse a spirit of detestation and hatred against one entire and the largest section of the Union. And like a notorious agitator upon another theatre, (Mr. Daniel O'Connell,) they would hunt down and proscribe from the pale of civilized society the inhabitants of that entire section. Allow me, Mr. President, to say, that whilst I recognize in the justly wounded feelings of the Minister of the United States at the court of St. James much to excuse the notice which he was provoked to take of that agitator, in my humble opinion, he would better have consulted the dignity of his station and of his country in treating him with contemptuous silence. That agitator would exclude us from European society—he who himself can only obtain a contraband admission, and is received with scornful repugnance into it! If he be no more desirous of our society than we are of his, he may rest assured that a state of eternal non-intercourse will exist between us. Yes, sir, I think the American Minister would have best pursued the dictates of true dignity by regarding the language of that member of the British House of Commons as the malignant ravings of the plunderer of his own country, and the libeler of a foreign and kindred people.

But the means to which I have already adverted are not the only ones which this third class of ultra-abolitionists are employing to effect their ultimate end. They began their operations by professing to employ only persuasive means in appealing to the humanity, and enlightening the understandings, of the slaveholding portion of the Union. If there were some kindness in this avowed motive, it must be acknowledged that there was rather a presumptuous display also of an assumed superiority in intelligence and knowledge. For some time they continued to make these appeals to our duty and our interest; but, impatient with the slow influence of their logic upon our stupid minds, they recently resolved to change their system of action. To the agency of their powers of persuasion, they now propose to substitute the powers of the ballot box; and he must be blind to what is passing before us, who does not perceive that the inevitable tendency of their proceedings is, if these should be found insufficient, to invoke, finally, the more potent powers of the bayonet.

Mr. President, it is at this alarming stage of the proceedings of the ultra-abolitionists that I would seriously invite every considerate man in the country solemnly to pause, and deliberately to reflect, not merely on our existing posture, but upon that dreadful precipice down which they would hurry us. It is because these ultra-abolitionists have ceased to employ the instruments of reason and persuasion, have made their cause political, and have appealed to the ballot box, that I am induced, upon this occasion, to address you.

There have been three epochs in the history of our country at which the spirit of abolition displayed itself. The first was immediately after the formation of the present federal government. When the Constitution was about going into operation, its powers were not well understood by the community at large, and remained to be accurately interpreted and defined. At that period numerous abolition societies were formed, comprising not merely the Society of Friends, but many other good men. Petitions were presented to Congress praying for the abolition of slavery. They were received without serious opposition, referred, and reported upon by a committee. The report stated that the general government had no power to abolish slavery as it existed in the several States, and that these States themselves had exclusive jurisdiction over the subject. The report was generally acquiesced in, and satisfaction and tranquillity ensued; the abolition societies thereafter limiting their exertions, in respect to the black population, to offices of humanity within the scope of existing laws.

The next period when the subject of slavery and abolition, incidentally, was brought into notice and discussion, was on the memorable occasion of the admission of the State of Missouri into the Union. The struggle was long, strenuous, and fearful. It is too recent to make it necessary to do more than merely advert to it, and to say that it was finally composed by one of those compromises characteristic of our institutions, and of which the Constitution itself is the most signal instance.

The third is that in which we now find ourselves, and to which various causes have contributed. The principal one, perhaps, is British emancipation in the islands adjacent to our continent. Confounding the totally different cases of the powers of the British Parliament and those of our

Congress, and the totally different conditions of the slaves in the British West India Islands and the slaves in the sovereign and independent States of this confederacy, superficial men have inferred from the undecided British experiment the practibility of the abolition of slavery in these States. All these are different. The powers of the British Parliament are unlimited, and often described to be omnipotent. The powers of the American Congress, on the contrary, are few, cautiously limited, scrupulously excluding all that are not granted, and above all, carefully and absolutely excluding all power over the existence or continuance of slavery in the several States. The slaves, too, upon which British legislation operated, were not in the bosom of the kingdom, but in remote and feeble colonies, having no voice in Parliament. The West India slaveholder was neither representative nor represented in that Parliament. And while I most fervently wish complete success to the British experiment of West India emancipation, I confess that I have fearful forebodings of a disastrous termination of it. Whatever it may be, I think it must be admitted that, if the British Parliament treated the West India slaves as freemen, it also treated the West India freemen as slaves. If, instead of these slaves being separated by a wide ocean from the parent country, three or four millions of African negro slaves had been dispersed over England, Scotland, Wales, and Ireland, and their owners had been members of the British Parliament—a case which would have presented some analogy to that of our own country—does any one believe that it would have been expedient or practicable to have emancipated them, leaving them to remain, with all their embittered feelings, in the United Kingdom, boundless as the powers of the British Parliament are?

*   *   *   *   *   *

And now, Mr. President, allow me to consider the several cases in which the authority of Congress is invoked by these abolition petitioners upon the subject of domestic slavery. The first relates to it as it exists in the District of Columbia. The following is the provision of the Constitution of the United States in reference to that matter·

"To exercise exclusive legislation in all cases whatsoever over such District (not exceeding ten miles square,) as may by cession of particular States, and the acceptance of Congress, become the seat of government of the United States."

This provision preceded, in point of time, the actual cessions which were made by the States of Maryland and Virginia. The object of the cession was to establish a seat of government of the United States, and the grant in the Constitution of exclusive legislation, must be understood, and should be always interpreted, as having relation to the object of the cession. It was with a full knowledge of this clause in the Constitution, that those two States ceded to the general government the ten miles square constituting the District of Columbia. In making the cession, they supposed that it was to be applied, and applied solely, to the purposes of a seat of government, for which it was asked. When it was made, slavery existed in both those commonwealths, and in the ceded territory, as it now continues to exist in all of them. Neither Maryland nor Virginia could have anticipated, that, whilst the institution remained within their respective limits, its abolition would be attempted by Congress without their consent. Neither of them would probably have made an unconditional cession if they could have anticipated such a result.

From the nature of the provision in the Constitution, and the avowed object of the acquisition of the territory, two duties arise on the part of Congress. The first is, to render the District available, comfortable, and convenient, as a seat of government of the whole Union; the other is, to govern the people within the District so as best to promote their happiness and prosperity. These objects are totally distinct in their nature, and, in interpreting and exercising the grant of the power of exclusive legislation, that distinction should be constantly borne in mind. Is it necessary, in order to render this place a comfortable seat of the general government, to abolish slavery within its limits? No one can or will advance such a proposition. The government has remained here near forty years without the slightest inconvenience from the presence of domestic slavery. Is it necessary to the well-being of the people of the District, that slavery should be abolished from amongst them? They not only neither ask nor desire, but are almost unanimously opposed to it. It exists here in the mildest and most mitigated form. In a population of 39,834, there were, at the last enumeration of the population of the United States, but 6,119 slaves. The number has not probably much increased since. They are dispersed over the ten miles square, engaged in the quiet pursuits of husbandry, or in menial offices in domestic life. If it were necessary to the efficiency of this place as a seat of the general government, to abolish slavery, which is utterly denied, the abolition should be confined to the necessity which prompts it, that is, to the limits of the city of Washington itself. Beyond those limits, persons concerned in the government of the United States have no more to do with the inhabitants of the District, than they have with the inhabitants of the adjacent counties of Maryland and Virginia which lie beyond the District.

To abolish slavery within the District of Columbia, whilst it remains in Virginia and Maryland, situated as that District is, within the very heart of those States, would expose them to great practical inconvenience and annoyance. The District would become a place of refuge and escape for fugitive slaves from the two States, and a place from which a spirit of discontent, insubordination and insurrection, might be fostered and encouraged in the two States. Suppose, as was at one time under consideration, Pennsylvania had granted ten miles square within its limits, for the purpose of a seat of the general government : could Congress, without a violation of good faith, have introduced and established slavery within the bosom of that Commonwealth in the ceded territory, after she had abolished it so long ago as the year 1780 ? Yet the inconvenience to Pennsylvania in the case supposed, would have been much less than that to Virginia and Maryland, in the case we are arguing.

It was upon this view of the subject that the Senate, at its last session, solemnly declared, that it would be a violation of implied faith, resulting from the transaction of the cession, to abolish slavery within the District of Columbia. And would it not be ? By implied faith, is meant, that when a grant is made for one avowed and declared purpose, known to the parties, the grant should not be perverted to another purpose, unavowed and undeclared, and injurious to the grantor. The grant in the case we are considering, of the territory of Columbia, was for a *seat of government*. Whatever power is necessary to accomplish that object, is carried along by the grant. But the abolition of slavery, is not necessary to the enjoyment of this site as a seat of the general government. The grant in the Constitution of exclusive power of legislation over the District, was made to insure the exercise of an exclusive authority of the general government, to render this place a safe and secure seat of government, and to promote the well-being of the inhabitants of the District. The power granted ought to be interpreted and exercised solely to the end for which it was granted. The language of the grant was necessarily broad, comprehensive, and exclusive, because all the exigencies which might arise to render this a secure seat of the general government, could not have been foreseen and provided for. The language may possibly be sufficiently comprehensive to include a power of abolition ; but it would not at all thence follow, that the power could be rightfully exercised. The case may be resembled to that of a plenipotentiary invested with a plenary power, but who at the same time has positive instructions from his government as to the kind of treaty which he is to negotiate and conclude. If he violates those instructions, and concludes a different treaty, his government is not bound by it; and if the foreign government is aware of the violation, it acts in bad faith. Or it may be illustrated by an example drawn from private life. I am an endorser for my friend on a note discounted in bank. He applies to me to endorse another, to renew it, which I do, in blank. Now, this gives him power to make any other use of my note which he pleases. But if, instead of applying it to the intended purpose, he goes to a broker and sells it, thereby doubling my responsibility for him, he commits a breach of trust, and a violation of the good faith implied in the whole transaction.

*   *   *   *   *   *   *   *

The first impediment is the utter and absolute want of all power on the part of the general government to effect the purpose. The Constitution of the United States creates a limited government, comprising comparatively few powers, and leaving the residuary mass of political power in the possession of the several States. It is well known that the subject of slavery interposed one of the greatest difficulties in the formation of the Constitution. It was happily compromised and adjusted in a spirit of harmony and patriotism. According to that compromise, no power whatever was granted to the general government in respect to domestic slavery, but that which relates to taxation and representation, and the power to restore fugitive slaves to their lawful owners. All other power in regard to the institution of slavery was retained exclusively by the States, to be exercised by them severally, according to their respective views of their own peculiar interest. The Constitution of the

United States never could have been formed upon the principle of investing the general government with authority to abolish the institution at its pleasure. It never can be continued for a single day if the exercise of such a power be assumed or usurped.

But it may be contended by these ultra-abolitionists that their object is not to stimulate the action of the general government, but to operate upon the States themselves in which the institution of domestic slavery exists. If that be their object, why are these abolition societies and movements all confined to the free States? Why are the slave States wantonly and cruelly assailed? Why do the abolition presses teem with publications tending to excite hatred and animosity on the part of the inhabitants of the free States against those of the slave States? Why is Congress petitioned? The free States have no more power or right to interfere with institutions in the slave States, confided to the exclusive jurisdiction of those States, than they would have to interfere with institutions existing in any foreign country. What would be thought of the formation of societies in Great Britain, the issue of numerous inflammatory publications, and the sending out of lecturers throughout the kingdom, denouncing and aiming at the destruction of any of the institutions of France? Would they be regarded as proceedings warranted by a good neighborhood? Or what would be thought of the formation of societies in the slave States, the issue of violent and inflammatory tracts, and the deputation of missionaries, pouring out impassioned denunciations against institutions under the exclusive control of the free States? Is their purpose to appeal to our understandings, and to actuate our humanity? And do they expect to accomplish that purpose by holding us up to the scorn, and contempt, and detestation of the people of the free States and the whole civilized world? The slavery which exists amongst us is our affair, not theirs; and they have no more just concern with it than they have with slavery as it exists throughout the world. Why not leave it to us, as the common Constitution of our country has left it, to be dealt with, under the guidance of Providence, as best we may or can?

* * * * * * * *

I know that there is a visionary dogma which holds that negro slaves cannot be the subject of property. I shall not dwell long with this speculative abstraction. That is property which the law declares *to be* property. Two hundred years of legislation have sanctioned and sanctified negro slaves as property. Under all the forms of government which have existed upon this continent during that long space of time—under the British government—under the colonial government—under all the State constitutions and governments—and under the federal government itself—they have been deliberately and solemnly recognized as the legitimate subjects of property. To the wild speculations of theorists and innovators stands opposed the *fact*, that in an uninterrupted period of two hundred years' duration, under every form of human legislation, and by all the departments of human government, African negro slaves have been held and respected, have descended and been transferred, as lawful and indisputable property. They were treated as property in the very British example which is so triumphantly appealed to as worthy of our imitation. Although the West India planters had no voice in the united Parliament of the British Isles, an irresistible sense of justice extorted from that legislature the grant of twenty millions of pounds sterling to compensate the colonists for their loss of property.

* * * * * * * *

Sir, I am not in the habit of speaking lightly of the possibility of dissolving this happy Union. The Senate knows that I have deprecated allusions on ordinary occasions to that direful event. The country will testify that if there be anything in the history of my public career worthy of recollection, it is the truth and sincerity of my ardent devotion to its lasting preservation. But we should be false in our allegiance to it, if we did not discriminate between the imaginary and real dangers by which it may be assailed. Abolition should no longer be regarded as an imaginary danger. The Abolitionists, let me suppose, succeed in their present aim of uniting the inhabitants of the free States as one man against the inhabitants of the slave States. Union on the one side will beget union on the other; and this process of reciprocal consolidation will be attended with all the violent prejudices, embittered passions, and implacable animosities which ever degraded or deformed human nature. A virtual dissolution of the Union will have taken place, whilst the forms of its existence remain. The most valuable elements of union, mutual kindness, the feelings of sympathy, the fraternal bonds, which now happily unite us, will have been extinguished forever. One Section will stand in menacing and hostile array against the other. The collision of opinion will be quickly followed by the clash of arms. I will not attempt to describe scenes which now happily lie concealed from our view. Abolitionists themselves would shrink back in dismay and horror at the contemplation of desolated fields, conflagrated cities, murdered inhabitants, and the overthrow of the fairest fabric of human government that ever rose to animate the hopes of civilized man. Nor should these Abolitionists flatter themselves that, if they can succeed in their object of uniting the people of the free States, they will enter the contest with a numerical superiority that must insure victory. All history and experience proves the hazard and uncertainty of war. And we are admonished by holy writ that the "race is not to the swift, nor the battle to the strong." But if they were to conquer, whom would they conquer? A foreign foe—one who had insulted our flag, invaded our shores, and laid our country waste? No, sir; no, sir. It would be a conquest without laurels, without glory—a self, a suicidal conquest—a conquest of brothers over brothers, achieved by one over another portion of the descendants of common ancestors, who nobly pledging their lives, their fortunes, and their sacred honor, had fought and bled, side by side, in many a hard battle on land and ocean, severed our country from the British Crown, and established our national independence.

The inhabitants of the slaves States are sometimes accused by their Northern brethren with displaying too much rashness and sensibility to the operations and proceedings of Abolitionists. But, before they can be rightly judged, there should be a reversal of conditions. Let me suppose that the people of the slave States were to form societies, subsidize presses, make large pecuniary contributions, send forth numerous missionaries throughout all their own borders, and enter into machinations to burn the beautiful capitals, destroy the productive manufactories, and sink in the ocean the gallant ships of the Northern States. Would these incendary proceedings be regarded as neighborly and friendly, and consistent with the fraternal sentiments which should ever be cherished by one portion of the Union towards another? Would they excite no emotion? occasion no manifestations of dissatisfaction, nor lead to any acts of retaliatory violence? But the supposed case falls far short of the actual one in a most essential circumstance. In no contingency could these capitals, manufactories, and ships, rise in rebellion and massacre inhabitants of the Northern States.

I am, Mr. President, no friend of slavery. The Searcher of all Hearts knows that every pulsation of mine beats high and strong in the cause of civil liberty. Wherever it is safe and practicable, I desire to see every portion of the human family in the enjoyment of it. But I prefer the liberty of my own country to that of any other people, and the liberty of my own race to that of any other race. The liberty of the descendants of Africa in the United States is incompatible with the safety and liberty of the European descendants. There slavery forms an exception—an exception resulting from a stern and inexorable necessity—to the general liberty in the United States. We did not originate, nor are we responsible for, this necessity. Their liberty, if it were possible, could only be established by violating the incontestable powers of the States, and subverting the Union; and beneath the ruins of the Union would be buried, sooner or later, the liberty of both races.

But if one dark spot exists on our political horizon, is it not obscured by the bright and effulgent and cheering light that beams all around us? Was ever a people before so blessed as we are, if true to ourselves? Did ever any other nation contain within its bosom so many elements of prosperity, of greatness, and of glory? Our only real danger lies ahead, conspicuous, elevated, and visible. It was clearly discerned at the commencement, and distinctly seen throughout our whole career. Shall we wantonly run upon it, and destroy all the glorious anticipations of the high destiny that awaits us? I beseech the Abolitionists themselves solemnly to pause in their mad and fatal course. Amidst the infinite variety of objects of humanity and benevolence which invite the employment of their energies, let them select some one more harmless, that does not threaten to deluge our country in blood. I call upon that small portion of the clergy which has lent itself to these wild and ruinous schemes, not to forget the holy nature of the divine mission of the founder of our religion, and to profit by his peaceful examples. I intreat that portion of my countrywomen who have given their countenance to abolition, to remember that they are ever most loved and honored when moving in their own appropriate and delightful sphere, and to reflect that the ink which they shed in subscribing with their fair hands Abolition petitions, may prove but the prelude to the shedding of the blood of their brethren. I adjure all the inhabitants of the free States to rebuke and discountenance, by their opinion and their example, measures which must inevitably lead to the most calamitous consequences. And let us all, as countrymen, as friends, and as brothers, cherish in unfading memory the motto which bore our ancestors triumphantly through all the trials of the Revolution, as, if adhered to, it will conduct their posterity through all that may, in the dispensations of Providence, be reserved for them.

CHAPTER XII.

THE AGITATION IN 1847 AND 1850.

In 1847, Mr. Calhoun introduced the following Resolution in the Senate:

"*Resolved,* That it is a fundamental principle in our political creed that a people, in framing a Constitution, have the unconditional right to form and adopt the government which they may think best calculated to secure their liberty, prosperity, and happiness; and that, in conformity thereto, no other condition is imposed by the federal Constitution on a State, in order to be admitted into this Union, except that its Constitution shall be republican; and that the imposition of any other by Congress would not only be in violation of the Constitution, but in direct conflict with the principle on which our political system rests."

Upon this resolution Mr. Calhoun offered some highly striking remarks,

"Mr. President: Not only is that proposition grossly inconsistent with the Constitution, but the other, which undertakes to say that no State shall be admitted into this Union which shall not prohibit by its Constitution the existence of slaves, is equally a great outrage against the Constitution of the United States. Sir, I hold it to be a fundamental principle of our political system that the people have a right to establish what government they may think proper for themselves; that every State about to become a member of this Union has a right to form its own government as it pleases; and that, in order to be admitted, there is but one qualification, and that is, that the government shall be republican. There is no express provision to that effect, but it results from that important section which guarantees to every State in this Union a republican form of government. Now, sir, what is proposed? It is proposed, from a vague, indefinite, erroneous, and most dangerous conception of private individual liberty, to overrule this great common liberty which the people have of framing their own Constitution! Sir, the right of self-government on the part of individuals is not near so easily to be established by any course of reasoning as the right of a community or State to self-government. And yet, sir, there are men of such delicate feeling on the subject of liberty—men who cannot possibly bear what they call slavery in one section of the country, although not so much slavery as an institution indispensable for the good of both races—men so squeamish on this point, that they are ready to strike down the higher right of a community to govern themselves, in order to maintain the absolute right of individuals in every possible condition to govern themselves!"

In 1848 Mr. Calhoun said:

*   *   *   *   *   *

"There is a very striking difference between the position in which the slaveholding and non-slaveholding States stand in reference to the subject under consideration. The former desire no action of the Government; demand no law to give them any advantage in the Territory about to be established; are willing to leave it, and other Territories belonging to the United States, open to all their citizens, so long as they continue to be Territories, and when they cease to be so, to leave it to their inhabitants to form such governments as may suit them, without restriction or condition, except that imposed by the Constitution, as a prerequisite for admission into the Union. In short, they are willing to leave the whole subject where the Constitution and the great and fundamental principles of self-government place it. On the contrary, the non-slaveholding States, instead of being willing to leave it on this broad and equal foundation, demand the interposition of the Government, and the passage of an act to exclude the citizens of the slaveholding States from emigrating with their property into the Territory, in order to give their citizens, and those they may permit, the exclusive right of settling it, while it remains in that condition, preparatory to subjecting it to like restrictions and conditions when it becomes a State."

* * * * * *

"But I go further, and hold that justice and the Constitution are the easiest and the safest guard on which the question can be settled, regarded in reference to party. It may be settled on that ground simply by non-action—by leaving the Territories free and open to the emigration of all the world so long as they continue so; and when they become States to adopt whatever Constitution they please, with the single restriction, to be republican, in order to their admission into the Union. If a party cannot safely take this broad and solid position, and successfully maintain it, what other can it take and maintain? If it cannot maintain itself by an appeal to the great principles of justice, the Constitution, and self-government, to what other, sufficiently strong to uphold them in public opinion, can they appeal? I greatly mistake the character of the people of this Union, if such an appeal would not prove successful, if either party should have the magnanimity to step forward and boldly make it. It would, in my opinion, be received with shouts of approbation by the patriotic and intelligent in every quarter. There is a deep feeling pervading the country that the Union and our political institutions are in danger, which such a course would dispel."

January 12, 1848. In the Senate of the United States,

the following resolutions, submitted by Mr. Dickinson on the 14th ultimo, came up:

"*Resolved*, That true policy requires the government of the United States to strengthen its political and commercial relations upon this continent, by the annexation of such contiguous territory as may conduce to that end, and can be justly obtained; and that neither in such acquisition nor in the territorial organization thereof can any conditions be constitutionally imposed, or institutions be provided for or established, inconsistent with the right of the people thereof to form a free sovereign State, with the powers and privileges of the original members of the confederacy.

"*Resolved*, That, in organizing a territorial government for territories belonging to the United States, the principles of self-government upon which our federative system rests will be best promoted, the true spirit and meaning of the Constitution be observed, and the confederacy strengthened, by leaving all questions concerning the domestic policy therein to the legislatures chosen by the people thereof."

Mr. Dickinson said:—The second resolution declares that the principle of self-government upon which the federative system rests will be best promoted, the true spirit and meaning of the Constitution be observed, and the confederacy strengthened, by leaving all questions concerning the domestic regulation of territory to the legislatures chosen by the people thereof.

It must be conceded by all, that Congress has no inherent power over this subject, and no more right to legislate concerning it than the British Parliament, unless such authority is delegated by the Constitution. The only clause of the Constitution which is supposed to confer upon Congress the right to legislate for the people of a territory, is as follows:

" The Congress shall have power to dispose of, and make

all needful rules and regulations respecting the territory or other property belonging to the United States," &c.

In providing legislation for the District of Columbia, and for places occupied by the government of the United States for fortifications and other erections required by the public service, the Constitution **thus** confers the power upon Congress:

" To exercise exclusive legislation in all cases whatever, in such district (not exceeding ten miles square) as may, by the cession of particular States, and the acceptance of Congress, become the seat of the government of the United States, and to exercise like authority over all places purchased, by the consent of the legislature of the State in which the same shall be, for the erection of forts, magazines, arsenals, dock-yards, and other needful buildings."

By the clause of the Constitution first above cited, it is evident that territory is mentioned in its material, and not in its political sense, for it is classed with "other property," and Congress is authorized to dispose of and make all needful rules and regulations respecting both. In the other section they are separated, and Congress is authorized to legislate over all places occupied for public structures, but no such authority is extended to territory. The language of the Constitution is that of great precision—free from repetition—and every word was well weighed in its positive and relative sense. And if its framers had supposed the phrase "needful rules and regulations" authorized legislation over places belonging to the United States, and used for public service, they would scarcely have authorized legislation over such places in express language in another section. Again, in providing legislation for the District of Columbia, Congress is authorized to "exercise exclusive legislation" over it. Now, if the words "needful rules and regulations" were deemed proper and apt language to confer legislative authority over the internal affairs of a territory, why were they not employed to authorize legislation over the District? And to reverse the order of the inquiry, if it was intended to confer upon Congress the power to legislate over territory, why was it not given in the same express terms as in authorizing legislation for the District? From this view, there is little doubt that a strict construction would deny to Congress the right to legislate for the domestic affairs of the people of territory without their consent.

Congress has, however, upon various occasions, exercised legislative power over the subject, especially in incorporating into the law organizing territories the provisions of the Ordinance of 1787; and this has been acquiesced in by the people of the territory. This Ordinance was framed under the old confederacy, for the government of the Northwestern Territory, and the sixth article forbade slavery or involuntary servitude therein. Its validity has often been questioned, and its adoption was pronounced by Mr. Madison to be "without the least color of constitutional law." But whether authorized or not, having been passed before the adoption of the Constitution, the act has no authority as a precedent for like practice under it.

Extract from the speech of Henry Clay, in the United States Senate, February 5th and 6th, 1850.

Mr. Clay said: When I came to consider the subject, and to compare the provisions of the line of 36° 30'—the Missouri compromise line—with the plan which I have proposed for the accommodation of this question, said I to myself, if I offer the line of 36° 30', to interdict the question of slavery north of it, and to leave it unsettled and open south of it, I offer that which is illusory to the South—I offer that which will deceive them, if they suppose that slavery will be received south of that line. It is better for them—I said to myself—it is better for the South, that there should be non-action as to slavery both north and south of the line—far better that there should be non-action both sides of the line, than that there should be action by the interdiction on the one side, without action for the admission upon the other side of the line. Is it not so? What is there gained by the South, if the Missouri line is extended to the Pacific, with the interdiction of slavery north of it? Why, the very argument which has been most often and most seriously urged by the South has been this: we do not want Congress to legislate upon the subject of slavery at all; you ought not to touch it. You have no power over it. I do not concur, as is well known from what I have said upon that question, in this view of the subject; but that is the Southern argument. We do not want you, say they, to legislate upon the subject of slavery. But if you adopt the Missouri line, and thus interdict slavery north of that line, you do legislate upon the subject of slavery, and you legislate for its restriction without a corresponding equivalent of legislation south of that line for its admission; for I insist that if there be legislation interdicting slavery north of the line, then the principles of equality would require that there should be legislation admitting slavery south of the line.

I have said that I never could vote for it myself, and I repeat that I never can, and never will vote, and no earthly power will ever make me vote, to spread slavery over territory where it does not exist. Still, if there be a majority who are for interdicting slavery north of the line, there ought to be a majority, if justice is done to the South, to admit slavery south of the line. And if there be a majority to accomplish both of these purposes, although I cannot concur in their action, yet I shall be one of the last to create any disturbance; I shall be one of the first to acquiesce in that legislation, although it is contrary to my own judgment and to my own conscience.

I hope, then, to keep the whole of these matters untouched by any legislation of Congress upon the subject of slavery, leaving it open and undecided. Non-action by Congress is best for the South, and best for all the views which the South have disclosed to us from time to time as corresponding to their wishes. I know it has been said with regard to the territories, and especially has it been said with regard to California, that non-legislation upon the part of Congress implies the same thing as the exclusion of slavery. That we cannot help. That Congress is not responsible for. If nature has pronounced the doom of slavery in these territories—if she has declared, by her immutable laws, that slavery cannot and shall not be introduced there—who can you reproach but nature and nature's God? Congress you cannot. Congress abstains. Congress is passive. Congress is non-acting, south and north of the line; or rather if Congress agrees to the plan which I propose, extending no line, it leaves the entire theatre of the whole cession of these territories untouched by legislative enactments, either to exclude or admit slavery. Well, I ask again, if you will listen to the voice of calm and dispassionate reason—I ask of any man of the South, to rise and tell me if it is not better for that section of the Union, that Congress should remain passive upon both sides of the ideal line, rather than that we should interdict slavery upon the one side of that line and be passive upon the other side of that line?

Extract from Daniel Webster's speech in the United States Senate, March 7th, 1850.

Now, as to California and New Mexico, I hold slavery to be excluded from those territories by a law even superior to that which admits and sanctions it in Texas—I mean the law of nature, of physical geography—the law of the formation of the earth. That law settles forever, with a strength beyond all terms of human enactment, that slavery cannot exist in

California or New Mexico. Understand me, sir,—I mean slavery as we regard it; slaves in gross, of the colored race, transferable by sale and delivery, like other property.

* * * * * * * *

I look upon it, therefore, as a fixed fact, to use an expression current at this day, that both California and New Mexico are destined to be free, so far as they are settled at all, which I believe, especially in regard to New Mexico, will be very little for a great length of time—free by the arrangement of things by the Power above us. I have therefore to say, in this respect also, that this country is fixed for freedom, to as many persons as shall ever live there, by as irrepealable, and a more irrepealable law, than the law that attaches to the right of holding slaves in Texas; and I will say further, that if a resolution, or a law, were now before us, to provide a territorial government for New Mexico, I would not vote to put any prohibition into it whatever. The use of such a prohibition would be idle, as it respects any effect it would have upon the territory; and I would not take pains to reaffirm an ordinance of nature, nor to re-enact the will of God. And I would put in no Wilmot proviso, for the purpose of a taunt or a reproach. I would put into it no evidence of the votes of superior power, to wound the pride, even whether a just pride, a rational pride, or an irrational pride—to wound the pride of the gentlemen who belong to the Southern States. I have no such object, no such purpose. They would think it a taunt, an indignity. They would think it to be an act taking away from them what they regard a proper equality of privilege; and whether they expect to realize any benefit from it or not, they would think it a theoretic wrong—that something more or less derogatory to their character and their rights had taken place. I propose to inflict no such wound upon anybody, unless something essentially important to the country, and efficient to the preservation of liberty and freedom, is to be effected. Therefore I repeat, sir— and I repeat it because I wish it to be understood—that I do not propose to address the Senate often on this subject. I desire to pour out all my heart in as plain a manner as possible; and I say again, that if a proposition were now here for a government for New Mexico, and it was moved to insert a provision for a prohibition of slavery, I would not vote for it.

Now, Mr. President, I have established, so far as I proposed to go into any line of observation to establish, the proposition with which I set out, and upon which I propose to stand or fall, and that is, that the whole territory of the States in the United States, or in the newly-acquired territory of the United States, has a fixed and settled character, now fixed and settled by law, which can not be repealed in the case of Texas without a violation of public faith, and can not be repealed by any human power in regard to California or New Mexico; that, under one or other of these laws, every foot of territory in the States, or in the Territories, has now received a fixed and decided character.

Sir, if we were now making a government for New Mexico, and anybody should propose a Wilmot proviso, I should treat it exactly as Mr. Polk treated that provision for excluding slavery from Oregon. Mr. Polk was known to be in opinion decidedly averse to the Wilmot proviso; but he felt the necessity of establishing a government for the Territory of Oregon, and, though the proviso was there, he knew it would be entirely nugatory; and, since it must be entirely nugatory, since it took away no right, no describable, no estimable, no weighable, or tangible right of the South, he said he would sign the bill for the sake of enacting a law to form a government in that Territory, and let that entirely useless, and, in that connection, entirely senseless, proviso remain. For myself, I will say that we hear much of the annexation of Canada; and if there be any man, any of the northern democracy, or any one of the free-soil party, who supposes it necessary to insert a Wilmot proviso in a territorial government for New Mexico, that man will of course be of opinion that it is necessary to protect the everlasting snows of Canada from the foot of slavery, by the same overpowering wing of an act of Congress.

Then, sir, there are those abolition societies, of which I am unwilling to speak, but in regard to which I have very clear notions and opinions. I do not think them useful. I think their operations for the last twenty years have produced nothing good or valuable. At the same time, I know thousands of them are honest and good men; perfectly well-meaning men. They have excited feelings; they think they must do something for the cause of liberty; and in their sphere of action, they do not see what else they can do, than to contribute to an abolition press, or an abolition society, or to pay an abolition lecturer. I do not mean to impute gross motives even to the leaders of these societies, but I am not blind to the consequences. I cannot but see what mischiefs their interference with the South has produced. And is it not plain to every man? Let any gentleman who doubts of that, recur to the debates in the Virginia House of Delegates in 1832, and he will see with what freedom a proposition, made by Mr. Randolph, for the gradual abolition of slavery was discussed in that body. Every one spoke of slavery as he thought; very ignominious and disparaging names and epithets were applied to it. The debates in the House of Delegates on that occasion, I believe, were all published. They were read by every colored man who could read, and if there were any who could not read, those debates were read to them by others. At that time Virginia was not unwilling nor afraid to discuss this question, and to let that part of her population know as much of it as they could learn. That was in 1832. As has been said by the honorable member from

Carolina, these abolition societies commenced their course of action in 1835. It is said—I do not know how true it may be—that they sent incendiary publications into the slave States; at any event, they attempted to arouse, and did arouse, a very strong feeling; in other words, they created great agitation in the North against Southern slavery. Well, what was the result? The bonds of the slaves were bound more firmly than before; their rivets were more strongly fastened. Public opinion, which in Virginia had begun to be exhibited against slavery, and was opening out for the discussion of the question, drew back and shut itself up in its castle. I wish to know whether any body in Virginia can, now, talk as Mr. Randolph, Gov. McDowell, and others talked there, openly, and sent their remarks to the press, in 1832. We all know the fact, and we all know the cause, and everything that this agitating people have done, has been, not to enlarge, but to restrain, not to set free, but to bind faster, the slave population of the South. That is my judgment. Sir, as I have said, I know many abolitionists in my own neighborhood, very honest, good people, misled, as I think, by strange enthusiasm; but they wish to do something, and they are called on to contribute, and they do contribute; and it is my firm opinion this day, that within the last twenty years, as much money has been collected and paid to the abolition societies, abolition presses, and abolition lecturers, as would purchase the freedom of every slave—man, woman, and child—in the State of Maryland, and send them all to Liberia. I have no doubt of it. But I have yet to learn that the benevolence of these abolition societies has at any time taken that particular turn.

Extract from Hon. John C. Calhoun's speech in the Senate, June 27th, 1848.

But there is one precedent referred to by the Senator

unconnected with the power, and on that account requires particular notice. I refer to the ordinance of 1787, which was adopted by the old Congress of the Confederation while the Convention that framed the Constitution was in session, and about one year before its adoption, and of course on the very eve of the expiration of the old Confederation. Against its introduction, I might object that the act of the Congress of the Confederation cannot rightfully form precedents for this government; but I waive that. I waive also the objection that the act was consummated when that government was *in extremis*, and could hardly be considered *compos mentis*. I waive also the fact that the ordinance assumed the form of a compact, and was adopted when only eight States were present, when the Articles of Confederation required nine to form compacts. I waive also the fact, that Mr. Madison declared that the act was without shadow of constitutional authority, and shall proceed to show, from the history of its adoption, that it cannot justly be considered of any binding force.

Virginia made the cession of the Territory north of the Ohio, and lying between it and the Mississippi and the lakes, in 1784. It now contains the States of Ohio, Indiana, Illinois, Michigan, Wisconsin, and a very considerable extent of territory lying North of the latter. Shortly after the cession, a committee of three was raised, of whom Mr. Jefferson was one. They reported an ordinance for the establishment of the Territory, containing, among other provisions, one, of which Mr. Jefferson was the author, excluding slavery from the Territory after the year 1800. It was reported to Congress, but this provision was struck out. On the question of striking out, every Southern State present voted in favor of it; and what is more striking, every Southern delegate voted the same way, Mr. Jefferson alone excepted. The ordinance was adopted without the provision. At the next session, Rufus King, then a member of the old Congress, moved a proposition, very much in the same shape as the sixth article (that which excludes slavery) in the ordinance as it now stands, with the exception of its proviso. It was referred to a committee, but there was no action on it. A committee was moved the next or the subsequent year, which reported without including or noticing Mr. King's proposition. Mr. Dane was a member of that committee, and proposed a provision the same as that in the ordinance as it passed, but the committee reported without including it. Finally, another committee was raised, at the head of which was Mr. Carrington, of Virginia, and of which Mr. Dane was also a member. That committee reported without including the amendment previously proposed by him. Mr. Dane moved his proposition, which was adopted, and the report of the committee thus amended became the Ordinance of 1787.

It may be inferred from this brief historical sketch, that the ordinance was a compromise between the Southern and Northern States, of which the terms were, that slavery should be excluded from Territory upon condition that fugitive slaves, who might take refuge in the Territory should be delivered up to their owners, as stipulated in the proviso of the 6th article of the Ordinance. It is manifest, from what has been stated, that the South was unitedly and obstinately opposed to the provision when first moved; that the proposition of Mr. King, without the proviso, was in like manner resisted by the South, as may be inferred from its entire want of success, and that it never could be brought to agree to it until the provision for the delivery up of fugitive slaves was incorporated in it. But it is well understood that a compromise involves not a surrender, but simply a waiver of the right or power; and hence, in the case of individuals, it is a well established legal principle, that an offer to settle by compromise a litigated claim, is no evidence against the justice of the claim on the side of the party making it. The South, to her honor, has observed with fidelity her engagements under this compromise; in proof of which, I appeal to the precedents cited by the Senator from New York, intended by him to establish the fact of her acquiescence in the Ordinance. I admit that she has acquiesced in the several acts of Congress to carry it into effect; but the Senator is mistaken in supposing that it is proof of a surrender, on her part, of the power over the territories which he claims for Congress. No, she never has, and I trust never will, make such a surrender. Instead of that, it is conclusive proof of her fidelity to her engagements. She has never attempted to set aside the ordinance, or to deprive the territory, and the States erected within its limits, of any right or advantage it was intended to confer. But I regret that as much cannot be said in favor of the fidelity with which it has been observed on their part. With the single exception of the State of Illinois—be it said to her honor—every other State erected within its limits has pursued a course, and adopted measures, which have rendered the stipulations of the proviso to deliver up fugitive slaves nugatory. Wisconsin may also be an exception, as she has just entered the Union, and has hardly had time to act on the subject. They have gone further, and suffered individuals to form combinations, without an effort to suppress them, for the purpose of enticing and seducing the slaves to leave their masters, and to run them into Canada beyond the reach of our laws—in open violation, not only of the stipulations of the ordinance, but of the Constitution itself. If I express myself strongly, it is not for the purpose of producing excitement, but to draw the attention of the Senate forcibly to the subject. My object is to lay bare the subject under consideration, just as a surgeon probes to the bottom and lays open a wound, not to cause pain to his patient, but for the purpose of healing it.

* * * * * * *

I come now to another precedent of a similar character, but differing in this, that it took place under this government, and not under that of the old confederation; I refer to what is known as the Missouri compromise. It is more recent, and better known, and may be more readily despatched.

After an arduous struggle of more than a year, on the question whether Missouri should come into the Union, with or without restrictions prohibiting slavery, a compromise line was adopted between the North and the South; but it was done under circumstances which made it nowise obligatory upon the latter. It is true, it was moved by one of her distinguished citizens, [Mr. Clay,] but it is equally so, that it was carried by the almost united vote of the North against the almost united vote of the South; and was thus imposed on the latter by superior numbers, in opposition to her strenuous efforts. The South has never given her sanction to it, or assented to the power it asserted. She was voted down, and has simply acquiesced in an arrangement which she has not had the power to reverse, and which she could not attempt to do without disturbing the peace and harmony of the Union—to which she has ever been averse. Acting on this principle, she permitted the Territory of Iowa to be formed, and the State to be admitted into the Union, under the compromise, without objection; and that is now quoted by the Senator from New York to prove her surrender of the power he claims for Congress.

To add to the strength of this claim, the advocates of the power hold up the name of Jefferson in its favor, and go so far as to call him the author of the so-called Wilmot proviso, which is but a general expression of a 'power of which the Missouri compromise is a case of its application. If we may judge by his opinion of that case, what his opinion was of the principle, instead of being the author of the proviso, or being in its favor, no one could be more deadly hostile to it. In a letter addressed to the elder Adams, in 1819, in answer to one from him, he uses these remarkable expressions in reference to the Missouri question:

"The banks, bankrupt law, manufactures, Spanish treaty, are nothing. These are occurrences which, like waves in a storm, will pass under the ship. But the Missouri question is a breaker on which we lose the Missouri country by revolt, and what more, God only knows."

To understand the full force of these expressions, it must be borne in mind, that the questions enumerated were the great and exciting political questions of the day on which parties divided. The banks and bankrupt law had long been so. Manufactures (or what has since been called the protective tariff) was at the time a subject of great excitement, as was the Spanish treaty; that is, the treaty by which Florida was ceded to the Union, and by which the western boundary between Mexico and the United States was settled, from the Gulf of Mexico to the Pacific Ocean. All these exciting party questions of the day, Mr. Jefferson regarded as nothing compared with the Missouri question. He looked on all of them as, in their nature, fugitive; and, to use his own forcible expression, "would pass off under the ship of state like waves in a storm." Not so that fatal question. It was a breaker on which it was destined to be stranded; and yet, his name is quoted by the incendiaries of the present day in support of, and as the author of, a proviso which would give indefinite and universal extension of this fatal question to all the territories. It was compromised the next year by the adoption of the line to which I have referred. Mr. Holmes, of Maine, long a member of this body, who voted for the measure, addressed a letter to Mr. Jefferson, enclosing a copy of his speech on the occasion. It drew out an answer from him which ought to be treasured up in the heart of every man who loves the country and its institutions. It is brief: I will send it to the Secretary to be read. The time of the Senate cannot be better occupied than in listening to it:

"MONTICELLO, *April* 22, 1820.

"I thank you, dear sir, for the copy you have been so kind as to send me of the letter to your constituents on the Missouri question. It is a perfect justification to them. I had for a long time ceased to read newspapers, or pay any attention to public affairs, confident they were in good hands, and content to be a passenger in our bark to the shore from which I am not distant. But this momentous question, like a fire-bell in the night, awakened and filled me with terror. I considered it at once as the knell of the Union. It is hushed, indeed, for the moment; but this is a reprieve only, not a final sentence. A geographical line, coinciding with a marked principle, moral and political, once conceived and held up to the angry passions of men, will never be obliterated; and every new irritation will mark it deeper and deeper. I can say, with conscious truth, that there is not a man on earth who would sacrifice more than I would to relieve us from this heavy reproach, in any *practicable* way. The cession of that kind of property (for so it is misnamed) is a bagatelle, which would not cost me a second thought, if, in that way, a general emancipation and *expatriation* could be effected; and gradually, and with due sacrifices, I think it might be. But as it is, we have the wolf by the ears, and we can neither hold him, nor safely let him go. Justice is in one scale, and self-preservation in the other. Of one thing I am certain, that as the free passage of slaves from one State to another would not make a slave of a single human being who would not be so without it, so their diffusion over a greater surface would make them individually happier, and proportionally facilitate the accomplishment of their emancipation, by dividing the burden on a greater number of coadjutors. An absti nence, too, from this act of power, would remove the jealousy excited by the undertaking of Congress to regulate the condition of the different descriptions of men composing a State. This certainly is the exclusive right of every State, which nothing in the Constitution has taken from them, and given to the general government. Could Congress, for example, say that the non-freemen of Connecticut shall be freemen, or that they shall not emigrate into any other State?

"I regret that I am now to die in the belief, that the useless sacrifice of themselves by the generation of 1776, to acquire self-government and happiness to their country, is to be thrown away by the unwise and unworthy passions of their sons, and that my only consolation is to be, that I live not, to weep over it. If they would but dispassionately weigh the blessings they will throw away, against an abstract principle, more likely to be effected by union than by secession, they would pause before they would perpetrate this act of suicide on themselves, and of treason against the hopes of the world. To yourself as the faithful advocate of the Union, I tender the offering of my high esteem and respect. "THOMAS JEFFERSON."

"JOHN HOLMES, Esq."

Mark his prophetic words! Mark his profound reasoning!

"It [the question] is hushed *for the moment*. But this is a *reprieve only*, not a *final sentence*. A geographical line coinciding with a marked principle, moral and political, *once conceived and held up to the angry passions of men, will never be obliterated, and every new irritation will mark it deeper and deeper.*"

Twenty-eight years have passed since these remarkable words were penned, and there is not a thought which time has not thus far verified, and it is to be feared will continue to verify until the whole will be fulfilled. Certain it is, that he regarded the compromise line as utterly inadequate to arrest that fatal course of events which his keen sagacity anticipated from the question. It was but a "reprieve." Mark the deeply melancholy impression which it made on his mind:

"I regret that I am to die in the belief that the useless sacrifice of themselves by the generation of 1776, to acquire self-government and happiness for themselves, is to be thrown away by the unwise and unworthy passions of their sons, and that my only consolation is to be, that I shall live not to weep over it."

Can any one believe, after listening to this letter, that Jefferson is the author of the so-called Wilmot proviso, or ever favored it? And yet there are at this time strenuous efforts making in the North to form a purely sectional party on it, and that, too, under the sanction of those who profess the highest veneration for his character and principles!

* * * * * *

I have now concluded the discussion, so far as it relates to the power; and have, I trust, established, beyond controversy, that the Territories are free, and open to all of the citizens of the United States, and that there is no power, under any aspect the subject can be viewed in, by which the citizens of the South can be excluded from emigrating with their property into any of them. I have advanced no argument which I do not believe to be true, nor pushed any one beyond what truth would strictly warrant. But, if mistaken, if my arguments, instead of being sound and true, as I hold them beyond controversy to be, should turn out to be a mere mass of sophisms; and if, in consequence, the barrier opposed by the want of power, should be surmounted, there is another still in the way that cannot be. The mere possession of power, is not, of itself, sufficient to justify its exercise. It must be, in addition, shown, that in the given case it can be rightfully and justly exercised. Under our system, the first inquiry is, Does the Constitution authorize the exercise of the power? If that be decided in the affirmative, the next is, Can it be rightfully and justly exercised under the circumstances? And it is not until that, too, is decided in the affirmative, that the question of the expediency of exercising it is presented for consideration.

Now, I put the question solemnly to the Senators from the North: Can you rightly and justly exclude the South from the territories of the United States, and monopolize them for yourselves, even if, in your opinion, you should have the power? It is this question I wish to press on your attention, with all due solemnity and decorum. The North and the South stand in the relation of partners in a common Union, with equal dignity and equal rights. We of the South have contributed our full share of funds, and shed our full share of blood, for the acquisition of our territories. Can you, then, on any principle of equity and justice, deprive us of our full share in their benefit and advantages? Are you ready to affirm, that a majority of the partners in a joint concern have the right to monopolize its benefits, to the exclusion of the minority, even in cases where they have contributed their full share to the concern?

OPINIONS OF MESSRS. CASS, DICKINSON, AND TOOMBS.

In the Senate, 1850, Mr. Cass said: We are all aware that there are various clauses of the Constitution, and various other sources, *foreign and domestic*, whence this right of unlimited legislation over the territories is sought to be deduced. One of these, at least, is an express constitutional grant of power, and if it fairly includes the authority *to bind the territories in all cases whatsoever*, then there is an end of this question, and we may pass this proviso, and regulate all their other concerns at our pleasure. But there are other sources, accepted or rejected, as minds differently constituted take part in this controversy, whence this right is derived indirectly, as necessary to the exercise of some power found in the Constitution, or of some other power found out of the Constitution. It will hardly be denied— the time for denial has not yet come, though appearances indicate it as fast approaching—that these indirect or incidental powers are to be employed no further than is necessary to meet the occasion which calls them into action. Derivative in their nature, they are limited in their exercise. They cannot go beyond the legitimate object which is sought to be attained. If the necessity for social order in the Territories, as many, perhaps as most of the speakers contend, is the true foundation of the right of Congress to legislate over them, it is a right which extends no further than may be necessary and proper to fulfill this first duty of society. The means must be proper for the end, and proportioned to it; and if this end can be obtained by the establishment of local governments, there ceases the constitutional action of Congress, and the internal legislation should be committed to the people to be affected by it. It is essential, therefore, to ascertain whence this power comes, that we may ascertain how far it may go; essential, that we may not violate the Constitution; essential, that we may not violate a fundamental principle of freedom, the unalienable connection between representation and internal legislation; and essential, that the people of the Territories may conduct their own concerns in their own way—the very cardinal doctrine of American freedom.

*　　*　　*　　*　　*　　*　　*　　*

There is no clause in the Constitution which gives to Congress express power to pass any law respecting slavery in the Territories. The authority is deduced from various sources, which I propose to examine by and by. But every construction which would give to a foreign legislature jurisdiction over this subject of slavery—by foreign I mean not elected by the people to be affected by its acts, nor responsible to them—would equally give it jurisdiction over every other department of life, social and political, in the territories: over the relations of husband and wife, of parent and child, of guardian and ward, as well as over the relations of master and servant; and embracing within the sphere of its operations the whole circle of human rights, personal and political—life, liberty, and property, in all their various modes of enjoyment. I say "the power of Congress over slavery;" for, if we have power to abolish it, or to exclude it, we have power to institute it. We possess complete jurisdiction over the subject; for there is no intellect, however acute, which can so limit the legislative right of action, if it exist at all, as to apply it to the exclusion of slavery, and withhold it from its institution. If any one doubts this proposition, let him turn to the Constitution and show the limitation. Before I can believe that such a power was granted, so remote from the objects of the government which the framers of the Constitution sought to establish, belonging exclusively to the local questions affecting the different communities into which we are divided, I must abandon many of the illusions I have cherished respecting the wisdom of the statesmen who composed the Convention of 1787.

*　*　*　*　*　*　*　*

Reverting to the proposition that Congress has unlimited power of legislation over the territories, the first reflection which strikes the inquirer is, that if this power were intended to be granted, nothing was more easy than for the Convention to place the subject beyond doubt by a plain expression of the object.

Extracts of Speech of Mr. Houston, of Texas, on Mr. Clay's compromise Resolutions, Feb. 8, 1850.

Mr. Houston said, the North contend that they have a right to interfere with the subject of slavery, hence the Wilmot proviso. The South contend that the North has no such right—no right to interfere with the subject of slavery anywhere; and hence the principle is contended for that Congress does not possess this power as applicable to the territories—no power arising from the terms of the union between the North and the South—none growing out of the Constitution by which they are bound together. Nor do I believe that Congress has, under the Constitution, any authority to impose upon States asking for admission into the Union any condition whatever, other than that of having a republican form of government. In this view I am sustained by high authority—no less than that of a statesman of long experience and distinguished reputation; I allude to the senator from South Carolina, who is now absent from his seat [Mr. Calhoun]; and in mentioning him, permit me to express my sincere regret for the cause which has withheld him from the discharge of his duties in this House. No one feels more sympathy for his physical sufferings than myself. That gentleman, in laying down his principles upon this subject in 1847, declared them, in a resolution of that day, almost in the terms of the resolution just read. I had not the benefit of the light of that resolution when I drew the one submitted by me; but I believe, had I possessed it, I could not have been more fortunate in the expression of the very view which I entertained.

*   *   *   *   *   *   *   *

I regret that the disposition to interfere with the institution of slavery, to inhibit the exercise of their rights to the Southern States and people; rights which all free people have to regulate their own domestic institutions—exists at all at the North; that any should wish to interfere with, or obstruct, the rights of the people of the territories to adopt such form of republican government as they may choose; for they would, subsequently to their admission to the Union as States, have the obvious right to modify their constitution so as to adopt or prohibit slavery according to their own will and pleasure. But I do not charge this disposition upon the people of the North, and to do so is, I think, to discourage our friends there, and to misinform and mislead the South. We ought to draw the line distinctly between those who are disposed to support the Constitution by sustaining the rights of the South, and those who are willing to carry on a crusade against rights pre-existent to the Constitution of the Union itself.

If the power, Mr. President, is not clearly and definitely given to the Congress of the United States to legislate upon the subject of the territorial governments, it strikes me that there is great force in the position, that to assume it would be to violate a fundamental principle of our government, which is, that the people (by which I understand the people of the territories as well as the people of the States) have the right of self-government under the Constitution. Congress has the power to make needful rules and regulations for the territories and other property of the United States; but these rules are temporary. They may apportion the land, and they have a right to do whatever may be necessary in order to dispose of it. They may provide for the boundaries of the territories, in order to give them compactness and judicious dimensions, and they have power to authorize the formation of territorial governments, to exist no longer than until it may be convenient for the people to legislate for themselves. Such are the powers necessarily resulting from authority delegated by the Constitution to Congress, but beyond this, I think, we cannot safely go.

Extract from the Speech of Mr. R. Toombs, of Georgia, in the House of Representatives, February 27th, 1850.

Mr. Toombs said: * * * *

Those who claim the power in Congress to exclude slavery from the territories rely rather on authority than principle to support it. They affirm, with singular ignorance of, or want of fidelity to, the facts, that Congress has from the beginning of the government uniformly claimed and repeatedly exercised the power to discourage slavery and to exclude it from the territories. My investigation of the subject has satisfied my own mind that neither position is sustained by a single precedent. I exclude, of course, legislation prohibiting the African slave trade; and I hold the ordinance of 1787 not to be within the principle asserted. For the first thirty years of our history this general duty to protect this great interest equally with every other, was universally admitted and fairly performed by every department of the government. The act of 1793 was passed to secure the delivery up of fugitives from labor escaping to the non-slaveholding States: your navigation laws authorized their transportation on the high seas. The government demanded and repeatedly received compensation for the owners of slaves for injuries sustained in these lawful voyages by the interference of foreign governments. It not only protected us upon the high seas, but followed us to foreign lands where we had been driven by the dangers of the sea, and protected slave property when thus cast even within the jurisdiction of hostile municipal laws. The slave property of our people was protected against the incursions of Indians by our military power and public treaties. The citizens of Georgia have received hundreds of thousands of dollars through your treaties for Indian depredations upon this species of property. That clause of the treaty of Ghent, which provided compensation for property destroyed or taken by the British government, placed slavery precisely upon the same ground with other property; and a New England man [Mr. Adams] ably and faithfully maintained the rights of the slaveholder under it at the Court of St. James. Then the government was administered according to the Constitution, and not according to what is now called "the spirit of the age." Those legislators looked for political powers and public duties in the organic law which political communities had laid down for their guidance and government. Humanity-mongers, atheistical socialists, who would upturn the moral, social, and political foundations of society, who would substitute the folly of men for the wisdom of God, were then justly considered as the enemies of the human race, and as deserving the contempt, if not the execration, of all mankind.

Until the year 1820 your territorial legislation was marked by the same general spirit of fairness and justice. Notwithstanding the constant assertions to the contrary by gentlemen from the North, up to that period no act was ever passed by Congress maintaining or asserting the primary constitutional power to prevent any citizen of the United States owning slaves from removing with them to our territories, and there receiving legal protection for this property. Until that time such persons did so remove into all the territories owned or acquired by the United States, except the Northwest Territory, and were there adequately protected. The action of Congress in reference to the ordinance of 1787 does not contravene this principle. That ordinance was passed on the 13th of July, 1787, before the adoption of our present Constitution. It purported on its face to be a perpetual compact between the State of Virginia, the people of the territory, and the then government of the United States, and unalterable, except by the consent of all the parties. When Congress met for the first time under the new government, on the 4th of March, 1789, it found the government thus established by virtue of this ordinance in actual operation; and on the 7th of August, 1789, it passed a law making the offices of Governor and Secretary of the Territory conform to the Constitution of the new government. It did nothing more. It made no reference to the sixth and last section of the ordinance which inhibited slavery. The division of that territory was provided for in the ordinance; at each division, the whole of the ordinance was assigned by Congress to each of its parts. This is the whole sum and substance of the free-soil claim to legislative precedents. Congress did not assert the right to alter a solemn compact entered into with the former government, but gave its consent by its legislation to the governments established and provided for in the compact. If the original compact was void for want of power in the old government to make it, as Mr. Madison supposed, Congress may not have been bound to accept it—it certainly had no power to alter it. From these facts and principles it is clear that the legislation for the Northwest Territory does not conflict with the principle which I assert, and does not afford precedents for the hostile legislation of Congress against slavery in the territories. That such was neither the principle nor the policy upon which the act of the 7th of August, 1789, was based, is further shown by the subsequent action of the same Congress. On the 2d of April, 1790, Congress, by a formal act, accepted the cession made by North Carolina of her western lands (now the State of Tennessee) with this clause in the deed of cession, "That no regulations made or to be made by Congress shall tend to emancipate slaves" in the ceded territory; and on the 26th of May, 1790, passed a territorial bill for the government of all the territory claimed by the United States south of the Ohio river. The description of this territory included all the lands ceded by North Carolina, but it included a great deal more. Its boundaries were left indefinite, because there were conflicting claims to all the rest of the territory. But this act put the whole country claimed by the United States south of the Ohio under this pro-slavery clause of the North Carolina deed. The whole action of the first Congress in relation to slavery in the territories of the United States seems to have been this; It acquiesced in a government for the Northwest Territory based upon a pre-existing anti-slavery ordinance, created a government for the country ceded by North Carolina in conformity with the pro-slavery clause in her deed, and extended this pro-slavery clause to all the rest of the territory claimed by the United States south of the Ohio river. This legislation vindicates the first Congress from all imputation of having established the precedent claimed by the friends of legislative exclusion.

The next territorial act which was passed was that of the 7th of April, 1798. It was the first act of territorial legislation which had to rest solely upon original, primary, constitutional power over the subject. It established a government over the territory included within the boundaries of a line drawn due east from the mouth of the Yazoo river to the Chattahoochee river, then down that river to the thirty-first degree of north latitude, then west on that line to the Mississippi river, then up the Mississippi to the beginning. This territory was within the boundary of the United States as defined by the treaty of Paris, and was not within the boundary of any of the States. The charter of Georgia limited her boundary on the south to the Altamaha river. In 1763, after the surrender of her charter, her limits were extended by the Crown to the St. Mary's river, and west on the thirty-first degree of north latitude to the Mississippi. In 1764, on the recommendation of the Board of Trade, her boundary was again altered, and that portion of territory within the boundaries which I have described was annexed to West Florida, and thus it stood at the Revolution and the treaty of peace. Therefore the United States claimed it as common property, and, in 1798, passed the act now under review for its government. In that act she neither claimed nor exerted any power to prohibit slavery in it. And the question came directly before Congress, the ordinance of 1787 in terms was applied to this territory, expressly "excepting and excluding the last article of the ordinance," which is the article excluding slavery from the Northwest Territory. This is a precedent directly in point, and is against the exercise of the power now claimed. In 1802, Georgia ceded her western lands, she protected slavery in her grant, and the Government complied with her stipulations.

In 1803 the United States acquired Louisiana from France by purchase. There is no special reference to slavery in the treaty; it was protected only under the general term of property. This acquisition was soon after the treaty divided into two Territories—the Orleans and the Louisiana Territories—over both of which governments were established. The law of slavery obtained in the whole country at the time we acquired it. Congress prohibited the foreign and domestic slave trade in these Territories, but gave the protection of its laws to slave owners emigrating thither with their slaves. Upon the admission of Louisiana into the Union, a new government was established by Congress over the rest of the country under the name of the Missouri Territory. This act also attempted no exclusion; slaveholders emigrated to the country with their slaves, and were protected by their government. In 1819 Florida was acquired by purchase; its laws recognized and protected slavery at the time of the acquisition. The United States extended the same recognition and protection.

I have thus briefly reviewed the whole territorial legislation of Congress from the beginning of the government until 1820, and it sustains my proposition, that within that period there was no precedent where Congress had exercised, or attempted to exercise, any primary constitutional power to prevent slaveholders from emigrating, with their slave property, to any portion of the public lands; and that it had extended the protection of its laws and its arms over such persons, in all cases except in the Northwest Territory, where it was fettered and restrained by an organic law established before the formation of our present Constitution.

Extract from a speech of Hon. Chester Butler, of Pennsylvania, in the House of Representatives, June 8, 1850:

Mr. Butler said—Sir, I must be permitted to express my dissent from each of these extravagant propositions. I do not believe, that, to hold slaves is to be involved in moral guilt, in sin. To believe this, would be a surrender of the whole question, for no law or constitution should be permitted to exist, creating or sustaining an unholy institution. In my judgment, slavery is not an unmitigated evil, nor is it an unalloyed good. Like most of the institutions of men, it contains a mixture of the ingredients of good and evil. It has its advantages, its comforts, its conveniences and its benefits, to both of the parties, who stand to each other in the relation of master and servant, as well the opposites of these characteristics; and, like other institutions of this world, it depends in its practical working for good or for evil, not upon any abstract principle of right or wrong, freedom or bondage, but upon the character of those among whom it exists, and the manner in which the power and the duties of the superiors are exercised and discharged. Theoretically, slavery may be wrong, as it is an invasion of an absolute right of the enslaved. The original abstract right of every human being, of every hue and complexion, to personal liberty, is, I believe, denied by no one. To deprive any human being of his personal liberty, except for crime, and by due course of law, and to reduce him to the condition of a slave, is a grievous wrong. It by no means follows, however, that this admitted right should, under all circumstances, be at once vindicated by restoring the slave to freedom ; nor is it true that the master, who refuses thus to vindicate the right by setting free his bondsman, without regard to surrounding circumstances and fitness of things, or to obligations resting upon himself to society, and to the slave himself, is guilty of a grievous wrong, or a wrong of any kind. If there is an unyielding obligation upon one master to free his slaves, because of this abstract right, it must rest upon all slaveholders alike : no one need be told of the disastrous consequences which would follow the practical application of this doctrine by immediate emancipation in our southern States. Such a course of proceeding there, would be unjust and cruel to the slaves themselves ; it would destroy slavery by destroying the slaves. To use a favorite illustration, it would be like plunging the knife to the heart of the patient in attempting to remove a blemish from the surface.

Slavery exists, and always has existed, among the different nations of the earth, from the earliest period in the history of man, among the uncivilized and barbarous, as well as the uncultivated and refined ; and while, with the former, the treatment of the slave is oppressive and cruel, with the latter his condition is much meliorated and improved, being modified by, and made to partake, in some measure, of the civilization, if not the cultivation, of those among whom his lot is cast. Compared with the slaves of other countries, and, it is said, even with the free peasantry of some, the condition of our southern slaves is greatly superior, in all that constitute the substantial comforts and happiness of life. And, sir, if slavery is to exist at all, it can be in no better form, at least, no better has ever been suggested, than that which prevails in our southern States ;

nor, in my judgment, is there any people, anywhere, in whose character for intelligence, benevolence and humanity, the most exacting friend of the negro race can hope to find stronger pledges against the abuse of power over those who are bound to their service, or surer guarantees that their duties and obligations towards them would be faithfully performed, than are found in that of our southern fellow-citizens. The relation of master and servant, imposes reciprocal duties and obligations upon the parties—service and obedience being due from the servant, care and protection from the master. When these mutual duties and obligations are faithfully observed, philanthropy has little to weep over in contemplating the condition of the servant.

*　　*　　*　　*　　*　　*

Mr. Chairman, I cannot read the second section of the fourth article of the Constitution without coming to the conclusion that it was intended the fugitives from service or labor, that is slavery, there spoken of, were to be delivered up promptly and summarily, and without the delay of a formal trial by jury. This same section provides that fugitives from justice shall, on demand of the executive authority of a State, "be delivered up, to be removed," &c. With regard to fugitives from service or labor, the provision is, they shall not " be discharged from such service or labor, but shall *be delivered up* on claim of the party to whom such service or labor may be due." In neither case is it said by whom or by what authority they shall be delivered up. In the case of fugitives from justice, the delivery up has always been done by the executive of one State upon the demand of the executive of another State; but in the case of fugitives from service, such has not been the practice, though the words are almost identical. The delivery up is to be done by somebody. Clearly it is not the duty of each individual citizen to do it. It must devolve on the State authority, or on that of the United States, and it is understood that it belongs exclusively to the latter. But though a State cannot perform this duty devolved by the Constitution somewhere, she has no right to interpose improper and embarrassing obstacles in the way of such delivery up of a fugitive by proper authority. If she does so she transcends her duty, and is liable to the charge of not standing faithfully by the compromises of the Constitution.

*　*　*　*　*　*　*　*

The duty to deliver up is clear, and can only be evaded by a breach of the Constitution or by its alteration. As long as it remains I am willing to acknowledge the obligation, and to vote for any feasible and judicious plan by which this duty can be performed, and the constitutional obligation be maintained and discharged. I am for the Constitution as it stands, as long as it stands, and for the Union as our fathers made it, and do not mean, by any act of mine, either of commission or omission, to jeopard either. My feelings of attachment to the Union are still strong, but I must confess to some diminution of their intensity during the agitation of this slavery question. I much fear that if it were the object of gentlemen to produce a like effect upon the minds of the people generally, they may have accomplished their purpose. Still I would sacrifice much to maintain it, if sacrifice were necessary. I do not, however, perceive any great danger, for the causes alleged seem inadequate. Some, however, can snuff dissolution in every gale, and find evidences of its approach when others cannot discover any signs of danger. The distinguished senator from South Carolina, now dead, could see it in the action of the religious bodies of the country. True, sir, there has been something of the kind in one of the most numerous denominations in the country. Speaking of the snapping of their religious cords, Mr. Calhoun can say, "that of the Presbyterian is not entirely snapped, but some of its strands have given away." The correctness of this statement with regard to the Presbyterian Church, I must be permitted to question. This church has ever been distinguished for its devotion to freedom; both political and religious, and it will be one of the last to do anything tending towards a subversion of the institutions of the country, to the formation of which their ancestors of the same faith so largely contributed. I will cite the report and resolutions of the General Assembly, adopted at Cincinnati, in May, 1845, in support of the views I have advanced on the moral aspect of slavery, and as evidence of the attachment this church, north and south, bears to the Union of the States. I can only refer to the report: the resolutions adopted by a vote of 168 yeas to 13 nays, are as follows, viz.:

"*Resolved*, 1st, That the General Assembly of the Presbyterian Church in the United States was originally organized, and has since continued the bond of Union in the church, upon the conceded principle that the existence of domestic slavery, under the circumstances in which it is found in the southern portion of the country, is no bar to Christian communion.

"*Resolved*, 2d, That the petitions that ask the Assembly to make the holding of slaves itself a matter of discipline, do virtually require this judicatory to dissolve itself, and abandon the organization under which, by the Divine blessing, it has so long prospered. The tendency is evidently to separate the northern from the southern portion of the Church; a result which every good citizen must deplore, as tending to the dissolution of the Union of our beloved country, and which every enlightened Christian will oppose as bringing about a ruinous and unnecessary schism between brethren who maintain a common faith."

These patriotic and Christian-like sentiments have never been changed or withdrawn at any subsequent period, as I am informed by the best authority; and I am happy to add, there is no fear that they ever will be. They are worthy the church, and do honor to the heads and hearts of the members of the Assembly by which they were so unanimously adopted. There are no elements of political disunion in this church; no snapping of any strands, however delicate, forming her religious cords, to draw forth from the patriot Christian

"Such tears as patriots shed for dying laws."

In the preservation of the Union of these States lie all our hopes of happiness as a people—of our peace, prosperity, and strength, as a nation. What patriotism is to the citizens of other countries, unionism should be to us—the noblest passion that animates man in the character of a citizen. Attachment and devotion to the Constitution and to the Union is a deeply-seated feeling in the heart of every American. It should be cherished and fostered with care, as a vital principle, never to be surrendered until every sentiment of civil liberty shall be extinguished forever.

Extract from the speech of Mr. Thomas Ross, of Pennsylvania, in the House of Representatives, April 10, 1850.

Mr. Ross said: Congress has no constitutional power either to establish or to prohibit slavery in the States or territories. And I will further say, that even if Congress had the constitutional power, it would be unwise, inexpedient, and highly improper to exercise that power.

In justice to myself, I will, in a few words, give my reasons for this opinion. Each State was an independent sovereignty when she entered the confederacy, so far, at least, as regarded the objects of property, and the domestic and social institutions of her people; and she surrendered no part of that sovereignty by becoming a member of the Union. The general government was established for certain specified objects, and its powers are limited by the constitutional grant which created it; but to the States themselves belong all powers not expressly delegated, or which, by necessary implication, do not arise from some express grant. At the time of the adoption of the Constitution, negro slavery, I believe, existed in all the States but one, which then formed the Union; and no power was given to the general government to control, regulate, prohibit, or establish slavery. That power not being granted, was vested in the States themselves. The Constitution, however, recognized slavery as one of the institutions of the country, and made provision for the protection of slave property. There was no grant, therefore, of *power* of any kind on the subject of slavery made by the States to the general government; but there was a binding *obligation* entered into by the free States, or by such as might become free, that the general government should protect slave property. It seems to me, therefore, that as the States delegated to the general government no power of any kind over the question of slavery, Congress, which derives all its powers from the Constitution, possesses no authority either to establish or prohibit slavery in the States or territories. In regard to the territories, Mr. Chairman, the general government is but the trustee of the States; and it has no power to make any rule or regulation which will throw open the territories to settlement by the people of one section of the Union to the exclusion of the people of another. The beneficiary interest of the territories is in the people of all the States—slave States as well as free— and the general government, as the trustee, is bound to execute the trust for the common benefit of all. Any legislation by Congress, prohibiting slavery in the territories, would, therefore, be not only an assumption of power not delegated, but would be a violation of the trust which the Constitution vested in the general government.

But, sir, I further hold, that the general government has no power to prohibit, by any legislative act, the introduction into the territories of any species of property which the Constitution of the United States has recognized as property. Property in slaves is not only recognized by the Constitution, but guarantees are given for its protection. The power, therefore, which is given to Congress by the third section of the fourth article, to make "all needful rules and regulations respecting the territory or other property belonging to the United States," is merely a right to regulate, but not a power to abolish that which the Constitution has recognized as property. An obligation to protect or regulate gives no power to prohibit or to destroy. And thus, while we have the constitutional power to pass laws for the protection and regulation of slave property in the territories, we have no power to make any legislative enactment for its prohibition, whether in the States or territories. In a word, sir, the Constitution of the United States is the Constitution of the territories, and as that Constitution recognizes the right of property in slaves, any prohibition by Congress of that right would be in violation of the Constitution, which is the supreme law of the land.

Extract from the Southern Address published in 1830, said to have been drawn by Mr. Calhoun:

We do not deem it necessary, looking to the object of this address, to examine the question so fully discussed at the last session, whether Congress has the right to exclude the citizens of the South from immigrating with their property into territories belonging to the confederated States of the Union. What we propose in this connection is, to make a few remarks on what the North alleges, erroneously, to be the issue between us and them.

So far from maintaining the doctrine, which the issue implies, we hold that the Federal Government has no right to extend or restrict slavery, no more than to establish or abolish it; nor has it any right whatever to distinguish between the domestic institutions of one State, or section, and another, in order to favor the one and discourage the other. As the federal representatives of each and all the States, it is bound to deal out, within the sphere of its powers, equal and exact justice and favor to all. To act otherwise, to undertake to discriminate between the domestic institutions of one and another, would be to act in total subversion of the end for which it was established—to be the common protector and guardian of all. Entertaining these opinions, we ask not, as the North alleges we do, for the extension of slavery. That would make a discrimination in our favor, as unjust and unconstitutional as the discrimination they ask against us in their favor. It is not for them nor for the federal government to determine whether our domestic institution is good or bad, or whether it should be repressed or preserved. It belongs to us, and us only, to decide such questions. What, then, we do insist on is, not to extend slavery, but that we shall not be prohibited from immigrating with our property into the territories of the United States because we are slaveholders; or, in other words, that we shall not on that account be disfranchised of a privilege possessed by all others, citizens and foreigners, without discrimination as to character, profession, or color. All, whether savage, barbarian, or civilized, may freely enter and remain, we only being " excluded."

CHAPTER XIII.

THE DRED SCOTT CASE.

Extract from the opinion of the Court by Chief Justice Taney; also from the opinion of Judge Daniels; and from a Pennsylvania case declaring a negro not a citizen.

TANEY, C. J. * * * * * The question is simply this: Can a negro, whose ancestors were imported into this country, and sold as slaves, become a member of the political community formed and brought into existence by the Constitution of the United States, and as such, become entitled to all the rights, and privileges, and immunities, guaranteed by that instrument to the citizen? One of which rights is the privilege of suing in a court of the United States, in the cases specified in the Constitution.

It will be observed, that the plea applies to that class of persons only whose ancestors were negroes of the African race, and imported into this country, and sold and held as slaves. The only matter in issue before the court, therefore, is, whether the descendants of such slaves, when they shall be emancipated, or who are born of parents who had become free before their birth, are citizens of a State, in the sense in which the word citizen is used in the Constitution of the United States. And this being the only matter in dispute on the pleadings, the court must be understood as speaking, in this opinion, of that class only; that is, of those persons who are the descendants of Africans who were imported into this country and sold as slaves.

*   *   *   *   *   *

The words "people of the United States" and "citizens" are synonymous terms, and mean the same thing. They both describe the political body who, according to our republican institutions, form the sovereignty, and who hold the power and conduct the government through their representatives. They are what we familiarly call the "sovereign people," and every citizen is one of this people, and a constituent member of this sovereignty. The question before us is, Whether the class of persons described in the plea in abatement compose a portion of this people, and are constituent members of this sovereignty? We think they are not, and that they are not included, and were not intended to be included, under the word "citizens" in the Constitution, and can therefore claim none of the rights and privileges which that instrument provides for and secures to citizens of the United States. On the contrary, they were at that time considered as a subordinate and inferior class of beings, who had been subjugated by the dominant race, and, whether emancipated or not, yet remain subject to their authority, and had no rights or privileges but such as those who held the power and the government might choose to grant them.

It is not the province of the court to decide upon the justice or injustice, the policy or impolicy, of these laws. The decision of that question belonged to the political, or law-making power; to those who formed the sovereignty and framed the Constitution. The duty of the court is to interpret the instrument they have framed, with the best lights we can obtain on the subject, and to administer it as we find it, according to its true intent and meaning when it was adopted.

*   *   *   *   *   *

In the opinion of the court, the legislation and histories of the times, and the language used in the Declaration of Independence, show that neither the class of persons who had been imported as slaves, nor their descendants, whether they had become free or not, were then acknowledged as a part of the people, nor intended to be included in the general words used in that memorable instrument.

It is difficult at this day to realize the state of public opinion in relation to that unfortunate race, which prevailed in the civilized and enlightened portions of the world at the time of the Declaration of Independence, and when the Constitution of the United States was framed and adopted. But the public history of every European nation displays it in a manner too plain to be mistaken.

They had for more than a century before been regarded as beings of an inferior order, and altogether unfit to associate with the white race, either in social or political relations; and so far inferior, that they had no rights which the white man was bound to respect; and that the negro might justly and lawfully be reduced to slavery for his benefit. He was bought and sold, and treated as an ordinary article of merchandise and traffic, whenever a profit could be made by it. This opinion was at that time fixed and universal in the civilized portion of the white race. It was regarded as an axiom in morals as well as in politics, which no one thought of disputing, or supposed to be open to dispute; and men in every grade and position in society daily and habitually acted upon it in their private pursuits, as well as in matters of public concern, without doubting for a moment the correctness of this opinion.

And in no nation was this opinion more firmly fixed or more uniformly acted upon than by the English government and English people. They not only seized them on the coast of Africa, and sold them or held them in slavery for their own use; but they took them as ordinary articles of merchandise to every country where they could make a profit on them, and even far more extensively engaged in this commerce than any other nation in the world.

The opinion thus entertained and acted upon in England was naturally impressed upon the colonies they founded on this side of the Atlantic. And accordingly, a negro of the African race was regarded by them as an article of property, and held, and bought, and sold as such in every one of the thirteen colonies which united in the Declaration of Independence, and afterwards formed the Constitution of the United States. The slaves were more or less numerous in the different colonies, as slave labor was found more or less profitable. But no one seems to have doubted the correctness of the prevailing opinion of the time. The legislation of the different colonies furnished positive and indisputable proof of this fact.

It would be tedious, in this opinion, to enumerate the various laws they passed upon this subject. It will be sufficient, as a sample of the legislation which then generally prevailed throughout the British colonies, to give the laws of two of them, one being still a large slaveholding State, and the other the first State in which slavery ceased to exist.

The Province of Maryland, in 1717, (ch. 13, s. 5,) passed a law declaring "that if any free negro or mulatto intermarry with any white woman, or any white man shall intermarry with any negro or mulatto woman, such negro or mulatto shall become a slave during life, excepting mulattoes born of white women, who, for such intermarriage, shall only become servants for seven years, to be disposed of as the justices of the county court, where such marriage so happens, shall think fit, to be applied by them toward the support of a public school within the said county. And any white man or white woman, who shall intermarry as aforesaid, with any negro or mulatto, such white man or white woman shall become a servant for or during the term of seven years, and shall be disposed of by the justices as aforesaid, and be applied to the uses aforesaid."

The other colonial law to which we refer, was passed by Massachusetts, in 1705, (ch. 6.) It is entitled "An Act for the better preventing of a spurious and mixed issue," &c., and it provides "that if any negro or mulatto shall presume to strike or smite any person of the English or other Christian nation, such negro or mulatto shall be severely whipped, at the discretion of the justice before whom the offender shall be convicted."

And "that none of her Majesty's English or Scottish subjects, nor of any other Christian nation within this province, shall contract matrimony with any negro or mulatto; nor shall any person duly authorized to solemnize marriage, presume to join any such in marriage, on pain of forfeiting the sum of fifty pounds, one moiety thereof to her Majesty, for and toward the support of the government within this province, and the other moiety to him or them who shall inform and sue for the same, in any of her Majesty's courts of record within the province, by bill, plaint, or information."

*   *   *   *   *   *

The language of the Declaration of Independence is equally conclusive. It begins by declaring, that "When, in the course of human events, it becomes necessary for one people to dissolve the political bands which have connected them with another, and to assume among the powers of the earth the separate and equal station to which the laws of nature, and nature's God, entitled them, a decent respect for the opinions of mankind require that they should declare the causes which impel them to the separation."

It then proceeds to say: "We hold these truths to be self-evident—That all men are created equal; that they are endowed by their Creator with certain inalienable rights; that among them is life, liberty, and the pursuit of happiness; that, to secure these rights, governments are instituted, deriving their just powers from the consent of the governed."

The general words, above quoted, would seem to embrace the whole human family; and if they were used in a similar instrument at this day, would be so understood. But it is too clear for dispute, that the enslaved African race were not intended to be included, and formed no part of the people who framed and adopted this Declaration; for if the language, as understood in that day, would embrace them, the conduct of the distinguished men who framed the Declaration of Independence would have been utterly and flagrantly inconsistent with principles they asserted; and instead of the sympathy of mankind to which they so confidently appealed, they would have deserved and received universal rebuke and reprobation.

Yet, the men who framed this Declaration were great men—high in literary acquirements—high in their sense of honor, and incapable of asserting principles inconsistent with those on which they were acting. They perfectly understood the meaning of the language they used, and how it would be understood by others; and they knew that it would not, in any part of the civilized world, be supposed to embrace the negro race, which, by common consent, had been excluded from civilized government and the family of nations, and doomed to slavery. They spoke and acted according to the then established doctrine and principles, and in the ordinary language of the day, and no one misunderstood them. The unhappy black race were separated from the white by indelible marks, and laws long before established, and were never thought or spoken of except as property, and when the claims of the owners, or the profit of the trader, were supposed to need protection.

This state of public opinion had received or undergone no change when the Constitution was adopted, as is equally evident from its provisions and language.

* * * * * *

And if we turn to the legislation of the States where slavery had worn out, or measures taken for its speedy abolition, we shall find the same opinions and principles, equally fixed and equally acted upon.

Thus, Massachusetts, in 1786, passed a law similar to the Colonial one, of which we have spoken. The law of 1786, like the law of 1705, forbids the marriage of any white person to any negro, Indian, or mulatto, and inflicts a penalty of fifty pounds upon any one who shall join them in marriage; and declares all such marriages absolutely null and void, and degrades thus the unhappy issue of the marriage, by fixing upon it the stain of bastardy. And this mark of degradation was renewed, and again impressed upon the race, in the careful and deliberate preparation of their revised code, published in 1836. This code forbids any person from joining in marriage any white person with any Indian, negro, or mulatto, and subjects the party who shall offend in this respect, to imprisonment, not exceeding six months, in the common jail, or to hard labor, and to a fine not less than fifty or more than two thousand dollars; and, like the law of 1786, it declares the marriages absolutely null and void. It will be seen that the punishment is increased by the code upon the person who shall marry them, by adding imprisonment to a pecuniary penalty.

So, too, in Connecticut. We refer more particularly to the legislation of this State, because it was not only among the first to put an end to slavery within its own territory, but was the first to fix a mark of reprobation upon the African slave trade. The law last mentioned was passed in October 1788, about nine months after the State had ratified and adopted the present Constitution of the United States; and by that law it prohibited its own citizens, under severe penalties, from engaging in the trade, and declared all policies of insurance on the vessel or cargo made in the State to be null and void. But, up to time of the adoption of the Constitution, there is nothing in the legislation of the State indicating any change of opinion as to the relative rights and positions of the white and black races in this country, or indicating that it meant to place the latter, when free, upon a level with its citizens. And certainly nothing which would have led the slaveholding States to suppose that Connecticut designed to claim for them, under the new Constitution, the equal rights and privileges, and rank of citizens, in every other State.

The first step taken by Connecticut upon this subject was as early as 1774, when it passed an act forbidding the further importation of slaves into the State. But the section containing the prohibition is introduced by the following preamble:

"And whereas the increase of slaves into this State is injurious to the poor, and inconvenient."

This recital would appear to have been carefully introduced, in order to prevent any misunderstanding of the motive which induced the legislature to pass the law, and place it distinctly upon the interest and convenience of the white population—excluding the inference that it might have been intended, in any degree, for the benefit of the other.

And in the act of 1784, by which the issue of slaves, born after the time therein mentioned, were to be free at a certain age, the section is again introduced by a preamble assigning a similar motive for the act. It is in these words:

"Whereas, sound policy requires that the abolition of slavery should be effected as soon as may be consistent with the rights of individuals and the public safety and welfare,"
—showing that the right of property in the master was to be protected, and that the measure was one of policy, and to prevent the injury and inconvenience to the whites, of a a slave population in the State.

And still further pursuing its legislation, we find that in

the same statute passed in 1774, which prohibited the further importation of slaves into the State, there is also a provision by which any negro, Indian, or mulatto servant, who was found wandering out of the town or place to which he belonged, without a written pass such as therein described, was made liable to be seized by any one, and taken before the next authority, to be examined and delivered up to his master, who was required to pay the charge which had accrued thereby. And a subsequent section of the same law provided, that if any free negro shall travel without such pass, and shall be stopped, seized, or taken up, he shall pay all charges arising thereby. And this law was in full operation when the Constitution of the United States was adopted, and was not repealed till 1797. So that up to that time free negroes and mulattoes were associated with servants and slaves in the police regulations established by the laws of the State.

And again, in 1833, Connecticut passed another law which made it penal to set up or establish any school in that State for the instruction of persons of the African race, not inhabitants of the State, or to instruct or teach in any such school or institution, or board or harbor for that purpose, any such person, without the previous consent in writing of the civil authority of the town in which such school or institution might be.

And it appears by the case of Crandell v. the State, reported in 10 Conn. Rep., 340, that upon an information filed against Prudence Crandell for a violation of this law, one of the points raised in the defense was, that the law was a violation of the Constitution of the United States; and that the persons instructed, although of the African race, were citizens of other States, and therefore entitled to the rights and privileges of citizens in the State of Connecticut. But Chief Justice Dagget, before whom the case was tried, held, that persons of that description were not citizens of a

State within the meaning of the word citizen in the Constitution of the United States, and were not therefore entitled to the privileges and immunities of citizens in other States.

We extract the following from the opinion of Judge Daniels in the same case:

The power of Congress to impose the prohibition in the eighth section of the act of 1820, has been advocated upon an attempted construction of the second clause of the third section of the fourth article of the Constitution, which declares that "Congress shall have power to dispose of and to make all needful rules and regulations respecting the *territory* and *other property belonging* to the United States,"

In the discussion in both houses of Congress, at the time of adopting the eighth section of the act of 1820, great weight was given to the peculiar language of this clause, viz., *territory* and *other property belonging* to the United States, as going to show that power of disposing of and regulating, thereby vested in Congress, was restricted to a *proprietary interest in the territory of land* comprised therein, and did not extend to the personal or political rights of citizens or settlers, inasmuch as this phrase in the Constitution, "*territory or other property*," identified *territory* with *property*, and inasmuch as *citizens* or *persons* could not be property, and especially were not property *belonging* to the United States. And upon every principle of reason or necessity, this power to dispose of and to regulate the *territory* of the nation could be designed to extend no further to its preservation and appropriation to the uses of those to whom it belonged, viz., the nation. Scarcely anything more illogical or extravagant can be imagined than the attempt to deduce from this provision in the Constitution a power to destroy or in any wise to impair the civil and political rights of the citizens of the United States, and much more so the power to establish inequalities amongst those citizens by creating privileges in one class of those cit ens, and by the disfranchisement of other portions or classes by degrading them from the position they previously occupied.

There can exist no rational or natural connection or affinity between a pretension like this and the power vested by the Constitution in Congress with regard to the territories; on the contrary, there is an absolute incongruity between them.

But whatever the power vested by Congress, and whatever the precise subject to which that power extended, it is clear that the power related to a subject appertaining to the *United States*, and one to be disposed of and regulated for the benefit and under the authority of the *United States*. Congress was made simply the agent or *trustee* for the United States, upon equal grounds, legal or equitable. Congress could not appropriate that subject to any one class or portion of the people to the exclusion of others politically and constitutionally equals; but every citizen would, if any *one* could claim it, have the like rights of purchase, settlement, occupation, or any other right in their national territory.

Nothing can be more conclusive to show the equality of this with every other right in all the citizens of the United States, and the iniquity and absurdity of the pretensions to exclude or to disfranchise a portion of them because they are the owners of slaves, than the fact that the same instrument, which imparts to Congress its very existence, and its very functions, guarantees to the slaveholder the title to his property, and gives him the right to reclaim his property throughout the country; and, further, that the only private property which the Constitution has *specifically recognized*, and has imposed it as a direct obligation both on the States and the federal government to protect and *enforce*, is the property of the master in his slave: no other right of property is placed by the Constitution on the same high ground, nor shielded by a similar guarantee.

Can there be imputed to the sages and patriots by whom the Constitution was framed, or can there be detected in the text of that Constitution, or in any rational construction or implication deducible therefrom, a contradiction so palpable as would exist between a pledge to the slaveholder of an equality with his fellow-citizens, and of the formal and solemn assurance for the security and enjoyment of his property, and a warrant given as it were *uno flatu* to another, to rob him of that property, or to subject him to proscription and disfranchisement for possessing, or for endeavoring to retain it? The injustice and extravagance necessarily implied in a supposition like this, cannot be rationally imputed to the patriotic or the honest, or to those who were merely sane.

A conclusion in favor of the prohibitory power in Congress, as asserted in the eighth section of the act of 1820, has been attempted, as deducible from the precedent of the ordinance of the Convention of 1787, concerning the cession by Virginia of the territory northwest of the Ohio: the provision in which ordinance relative to slavery, it has been attempted to impose upon other and subsequently acquired territory.

The first circumstance which, in the consideration of this provision, impresses itself upon my mind, is its utter futility and want of authority. This court has, in repeated instances, ruled, that whatever may have been the force accorded to this ordinance of 1787 at the period of its enactment, its authority and effect ceased, and yielded to the paramount authority of the Constitution, from the period of the adoption of the latter. Such is the principle ruled in the cases of Pollard's Lessee v. Hagan, (3 How, 212); Parmoli v. The First Municipality of New Orleans, (3 How, 589;) Strader v. Graham, (16 How, 82). But apart from the superior control of the Constitution, and anterior to the adoption of that instrument, it is obvious that the inhibition in question never had and never could have any legitimate and binding force.

We may seek in vain for any power in the Convention, either to require or to accept a condition or restriction upon the cession like that insisted on—a condition inconsistent with, and destructive of, the object of the grant. The cession was, as recommended by the old Congress in 1780, made originally and completed *in terms to the United States*, and for the benefit of the United States: i. e., for *the people, all the people*, of the United States: the condition subsequently sought to be annexed in 1787, (declared, too, to be perpetual and immutable,) being contradictory to the terms and destructive of the purposes of the cession, and after the cession was consummated, and the powers of the ceding party terminated, and the rights of *the* grantees, *the people of the United States*, vested, must necessarily, so far, have been *ab initio* void.

With respect to the powers of the Convention to impose this inhibition, it seems to be pertinent in this place to recur to the opinion of one cotemporary with the establishment of the government, and whose distinguished services in the formation and adoption of our national charter, point him out as the *artifex maximus* of our federal system. James Madison, in the year 1819, speaking with reference to the prohibitory law claimed by Congress, then threatening the very existence of the Union, remarks of the language of the second clause of the third section of article fourth of the Constitution, "that it cannot be well extended beyond a power over the territory *as property*, and the power to make provisions really needful or necessary for the government of settlers, until ripe for admission into the Union."

Again he says, " with respect to what has taken place in

the Northwestern Territory, it may be observed, that the ordinance giving it its distinctive character on the subject of slaveholding proceeded from the old Congress, acting with the best intentions, but under a charter which contains no shadow of the authority exercised; and it remains to be decided how far the States formed in that territory, and admitted into the Union, are on a different footing from its other members as to their legislative sovereignty. As to the power of admitting new States into the federal compact, the questions offering themselves are, whether Congress can attach conditions, or the new States concur in conditions, which after admission would *abridge* or *enlarge* the constitutional rights of legislation common to other States: whether Congress can, by a compact with a new State, take power to or from itself, or place the new member above or below the equal rank and rights preserved by the others; whether all such stipulations, expressed or implied, would not be nullities, and be so pronounced when brought to a practical test. It falls within the scope of our inquiry to state the fact, that there was a proposition in the Convention to discriminate between the old and the new States by an article in the Constitution. The proposition, happily, was rejected. The effect of such a discrimination is sufficiently evident."

In support of the ordinance of 1787, there may be adduced the semblance, at least, of obligation deducible from compact, the *form* of assent or agreement between the grantor and grantee; but this form, or similitude, as is justly remarked by Mr. Madison, is rendered null by the absence of power or authority in the contracting parties, and by the more intrinsic and essential defect of incompatibility with the rights and avowed purposes of those parties, and with their relative duties and obligations to others. If, then, with the attendant *formalities* of assent, or compact, the restrictive power claimed was void as to the immediate subject of the ordinance, how much more unfounded must be the pretensions of such a power as derived from that source, (viz., the ordinance of 1787,) with respect to territory acquired by purchase or conquest under the supreme authority of the Constitution—territory not the subject of *mere donation*, but obtained *in the name of all, by the combined efforts and resources of all*, and with no condition annexed or pretended.

Synopsis of the case of Hobbs and others, against Fogg, in the Supreme Court of Pennsylvania, in 1837, (6 Watts, 553.)

The plaintiff below, Fogg, was a colored man, or mulatto, and offered his vote at a general election in the township of Greenfield, Luzerne county, which was refused by the Board of Election. He then brought his action to recover damages against the Board, and "to maintain his rights as a citizen and freeman of the State." The case arose under the old Constitution, which declared that "*every freeman*, of the full age of twenty-one years," &c., "shall enjoy the rights of an elector." The present Constitution prefixes the word *white* to the word *freeman*.

The facts of the case were admitted, and the court below directed judgment for the plaintiff.

In the Supreme Court, the case was argued by Hon. John N. Conyngham and Hon. H. B. Wright, for plaintiffs in error; and by Hon. Luther Kidder and —— Greenough, for defendant in error. The opinion of the Court was delivered by Chief Justice Gibson, from which we make the following extract. It will be seen that it takes the same ground, as to the citizenship of the negro, as does the Dred Scott case.

Gibson C. J. * * * * But in addition to interpretation from usage, this antecedent legislation furnishes other proofs that no colored race was party to our social compact. As was justly remarked by President Fox, in the matter of the late contested election, our ancestors settled the province as a community of white men, whence an unconquerable prejudice of caste, which has come down to our day, insomuch that a suspicion of tint still has the unjust effect of sinking the subject of it below the common level. Consistently with this prejudice, is it to be credited that parity of rank would be allowed to such a race? Let the question be answered by the statute of 1726, which denominated it an idle and a slothful people; which directed the magistrates to bind out free negroes for laziness or vagrancy; which forbade them to harbor Indian or mulatto slaves, on pain of stripes; which annexed to the interdict with a marriage with white, the penalty of reduction to slavery; which punished them for tippling, with stripes; and even a white person with servitude for intermarriage with a negro. If freemen, in a political sense, were subjects of those cruel and degrading oppressions, what must have been the lot of their brethren in bondage? It is also true, that degrading positions were sometimes assigned to white men, but never as members of a caste. Insolvent debtors, to indicate the worst of them, were compelled to make satisfaction by servitude; but that was borrowed from a kindred and still less rational principle of the common law. This act of 1726, however, remained in force until it was repealed by the emancipating act of 1780; and it is irrational to believe that the progress of liberal sentiments was so rapid in the next ten years, as to produce a determination in the Convention of 1790, to raise this depressed race to the level of the white one. If such were its purpose, it is strange that the word chosen to effect it should have been the very one chosen by the Convention of 1776, to designate a white elector. "Every *freeman*," it is said, chap. ii, sec. 6, "of the full age of twenty-one years before the day of election, and having paid taxes during that time, shall enjoy the rights of an elector."

Now if the word freeman was not potent enough to admit a free negro to suffrage under the first Constitution, it is difficult to discern a degree of magic in the intervening plan of emancipation, sufficient to give it adequate potency in the apprehension of the Convention under the second.

The only thing in the history of the Convention which casts a doubt upon the intent, is the fact, that the word white was prefixed to the word freeman in the report of the committee, and subsequently struck out; probably because it was thought superfluous, or still more probably, because it was feared respectable men of dark complexion would be often insulted at the polls, by objections to their color. I have heard it said, that Mr. Gallatin sustained his motion to strike out on the latter ground. Whatever the motion, the disseverance is insufficient to warp the interpretation of a word on such settled and determinate meaning as the one which remained. A legislative body speaks to the judiciary only through its final act, and expresses its will only in the words of it; and though their meaning may be influenced by the sense in which they have usually been applied to intrinsic matters, we cannot receive an explanation of them from what has been moved or said in debate. Were he even disposed to pry into the motives of the members, it would be impossible for him to ascertain them; and in attempting to discover the ground on which the conclusion was attained, it is not probable that a member of the majority could indicate anything that was common to all. Previous propositions are merged in the act of consummation, and the interpreter of it must look to that alone.

I have thought it fair to treat the question as it stands, affected by our own municipal regulations, without illustration from those of other States, where the condition of the race has been still less favored. Yet it is proper to say that the second section of the fourth article of the federal Constitution presents an obstacle to the political freedom of the negro, which seems to be insuperable. It is to be remembered that citizenship as well as freedom is a constitutional qualification; and how it could be conferred so as to overbear the laws imposing countless disabilities on him in other States, is a problem of difficult solution. In this aspect the question becomes one not of intention, but of power; and of power so doubtful as to forbid the exercise of it. Every man must lament the necessity of these disabilities; but slavery is to be dealt with by those whose existence depends on the skill with which it is treated. Considerations of mere humanity, however, belong to a class with which, as judges, we have nothing to do; *and interpreting the Constitution in the spirit of our institutions, we are bound to pronounce that men of color are destitute of title to the elective franchise.* Their blood, however, may become so diluted in successive descents as to lose its distinctive character, and then both policy and justice require that previous disabilities should cease. By the amended Constitution of North Carolina, no free negro, mulatto, or free person of mixed blood, descended from negro ancestors, to the fourth generation inclusive, though one ancestor of each generation may have been a white person, shall vote for members of the legislature.

I regret to say, no similar regulation for practical purposes has been attempted here, in consequence of which every case of disputed color must be determined by no particular rule, but by the discretion of the judges, and thus a great constitutional right, even under the proposed amendments of the Constitution, will be left a sport of caprice. In conclusion, we are of opinion the court erred in directing that the plaintiff could have his action against the defendant for the rejection of his vote.

Judgment reversed.

Extract from the opinion of Judge Story.

The Supreme Court of the United States in the case of Prigg vs. the Commonwealth of Pennsylvania, 16th Peters' Rep., wherein Judge Story, in delivering the opinion of the court, says:

"It is historically well known that the clause in the Constitution of the United States, relating to persons owing service and labor in one State escaping into other States, was to secure to the citizens of the slaveholding States the complete right and title of ownership in their slaves, as property, in every State in the Union into which they might escape from the State where they were held in servitude. The full recognition of this right and title was indispensable to the security of this species of property in all the slaveholding States; and, indeed, was so vital to the preservation of their domestic interests and institutions, that it cannot be doubted that it is constituted a fundamental article, without the adoption of which the Union could not have been formed. Its true design was to guard against the doctrines and principles prevailing in the non-slaveholding States, by preventing them from intermeddling with, or obstructing, or abolishing the rights of the owners of slaves.

*   *   *   *   *   *

"The clause in the Constitution of the United States, relating to fugitives from labor, manifestly contemplates the existence of a positive, unqualified right on the part of the owner of the slave, which no State law or regulation can in any way qualify, regulate, control, or restrain.

*   *   *   *   *   *   *

"The owner of a fugitive slave has the same right to seize, and to take him in a State to which he has escaped or fled that he had in the State from which he escaped; and it is well known that this right to seize or recapture is universally acknowledged in all the slaveholding States. The court have not the slightest hesitation in holding, that under and in virtue of the Constitution, the owner of the slave is clothed with authority in every State of the Union to seize and recapture his slave, wherever he can do it without any breach of the peace, or illegal violence.

*　　*　　*　　*　　*　　*　　*　　*

"The right to seize and retake fugitive slaves, and the duty to deliver them up, in whatever State of the Union they may be found, is, under the Constitution, recognized as an absolute positive right and duty, pervading the whole Union with an equal and supreme force; uncontrolled and uncontrollable by State sovereignty or State legislation. The right and duty are co-extensive and uniform in remedy and operation throughout the whole Union. The owner has the same security, and the same remedial justice, and the same exemption from State regulations and control, through however many States he may pass with the fugitive slave in his possession, *in transitu*, to his domicile."

Here the Supreme Court emphatically declare that this clause in the Constitution manifestly contemplates the existence of a positive, unqualified right on the part of the owner of a slave, which no State law or regulation can control, and without which the Union could not have been formed, and, further, that the right to seize and retake fugitive slaves, in whatever State of the Union they may be found, is an absolute, positive right. But we are not left simply with this constitutional provision, for Congress, in 1793, passed an act designed to put the provision into practical operation, the last two sections of which are as follows:

"SEC. 3. *And be it also enacted*, That when a person held to labor in any of the United States, or in either of the territories on the northwest, or south of the river Ohio, under the laws thereof, shall escape into any other of the said States or territories, the person to whom such labor or service may be due, his agent or attorney is hereby empowered to seize or arrest such fugitive from labor, and to take him or her before any judge of the circuit or district courts of the United States, residing or being within the State, or before any magistrate of a county, city, or town corporate, wherein such seizure or arrest shall be made, and upon proof to the satisfaction of such judge or magistrate, either by oral testimony or affidavit taken before and certified by a magistrate of any such State or territory, that the person so seized or arrested, doth, under the laws of the State or territory from which she or he fled, owe service or labor to the person claiming him or her, it shall be the duty of the judge or magistrate to give a certificate thereof to such claimant, his agent or attorney, which shall be sufficient warrant for removing the said fugitive from labor to the State or territory from which he or she fled.

"SEC. 4. *And be it further enacted,* That any person who shall knowingly and willingly obstruct and hinder such claimant, his agent or attorney, in so seizing or arresting such fugitive from labor, or shall rescue such fugitive from such claimant, his agent or attorney, when so arrested, pursuant to the authority herein given or declared, or shall harbor or conceal such person after notice that he or she was a fugitive from labor as aforesaid, shall, for either of the said offenses, forfeit and pay the sum of five hundred dollars. Which penalty may be recovered by and for the benefit of such claimant, by action of debt, in any court proper to try the same; saving, moreover, to the person claiming such labor or service, his right of action for or on account of the said injuries or either of them."

CHAPTER XIV.

INAUGURAL ADDRESSES OF WASHINGTON, ADAMS, JEFFERSON, AND MADISON; AND THE FAREWELL ADDRESSES OF WASHINGTON AND JACKSON.

THE oath of office having, on Thursday, April 30, 1789, been administered by the Chancellor of the State of New York, in the presence of the Senate and House of Representatives, to George Washington, President of the United States, he then made the following Inaugural Address:

Fellow-Citizens of the Senate, and
  of the House of Representatives:

Among the vicissitudes incident to life, no event could have filled me with greater anxieties than that of which the notification was transmitted by your order, and received on the fourteenth day of the present month. On the one hand, I was summoned by my country, whose voice I can never hear but with veneration and love, from a retreat which I had chosen with the fondest predilection, and, in my flattering hopes, with an immutable decision, as the asylum of my declining years; a retreat which was rendered every day more necessary, as well as more dear to me, by the addition of habit to inclination, and of frequent interruptions in my health, to the gradual waste committed on it by time. On the other hand, the magnitude and difficulty of the trust to which the voice of my country called me, being sufficient to awaken in the wisest and most experienced of her citizens a distrustful scrutiny into his qualifications, could not but overwhelm with despondence one, who, inheriting inferior endowments from nature, and unpracticed in the duties of civil administration, ought to be peculiarly conscious of his own deficiencies. In this conflict of emotions, all I dare aver, is, that it has been my faithful study to collect my duty from a just appreciation of every circumstance by which it might be affected. All I dare hope, is, that if, in executing this task, I have been too much swayed by a grateful remembrance of former instances, or by an affectionate sensibility to this transcendent proof, of the confidence of my fellow-citizens, and have thence too little consulted my incapacity as well as disinclination for the weighty and untried cares before me, my error will be palliated by the motives which misled me, and its consequences be judged by my country, with some share of the partiality in which they originated.

Such being the impressions under which I have, in obedience to the public summons, repaired to the present station, it would be peculiarly improper to omit, in this first official act, my fervent supplications to that Almighty Being who rules over the universe—who presides in the councils of nations, and whose providential aids can supply every human defect—that his benediction may consecrate to the liberties and happiness of the people of the United States, a government instituted by themselves for these essential purposes, and may enable every instrument employed in its administration to execute with success the functions allotted to his charge. In tendering this homage to the Great Author of every public and private good, I assure myself that it expresses your sentiments not less than my own; nor those of my fellow-citizens at large, less than either. No people can be bound to acknowledge and adore the invisible hand which conducts the affairs of men, more than the people of the United States. Every step by which they have advanced to the character of an independent nation, seems to have been distinguished by some token of providential agency; and in the important revolution just accomplished in the system of their united government, the tranquil deliberations, and voluntary consent of so many distinct communities, from which the event has resulted, cannot be compared with the means by which most governments have been established, without some return of pious gratitude, along with an humble anticipation of the future blessings which the past seem to presage. These reflections, arising out of the present crisis, have forced themselves too strongly on my mind to be suppressed. You will join with me, I trust, in thinking that there are none, under the influence of which the proceedings of a new and free government can more auspiciously commence.

By the article establishing the executive department, it is made the duty of the President "to recommend to your consideration such measures as he shall judge necessary and expedient." The circumstances under which I now meet you will acquit me from entering into that subject, further than to refer to the great constitutional charter under which you are assembled; and which, in defining your powers, designates the objects to which your attention is to be given. It will be more consistent with those circumstances, and far more congenial with the feelings which actuate me, to substitute, in place of a recommendation of particular measures, the tribute that is due to the talents, the rectitude, and the patriotism, which adorn the characters selected to devise and adopt them. In these honorable qualifications I behold the surest pledges that, as on one side, no local prejudices or attachments, no separate views or party animosities, will misdirect the comprehensive and equal eye which ought to watch over this great assemblage of communities and interests; so, on another, that the foundations of our national policy will be laid in the pure and immutable principles of private morality; and the preeminence of free government be exemplified by all the attributes which can win the affections of its citizens, and command the respect of the world. I dwell on this prospect with every satisfaction which an ardent love for my country can inspire: since there is no truth more thoroughly established, than that there exists in the economy and course of nature an indissoluble union between virtue and happiness—between duty and advantage—between the genuine maxims of an honest and magnanimous policy, and the solid rewards of public prosperity and felicity; since we ought to be no less persuaded that the propitious smiles of Heaven can never be expected on a nation that disregards the eternal rules of order and right, which Heaven itself has ordained; and since the preservation of the sacred fire of liberty, and the destiny of the republican model of government, are justly considered as deeply, perhaps as finally, staked, on the experiment intrusted to the hands of the American people.

Besides the ordinary objects submitted to your care, it will remain with your judgment to decide how far an exercise of the occasional power delegated by the fifth article of the Constitution, is rendered expedient at the present juncture, by the nature of objections which have been urged against the system, or by the degree of inquietude which has given birth to them. Instead of undertaking particular recommendations on this subject, in which I could be guided by no lights derived from official opportunities, I shall again give way to my entire confidence in your discernment and pursuit of the public good; for, I assure myself, that whilst you carefully avoid every alteration which might endanger the benefits of an united and effective government, or which ought to await the future lessons of experience, a reverence for the characteristic rights of freemen, and a regard for the public harmony, will sufficiently influence your deliberations on the question, how far the former can be more impregnably fortified, or the latter be safely and advantageously promoted.

To the preceding observations I have one to add, which will be most properly addressed to the House of Representatives. It concerns myself, and will, therefore, be as brief as possible. When I was first honored with a call into the service of my country, then on the eve of an arduous struggle for its liberties, the light in which I contemplated my duty required that I should renounce every pecuniary compensation. From this resolution I have in no instance departed; and being still under the impressions which produced it, I must decline, as inapplicable to myself, any share in the personal emoluments which may be indispensably included in a permanent provision for the executive department; and must accordingly pray that the pecuniary estimates for the station in which I am placed, may, during my continuance in it, be limited to such actual expenditures as the public good may be thought to require.

Having thus imparted to you my sentiments, as they have been awakened by the occasion which brings us together, I shall take my present leave; but not without resorting once more to the benign Parent of the human race in humble supplication, that, since he has been pleased to favor the American people with opportunities for deliberating in perfect tranquillity, and dispositions for deciding, with unparalleled unanimity, on a form of government for the security of their Union, and the advancement of their happiness, so his Divine blessing may be equally conspicuous in the enlarged views, the temperate consultations, and the wise measures, on which the success of this government must depend. G. WASHINGTON.

April 30, 1789

INAUGURAL ADDRESS OF JOHN ADAMS, PRESIDENT OF THE UNITED STATES.

March 4, 1797.

When it was first perceived, in early times, that no middle course for America remained between unlimited submission to a foreign legislature and a total independence of its claims, men of reflection were less apprehensive of danger from the formidable power of fleets and armies they must determine to resist, than from those contests and dissensions which would certainly arise concerning the forms of government to be instituted over the whole and over the parts of this extensive country. Relying, however, on the purity of their intentions, the justice of their cause, and the integrity and intelligence of the people, under an overruling Providence, which had so signally protected this country from the first, the representatives of this nation, then consisting of little more than half its present number, not only broke to pieces the chains which were forging, and the rod of iron that was lifted up, but frankly cut asunder the ties which had bound them, and launched into an ocean of uncertainty.

The zeal and ardor of the people, during the revolutionary war, supplying the place of government, commanded a degree of order, sufficient at least for the temporary preservation of society. The Confederation, which was early felt to be necessary, was prepared from the models of the Batavian and Helvetic confederacies—the only examples which remain, with any detail and precision, in history, and certainly the only ones which the people at large had ever considered. But, reflecting on the striking difference, in so many particulars, between this country and those where a courier may go from the seat of government to the frontier in a single day, it was then certainly foreseen, by some who assisted in Congress at the formation of it, that it could not be durable.

Negligence of its regulations, inattention to its recommendations, if not disobedience to its authority, not only in individuals, but in States, soon appeared, with their melancholy consequences: universal languor; jealousies and rivalries of States; decline of navigation and commerce; discouragement of necessary manufactures; universal fall in the value of lands and their produce; contempt of public and private faith; loss of consideration and credit with foreign nations; and, at length, in discontents, animosities, combinations, partial conventions, and insurrection, threatening some great national calamity.

In this dangerous crisis, the people of America were not abandoned by their usual good sense, presence of mind, resolution, or integrity. Measures were pursued to concert a plan to form a more perfect union, establish justice, ensure domestic tranquillity, provide for the common defense, promote the general welfare, and secure the blessings of liberty, The public disquisitions, discussions, and deliberations, issued in the present happy constitution of government.

Employed in the service of my country abroad during the whole course of these transactions, I first saw the Constitution of the United States in a foreign country. Irritated by no literary altercation, animated by no public debate, heated by no party animosity, I read it with great satisfaction, as the result of good heads, prompted by good hearts—as an experiment, better adapted to the genius, character, situation, and relations, of this nation and country, than any which had ever been proposed or suggested. In its general principles and great outlines, it was conformable to such a system of government as I had ever most esteemed, and in some States, my own native State in particular, had contributed to establish. Claiming a right of suffrage, in common with my fellow-citizens, in the adoption or rejection of a Constitution which was to rule me and my posterity, as well as them and theirs, I did not hesitate to express my approbation of it, on all occasions, in public and in private. It was not then, nor has been since, any objection to it, in my mind, that the executive and Senate were not more permanent. Nor have I ever entertained a thought of promoting any alteration in it, but such as the people themselves, in the course of their experience, should see and feel to be necessary or expedient, and, by their representatives in Congress and the State legislatures, according to the Constitution itself, adopt and ordain.

Returning to the bosom of my country, after a painful separation from it, for ten years, I had the honor to be elected to a station under the new order of things, and I have repeatedly laid myself under the most serious obligations to support the Constitution. The operation of it has equalled the most sanguine expectations of its friends; and, from an habitual attention to it, satisfaction in its administration, and delight in its effects upon the peace, order, prosperity and happiness of the nation, I have acquired an habitual attachment to it and veneration for it.

What other form of government, indeed, can so well deserve our esteem and love?

There may be little solidity in an ancient idea, that congregations of men into cities and nations are the most pleasing objects in the sight of superior intelligences; but this is very certain, that, to a benevolent human mind, there can be no spectacle presented by any nation more pleasing, more noble, majestic, or august, than an assembly like that which has so often been seen in this and the other chamber of Congress, of a government in which the executive authority, as well as that of all the branches of the legislature, are exercised by citizens selected, at regular periods, by their neighbors, to make and execute laws for the general good. Can anything essential, anything more than mere ornament and decoration, be added to this by robes and diamonds? Can authority be more amiable and respectable when it descends from accidents, or institutions established in remote antiquity, than when it springs fresh from the hearts and judgments of an honest and enlightened people? For it is the people only that are represented: it is their power and majesty that is reflected, and only for their good, in every legitimate government, under whatever form it may appear. The existence of such a government as ours, for any length of time, is a full proof of a general dissemination of knowledge and virtue throughout the whole body of the people. And what object or consideration more pleasing than this can be presented to the human mind? If national pride is ever justifiable, or excusable, it is when it springs, not from power or riches, grandeur or glory, but from conviction of national innocence, information, and benevolence.

In the midst of these pleasing ideas, we should be unfaithful to ourselves if we should ever lose sight of the danger to our liberties—if anything partial or extraneous should infect the purity of our free, fair, virtuous, and independent elections. If an election is to be determined by a majority of a single vote, and that can be secured by a party, through artifice or corruption, the government may be the choice of a party, for its own ends—not of the nation, for the national good. If that solitary suffrage can be obtained by foreign nations by flattery or menaces, by fraud or violence, by terror, intrigue, or venality, the government may not be the choice of the American people, but of foreign nations. It may be foreign nations who govern us, and not we the people who govern ourselves. And candid men will acknowledge, that, in such cases, choice would have little advantage to boast of, over lot or chance.

Such is the amiable and interesting system of government (and such are some of the abuses to which it may be exposed) which the people of America have exhibited to the admiration and anxiety of the wise and virtuous of all nations, for eight years, under the administration of a citizen, who, by a long course of great actions, regulated by prudence, justice, temperance, and fortitude, conducting a people inspired with the same virtues, and animated with the same ardent patriotism and love of liberty, to independence and peace, to increasing wealth and unexampled prosperity, has merited the gratitude of his fellow-citizens, commanded the highest praises of foreign nations, and secured immortal glory with posterity.

In that retirement which is his voluntary choice, may he long live to enjoy the delicious recollection of his services, the gratitude of mankind, the happy fruits of them to himself and the world, which are daily increasing, and that splendid prospect of the future fortunes of this country which is opening from year to year. His name may be still a rampart, and the knowledge that he lives a bulwark, against all open or secret enemies of his country's peace. This example has been recommended to the imitation of his successors, by both houses of Congress and by the voice of the legislatures and the people throughout the nation.

On this subject it might become me better to be silent, or to speak with diffidence; but, as something may be expected, the occasion, I hope, will be admitted as an apology, if I venture to say, That—

If a preference, upon principle, of a free republican government, formed upon long and serious reflection, after a diligent and impartial inquiry after truth; if an attachment to the Constitution of the United States, and a conscientious determination to support it, until it shall be 'altered by the judgments and wishes of the people, expressed in the mode prescribed in it; if a respectable attention to the constitutions of the individual States, and a constant caution and delicacy towards the State governments; if an equal and impartial regard to the rights, interest, honor, and happiness, of all the States in the Union, without preference or

regard to a northern or southern, an eastern or western
position, their various political opinions on unessential
points, or their personal attachments; if a love of virtuous
men, of all parties and denominations; if a love of science
and letters, and a wish to patronize every rational effort to
encourage schools, colleges, universities, academies, and
every institution for propagating knowledge, virtue, and religion, among all classes of the people, not only for their
benign influence on the happiness of life in all its stages
and classes, and of society in all its forms, but as the only
means of preserving our Constitution from its natural
enemies, the spirit of sophistry, the spirit of party, the spirit
of intrigue, the profligacy of corruption, and the pestilence
of foreign influence, which is the angel of destruction to
elective governments; if a love of equal laws, of justice,
and humanity, in the interior administration; if an inclination to improve agriculture, commerce, and manufactures
for necessity, convenience, and defense; if a spirit of equity
and humanity towards the aboriginal nations of America,
and a disposition to meliorate their condition, by inclining
them to be more friendly to us, and our citizens to be more
friendly to them; if an inflexible determination to maintain
peace and inviolable faith with all nations, and that system
of neutrality and impartiality among the belligerent powers
of Europe which has been adopted by this government, and
so solemnly sanctioned by both houses of Congress, and
applauded by the legislatures of the States and the public
opinion, until it shall be otherwise ordained by Congress;
if a personal esteem for the French nation, formed in a residence of seven years chiefly among them, and a sincere desire to preserve the friendship which has been so much for
the honor and interest of both nations; if, while the conscious honor and integrity of the people of America, and
the internal sentiment of their own power and energies,
must be preserved, an earnest endeavor to investigate every

just cause, and remove every colorable pretense of complaint; if an intention to pursue, by amicable negotiation, a reparation for the injuries that have been committed on the commerce of our fellow-citizens, by whatever nation, and if success cannot be obtained, to lay the facts before the legislature, that they may consider what further measures the honor and interest of the government and its constituents demand; if a resolution to do justice, as far as may depend upon me, at all times and to all nations, and maintain peace, friendship, and benevolence, with all the world; if an unshaken confidence in the honor, spirit, and resources of the American people, on which I have so often hazarded my all, and never been deceived; if elevated ideas of the high destinies, of this country, and of my own duties toward it, founded on a knowledge of the moral principles and intellectual improvements of the people, deeply engraven on my mind in early life, and not obscured, but exalted, by experience and age; and, with humble reverence, I feel it to be my duty to add, if a veneration for the religion of a people who profess and call themselves Christians, and a fixed resolution to consider a decent respect for Christianity among the best recommendations for the public service,—can enable me, in any degree, to comply with your wishes, it shall be my strenuous endeavor that this sagacious injunction of the two houses shall not be without effect.

With this great example before me—with the sense and spirit, the faith and honor, the duty and interest, of the same American people, pledged to support the Constitution of the United States, I entertain no doubt of its continuance in all its energy, and my mind is prepared, without hesitation, to lay myself under the most solemn obligations to support it to the utmost of my power.

And may that Being who is supreme over all, the Patron of order, the Fountain of justice, and the Protector, in all ages of the world, of virtuous liberty, continue His blessing upon this nation and its government, and give it all possible success and duration consistent with the ends of His providence.

INAUGURAL ADDRESS OF THOMAS JEFFERSON, PRESIDENT OF THE UNITED STATES,

At his first term of office, March 4, 1801.

Friends and fellow-citizens :—Called upon to undertake the duties of the first executive office of our country, I avail myself of the presence of that portion of my fellow citizens which is here assembled, to express my grateful thanks for the favor with which they have been pleased to look towards me, to declare a sincere consciousness that the task is above my talents, and that I approach it with those anxious and awful presentiments which the greatness of the charge, and the weakness of my powers, so justly inspire. A rising nation, spread over a wide and fruitful land; traversing all the seas with the rich productions of their industry ; engaged in commerce with nations who feel power, and forget right ; advancing rapidly to destinies beyond the reach of mortal eye—when I contemplate these transcendent objects, and see the honor, the happiness, and the hopes of this beloved country, committed to the issue and the auspices of this day, I shrink from the contemplation, and humble myself before the magnitude of the undertaking. Utterly, indeed, should I despair, did not the presence of many whom I here see, remind me, that, in the other high authorities provided by our Constitution, I shall find resources of wisdom, of virtue, and of zeal, on which to rely under all difficulties. To you, then, gentlemen, who are charged with the sovereign functions of legislation, and to those associated with you, I look with encouragement for that guidance and support which may enable us to steer with safety the vessel in which we are all embarked, amidst the conflicting elements of a troubled world.

During the contest of opinion through which we have passed, the animation of discussions and of exertions has sometimes worn an aspect which might impose on strangers unused to think freely, and to speak and to write what they may think; but, this being now decided by the voice of the nation, announced, according to the rules of the Constitution, all will, of course, arrange themselves under the will of the law, and unite in common efforts for the common good. All, too, will bear in mind this sacred principle, that, though the will of the majority is in all cases to prevail, that will, to be rightful, must be reasonable; that the minority possess their equal rights, which equal laws must protect, and to violate would be oppression. Let us, then, fellow-citizens, unite, with one heart and one mind; let us restore to social intercourse, that harmony and affection, without which liberty, and even life itself, are but dreary things. And let us reflect, that, having banished from our land that religious intolerance under which mankind so long bled and suffered, we have yet gained little, if we countenance a political intolerance as despotic, as wicked, and capable of as bitter and bloody persecutions. During the throes and convulsions of the ancient world; during the agonizing spasms of infuriated man, seeking, through blood and slaughter, his long-lost liberty, it was not wonderful that the agitation of the billows should reach even this distant and peaceful shore; that this should be more felt and feared by some, and less by others, and should divide opinions as to measures of safety; but every difference of opinion is not a difference of principle. We have called by different names brethren of the same principle. We are all republicans; we are all federalists. If there be any among us who would wish to dissolve this Union, or to change its republican form, let them stand, undisturbed, as monuments of the safety with which *error of opinion may be tolerated, where reason is left free to combat it.* I know, indeed, that some honest men fear that a republican government cannot be strong—that this government is not strong enough. But would the honest patriot, in the full tide of successful experiment, abandon a government which has so far kept us free and firm, on the theoretic and visionary fear, that this government, the world's best hope, may, by possibility, want energy to preserve itself? I trust not. I believe this, on the contrary, the strongest government on earth. I believe it the only one where every man, at the call of the law, would fly to the standard of the law, and would meet invasions of the public order as his own personal concern. Sometimes, it is said, that man cannot be trusted with the government of himself. Can he then be trusted with the government of others? Or, have we found angels, in the form of kings, to govern him? Let history answer this question.

Let us, then, with courage and confidence pursue our own federal and republican principles—our attachment to union and representative government. Kindly separated by nature and a wide ocean from the exterminating havoc of one quarter of the globe; too high-minded to endure the degradations of the others; possessing a chosen country, with room enough for our descendants to the hundredth and thousandth generation; entertaining a due sense of our equal right to the use of our own faculties, to the acquisitions of our own industry, to honor and confidence from our fellow-citizens, resulting, not from birth, but from our actions, and their sense of them; enlightened by a benign religion, professed, indeed, and practiced in various forms, yet all of them inculcating honesty, truth, temperance, gratitude, and the love of man; acknowledging and adoring an over-ruling Providence, which, by all its dispensations, proves that it delights in the happiness of man here, and his greater happiness hereafter—with all these blessings, what more is necessary to make us a happy and prosperous people? Still one thing more, fellow-citizens: a wise and frugal government, which shall restrain men from injuring one another, shall leave them otherwise free to regulate their own pursuits of industry and improvement, and shall not take from the mouth of labor the bread it has earned. This is the sum of good government, and this is necessary to close the circle of our felicities.

About to enter, fellow-citizens, on the exercise of duties which comprehend everything dear and valuable to you, it is proper you should understand what I deem the essential principles of our government, and consequently, those which ought to shape its administration. I will compress them within the narrowest compass they will bear—stating the general principle, but not all its limitations. Equal and exact justice to all men, of whatever state or persuasion, religious or political; peace, commerce, and honest friendship with all nations, entangling alliances with none; the support of the State governments in all their rights, as the most competent administrations for our domestic concerns, and the surest bulwarks against anti-republican tendencies; the preservation of the general government in its whole constitutional vigor, as the sheet-anchor of our peace at home and safety abroad; a jealous care of the right of election by the people; a mild and safe corrective of abuses which are lopped by the sword of revolution, where peaceable remedies are unprovided; absolute acquiescence in the decisions of the majority, the vital principle of republics, from which is no appeal but to force, the vital principle and immediate parent of despotism; a well-disciplined militia, our best reliance in peace, and for the first moments of war, till regulars may relieve them; the supremacy of the civil over the military authority; economy in the public expense, that labor may be lightly burdened; the honest payment of our debts, and sacred preservation of the public faith; encouragement of agriculture, and of commerce as its handmaid; the diffusion of information, and arraignment of all abuses at the bar of the public reason; freedom of religion, freedom of the press, and freedom of person, under the protection of the habeas corpus; and trial by juries impartially selected. These principles form the bright constellation which has gone before us, and guided our steps through an age of revolution and reformation. The wisdom of our sages and blood of our heroes have been devoted to their attainment. They should be the creed of our political faith, the text of civic instruction, the touch-stone by which to try the services of those we trust; and should we wander from them in moments of error or of alarm, let us hasten to retrace our steps, and to regain the road which alone leads to peace, liberty, and safety.

I repair, then, fellow-citizens, to the post you have assigned me. With experience enough in subordinate offices to have seen the difficulties of this, the greatest of all, I have learned to expect that it will rarely fall to the lot of imperfect man to retire from this station with the reputation and the favor which brought him into it. Without pretensions to that high confidence you reposed in our first and greatest revolutionary character, whose pre-eminent services had entitled him to the first place in his country's love, and destined for him the fairest page in the volume of faithful history, I ask so much confidence only as may give firmness and effect to the legal administration of your affairs. I shall often go wrong, through defect of judgment. When right, I shall often be thought wrong by those whose positions will not command a view of the whole ground. I ask your indulgence for my own errors, which will never be intentional, and your support against the errors of others, who may condemn what they would not if seen in all its parts. The approbation implied by your suffrage is a great consolation to me for the past; and my future solicitude will be, to retain the good opinion of those who have bestowed it in advance, to conciliate that of others by doing them all the good in my power, and to be instrumental to the happiness and freedom of all.

Relying, then, on the patronage of your good will, I advance with obedience to the work, ready to retire from it whenever you become sensible how much better choices it is in your power to make. And may that Infinite Power which rules the destinies of the universe, lead our councils to what is best, and give them a favorable issue for your peace and prosperity.

INAUGURAL ADDRESS OF THOMAS JEFFERSON, PRESIDENT OF THE UNITED STATES,

At his second term of office, March 4, 1805.

Proceeding, fellow-citizens, to that qualification which the Constitution requires before my entrance on the charge again conferred on me, it is my duty to express the deep sense I entertain of this new proof of confidence from my fellow-citizens at large, and the zeal with which it inspires me so to conduct myself as may best satisfy their just expectations.

On taking this station, on a former occasion, I declared the principles on which I believed it my duty to administer the affairs of our commonwealth. My conscience tells me I have, on every occasion, acted up to that declaration, according to its obvious import, and to the understanding of every candid mind.

In the transaction of your foreign affairs, we have endeavored to cultivate the friendship of all nations, and especially of those with which we have the most important relations. We have done them justice on all occasions, favor where favor was lawful, and cherished mutual interests and intercourse on fair and equal terms. We are firmly convinced, and we act on that conviction, that with nations as with individuals, our interest, soundly calculated, will ever be found inseparable from our moral duties; and history bears witness to the fact, that a just nation is trusted on its word when recourse is had to armaments and wars to bridle others.

At home, fellow-citizens, you best know whether we have done well or ill. The suppression of unnecessary offices, of useless establishments and expenses enabled us to discontinue our internal taxes. These, covering our land with officers, and opening our doors to their intrusions, had already begun that process of domiciliary vexation which, once entered, is scarcely to be restrained from reaching successively, every article of property and produce. If, among these taxes, some minor ones fell, which had not been inconvenient, it was because their amount would not have paid the officers who collected them, and because, if they had any merit, the State authorities might adopt them instead of others less approved.

The remaining revenue, on the consumption of foreign articles, is paid chiefly by those who can afford to add foreign luxuries to domestic comforts. Being collected on our seaboard and frontiers only, and incorporated with the transactions of our mercantile citizens, it may be the pleasure and the pride of an American to ask, what farmer, what mechanic, what laborer, ever sees a tax-gatherer of the United States? These contributions enable us to support the current expenses of the government; to fulfil contracts with foreign nations; to extinguish the native right of soil within our limits; to extend those limits; and to apply such a surplus to our public debts as places at a short day their final redemption; and that redemption once effected, the revenue thereby liberated may, by a just repartition of it among the States, and a corresponding amendment of the Constitution, be applied, *in time of peace*, to rivers, canals, roads, arts, manufactures, education, and other great objects, within each State. *In time of war*, if injustice by ourselves or others must sometimes produce war, increased, as the same revenue will be, by increased population and consumption, and aided by other resources reserved for that crisis, it may meet, within the year, all the expenses of the year, without encroaching on the rights of future generations, by burdening them with the debts of the past. War will then be but a suspension of useful works; and a return to a state of peace, a return to the progress of improvement.

I have said, fellow-citizens, that the income reserved had enabled us to extend our limits; but that extension may possibly pay for itself before we are called on, and, in the mean time, may keep down the accruing interest; in all events, it will replace the advances we shall have made. I know that the acquisition of Louisiana has been disapproved by some, from a candid apprehension that the enlargement of our territory would endanger its union. But who can limit the extent to which the federative principle may operate effectively? The larger our associations, the less will it be shaken by local passions; and, in any view, is it not better that the opposite bank of the Mississippi should be settled by our own brethren and children than by strangers of another family? With which should we be most likely to live in harmony and friendly intercourse?

In matters of religion, I have considered that its free exercise is placed by the Constitution independent of the powers of the general government. I have therefore undertaken, on no occasion, to prescribe the religious exercises suited to it, but have left them, as the Constitution found them, under the direction and discipline of the church or State authorities acknowledged by the several religious societies.

The aboriginal inhabitants of these countries I have regarded with the commiseration their history inspires. Endowed with the faculties and the rights of men, breathing an ardent love of liberty and independence, and occupying a country which left them no desire but to be undisturbed, the stream of overflowing population from other regions directed itself on these shores. Without power to divert, or habits to contend against it, they have been overwhelmed by the current, or driven before it. Now reduced within limits too narrow for the hunter state, humanity enjoins us to teach them agriculture and the domestic arts, to encourage them to that industry which alone can enable them to maintain their place in existence, and to prepare them, in time, for that state of society which to bodily comforts adds the improvement of the mind and morals. We have, therefore, liberally furnished them with the implements of husbandry and household use: we have placed among them instructors in the arts of first necessity; and they are covered with the ægis of the law against aggressors from among ourselves.

But the endeavors to enlighten them on the fate which awaits their present course of life, to induce them to exercise their reason, follow its dictates, and change their pursuits with the change of circumstances, have powerful obstacles to encounter. They are combated by the habits of their bodies, prejudices of their minds, ignorance, pride, and the influence of interested and crafty individuals among them, who feel themselves something in the present order of things, and fear to become nothing in any other. These persons inculcate a sanctimonious reverence for the customs of their ancestors; that whatsoever they did must be done through all time; that reason is a false guide, and to advance under its counsel in their physical, moral, or political condition, is perilous innovation; that their duty is to remain as the Creator made them—ignorance being safety, and knowledge full of danger. In short, my friends, among them, also, is seen the action and counteraction of good sense and of bigotry. They, too, have their anti-philosophists, who find an interest in keeping things in their present state, who dread reformation, and exert all their faculties to maintain the ascendency of habit over the duty of improving our reason and obeying its mandates.

In giving these outlines, I do not mean, fellow-citizens, to arrogate to myself the merit of the measures: that is due, in the first place, to the reflecting character of our citizens at large, who, by the weight of public opinion, influence and strengthen the public measures. It is due to the sound discretion with which they select from among themselves those to whom they confide the legislative duties. It is due to the zeal and wisdom of the characters thus selected, who lay the foundations of public happiness in wholesome laws, the execution of which alone remains for others. And it is due to the able and faithful auxiliaries whose patriotism has associated them with me in the executive functions.

During this course of administration, and in order to disturb it, the artillery of the press has been leveled against us, charged with whatsoever its licentiousness could devise or dare. These abuses of an institution so important to freedom and science are deeply to be regretted, inasmuch as they tend to lessen its usefulness and to sap its safety. They might, indeed, have been corrected by the wholesome punishments reserved to and provided by the laws of the several States against falsehood and defamation; but public duties, more urgent, press on the time of public servants, and the offenders have therefore been left to find their punishment in the public indignation.

Nor was it uninteresting to the world, that an experiment should be fairly and fully made, whether freedom of discussion, unaided by power, is not sufficient for the propagation and protection of truth? Whether a government, conducting itself in the true spirit of its constitution, with zeal and purity, and doing no act which it would be unwilling the whole world should witness, can be written down by falsehood and defamation? The experiment has been tried. You have witnessed the scene. Our fellow-citizens looked on cool and collected. They saw the latent source from which these outrages proceeded. They gathered around their public functionaries; and, when the Constitution called them to the decision by suffrage, they pronounced their verdict honorable to those who had served them, and consolatory to the friend of man, who believes that he may be trusted with the control of his own affairs.

No inference is here intended that the laws provided by the States against false and defamatory publications should not be enforced. He who has time, renders a service to public morals and public tranquillity in reforming these abuses by the salutary coercions of the law. But the experiment is noted to prove that, since truth and reason have maintained their ground against false opinions, in league with false facts, the press, confined to truth, needs no other legal restraint. The public judgment will correct false reasonings and opinions, on a full hearing of all parties; and no other definite line can be drawn between the inestimable liberty of the press and its demoralizing licentiousness. If there be still improprieties which this rule would not restrain, its supplement must be sought in the censorship of public opinion.

Contemplating the union of sentiment now manifested so generally, as auguring harmony and happiness to our future course, I offer to our country sincere congratulations. With those, too, not yet rallied to the same point, the disposition to do so is gaining strength. Facts are piercing through the veil drawn over them; and our doubting brethren will at length see that the mass of their fellow-citizens, with whom they cannot yet resolve to act, as to principles and measures, think as they think, and desire what they desire;

that our wish, as well as theirs, is, that the public efforts may be directed honestly to the public good, that peace be cultivated, civil and religious liberty unassailed, law and order preserved, equality of rights maintained, and that state of property, equal or unequal, which results to every man from his own industry or that of his father's. When satisfied of these views, it is not in human nature that they should not approve and support them. In the mean time, let us cherish them with patient affection; let us do them justice, and more than justice, in all competitions of interest—and we need not doubt that truth, reason, and their own interests, will at length prevail—will gather them into the fold of their country, and will complete that entire union of opinion which gives to a nation the blessing of harmony, and the benefit of all its strength.

I shall now enter on the duties to which my fellow-citizens have again called me, and shall proceed in the spirit of those principles which they have approved. I fear not that any motives of interest may lead me astray. I am sensible of no passion which could seduce me, knowingly, from the path of justice; but the weaknesses of human nature, and the limits of my own understanding, will produce errors of judgment sometimes injurious to your interests. I shall need, therefore, all the indulgence which I have heretofore experienced from my constituents. The want of it will certainly not lessen with increasing years. I shall need, too, the favor of that Being in whose hands we are; who led our fathers, as Israel of old, from their native land, and planted them in a country flowing with all the necessaries and comforts of life; who has covered our infancy with his providence, and our riper years with his wisdom and power; and to whose goodness I ask you to join in supplications with me, that he will so enlighten the minds of your servants, guide their councils, and prosper their measures, that whatsoever they do shall result in your good, and shall secure to you the peace, friendship, and approbation of all nations.

INAUGURAL ADDRESS OF JAMES MADISON, PRESIDENT OF THE UNITED STATES.

At his First Term of Office, March 4, 1809.

Gentlemen of the Senate,
and of the House of Representatives:

Unwilling to depart from examples of the most revered authority, I avail myself of the occasion now presented, to express the profound impression made on me, by the call of my country, to the station, to the duties of which I am about to pledge myself, by the most solemn of sanctions. So distinguished a mark of confidence, proceeding from the deliberate and tranquil suffrage of a free and virtuous nation, would, under any circumstances, have commanded my gratitude and devotion, as well as filled me with an awful sense of the trust to be assumed. Under the various circumstances which give peculiar solemnity to the existing period, I feel that both the honor and the responsibility allotted to me, are inexpressibly enhanced.

The present situation of the world is, indeed, without a parallel; and that of our country full of difficulties. The pressure of these two is the more severely felt, because they have fallen upon us at a moment when national prosperity, being at a height not before attained, the contrast resulting from this change has been rendered the more striking. Under the benign influence of our republican institutions, and the maintenance of peace with all nations, whilst so many of them were engaged in bloody and wasteful wars, the fruits of a just policy were enjoyed in an unrivaled growth of our faculties and resources. Proofs of this were even in the improvements of agriculture; in the successful enterprises of commerce; in the progress of manufactures and useful arts; in the increase of the public revenue, and the use made of it in reducing the public debt; and in the valuable works and establishments everywhere multiplying over the face of our land.

It is a precious reflection, that the transition from this prosperous condition of our country, to the scene which has for some time been distressing us, is not chargeable on any unwarrantable views, nor, as I trust, on any involuntary errors in the public councils. Indulging no passions which trespass on the rights or the repose of other nations, it has been the true glory of the United States to cultivate peace, by observing justice, and to entitle themselves to the respect of the nations at war, by fulfilling their neutral obligations with the most scrupulous impartiality. If there be candor in the world, the truth of these assertions will not be questioned. Posterity, at least, will do justice to them.

This unexceptionable course could not avail against the injustice and violence of the belligerent powers. In their rage against each other, or impelled by more direct motives, principles of retaliation have been introduced, equally contrary to universal reason and acknowledged law. How long their arbitrary edicts will be continued, in spite of the demonstrations that not even a pretext for them has been given by the United States, and of the fair and liberal attempts to induce a revocation of them, cannot be anticipated. Assuring myself that, under every vicissitude, the determined spirit and united councils of the nation will be safeguards to its honor and its essential interests, I repair to the post assigned me, with no other discouragement than what springs from my own inadequacy to its high duties If I do not sink under the weight of this deep conviction, it is because I find some support in a consciousness of the purposes, and a confidence in the principles which I bring with me into this arduous service.

To cherish peace and friendly intercourse with all nations, having correspondent dispositions; to maintain sincere neutrality towards belligerent nations; to prefer, in all cases, amicable discussion and reasonable accommodation of differences, to a decision of them by an appeal to arms; to exclude foreign intrigues and foreign partialities, so degrading to all countries, and so baneful to free ones; to foster a spirit of independence; too just to invade the rights of others; too proud to surrender our own; too liberal to indulge unworthy prejudices ourselves, and too elevated not to look down upon them in others; to hold the union of the States as the basis of their peace and happiness; to support the Constitution, which is the cement of the Union, as well in its limitations as in its authorities; to respect the rights and authorities reserved to the States and to the people, as equally incorporated with, and essential to the success of the general system; to avoid the slightest interference with the rights of conscience, or the functions of religion, so wisely exempted from civil jurisdiction; to preserve, to their full energy, the other salutary provisions in behalf of private and personal rights, and of the freedom of the press; to observe economy in public expenditures; to liberate the public resources by an honorable discharge of the public debts; to keep within the requisite limits a standing military force, always remembering that an armed and trained militia is the firmest bulwark of republics; that without standing armies their liberty can never be in danger, nor, with large ones, safe; to promote, by authorized means, improvements friendly to agriculture, to manufactures, and to external as well as internal commerce; to favor, in like manner, the advancement of science and the diffusion of information, as the best aliment to true liberty; to carry on the benevolent plans which have been so meritoriously applied to the conversion of our aboriginal neighbors, from the degradation and wretchedness of savage life, to a participation of the improvements of which the human mind and manners are susceptible in a civilized state : as far as sentiments and intentions such as these can aid the fulfilment of my duty, they will be a resource which cannot fail me.

It is my good fortune, moreover, to have the path in which I am to tread, lighted by examples of illustrious services, successfully rendered in the most trying difficulties, by those who have marched before me. Of those of my immediate predecessor, it might least become me here to speak— I may, however, be pardoned for not suppressing the sympathy with which my heart is full, in the rich reward he enjoys in the benedictions of a beloved country, gratefully bestowed for exalted talents, zealously devoted through a long career to the advancement of its highest interest and happiness. But the source to which I look for the aids which alone can supply my deficiencies, is in the well-tried intelligence and virtue of my fellow-citizens, and in the councils of those representing them in the other departments associated in the care of the national interests. In these my confidence will, under every difficulty, be best placed ; next to that which we have all been encouraged to feel in the guardianship and guidance of that Almighty Being, whose power regulates the destiny of nations, whose blessings have been so conspicuously dispensed to this rising Republic, and to whom we are bound to address our devout gratitude for the past, as well as our fervent supplications and best hopes for the future.

FAREWELL ADDRESS OF GEORGE WASHINGTON, PRESIDENT, TO THE PEOPLE OF THE UNITED STATES.
September 17, 1796.

Friends and Fellow-citizens:

The period for a new election of a citizen to administer the executive government of the United States being not far distant, and the time actually arrived when your thoughts must be employed in designating the person who is to be clothed with that important trust, it appears to me proper, especially as it may conduce to a more distinct expression of the public voice, that I should now apprise you of the resolution I have formed, to decline being considered among the number of those out of whom a choice is to be made.

I beg you at the same time, to do me the justice to be assured that this resolution has not been taken without a strict regard to all the considerations appertaining to the relation which binds a dutiful citizen to his country; and that, in withdrawing the tender of service which silence, in my situation, might imply, I am influenced by no diminution of zeal for your future interests, no deficiency of grateful respect for your past kindness, but am supported by a full conviction that the step is compatible with both.

The acceptance of, and continuance hitherto in, the office to which your suffrages have twice called me, have been a uniform sacrifice of inclination to the opinion of duty, and to a deference for what appeared to be your desire. I constantly hoped that it would have been much earlier in my power, consistently with motives which I was not at liberty to disregard, to return to that retirement from which I have been reluctantly drawn. The strength of my inclination to do this, previous to the last election, had even led to the preparation of an address to declare it to you; but mature reflection on the then perplexed and critical posture of our affairs with foreign nations, and the unanimous advice of persons entitled to my confidence, impelled me to abandon the idea.

I rejoice that the state of your concerns, external as well as internal, no longer renders the pursuit of inclination incompatible with the sentiment of duty or propriety; and am persuaded, whatever partiality may be retained for my services, that, in the present circumstances of our country, you will not disapprove my determination to retire.

The impressions with which I first undertook the arduous

trust were explained on the proper occasion. In the discharge of this trust, I will only say, that I have with good intentions contributed towards the organization and administration of the government the best exertions of which a very fallible judgment was capable. Not unconscious in the outset of the inferiority of my qualifications, experience, in my own eyes—perhaps still more in the eyes of others—has strengthened the motives to diffidence of myself; and every day the increasing weight of years admonishes me, more and more, that the shade of retirement is as necessary to me as it will be welcome. Satisfied that if any circumstances have given peculiar value to my services, they were temporary, I have the consolation to believe, that while choice and prudence invite me to quit the political scene, patriotism does not forbid it.

In looking forward to the moment which is intended to terminate the career of my public life, my feelings do not permit me to suspend the deep acknowledgment of that debt of gratitude which I owe to my beloved country for the many honors it has conferred upon me; still more for the steadfast confidence with which it has supported me; and for the opportunities I have thence enjoyed of manifesting my inviolable attachment, by services faithful and persevering, though in usefulness unequal to my zeal. If benefits have resulted to our country from these services, let it always be remembered to your praise, and as an instructive example in our annals, that, under circumstances in which the passions, agitated in every direction, were liable to mislead; amidst appearances sometimes dubious, vicissitudes of fortune often discouraging; in situations in which, not unfrequently, want of success has countenanced the spirit of criticism—the constancy of your support was the essential prop of the efforts, and a guarantee of the plans, by which they were effected. Profoundly penetrated with this idea, I shall carry it with me to my grave, as a strong incitement to unceasing vows,

that Heaven may continue to you the choicest tokens of its
beneficence; that your union and brotherly affection may
be perpetual; that the free Constitution, which is the work
of your hands, may be sacredly maintained; that its administration, in every department, may be stamped with wisdom
and virtue; that, in fine, the happiness of the people of these
States, under the auspices of liberty, may be made complete,
by so careful a preservation and so prudent a use of this
blessing as will acquire to them the glory of recommending
it to the applause, the affection, and the adoption of every
nation which is yet a stranger to it.

Here, perhaps, I ought to stop; but a solicitude for your
welfare, which cannot end but with my life, and the apprehension of danger natural to that solicitude, urge me, on an
occasion like the present, to offer to your solemn contemplation, and to recommend to your frequent review, some sentiments, which are the result of much reflection, of no inconsiderable observation, and which appear to me all-important to the permanency of your felicity as a people.
These will be afforded to you with the more freedom, as you
can only see in them the disinterested warnings of a parting
friend, who can possibly have no personal motive to bias his
counsel; nor can I forget, as an encouragement to it, your
indulgent reception of my sentiments on a former and not
dissimilar occasion.

Interwoven as is the love of liberty with every ligament
of your hearts, no recommendation of mine is necessary to
fortify or confirm the attachment.

The unity of government, which constitutes you one
people, is also now dear to you. It is justly so; for it is a
main pillar in the edifice of your real independence—the
support of your tranquillity at home, your peace abroad, of
your safety, of your prosperity, of that very liberty which
you so highly prize. But as it is easy to foresee, that from
different causes and from different quarters, much pains will

be taken, many artifices employed, to weaken in your minds the conviction of this truth; as this is the point in your political fortress against which the batteries of internal and external enemies will be most confidently and actively (though often covertly and insidiously) directed—it is of infinite moment that you should properly estimate the immense value of your national union to your collective and individual happiness; that you should cherish a cordial, habitual, and immovable attachment to it; accustoming yourselves to think and speak of it as of the palladium of your political safety and prosperity; watching for its preservation with jealous anxiety; discountenancing whatever may suggest even a suspicion that it can, in any event, be abandoned; and indignantly frowning upon the first dawning of every attempt to alienate any portion of our country from the rest, or to enfeeble the sacred ties which now link together the various parts.

For this you have every inducement of sympathy and interest. Citizens by birth or choice, of a common country, that country has a right to concentrate your affections. The name of *American*, which belongs to you in your national capacity, must always exalt the just pride of patriotism, more than any appellation derived from local discriminations. With slight shades of difference, you have the same religion, manners, habits, and political principles. You have, in a common cause, fought and triumphed together; the independence and liberty you possess are the work of joint counsels and joint efforts, of common dangers, sufferings, and successes.

But these considerations, however powerfully they address themselves to your sensibility, are greatly outweighed by those which apply more immediately to your interest; here every portion of our country finds the most commanding motives for carefully guarding and preserving the union of the whole.

The North, in an unrestrained intercourse with the South, protected by the equal laws of a common government, finds, in the productions of the latter, great additional resources of maritime and commercial enterprise, and precious materials of manufacturing industry. The South, in the same intercourse, benefiting by the agency of the North, sees its agriculture grow, and its commerce expand. Turning partly into its own channels the seamen of the North, it finds its particular navigation invigorated; and while it contributes, in different ways, to nourish and increase the general mass of national navigation, it looks forward to the protection of a maritime strength to which itself is unequally adapted. The East, in like intercourse with the West, already finds, and in the progressive improvement of interior communication, by land and water, will more and more find, a valuable vent for the commodities which it brings from abroad, or manufactures at home. The West derives from the East supplies requisite to its growth and comfort; and what is perhaps of still greater consequence, it must, of necessity, owe the secure enjoyment of indispensable outlets for its own productions, to the weight, influence, and the future maritime strength of the Atlantic side of the Union, directed by an indissoluble community of interest as one nation. Any other tenure by which the West can hold this essential advantage, whether derived from its own separate strength, or from an apostate and unnatural connection with any foreign power, must be intrinsically precarious.

While, then, every part of our country thus feels an immediate and particular interest in union, all the parts combined cannot fail to find, in the united mass of means and efforts, greater strength, greater resource, proportionably greater security from external danger, a less frequent interruption of their peace by foreign nations; and what is of inestimable value, they must derive from union an exemption from those broils and wars between themselves, which so frequently afflict neighboring countries, not tied together by the same government; which their own rivalships alone would be sufficient to produce, but which opposite foreign alliances, attachments, and intrigues, would stimulate and imbitter. Hence, likewise, they will avoid the necessity of those overgrown military establishments, which, under any form of government, are inauspicious to liberty, and which are to be regarded as particularly hostile to republican liberty; in this sense it is that your union ought to be considered as a main prop of your liberty, and that the love of one ought to endear to you the preservation of the other.

These considerations speak a persuasive language to every reflecting and virtuous mind, and exhibit the continuance of the Union as a primary object of patriotic desire. Is there a doubt, whether a common government can embrace so large a sphere? Let experience solve it. To listen to mere speculation, in such a case, were criminal. We are authorized to hope, that a proper organization of the whole, with the auxiliary agency of governments for the respective subdivisions, will afford a happy issue to the experiment. It is well worth a fair and full experiment. With such powerful and obvious motives to Union, affecting all parts of our country, while experience shall not have demonstrated its impracticability, there will always be reason to distrust the patriotism of those, who, in any quarter, may endeavor to weaken its bands.

In contemplating the causes which may disturb our Union, it occurs, as a matter of serious concern, that any ground should have been furnished for characterizing parties by geographical discriminations—Northern and Southern—Atlantic and Western: whence designing men may endeavor to excite a belief that there is a real difference of local interests and views. One of the expedients of party to acquire influence within particular districts, is to misrepresent the opinions and aims of other districts. You cannot shield yourselves too much against the jealousies and heart-burnings which spring from these misrepresentations; they tend to render alien to each other those who ought to be bound together by fraternal affection. The inhabitants of our western country have lately had a useful lesson on this head; they have seen in the negotiation by the Executive, and in the unanimous ratification by the Senate, of the treaty with Spain, and in the universal satisfaction at that event throughout the United States, a decisive proof how unfounded were the suspicions propagated among them, of a policy in the general government, and in the Atlantic States, unfriendly to their interests in regard to the Mississippi: they have been witnesses to the formation of two treaties—that with Great Britain, and that with Spain, which secures to them everything they could desire in respect to our foreign relations, towards confirming their prosperity. Will it not be their wisdom to rely for the preservation of these advantages on the Union by which they were procured? Will they not henceforth be deaf to those advisers, if such there are, who would sever them from their brethren, and connect them with aliens?

To the efficacy and permanency of your Union, a government for the whole is indispensable. No alliance, however strict, between the parts, can be an adequate substitute; they must inevitably experience the infractions and interruptions which all alliances, in all time, have experienced. Sensible of this momentous truth, you have improved upon your first essay, by the adoption of a Constitution of government better calculated than your former for an intimate Union, and for the efficacious management of your common concerns. This government, the offspring of our own choice, uninfluenced and unawed, adopted upon full investigation and mature deliberation, completely free in its principles, in the distribution of its powers, uniting security with energy, and containing within itself a provision for its own amendment, has a just claim to your confidence and your support. Respect for its authority, compliance with its laws, acquiescence in its measures, are duties enjoined by the fundamental maxims of true liberty. The basis of our political systems, is the right of the people to make and to alter their constitutions of government; but the Constitution, which at any time exists, till changed by an explicit and authentic act of the whole people, is sacredly obligatory upon all. The very idea of the power and the right of the people to establish government, presupposes the duty of every individual to obey the established government.

All obstructions to the execution of the laws, all combinations and associations, under whatever plausible character, with the real design to direct, control, counteract or awe the regular deliberation and action of the constituted authorities, are destructive to this fundamental principle, and of fatal tendency. They serve to organize faction, to give it an artificial and extraordinary force, to put, in the place of the delegated will of the nation, the will of a party, often a small but artful and enterprising minority of the community; and, according to the alternate triumphs of different parties, to make the public administration the mirror of the ill-concerted and incongruous projects of faction, rather than the organ of consistent and wholesome plans, digested by common counsels, and modified by mutual interests.

However combinations or associations of the above description may now and then answer popular ends, they are likely, in the course of time and things, to become potent engines by which cunning, ambitious, and unprincipled men will be enabled to subvert the power of the people, and to usurp for themselves the reins of government; destroying, afterwards, the very engines which had lifted them to unjust dominion.

Towards the preservation of your government, and the

permanency of your present happy state, it is requisite, not only that you steadily discountenance irregular oppositions to its acknowledged authority, but also that you resist with care the spirit of innovation upon its principles, however specious the pretexts. One method of assault may be to effect, in the forms of the Constitution, alterations which will impair the energy of the system, and thus to undermine what cannot be directly overthrown. In all the changes to which you may be invited, remember that time and habit are at least as necessary to fix the true character of governments, as of other human institutions; that experience is the surest standard by which to test the real tendency of the existing Constitution of a country; that facility in changes, upon the credit of mere hypothesis and opinion, exposes to perpetual change, from the endless variety of hypothesis and opinion; and remember, especially, that for the efficient management of your common interests, in a country so extensive as ours, a government of as much vigor as is consistent with the perfect security of liberty, is indispensable. Liberty itself will find in such a government, with powers properly distributed and adjusted, its surest guardian. It is, indeed, little else than a name, where the government is too feeble to withstand the enterprises of faction, to confine each member of the society within the limits prescribed by the laws, and to maintain all in the secure and tranquil enjoyment of the rights of person and property.

I have already intimated to you the danger of parties in the State, with particular reference to the founding of them on geographical discriminations. Let me now take a more comprehensive view, and warn you, in the most solemn manner, against the baneful effects of the spirit of party generally.

This spirit, unfortunately, is inseparable from our nature, having its root in the strongest passions of the human mind.

It exists under different shapes, in all governments, more or less stifled, controlled, or repressed; but in those of the popular form it is seen in its greatest rankness, and is truly their worst enemy.

The alternate domination of one faction over another, sharpened by the spirit of revenge, natural to party dissension, which, in different ages and countries, has perpetrated the most horrid enormities, is itself a frightful despotism. But this leads, at length, to a more formal and permanent despotism. The disorders and miseries which result, gradually incline the minds of men to seek security and repose in the absolute power of an individual; and, sooner or later the chief of some prevailing faction, more able or more fortunate than his competitors, turns this disposition to the purposes of his own elevation on the ruins of public liberty.

Without looking forward to an extremity of this kind, (which, nevertheless, ought not to be entirely out of sight,) the common and continual mischiefs of the spirit of party are sufficient to make it the interest and duty of a wise people to discourage and restrain it.

It tends always to distract the public councils, and enfeeble the public administration. It agitates the commmunity with ill-founded jealousies and false alarms; kindles the animosity of one part against another; foments, occasionally, riot and insurrection. It opens the door to foreign influence and corruption, which find a facilitated access to the government itself, through the channels of party passions. Thus the policy and the will of one country are subjected to the policy and will of another.

There is an opinion that parties, in free countries, are useful checks upon the administration of the government, and serve to keep alive the spirit of liberty. This, within certain limits, is probably true; and in governments of a monarchical cast, patriotism may look with indulgence, if not with favor, upon the spirit of party. But in those of the popular character, in governments purely elective, it is a spirit not to be encouraged. From their natural tendency, it is certain there will always be enough of that spirit for every salutary purpose. And there being constant danger of excess, the effort ought to be, by force of public opinion, to mitigate and assuage it. A fire not to be quenched, it demands a uniform vigilance to prevent its bursting into a flame, lest, instead of warming, it should consume.

It is important, likewise, that the habits of thinking, in a free country, should inspire caution in those intrusted with its administration, to confine themselves within their respective constitutional spheres, avoiding, in the exercise of the powers of one department, to encroach upon another. The spirit of encroachment tends to consolidate the powers of all the departments in one, and thus to create, whatever the form of government, a real despotism. A just estimate of that love of power, and proneness to abuse it, which predominates in the human heart, is sufficient to satisfy us of the truth of this position. The necessity of reciprocal checks in the exercise of political power, by dividing and distributing it into different depositaries, and constituting each the guardian of the public weal, against invasions by the others, has been evinced by experiments, ancient and modern; some of them in our own country, and under our own eyes. To preserve them must be as necessary as to institute them. If, in the opinion of the people, the distribution or modification of the constitutional powers be, in any particular, wrong, let it be corrected by an amendment in the way which the Constitution designates. But let there be no change by usurpation; for though this, in one instance, may be the instrument of good, it is the customary weapon by which free governments are destroyed. The precedent must always greatly overbalance, in permanent evil, any partial or transient benefit which the use can, at any time, yield.

Of all the dispositions and habits which lead to political prosperity, religion and morality are indispensable supports. In vain would that man claim the tribute of patriotism, who should labor to subvert these great pillars of human happiness, these firmest props of the duties of men and citizens. The mere politician, equally with the pious man, ought to respect and to cherish them. A volume could not trace all their connections with private and public felicity. Let it simply be asked, where is the security for property, for reputation, for life, if the sense of religious obligation *desert* the oaths which are the instruments of investigation in courts of justice? And let us with caution indulge the supposition, that morality can be maintained without religion. Whatever may be conceded to the influence of refined education on minds of peculiar structure, reason and experience both forbid us to expect that national morality can prevail in exclusion of religious principles.

It is substantially true, that virtue or morality is a necessary spring of popular government. The rule, indeed, extends with more or less force to every species of free government. Who, that is a sincere friend to it, can look with indifference upon attempts to shake the foundation of the fabric?

Promote, then, as an object of primary importance, institutions for the general diffusion of knowledge. In proportion as the structure of a government gives force to public opinion, it is essential that public opinion should be enlightened.

As a very important source of strength and security, cherish public credit. One method of preserving it is to use it as sparingly as possible; avoiding occasions of expense by cultivating peace, but remembering also that timely disbursements to prepare for danger, frequently prevent much greater disbursements to repel it; avoiding, likewise, the accumulation of debt, not only by shunning occasions of expense, but by vigorous exertions in time of peace to discharge the debts which unavoidable wars may have occasioned; not ungenerously throwing upon posterity the burden which we ourselves ought to bear. The execution of these maxims belongs to your representatives, but it is necessary that public opinion should co-operate. To facilitate to them the performance of their duty, it is essential that you should practically bear in mind, that towards the payment of debts there must be revenue; that to have revenue there must be taxes; that no taxes can be devised, which are not more or less inconvenient and unpleasant; that the intrinsic embarrassment inseparable from the selection of the proper objects, (which is always a choice of difficulties,) ought to be a decisive motive for a candid construction of the conduct of the Government in making it, and for a spirit of acquiescence in the measures for obtaining revenue, which the public exigencies may at any time dictate.

Observe good faith and justice towards all nations; cultivate peace and harmony with all; religion and morality enjoin this conduct; and can it be that good policy does not equally enjoin it? It will be worthy of a free, enlightened, and, at no distant period, a great nation, to give to mankind the magnanimous and too novel example of a people always guided by an exalted justice and benevolence. Who can doubt that, in the course of time and things, the fruits of such a plan would richly repay any temporary advantages which might be lost by a steady adherence to it? Can it be that Providence has not connected the permanent felicity of a nation with its virtue? The experiment, at least, is recommended by every sentiment which ennobles human nature. Alas! is it rendered impossible by its vices?

In the execution of such a plan, nothing is more essential than that permanent inveterate antipathies against particular nations, and passionate attachments for others, should be excluded; and that, in place of them, just and amicable feelings towards all should be cultivated. The nation which indulges towards another an habitual hatred, or an habitual fondness, is, in some degree, a slave. It is a slave to its animosity or to its affection; either of which is sufficient to lead it astray from its duty and its interest. Antipathy in one nation against another, disposes each more readily to offer insult and injury, to lay hold of slight causes of umbrage, and to be haughty and intractable, when accidental or trifling occasions of dispute occur. Hence frequent collisions, obstinate, envenomed, and bloody contests. The nation, prompted by ill-will and resentment, sometimes impels to war the Government, contrary to the best calculations of policy. The Government sometimes participates in the national propensity, and adopts, through passion, what reason would reject; at other times it makes the animosity of the nation, subservient to projects of hostility, instigated by pride, ambition, and other sinister and pernicious motives. The peace often, sometimes perhaps the liberty, of nations has been the victim.

So, likewise, a passionate attachment of one nation to another produces a variety of evils. Sympathy for the favorite nation, facilitating the illusion of an imaginary common interest, in cases where no real common interest exists, and infusing into one the enmities of the other, betrays the former into a participation in the quarrels and wars of the latter, without adequate inducement or justification. It leads also to concessions to the favorite nation of privileges denied to others, which is apt doubly to injure the nation making the concessions; by unnecessarily parting with what ought to have been retained, and by exciting jealousy, ill-will, and a disposition to retaliate, in the parties from whom equal privileges are withheld; and it gives to ambitious, corrupted, or deluded citizens (who devote themselves to the favorite nation) facility to betray, or sacrifice the interest of their own country, without odium; sometimes even with popularity; gilding with the appearance of a virtuous sense of obligation, a commendable deference for public opinion, or a laudable zeal for public good, the base or foolish compliances of ambition, corruption, or infatuation.

As avenues to foreign influence in innumerable ways, such attachments are particularly alarming to the truly enlightened and independent patriot. How many opportunities do they afford to tamper with domestic factions, to practice the art of seduction, to mislead public opinion, to influence or awe the public councils? Such an attachment of a small or weak, toward a great and powerful nation, dooms the former to be the satellite of the latter.

Against the insidious wiles of foreign influence (I conjure you to believe me, fellow-citizens) the jealousy of a free people ought to be *constantly* awake; since history and experience prove that foreign influence is one of the most baneful foes of republican government. But that jealousy, to be useful, must be impartial; else it becomes the instrument of the very influence to be avoided, instead of a defense against it. Excessive partiality for one foreign nation, and excessive dislike for another, cause those whom they actuate to see danger only on one side, and serve to vail, and even second, the arts of influence on the other. Real patriots, who may resist the intrigues of the favorite, are liable to become suspected and odious; while its tools and dupes usurp the applause and confidence of the people, to surrender their interests.

The great rule of conduct for us, in regard to foreign nations is, in extending our commercial relations, to have with them as little political connection as possible. So far as we have formed engagements, let them be fulfilled with perfect good faith. Here let us stop.

Europe has a set of primary interests, which to us have none, or a very remote relation. Hence she must be engaged in frequent controversies, the causes of which are essentially foreign to our concerns. Hence, therefore, it must be unwise in us to implicate ourselves, by artificial ties, in the ordinary vicissitudes of politics, or the ordinary combinations and collisions of her friendships or enmities.

Our detached and distant situation invites and enables us to pursue a different course. If we remain one people, under an efficient government, the period is not far off when we may defy material injury from external annoyance; when we may take such an attitude as will cause the neutrality we may at any time resolve upon, to be scrupulously respected; when belligerent nations, under the impossibility of making acquisitions upon us, will not lightly hazard the giving us provocation; when we may choose peace or war, as our interest, guided by justice, shall counsel.

Why forego the advantages of so peculiar a situation? Why quit our own to stand upon foreign ground? Why, by interweaving our destiny with that of any part of Europe, entangle our peace and prosperity in the toils of European ambition, rivalship, interest, humor, or caprice?

It is our true policy to steer clear of permanent alliances with any portion of the foreign world; so far, I mean, as we are now at liberty to do it; for let me not be understood as capable of patronizing infidelity to existing engagements. I hold the maxim no less applicable to public than to private affairs, that honesty is always the best policy. I repeat it, therefore, let those engagements be observed in their genuine sense. But in my opinion, it is unnecessary, and would be unwise, to extend them.

Taking care always to keep ourselves, by suitable establishments, in a respectable defensive posture, we may safely trust to temporary alliances for extraordinary emergencies.

Harmony, and a liberal intercourse with all nations, are recommended by policy, humanity, and interest. But even our commercial policy should hold an equal and impartial hand; neither seeking nor granting exclusive favors or preferences; consulting the natural course of things; diffusing and diversifying, by gentle means, the streams of commerce, but forcing nothing; establishing, with powers so disposed, in order to give trade a stable course, to define the rights of our merchants, and to enable the government to support them, conventional rules of intercourse, the best that present circumstances and mutual opinions will permit, but temporary, and liable to be, from time to time, abandoned, or varied, as experience and circumstances shall dictate; constantly keeping in view, that it is folly in one nation to look for disinterested favors from another; that it must pay, with a portion of its independence, for whatever it may accept under that character; that by such acceptance it may place itself in the condition of having given equivalents for nominal favors, and yet of being reproached with ingratitude for not giving more. There can be no greater error than to expect, or calculate upon, real favors, from nation to nation. It is an illusion which experience must cure, which a just pride ought to discard.

In offering to you, my countrymen, these counsels of an old and affectionate friend, I dare not hope they will make the strong and lasting impression I could wish; that they will control the usual current of the passions, or prevent our nation from running the course which has hitherto marked the destiny of nations; but if I may even flatter myself that they may be productive of some partial benefit, some occasional good; that they may now and then recur to moderate the fury of party spirit, to warn against the mischiefs of foreign intrigues, to guard against the impostures of pretended patriotism; this hope will be a full recompense for the solicitude for your welfare by which they have been dictated.

How far, in the discharge of my official duties, I have been guided by the principles which have been delineated, the public records, and other evidences of my conduct, must witness to you and the world. To myself, the assurance of my own conscience is, that I have at least believed myself to be guided by them.

In relation to the still subsisting war in Europe, my proclamation of the 22d of April, 1793, is the index to my plan. Sanctioned by your approving voice, and that of your representatives in both houses of Congress, the spirit of that measure has continually governed me, uninfluenced by any attempts to deter or divert me from it.

After deliberate examination, with the aid of the best lights I could obtain, I was well satisfied that our country, under all the circumstances of the case, had a right to take, and was bound in duty and interest to take, a neutral position. Having taken it, I determined, as far as should depend upon me, to maintain it with moderation, perseverance, and firmness.

The considerations which respect the right to hold this conduct, it is not necessary on this occasion to detail. I will only observe, that, according to my understanding of the matter, that right, so far from being denied by any of the belligerent powers, has been virtually admitted by all.

The duty of holding a neutral conduct may be inferred, without anything more, from the obligation which justice and humanity impose on every nation, in cases in which it is free to act, to maintain inviolate the relations of peace and amity towards other nations.

The inducements of interest, for observing that conduct, will best be referred to your own reflections and experience. With me, a predominant motive has been to endeavor to gain time to our country to settle and mature its yet recent institutions, and to progress, without interruption, to that degree of strength and consistency which is necessary to give it, humanly speaking, the command of its own fortunes.

Though in reviewing the incidents of my administration, I am unconscious of intentional error; I am, nevertheless, too sensible of my defects not to think it probable that I may have committed many errors. Whatever they may be, I fervently beseech the Almighty to avert or mitigate the evils to which they may tend. I shall also carry with me the hope, that my country will never cease to view them with indulgence; and that, after forty-five years of my life dedicated to its service with an upright zeal, the faults of incompetent abilities will be consigned to oblivion, as myself must soon be to the mansions of rest.

Relying on its kindness in this, as in other things, and actuated by that fervent love towards it which is so natural to a man who views in it the native soil of himself and his progenitors for several generations, I anticipate, with pleasing expectation, that retreat in which I promise myself to realize, without alloy, the sweet enjoyment of partaking, in the midst of my fellow-citizens, the benign influence of good laws under a free Government—the ever favorite object of my heart—and the happy reward, as I trust, of our mutual cares, labors, and dangers.

GEORGE WASHINGTON.

United States, September 17th, 1796.

Following the example of Washington, General Jackson issued a Farewell Address to the people of the United States, at his retiring from the Presidency; and, like that of Washington, it was principally devoted to the danger of disunion, and to the preservation of harmony and good feeling between the different sections of the country. General Washington only had to contemplate the danger of disunion, as a possibility, and as an event of future contingency; General Jackson had to confront it as a present, actual, subsisting danger, and therefore published the following

FAREWELL ADDRESS OF ANDREW JACKSON TO THE PEOPLE OF THE UNITED STATES.

Fellow-citizens.—Being about to retire finally from public life, I beg leave to offer you my grateful thanks for the many proofs of kindness and confidence which I have received at your hands. It has been my fortune, in the discharge of public duties, civil and military, frequently to have found myself in difficult and trying situations, where prompt decision and energetic action were necessary, and where the interest of the country required that high responsibilities should be fearlessly encountered; and it is with the deepest emotions of gratitude that I acknowledge the continued and unbroken confidence with which you have sustained me in every trial. My public life has been a long one, and I cannot hope that it has, at all times, been free from errors. But I have the consolation of knowing that, if mistakes have been committed, they have not seriously injured the country I so anxiously endeavored to serve; and at the moment when I surrender my last public trust, I I leave this great people prosperous and happy, in the full enjoyment of liberty and peace, and honored and respected by every nation of the world.

If my humble efforts have, in any degree, contributed to preserve to you these blessings, I have been more than rewarded by the honors you have heaped upon me, and, above all, by the generous confidence with which you have supported me in every peril, and with which you have continued to animate and cheer my path to the closing hour of my political life. The time has now come, when advanced age and a broken frame warn me to retire from public concerns; but the recollection of the many favors you have bestowed upon me is engraven upon my heart, and I have felt that I could not part from your service without making this public acknowledgment of the gratitude I owe you. And if I use the occasion to offer to you the counsels of age and experience, you will, I trust, receive them with the same indulgent kindness which you have so often extended to me; and will, at least, see in them an earnest desire to perpetuate, in this favored land, the blessings of liberty and equal law.

We have now lived almost fifty years under the constitution framed by the sages and patriots of the Revolution. The conflicts in which the nations of Europe were engaged during a great part of this period, the spirit in which they waged war against each other, and our intimate commercial connections with every part of the civilized world, rendered it a time of much difficulty for the Government of the United States. We have had our seasons of peace and of war, with all the evils which precede or follow a state of hostility with powerful nations. We encountered these trials with our constitution yet in its infancy, and under the disadvantages which a new and untried government must always feel when it is called upon to put forth its whole strength, without the lights of experience to guide it, or the weight of precedents to justify its measures. But we have passed triumphantly through all these difficulties. Our Constitution is no longer a doubtful experiment; and, at the end of nearly half a century, we find that it has preserved unimpaired the liberties of the people, secured the rights of property, and that our country has improved and is flourishing beyond any former example in the history of nations.

In our domestic concerns there is everything to encourage us; and, if you are true to yourselves, nothing can impede your march to the highest point of national prosperity. The States which had so long been retarded in their improvement by the Indian tribes residing in the midst of them, are at length relieved from the evil; and this unhappy race—the original dwellers in our land—are now placed in a situation where we may well hope that they will share in the blessings of civilization, and be saved from that degradation and destruction to which they were rapidly hastening while they remained in the States; and while the safety and comfort of our own citizens have been greatly promoted by their removal, the philanthropist will rejoice that the remnant of that ill-fated race has been at length placed beyond the reach of injury or oppression, and that the paternal care of the general government will hereafter watch over them and protect them.

If we turn to our relations with foreign powers, we find our condition equally gratifying. Actuated by the sincere desire to do justice to every nation, and to preserve the blessings of peace, our intercourse with them has been conducted on the part of this government in the spirit of frankness, and I take pleasure in saying that it has generally been met in a corresponding temper. Difficulties of old standing have been surmounted by friendly discussion and the mutual desire to be just; and the claims of our citizens, which had been long withheld, have at length been acknowledged and adjusted, and satisfactory arrangements made for their final payment; and, with a limited, and, I trust, a temporary exception, our relations with every foreign power are now of the most friendly character—our commerce continually expanding, and our flag respected in every quarter of the world.

These cheering and grateful prospects, and these multiplied favors, we owe, under Providence, to the adoption of the federal Constitution. It is no longer a question whether this great country can remain happily united, and flourish, under our present form of government. Experience, the unerring test of all human undertakings, has shown the wisdom and foresight of those who formed it; and has proved, that, in the union of these States, there is a sure foundation for the brightest hopes of freedom, and for the happiness of the people. At every hazard, and by every sacrifice, this Union must be preserved.

The necessity of watching with jealous anxiety for the preservation of the Union, was earnestly pressed upon his fellow-citizens, by the Father of his Country, in his farewell address. He has there told us, that, "while experience shall not have demonstrated its impracticability, there will always be reason to distrust the patriotism of those who, in any quarter, may endeavor to weaken its bands;" and he has cautioned us, in the strongest terms, against the formation of parties on geographical discriminations, as one of the means which might disturb our Union, and to which designing men would be likely to resort.

The lessons contained in this invaluable legacy of Washington to his countrymen, should be cherished in the heart of every citizen to the latest generation; and, perhaps, at no period of time could they be more usefully remembered than at the present moment. For, when we look upon the scenes that are passing around us, and dwell upon the pages of his parting address, his paternal counsels would seem to be not merely the offspring of wisdom and foresight, but the voice of prophecy, foretelling events, and warning us of the evil to come. Forty years have passed since this imperishable document was given to his countrymen. The federal Constitution was then regarded by him as an experiment, and he so speaks of it in his address, but an experiment upon the success of which the best hopes of his country depended; and we all know that he was prepared to lay down his life, if necessary, to secure to it a full and a fair trial. The trial has been made. It has succeeded beyond the proudest hopes of those who framed it. Every quarter of this widely extended nation has felt its blessings, and shared in the general prosperity produced by its adoption. But, amid this general prosperity and splendid success, the dangers of which he warned us are becoming every day more evident, and the signs of evil are sufficiently apparent to awaken the deepest anxiety in the bosom of the patriot. We behold systematic efforts publicly made to sow the seeds of discord between different parts of the United States, and to place party divisions directly upon geographical distinctions; to excite the *South* against the *North*, and the *North* against the *South*, and to force into the controversy the most delicate and exciting topics—topics upon which it is impossible that a large portion of the Union can ever speak without strong emotion. Appeals, too, are constantly made to sectional interests, in order to influence the election of the Chief Magistrate, as if it were desired that he should favor a particular quarter of the country, instead of fulfilling the duties of his station with impartial justice to all; and the possible dissolution of the Union has at length become an ordinary and familiar subject of discussion. Has the warning voice of Washington been forgotten? or have designs already been formed to sever the Union? Let it not be supposed that I impute to all of those who have taken an active part in these unwise and unprofitable discussions a want of patriotism or of public virtue. The honorable feeling of State pride, and local attachments, find a place in the bosoms of the most enlightened and pure. But while such men are conscious of their own integrity and honesty of purpose, they ought never to forget that the citizens of other States are their political brethren; and that, however mistaken they may be in their views, the great body of them are equally honest and upright with themselves. Mutual suspicions and reproaches may in time create mutual hostility, and artful and designing men will always be found, who are ready to foment these fatal divisions, and to inflame the natural jealousies of different sections of the country. The history of the world is full of such examples, and especially the history of re publics.

What have you to gain by division and dissension? Delude not yourselves with the belief that a breach once made may be afterwards repaired. If the Union is once severed, the line of separation will grow wider and wider, and the controversies which are now debated and settled in the halls of legislation will then be tried in fields of battle, and determined by the sword. Neither should you deceive yourselves with the hope that the first line of separation would be the permanent one, and that nothing but harmony and concord would be found in the new associations formed upon the dissolution of this Union. Local interests would still be found there, and unchastened ambition. And if the recollection of common dangers, in which the people of these United States stood side by side against the common foe; the memory of victories won by their united valor; the prosperity and happiness they have enjoyed under the present Constitution; the proud name they bear as citizens of this great republic: if all these recollections and proofs of common interest are not strong enough to bind us together as one people, what tie will hold united the new divisions of empire, when these bonds have been broken and this Union dissevered. The first line of separation would not last for a single generation; new fragments would be torn off; new leaders would spring up; and this great and glorious republic would soon be broken into a multitude of petty States, without commerce, without credit; jealous of one another; armed for mutual agression, loaded with taxes to pay armies and leaders; seeking aid against each other from foreign powers; insulted and trampled upon by the nations of Europe, until harassed with conflicts, and humbled and debased in spirit, they would be ready to submit to the absolute dominion of any military adventurer, and to surrender their liberty for the sake of repose. It is impossible to look on the consequences that would inevitably follow the destruction of this governmemt, and not feel indignant when we hear cold calculations about the value of the Union, and have so constantly before us a line of conduct so well calculated to weaken its ties.

There is too much at stake to allow pride or passion to influence your decision. Never for a moment believe that the great body of the citizens of any State or States can deliberately intend to do wrong. They may, under the influence of temporary excitement or misguided opinions, commit mistakes; they may be misled for a time by the suggestions of self-interest; but, in a community so enlightened and patriotic as the people of the United States, argument will soon make them sensible of their errors; and when convinced, they will be ready to repair them. If they have no higher or better motives to govern them, they will at least perceive that their own interest requires them to be just to others, as they hope to receive justice at their hands.

But, in order to maintain the Union unimpaired, it is absolutely necessary that the laws passed by the constituted authorities should be faithfully executed in every part of the country, and that every good citizen should, at all times, stand ready to put down, with the combined force of the nation, every attempt at unlawful resistance, under whatever pretext it may be made, or whatever shape it may assume. Unconstitutional or oppressive laws may, no doubt, be passed by Congress, either from erroneous views, or the want of due consideration; if they are within the reach of judicial authority, the remedy is easy and peaceful; and if, from the character of the law, it is an abuse of power not within the control of the judiciary, then free discussion and calm appeals to reason and to the justice of the people will not fail to redress the wrong. But until the law shall be declared void by the courts, or repealed by Congress, no individual, or combination of individuals, can be justified in forcibly resisting its execution. It is impossible that any government can continue to exist upon any other principles. It would cease to be a government, and be unworthy of the name, if it had not the power to enforce the execution of its own laws within its own sphere of action.

It is true that cases may be imagined disclosing such a settled purpose of usurpation and oppression, on the part of the government, as would justify an appeal to arms. These, however, are extreme cases, which we have no reason to apprehend in a government where the power is in the hands of a patriotic people; and no citizen who loves his country would, in any case whatever, resort to forcible resistance, unless he clearly saw that the time had come when a freeman should prefer death to submission ; for if such a struggle is once begun, and the citizens of one section of the country are arrayed in arms against those of another in doubtful conflict, let the battle result as it may, there will be an end of the Union, and with it an end to the hopes of freedom. The victory of the injured would not secure to them the blessings of liberty ; it would avenge their wrongs, but they would themselves share in the common ruin.

But the Constitution cannot be maintained, nor the Union preserved, in opposition to public feeling, by the mere exertion of the coercive powers confided to the general government. The foundations must be laid in the affections of the people ; in the security it gives to life, liberty, character, and property, in every quarter of the country ; and in the fraternal attachment which the citizens of the several States bear to one another, as members of one political family, mutually contributing to promote the happiness of each other. Hence, the citizens of every State should studiously avoid everything calculated to wound the sensibility or offend the just pride of the people of other States ; and they should frown upon any proceedings within their own borders likely to disturb the tranquillity of their political brethren in other portions of the Union. In a country so extensive as the United States, and with pursuits so varied, the internal regulations of the several States must frequently differ from one another in important particulars; and this difference is unavoidably increased by the varying principles upon which the American colonies were originally planted; principles which had taken deep root in their social relations before the Revolution, and therefore of necessity influencing their policy since they became free and independent States. But each State has the unquestionable right to regulate its own internal concerns according to its own pleasure; and while it does not interfere with the rights of the people of other States, or the rights of the Union, every State must be the sole judge of the measures proper to secure the safety of its citizens, and promote their happiness; and all efforts on the part of people of other States to cast odium upon their institutions, and all measures calculated to disturb their rights of property or to put in jeopardy their peace and internal tranquillity, are in direct opposition to the spirit in which the Union was formed, and must endanger its safety. Motives of philanthropy may be assigned for this unwarrantable interference; and weak men may persuade themselves for a moment that they are laboring in the cause of humanity, and asserting the rights of the human race; but every one, upon sober reflection, will see that nothing but mischief can come from these improper assaults upon the feelings and rights of others. Rest assured that the men found busy in this work of discord are not worthy of your confidence, and deserve your strongest reprobation.

In the legislation of Congress, also, and in every measure of the general government, justice to every portion of the United States should be faithfully observed. No free government can stand without virtue in the people, and a lofty spirit of patriotism; and if the sordid feelings of mere selfishness shall usurp the place which ought to be filled by public spirit, the legislation of Congress will soon be converted into a scramble for personal and sectional advantages.

Under our free institutions, the citizens of every quarter of our country are capable of attaining a high degree of prosperity and happiness, without seeking to profit themselves at the expense of others; and every such attempt must in the end fail to succeed, for the people in every part of the United States are too enlightened not to understand their own rights and interests, and to detect and defeat every effort to gain undue advantages over them; and when such designs are discovered, it naturally provokes resentments which cannot always be easily allayed. Justice, full and ample justice, to every portion of the United States, should be the ruling principle of every freeman, and should guide the deliberations of every public body, whether it be State or national.

It is well known that there have always been those amongst us who wish to enlarge the powers of the general government; and experience would seem to indicate that there is a tendency on the part of this government to overstep the boundaries marked out for it by the Constitution. Its legitimate authority is abundantly sufficient for all the purposes for which it was created; and its powers being expressly enumerated, there can be no justification for claiming anything beyond them. Every attempt to exercise power beyond these limits should be promptly and firmly opposed. For one evil example will lead to other measures still more mischievous; and if the principle of constructive powers, or supposed advantages, or temporary circumstances, shall ever be permitted to justify the assumption of a power not given by the Constitution, the general government will before long absorb all the powers of legislation, and you will have, in effect, but one consolidated government. From the extent of our country, its diversified interests, different pursuits, and different habits, it is too obvious for argument, that a single consolidated government would be wholly inadequate to watch over and protect its interests; and every friend of our free institutions should be always prepared to maintain unimpaired and in full vigor the rights and sovereignty of the States, and to confine the action of the general government strictly to the sphere of its appropriate duties.

There is, perhaps, no one of the powers conferred on the federal government so liable to abuse as the taxing power. The most productive and convenient sources of revenue were necessarily given to it, that it might be able to perform the important duties imposed upon it; and the taxes which it lays upon commerce being concealed from the real payer in the price of the article, they do not so readily attract the attention of the people as smaller sums demanded from them directly by the tax-gatherer. But the tax imposed on goods enhances by so much the price of the commodity to the consumer; and, as many of these duties are imposed on articles of necessity, which are daily used by the great body of the people, the money raised by these imposts is drawn from their pockets. Congress has no right, under the Constitution, to take money from the people, unless it is required to execute some one of the specific powers intrusted to the government; and if they raise more than is necessary for such purposes, it is an abuse of the power of taxation, and unjust and oppressive. It may, indeed, happen that the revenue will sometimes exceed the amount anticipated when the taxes were laid. When, however, this is ascertained, it is easy to reduce them, and, in such a case, it is unquestionably the duty of the government to reduce them; for no circumstances can justify it in assuming a power not given to it by the Constitution, nor in taking away the money of the people when it is not needed for the legitimate wants of the government.

Plain as these principles appear to be, you will yet find there is a constant effort to induce the general government to go beyond the limits of its taxing power, and to impose unnecessary burdens upon the people. Many powerful interests are continually at work to procure heavy duties on commerce, and to swell the revenue beyond the real necessities of the public service; and the country has already felt the injurious effects of their combined influence. They succeeded in obtaining a tariff of duties bearing most oppressively on the agricultural and laboring classes of society, and producing a revenue that could not be usefully employed within the range of the powers conferred upon Congress; and, in order to fasten upon the people this unjust and unequal system of taxation, extravagant schemes of internal improvements were got up in various quarters, to squander the money and to purchase support. Thus one unconstitutional measure was intended to be upheld by another, and the abuse of the power of taxation was to be maintained by usurping the power of expending the money in internal improvements. You cannot have forgotten the severe and doubtful struggle through which we passed, when the executive department of the government, by its veto, endeavored to arrest this prodigal scheme of injustice, and to bring back the legislation of Congress to the boundaries prescribed by the Constitution. The good sense and practical judgment of the people, when the subject was brought before them, sustained the course of the executive; and this plan of unconstitutional expenditures for the purposes of corrupt influence is, I trust, finally overthrown.

The result of this decision has been felt in the rapid extinguishment of the public debt, and the large accumulation of a surplus in the treasury, notwithstanding the tariff was reduced, and is now very far below the amount originally contemplated by its advocates. But, rely upon it, the design to collect an extravagant revenue, and to burden you with taxes beyond the economical wants of the government, is not yet abandoned. The various interests which have combined together to impose a heavy tariff, and to produce an overflowing treasury, are too strong, and have too much at stake, to surrender the contest. The corporations and wealthy individuals who are engaged in large manufacturing establishments desire a high tariff to increase their gains. Designing politicians will support it to conciliate their favor, and to obtain the means of profuse expenditure, for the purpose of purchasing influence in other quarters; and, since the people have decided that the federal government cannot be permitted to employ its income in internal improvements, efforts will be made to seduce and mislead the citizens of the several States, by holding out to them the deceitful prospect of benefits to be derived from a surplus revenue collected by the general government, and annually divided among the States; and if, encouraged by these fallacious hopes, the States should disregard the principles of economy which ought to characterize every republican government, and should indulge in lavish expenditures, exceeding their resources, they will, before long, find themselves oppressed with debts which they are unable to pay, and the temptation will become irresistible to support a high tariff in order to obtain a surplus for distribution. Do not allow yourselves, my fellow-citizens, to be misled on this subject. The federal government cannot collect a surplus for such purposes, without violating the principles of the Constitution, and assuming powers which have not been granted. It is, moreover, a system of injustice, and, if persisted in, will inevitably lead to corruption, and must end in ruin. The surplus revenue will be drawn from the pockets of the people, from the farmer, the mechanic, and the laboring classes of society; but who will receive it when distributed among the States, where it is to be disposed of by leading State politicians, who have friends to favor and political partisans to gratify? It will certainly not be returned to those who paid it, and who have most need of it, and are honestly entitled to it. There is but one safe rule; and that is, to confine the general government rigidly within the sphere of its appropriate duties. It has no power to raise a revenue or impose taxes except for the purposes enumerated in the Constitution; and if its income is found to exceed these wants, it should be forthwith reduced, and the burden of the people so far lightened.

In reviewing the conflicts which have taken place between different interests in the United States, and the policy pursued since the adoption of our present form of government, we find nothing that has produced such deep-seated evil as the course of legislation in relation to the currency. The Constitution of the United States unquestionably intended to secure to the people a circulating medium of gold and silver. But the establishment of a national bank by Congress, with the privilege of issuing paper money receivable in the payment of the public dues, and the unfortunate course of legislation in the several States upon the same subject, drove from circulation the constitutional currency, and substituted one of paper in its place.

It was not easy for men engaged in the ordinary pursuits of business, whose attention had not been particularly drawn to the subject, to foresee all the consequences of a currency exclusively of paper; and we ought not, on that account, to be surprised at the facility with which laws were obtained to carry into effect the paper system. Honest and even enlightened men are sometimes misled by the specious and plausible statements of the designing. But experience has now proved the mischiefs and dangers of a paper currency; and it rests with you to determine whether the proper remedy shall be applied.

The paper system being founded on public confidence, and having of itself no intrinsic value, it is liable to great and sudden fluctuations; thereby rendering property insecure, and the wages of labor unsteady and uncertain. The corporations which create the paper money cannot be relied upon to keep the circulating medium uniform in amount. In times of prosperity, when confidence is high, they are tempted, by the prospect of gain, or by the influence of those who hope to profit by it, to extend their issues of paper beyond the bounds of discretion and the reasonable demands of business. And when these issues have been pushed on, from day to day, until public confidence is at length shaken, then a reaction takes place, and they immediately withdraw the credits they have given, suddenly curtail their issues, and produce an unexpected and ruinous contraction of the circulating medium, which is felt by the whole community. The banks, by this means, save themselves, and the mischievous consequences of their imprudence or cupidity are visited upon the public. Nor does the evil stop here. These ebbs and flows in the currency, and these indiscreet extensions of credit, naturally engender a spirit of speculation injurious to the habits and character of the people. We have already seen its effects in the wild spirit of speculation in the public lands and various kinds of stock, which within the last year or two seized upon such a multitude of our citizens, and threatened to pervade all classes of society, and to withdraw their attention from the sober pursuits of honest industry. It is not by encouraging this spirit that we shall best preserve public virtue and promote the true interests of our country. But if your currency continues as exclusively paper as it now is, it will foster this eager desire to amass wealth without labor; it will multiply the number of dependents on bank accommodations and bank favors; the temptation to obtain money at any sacrifice will become stronger and stronger, and inevitably lead to corruption, which will find its way into your public councils, and destroy, at no distant day, the purity of your government. Some of the evils which arise from this system of paper, press with peculiar hardship upon the class of society least able to bear it. A portion of this currency frequently becomes depreciated or worthless, and all of it is easily counterfeited in such a manner as to require peculiar skill and much experience to distinguish the counterfeit from the genuine note. These frauds are most generally perpetrated in the smaller notes, which are used in the daily transactions of ordinary business; and the losses occasioned by them are commonly thrown upon the laboring classes of society, whose situation and pursuits put it out of their power to guard themselves from these impositions, and whose daily wages are necessary for their subsistence. It is the duty of every government so to regulate its currency as to protect this numerous class, as far as practicable, from the impositions of avarice and fraud. It is more especially the duty of the United States, where the government is emphatically the government of the people, and where this respectable portion of our citizens are so proudly distinguished from the laboring classes of all other nations, by their independent spirit, their love of liberty, their intelligence, and their high tone of moral character. Their industry, in peace, is the source of our wealth; and their bravery, in war, has covered us with glory; and the government of the United States will but ill discharge its duties, if it leaves them a prey to such dishonest impositions. Yet it is evident that their interests cannot be effectually protected, unless silver and gold are restored to circulation.

These views alone, of the paper currency, are sufficient to call for immediate reform; but there is another consideration which should still more strongly press it upon your attention.

Recent events have proved that the paper-money system of this country may be used as an engine to undermine your free institutions; and that those who desire to engross all power in the hands of the few, and to govern by corruption or force, are aware of its power, and prepared to employ it.

Your banks now furnish your only circulating medium, and money is plenty or scarce, according to the quantity of notes issued by them. While they have capitals not greatly disproportioned to each other, they are competitors in business, and no one of them can exercise dominion over the rest; and although, in the present state of the currency, these banks may and do operate injuriously upon the habits of business, the pecuniary concerns, and the moral tone of society, yet, from their number and dispersed situation, they cannot combine for the purposes of political influence; and, whatever may be the dispositions of some of them, their power of mischief must necessarily be confined to a narrow space, and felt only in their immediate neighborhoods.

But when the charter for the Bank of the United States was obtained from Congress, it perfected the schemes of the paper system, and gave to its advocates the position they have struggled to obtain, from the commencement of the federal government to the present hour. The immense capital and peculiar privileges bestowed upon it enabled it to exercise despotic sway over the other banks, in every part of the country. From its superior strength, it could seriously injure, if not destroy, the business of any one of them which might incur its resentment; and it openly claimed for itself the power of regulating the currency throughout the United States. In other words, it asserted (and it undoubtedly possessed) the power to make money plenty or scarce, at its pleasure, at any time, and in any quarter of the Union, by controlling the issues of other banks, and permitting an expansion, or compelling a general contraction, of the circulating medium, according to its own will. The other banking institutions were sensible of its strength, and they soon generally became its obedient instruments, ready at all times to execute its mandates; and with the banks necessarily went, also, that numerous class of persons in our commercial cities who depend altogether on bank credits for their solvency and means of business; and who are therefore obliged, for their own safety, to propitiate the favor of the money power by distinguished zeal and devotion in its service. The result of the ill-advised legislation which established this great monopoly was, to concentrate the whole moneyed power of the Union, with its boundless means of corruption and its numerous dependents, under the direction and command of one acknowledged head : thus organizing this particular interest as one body ; and securing to it unity and concert of action throughout the United States, and enabling it to bring forward, upon any occasion, its entire and undivided strength, to support or defeat any measure of the Government. In the hands of this formidable power, thus perfectly organized, was also placed unlimited dominion over the amount of the circulating medium, giving it the power to regulate the value of property and the fruits of labor in every quarter of the Union; and to bestow prosperity or bring ruin upon any city or section of the country, as might best comport with its own interest or policy.

We are not left to conjecture how the moneyed power, thus organized, and with such a weapon in its hands, would be likely to use it. The distress and alarm which pervaded and agitated the whole country when the Bank of the United States waged war upon the people, in order to compel them to submit to its demands, cannot yet be forgotten. The ruthless and unsparing temper with which whole cities and communities were oppressed, individuals impoverished and ruined, and a scene of cheerful prosperity suddenly changed into one of gloom and despondency, ought to be indelibly impressed on the memory of the people of the United States. If such was its power in a time of peace, what would it not have been in a season of war, with an enemy at your doors? No nation but the freemen of the United States could have come out victorious from such a contest; yet, if you had not conquered, the government would have passed from the hands of the many to the hands of the few; and this organized money power, from its secret conclave, would have dictated the choice of your highest offices, and compelled you to make peace or war, as best suited their own wishes. The forms of your government might, for a time, have remained, but its living spirit would have departed from it.

The distress and sufferings inflicted on the people by the bank are some of the fruits of that system of policy which is continually striving to enlarge the authority of the federal government beyond the limits fixed by the Constitution. The powers enumerated in that instrument do not confer on Congress the right to establish such a corporation as the Bank of the United States, and the evil consequences which followed may warn us of the danger of departing from the true rule of construction, and of permitting temporary circumstances, or the hope of better promoting the public welfare, to influence, in any degree, our decisions upon the extent of the authority of the general government. Let us abide by the Constitution as it is written, or amend it, in the constitutional mode, if it is found to be defective.

The severe lessons of experience will, I doubt not, be sufficient to prevent Congress from again chartering such a monopoly, even if the Constitution did not present an insuperable objection to it. But you must remember, my fellow-citizens, that eternal vigilance by the people is the price of liberty; and that you must pay the price if you wish to secure the blessing. It behooves you, therefore, to be watchful in your States, as well as in the federal government. The power which the moneyed interest can exercise, when concentrated under a single head, and with our present system of currency, was sufficiently demonstrated in the struggle made by the Bank of the United States. Defeated in the general government, the same class of intriguers and politicians will now resort to the States, and endeavor to obtain there the same organization which they failed to perpetuate in the Union; and with specious and deceitful plans of public advantages, and State interests, and State pride, they will endeavor to establish, in the different States, one moneyed institution, with overgrown capital, and exclusive privileges, sufficient to enable it to control the operations of the other banks. Such an institution will be pregnant with the same evils produced by the Bank of the United States, although its sphere of action is more confined; and, in the State in which it is chartered, the money power will be able to embody its whole strength, and to move together with undivided force to accomplish any object it may wish to attain. You have already had abundant evidence of its power to inflict injury upon the agricultural, mechanical, and laboring classes of society; and over those whose engagements in trade or speculation render them dependent on bank facilities, the dominion of the State monopoly will be absolute, and their obedience unlimited. With such a bank and a paper currency, the money power would, in a few years, govern the State and control its measures; and, if a sufficient number of States can be induced to create such establishments, the time will soon come when it will again take the field against the United States, and succeed in perfecting and perpetuating its organization by a charter from Congress.

It is one of the serious evils of our present system of banking, that it enables one class of society, and that by no means a numerous one, by its control over the currency, to act injuriously upon the interests of all the others, and to exercise more than its just proportion of influence in political affairs. The agricultural, the mechanical, and the laboring classes, have little or no share in the direction of the great moneyed corporations; and, from their habits, and the nature of their pursuits, they are incapable of forming extensive combinations to act together with united force. Such concert of action may sometimes be produced in a single city, or in a small district of country, by means of personal communications with each other; but they have no regular or active correspondence with those who are engaged in similar pursuits in distant places; they have but little patronage to give to the press, and exercise but a small share of influence over it; they have no crowd of dependents about them, who hope to grow rich without labor, by their countenance and favor, and who are, therefore, always ready to execute their wishes. The planter, the farmer, the mechanic, and the laborer, all know that their success depends upon their own industry and economy, and that they must not expect to become suddenly rich by the fruits of their toil. Yet these classes of society form the great body of the people of the United States; they are the bone and sinew of the country; men who love liberty, and desire nothing but equal rights and equal laws; and who, moreover, hold the great mass of our national wealth, although it is distributed in moderate amounts among the millions of freemen who possess it. But, with overwhelming numbers and wealth on their side, they are in constant danger of losing their fair influence in the government, and with difficulty maintain their just rights against the incessant efforts daily made to encroach upon them. The mischief springs from the power which the moneyed interest derives from a paper currency, which they are able to control; from the multitude of corporations, with exclusive privileges, which they have succeeded in obtaining in the different States, and which are employed altogether for their benefit; and, unless you become more watchful in your States, and check this spirit of monopoly and thirst for exclusive privileges, you will, in the end, find that the most important powers of government have been given or bartered away, and the control over your dearest interests has passed into the hands of these corporations.

The paper-money system and its natural associations—monopoly and exclusive privileges—have already struck their roots too deep in the soil; and it will require all your efforts to check its further growth, and to eradicate the evil. The men who profit by the abuses, and desire to perpetuate them, will continue to besiege the halls of legislation in the general government as well as in the States, and will seek, by every artifice, to mislead and deceive the public servants. It is to yourselves that you must look for safety, and the means of guarding and perpetuating your free institutions. In your hands is rightfully placed the sovereignty of the country, and to you every one placed in authority is ultimately responsible. It is always in your power to see that the wishes of the people are carried into faithful execution, and their will, when once made known, must, sooner or later, be obeyed. And while the people remain, as I trust they ever will, uncorrupted and incorruptible, and continue watchful and jealous of their rights, the government is safe, and the cause of freedom will continue to triumph over all its enemies.

But it will require steady and persevering exertions on your part to rid yourselves of the iniquities and mischiefs of the paper system, and to check the spirit of monoply and other abuses which have sprung up with it, and of which it is the main support. So many interests are united to resist all reform on this subject, that you must not hope the conflict will be a short one, nor success easy. My humble efforts have not been spared, during my administration of the government, to restore the constitutional currency of gold and silver; and something, I trust, has been done towards the accomplishment of this most desirable object. But enough yet remains to require all your energy and perseverance. The power, however, is in your hands, and the remedy must and will be applied, if you determine upon it.

While I am thus endeavoring to press upon your attention the principles which I deem of vital importance in the domestic concerns of the country, I ought not to pass over, without notice, the important considerations which should govern your policy towards foreign powers. It is unquestionably, our true interest to cultivate the most friendly understanding with every nation, and to avoid, by every honorable means, the calamities of war; and we shall best attain this object by frankness and sincerity in our foreign intercourse, by the prompt and faithful execution of treaties, and by justice and impartiality in our conduct to all. But no nation, however desirous of peace, can hope to escape occasional collisions with other powers; and the soundest dictates of policy require that we should place ourselves in a condition to assert our rights, if a resort to force should ever become necessary. Our local situation, our long line of sea-coast, indented by numerous bays, with deep rivers opening into the interior, as well as our extended and still increasing commerce, point to the navy as our natural means of defense. It will, in the end, be found to be the cheapest and most effectual; and now is the time, in a season of peace, and with an overflowing revenue, that we can, year after year, add to its strength, without increasing the burdens of the people. It is your true policy. For your navy will not only protect your rich and flourishing commerce in distant seas, but will enable you to reach and annoy the enemy, and will give to defense its greatest efficiency, by meeting danger at a distance from home. It is impossible, by any line of fortifications, to guard every point from attack against a hostile force advancing from the ocean and selecting its object; but they are indispensable to protect cities from bombardment, dock yards and naval arsenals from destruction; to give shelter to merchant vessels in time of war, and to single ships or weaker squadrons when pressed by superior force. Fortifications of this description cannot be too soon completed and armed, and placed in a condition of the most perfect preparation. The abundant means we now possess cannot be applied in any manner more useful to the country; and when this is done, and our naval force sufficiently strengthened, and our militia armed, we need not fear that any nation will wantonly insult us, or needlessly provoke hostilities. We shall more certainly preserve peace, when it is well understood that we are prepared for war.

In presenting to you, my fellow-citizens, these parting counsels, I have brought before you the leading principles upon which I endeavored to administer the government in the high office with which you twice honored me. Knowing that the path of freedom is continually beset by enemies, who often assume the disguise of friends, I have devoted the last hours of my public life to warn you of the dangers. The progress of the United States, under our free and happy institutions, has surpassed the most sanguine hopes of the founders of the republic. Our growth has been rapid beyond all former example, in numbers, in wealth, in knowledge, and all the useful arts which contribute to the comforts and conveniences of man; and from the earliest ages of history to the present day, there never have been thirteen millions of people associated in one political body, who enjoyed so much freedom and happiness as the people of these United States. You have no longer any cause to fear danger from abroad; your strength and power are well known throughout the civilized world, as well as the high and gallant bearing of your sons. It is from within, among yourselves, from cupidity, from corruption, from disappointed ambition, and inordinate thirst for power, that factions will be formed, and liberty endangered. It is against such designs, whatever disguise the actors may assume, that you have especially to guard yourselves. You have the highest of human trusts committed to your care. Providence has showered on this favored land blessings without number, and has chosen you, as the guardians of freedom, to preserve it for the benefit of the human race. May He who holds in his hands the destinies of nations, make you worthy of the favors he has bestowed, and enable you, with pure hearts and pure hands, and sleepless vigilance, to guard and defend, to the end of time, the great charge he has committed to your keeping.

My own race is nearly run; advanced age and failing health warn me that before long I must pass beyond the reach of human events, and cease to feel the vicissitudes of human affairs. I thank God that my life has been spent in a land of liberty, and that he has given me a heart to love my country with the affection of a son. And, filled with gratitude for your constant and unwavering kindness, I bid you a last and affectionate farewell.

ANDREW JACKSON.

March 4, 1837.

CHAPTER XV.

THE KANSAS-NEBRASKA BILL.

Soon after the organization of Congress in December, 1853, a Bill for the organization of the Territories of Kansas and Nebraska, was introduced in the Senate, and referred to the Committee on Territories, of which Senator Douglas, of Illinois, was chairman. On the 4th day of January, 1854, the committee reported a substitute for the entire Bill, together with a report, which, after reviewing the various provisions of the Bill, concluded as follows:

"From these provisions it is apparent that the compromise measures of 1850 affirm and rest upon the following propositions:

"*First.* That all questions pertaining to slavery in the territories, and in the new States to be formed therefrom, are to be left to the decision of the people residing therein, by their appropriate representatives, to be chosen by them for that purpose.

"*Second.* That all cases involving title to slaves and questions of personal freedom, are referred to the adjudication of the local tribunals, with the right of appeal to the Supreme Court of the United States.

"*Third.* That the provision of the Constitution of the United States, in respect to fugitives from service, is to be carried into faithful execution in all the organized territories, the same as in the States. The substitute for the Bill, which your committee have prepared, and which is commended to the favorable action of the Senate, proposes to carry these propositions and principles into practical operation, in the precise language of the compromise measures of 1850."

It will thus be seen that the report based the Bill upon the compromise of 1850, so far as the question of slavery was concerned, and hence it becomes necessary to refer to those measures, to determine what principle was settled by them.

On the 29th of January, 1850, while the slavery agitation was raging with great violence, threatening, indeed, the very existence of the government, Mr. Clay introduced into the Senate several resolutions upon the subject of slavery, intended to form a basis of settlement upon that subject. While these resolutions were pending, the Committee on Territories reported a Bill for the admission of California as a State, and one for the organization of the Territories of Utah and New Mexico, and the adjustment of the Texas boundary. On the 19th of April a select committee of thirteen was appointed, of which Mr. Clay was chairman, and to that committee was referred the various propositions before the Senate. On the 8th of May, Mr. Clay, from the committee of thirteen, submitted to the Senate a report, accompanied by a bill, containing the essential features of the two bills previously submitted by the Committee on Territories, excepting as to the powers of the territorial legislature over slavery. The tenth section of the bill reported by the Committee on Territories read as follows:

"*And be it further enacted*, That the legislative power of the territory shall extend to all rightful subjects of legislation consistent with the Constitution of the United States and the provisions of this act; but no law shall be passed interfering with the primary disposition of the soil."

To which Mr. Clay's committee added these words: "*nor in respect to African slavery.*"

On the 31st of July, the above clause added by Mr. Clay, was struck out by the Senate, thus conferring on the Territorial Legislature power over "all rightful subjects of legislation consistent with the Constitution of the United States."

We have thus arrived at the meaning of the report, accompanying the Kansas-Nebraska Bill, from the committee to the Senate, on the 4th of January, 1854, when they say that the Bill "proposes to carry these propositions and principles into practical operation in the precise language of the compromise measures of 1850." It is proper here to say, that when the compromise of 1850 was before the Senate, an attempt was made to engraft upon it an amendment, declaring in substance, that the territorial legislature could not prohibit the introduction of slaves—that slaves were recognized as property by the Constitution of the United States, and hence were entitled to the same protection as other property. Many Southern Senators took this view of the question; while, upon the other hand, Messrs. Seward, Chase, and others from the North, advocated the power of Congress to prohibit slavery in the territories, and offered amendments to that import. The Bill passed the Senate, however, in the shape already referred to, by a vote of 32 to 19.

When the Kansas-Nebraska bill came before the Senate for discussion, it was contended by some, that, in the shape it then was, it could not be carried into practical operation, inasmuch as it did not, in terms, repeal the act of Congress of March 6th, 1820, prohibiting slavery north of 36° 30', commonly, but mistakenly, called the Missouri compromise. We say, mistakenly called the Missouri compromise, because the compromise under which that State was admitted into the Union was passed in 1821, while the section prohibiting slavery north of 36° 30' was a part of an enabling act for the admission of Missouri, passed in 1820, but which really had nothing to do with its final admission. This fact, however, is immaterial, in point of principle, and we allude to it only to correct a popular error.

The question having thus arisen as to the prohibition of

slavery north of 36° 30′, Mr. Douglas, chairman of the committee on Territories, proposed an amendment, which was incorporated into the bill, as follows—the proviso at the close of the section being adopted on motion of Mr. Badger, of North Carolina:

"That the Constitution, and all laws of the United States which are not locally inapplicable, shall have the same force and effect within the said Territory of Nebraska as elsewhere in the United States, except the eighth section of the act preparatory to the admission of Missouri into the Union, approved March sixth, eighteen hundred and twenty, which, being inconsistent with the principle of non-intervention by Congress with slavery in the States and Territories, as recognized by the legislation of eighteen hundred and fifty, commonly called the compromise measures, is hereby declared inoperative and void; it being the true intent and meaning of this act, not to legislate slavery into any Territory or State, nor to exclude it therefrom, but to leave the people thereof perfectly free to form and regulate their domestic institutions in their own way, subject only to the Constitution of the United States: *Provided*, That nothing herein contained shall be construed to revive or put in force any law or regulation which may have existed prior to the act of sixth March, eighteen hundred and twenty, either protecting, establishing, prohibiting or abolishing slavery."

When this amendment was presented to the Senate it became the signal for opening anew the slavery agitation with redoubled fury. It was opposed by the anti-slavery sentiment of the North as a violation of a solemn compact;—as an attempt to tear down a sacred barrier between freedom and slavery for the purpose of spreading that institution over the virgin soil of the country. On the other hand it was contended that it was necessary in order to give full effect to the compromise of 1850; the spirit and intent of which was to withdraw from Congress all control over the question of slavery in the territories, and leave the people therein free to act as they pleased. We give no debates upon the bill for the reason that they are now, *in extenso,* within the reach and remembrance of all who take any interest in the matter. The bill passed the Senate on the 3d day of March, 1854, by the following vote:

Yeas—Messrs. Adams, Atchison, Badger, Bayard, Benjamin, Brodhead, Brown, Butler, Cass, Clay, Dawson, Dixon, Dodge of Iowa, Douglas, Evans, Fitzpatrick, Geyer, Gwin, Hunter, Johnson, Jones of Iowa, Jones of Tennessee, Mason, Morton, Norris, Pettit, Pratt, Rusk, Sebastian, Shields, Slidell, Stuart, Thompson of Kentucky, Thompson of New Jersey, Toucey, Weller, and Williams, —37.

Nays—Messrs. Bell, Chase, Dodge of Wisconsin, Fessenden, Fish, Foot, Hamlin, Houston, James, Seward, Smith, Sumner, Wade, and Walker,—14.

It was delayed in the House till the 23d day of May, when it passed that body, striking out what was called the Clayton amendment, restricting the rights of aliens so far as suffrage was concerned.

The following is the vote in the House:

	YEAS.	NAYS.
Democrats from Slave States	53	4
" " Free "	43	46
Whigs from Slave States	13	5
" " Free "	—	41
Total,	109	100

It was returned to the Senate, and on the 25th of May, the House amendment was concurred in by a vote of 36 to 13. On the 30th of May, it was signed by the President, and thus became the law under which those territories were organized.

It would seem that both the North and the South construed

the Kansas-Nebraska Bill alike, so far as the slavery question was concerned, at the time of its passage,—that the intention of Congress was to give to the people of the territories full power to dispose of this as well as other questions. It is now, however, contended by many, especially in the South, that such power cannot be exercised by a territorial legislature—that slavery may exist in the territories, under the protection of the Constitution of the United States, which recognizes it as property and is bound to protect all species of property alike. For this they rely upon the following points in the decision of the Court in the Dred Scott case.

"1. Congress can exercise no power over the rights of persons or property of a citizen in the Territory which is prohibited by the Constitution. The government and the citizen, whenever the Territory is open to settlement, both enter it with their respective rights defined and limited by the Constitution.

"2. Congress have no right to prohibit the citizens of any particular State or States from taking up their home there, while it permits citizens of other States to do so. Nor has it a right to give privileges to one class of citizens which it refuses to another. The Territory is acquired for their equal and common benefit—and if open to any, it must be open to all upon equal and the same terms.

"3. Every citizen has a right to take with him into the Territory any article of property which the Constitution of the United States recognizes as property.

"4. The Constitution of the United States recognizes slaves as property, and pledges the federal government to protect it. And Congress cannot exercise any more authority over property of that description than it may constitutionally exercise over property of any other kind.

"5. The act of Congress, therefore, prohibiting a citizen of the United States from taking with him his slaves when he removes to the Territory in question to reside, is an exercise of authority over private property which is not warranted by the Constitution."

To this it is replied, that while it is true that the owner of slaves may take them to a Territory as property, still he must submit to the local law of the Territory when he gets them there, be it friendly or otherwise.

Thus is the sentiment of the country divided into three great parties, which may be properly designated the Prohibitionists, the Protectionists and the Non-interventionists. The prospect for a speedy and peaceful settlement of the vexed question is by no means encouraging. Would that it were; for we presume no one will deny that the continued agitation of this delicate and disturbing question is a great public misfortune. It destroys fraternal relations between the States and embitters the minds of the people. It creates sectional discords and divisions, disturbs the national councils, and is gradually but surely alienating the affections of the citizens from their government. The political energies of the country, that should be spent in building up those great commercial, industrial, moral, and social institutions which constitute the monuments of national greatness and power, are exhausted in the business of engendering internal hatred, contentions and strife. Let it be the effort of every patriot to do away with this deplorable state of things,—to settle this question by the safe and wise principles our fathers established, there to rest forever undisturbed. Only thus will peace and harmony again be restored to the country—only thus shall we present to the world the spectacle of a great, free, and happy people, united as one family in interest, in affection, and aim; ever moving onward in the pathway of prosperity and progress, as well as in all that contitutes national greatness, glory, and renown.

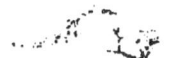

CHAPTER XVI.

NATIONAL CONVENTIONS.

THE first National Conventions of delegates elected by the people to nominate candidates for President and Vice-President, were held in 1840. Both the Whig and Democratic parties nominated in that way for that campaign. Previous to that period nominations were made by caucuses called by the members of Congress, in which they only were admitted to vote. Alleged abuses and intrigues led to the change of nominating, by delegates chosen from each congressional district. Up to 1848, no issue in reference to slavery seems to have been raised between the parties in their platforms; or, rather, up to that time no necessity seems to have arisen for the conventions to take particular notice of the subject. In the midst of the slavery agitation of that year, the two parties held their conventions. The Whig party nominated Gen. Zachary Taylor for President, and Millard Fillmore for Vice-President, and adjourned without laying down any platform. The Democratic convention nominated General Lewis Cass for President, and General William O. Butler for Vice-President, and passed the following resolution on the question of slavery:

"*Resolved*, That Congress has no power under the Constitution to interfere with or control the domestic institutions of the several States, and that such States are the sole and proper judges of everything appertaining to their own affairs, not prohibited by the Constitution; that all efforts of the abolitionists, or others, made to induce Congress to interfere with questions of slavery, or to take incipient steps in relation thereto, are calculated to lead to the most alarming and dangerous consequences; and that all such efforts have an inevitable tendency to diminish the happiness of the people, and endanger the stability and permanency of the Union, and ought not to be countenanced by any friend of our political institutions."

In 1852, the Democratic convention at Baltimore nominated General Franklin Pierce for President, and William R. King for Vice-President, and adopted the following resolutions referring to slavery:

"*Resolved*, That Congress has no power under the Constitution to interfere with or control the domestic institutions of the several States, and that such States are the sole and proper judges of everything appertaining to their own affairs, not prohibited by the Constitution; that all efforts of the abolitionists, or others, made to induce Congress to interfere with questions of slavery, or to take incipient steps in relation thereto, are calculated to lead to the most alarming and dangerous consequences; and that all such efforts have an inevitable tendency to diminish the happiness of the people, and endanger the stability and permanency of the Union, and ought not to be countenanced by any friend of our public institutions.

"*Resolved*, That the foregoing proposition covers, and was intended to embrace, the whole subject of slavery agitation in Congress, and therefore the Democratic party of the Union, standing on this national platform, will abide by, and adhere to, a faithful execution of the acts known as the compromise measures, settled by the last Congress—the act for reclaiming fugitives from service or labor included; which, being designed to carry out an express provision of the Constitution, cannot with fidelity thereto be repealed, or so changed as to destroy or impair its efficiency."

The Whig convention, at Baltimore, soon after, nominated General Winfield Scott for President, and William

R. Granam for Vice President, and adopted the following as their views. This was the last national convention ever held by that party:

"*Resolved,* That the series of resolutions known as the compromise, including the fugitive slave law, are received and acquiesced in by the Whig party of the United States as a settlement in principle and substance—*a final settlement*—of the dangerous and exciting subjects which they embrace; and so far as the fugitive slave law is concerned, we will maintain the same, and insist on its strict enforcement until time and experience shall demonstrate the necessity of further legislation against evasion or abuses, but not impairing its efficacy; and we deprecate all future agitation of the slavery question as dangerous to the peace, and we will discountenance all efforts at the renewal or continuance of such agitation in Congress, or out of it, whenever, wherever, or howsoever the attempt may be made, and will maintain this system of measures as policy essential to the nationality of the Whig party and the integrity of the Union."

In 1856, the Democratic convention at Cincinnati nominated James Buchanan for President, and John C. Breckenridge for Vice-President, and adopted the following resolution on the slavery question:

"*Resolved,* That the American Democracy recognize and adopt the principles contained in the organic laws establishing the Territories of Kansas and Nebraska as embodying the only sound and safe solution of the 'slavery question,' upon which the great national idea of the people of this whole country can repose in its determined conservatism of the Union,—non-interference by Congress with slavery in State and Territory, or in the District of Columbia;"

"That this was the basis of the Compromises of 1850, confirmed by both the Democratic and Whig parties in national conventions,—ratified by the people in the election of 1852,—and rightly applied to the organization of the

Territories in 1854; That by the uniform application of this democratic principle to the organization of Territories and to the admission of new States, with or without domestic slavery as they may elect, the equal rights of all will be preserved intact,—the original compacts of the Constitution maintained inviolate,—and the perpetuity and expansion of this Union insured to its utmost capacity of embracing in peace and harmony any future American State that may be constituted or annexed with a republican form of government."

The same year the Republican convention at Philadelphia nominated John C. Fremont for President, and William L. Dayton for Vice-President, and adopted the following as its platform on slavery.

"*Resolved*, That, with our republican fathers, who, when they had abolished slavery in all our national territory, ordained that no person shall be deprived of life, liberty, or property, without due process of law, it becomes our duty to maintain this provision of the Constitution against all attempts to violate it, for the purpose of establishing slavery in the United States, by positive legislation prohibiting its existence or extension therein.

"*Resolved*, That we deny the authority of Congress, of a territorial legislature, or any individual or association of individuals, to give legal existence to slavery in any territory of the United States, while the present Constitution shall be maintained.

Resolved, That the Constitution confers upon Congress sovereign power over the territories of the United States, for their government; and that, in the exercise of this power, it is both the duty and right of Congress to prohibit in the territories those twin relics of barbarism—polygamy and slavery."

The American convention nominated Millard Fillmore for President, and Andrew J. Donelson for Vice-President, and adopted, in substance, the principles of the compromise measures of 1850, as their platform on slavery.

In 1860, the Constitutional Union party, at Baltimore, nominated John Bell for President, and Edward Everett for Vice-President, adopting "*the Constitution* and enforcement of the laws" as a platform.

The Republican convention, at Chicago, nominated Abraham Lincoln for President, and Hannibal Hamlin for Vice-President, and adopted the following resolutions on slavery:

"*Resolved*, That the new dogma that the Constitution, of its own force, carries slavery into any or all the territories of the United States, is a dangerous political heresy, at variance with the explicit provisions of that instrument itself, with contemporaneous exposition, and with legislative and judicial precedent, is revolutionary in its tendency, and subversive of the peace and harmony of the country.

"*Resolved*, That the normal condition of all the territory of the United States is that of freedom; that as our republican fathers, when they had abolished slavery in all our national territory, ordained that no person should be deprived of life, liberty, or property, without due process of law, it becomes our duty, by legislation, whenever such legislation is necessary, to maintain this provision of the Constitution against all attempts to violate it; and we deny the authority of Congress, of a territorial legislature, or of any individuals, to give legal existence to slavery in any territory of the United States.

"*Resolved*, That we brand the recent re-opening of the African slave trade, under the cover of our national flag aided by perversions of judicial power, as a crime against humanity, a burning shame to our country and age, and we call upon Congress to take prompt and efficient measures for the total and final suppression of that execrable traffic."

NATIONAL CONVENTIONS. 493

The Democratic convention met at Charleston on the 18th of April. After a session of nearly two weeks, toward the close of which most of the delegates from eight southern States left the convention, an adjournment to meet at Baltimore, on the 18th of June, was agreed upon. The convention met, pursuant to adjournment, at Baltimore, and on the 23d of June, Stephen A. Douglas, of Illinois, was nominated for President, and Benjamin Fitzpatrick, of Alabama, for Vice-President. The following resolutions were adopted. Excepting the last one, these resolutions were passed at Charleston:

"*Resolved*, That we, the Democracy of the Union, in convention assembled, hereby declare our affirmation of the resolutions unanimously adopted and declared as a platform of principles by the Democratic convention at Cincinnati, in the year 1856, believing that Democratic principles are unchangeable in their nature when applied to the same subject matter, and we recommend as our only further resolutions, the following:

"*Resolved*, That it is in accordance with the interpretation of the Cincinnati platform, that during the existence of Territorial government, the measure of restriction, whatever it may be, imposed by the federal Constitution, or the power of the Territorial legislature, over the subject of the domestic relations, (as the same has been or shall hereafter be finally determined by the Supreme Court of the United States,) should be respected by all good citizens, and enforced with promptness and fidelity by every branch of the general government.

"*Resolved*, That it is the duty of the United States to afford ample and complete protection to all its citizens, at home or abroad, and whether native or foreign born.

"*Resolved*, That one of the necessities of the age, in a military, commercial and postal point of view, is speedy communication between the Atlantic and Pacific States, and the Democratic party pledge such constitutional enactment as will insure the construction of a railroad to the Pacific coast at the earliest practicable period.

"*Resolved*, That the Democratic party are in favor of the acquisition of the island of Cuba, on such terms as shall be honorable to ourselves and just to Spain.

"*Resolved*, That the enactments of State legislatures to defeat the faithful execution of the fugitive slave law, are hostile in character, subversive of the Constitution, and revolutionary in their effect.

Previous to the nomination of Mr. Douglas, a secession of about one hundred, both of Northern and Southern delegates, took place, who immediately met in Convention, and nominated John C. Breckenridge, of Kentucky, for President, and Joseph Lane, of Oregon, for Vice-President. This convention adopted the following platform, which is the same as adopted by the seceding delegates at Charleston:

"*Resolved*, That the platform adopted by the Democratic party at Cincinnati be affirmed, with the following explanatory resolutions:

"First—That the government of a Territory organized by an act of Congress, is provisional and temporary, and during its existence all citizens of the United States have an equal right to settle with their property in the Territory, without their rights, either of person or property, being destroyed or injured by congressional or territorial legislation.

"Second—That it is the duty of the federal government, in all its departments, to protect the rights of persons and property in the Territories, and wherever else its constitutional authority extends.

"Third—That when the settlers in a Territory having an adequate population, form a State Constitution, the right of sovereignty commences, and, being consummated by their admission into the Union, they stand on an equality with the people of other States, and a State thus organized ought to be admitted into the federal Union, whether its constitution prohibits or recognizes the institution of slavery.

"*Resolved*, That the Democratic party are in favor of the acquisition of the island of Cuba, on such terms as shall be honorable to ourselves and just to Spain, at the earliest practicable moment.

"*Resolved*, That the enactments of State legislatures to defeat the faithful execution of the fugitive slave law, are hostile in character, subversive of the Constitution, and revolutionary in their effect.

"*Resolved*, That the Democracy of the United States recognize it as the imperative duty of this government to protect the naturalized citizen in all his rights, whether at home or in foreign lands, to the same extent as its native born citizens.

"Whereas, One of the greatest necessities of the age, in a political, commercial, postal and military point of view, is a speedy communication between the Pacific and Atlantic coasts; therefore, be it

"*Resolved*, That the national Democratic party do hereby pledge themselves to use every means in their power to secure the passage of some bill, to the extent of their constitutional authority, by Congress, for the construction of a Pacific railroad from the Mississippi river to the Pacific ocean, at the earliest practicable moment.

Mr. Fitzpatrick refusing to accept the nomination for Vice-President with Mr. Douglas, the National Committee placed the name of Herschel V. Johnson, of Georgia, upon the ticket in his stead.

www.ingramcontent.com/pod-product-compliance
Lightning Source LLC
Chambersburg PA
CBHW021419300426
44114CB00010B/560